RAND McNALLY

Atlas of
World Geography

Editors
Brett R. Gover
Jon M. Leverenz
Ann T. Natunewicz

Art Direction
John C. Nelson

Design
Donna M. McGrath

Cover Design
Brian C. Doherty

Design Production
DePinto Graphic Design

Cartographic Direction
V. Patrick Healy

Cartographic Staff
Robert K. Argersinger
Lynn Jasmer
Patty A. Porter
James A. Purvis
L. Charlene Smith
James A. Wooden
David C. Zapenski

Research
Susan K. Hudson

Continental Thematic Maps
Thomas F. Vitacco
Marzee L. Eckhoff
Gwynn A. Lloyd
Robert L. Merrill
David R. Simmons
Ashley James Snyder
Barbara Benstead-Strassheim
Dara L. Thompson

Photo Research
Feldman and Associates, Inc.

Manufacturing Manager
Robert Sanders

Photograph Credits:

Front cover images provided by © 1997 PhotoDisc, Inc.

H. Armstrong Roberts: © R. Kord, 7, 11 (b); © Zefa, 100; © M. Schneiders, 108; © Smith/Zefa, 150 (b)

© Randall Hyman: 101

© Wolfgang Kaehler: 135

Odyssey Chicago: © R. Frerck, 152

Tony Stone Images: © K. Wood, 9 (t); © Mark Segal, 68; © David Frazier, 69; © Jacques Jangoux, 98 (t); © John Warden, 98 (b); © Owen Franken, 110; © John Lamb, 122 (t); © Yann Layma, 134; © Paul Chelsey, 153

Information Credits:

Volcano data, pages 9, 12, and 16: Tom Simkin, Smithsonian Institution Global Volcanism Program

Earthquake data, page 17: Paula Dunbar, National Geophysical Data Center, National Oceanic and Atmospheric Administration

Australia information, page 18: Australian Tourist Commission

Much of the information on the destruction of the Amazonian rain forest, page 101, was provided by Fred Engel of the Center for Earth and Planetary Science, National Air and Space Museum, Smithsonian Institution, Washington, D.C.

Atlas of World Geography

Copyright © 2000 by Rand McNally & Company
2001 Printing (1)

Published and printed in the United States of America

ISBN: 0-528-17790-0

For information about ordering *Atlas of World Geography*, call 1-800-678-7263; or visit our websites at:

www.randmcnally.com   www.K12online.com

Table of Contents

Using the Atlas — 4-6

Introduction to the Answer Section — 7

Questions and Answers
North America — 8-9
South America — 10-11
Europe — 12-13
Africa — 14-15
Asia — 16-17
Oceania (including Australia and New Zealand) — 18
World — 19

World Superlatives, Facts, and Rankings
The Universe and Solar System — 20-21
The Earth — 22-23
Continents and Islands — 24-25
Mountains, Volcanoes, and Earthquakes — 26-27
Oceans and Lakes — 28-29
Rivers — 30-31
Climate and Weather — 32-33
Population — 34-35
The World's Most Populous Cities — 36-38
Countries and Flags of the World — 39-50

Introduction to the Maps and Legend — 51

World Patterns
World, Political — 52-53
World, Physical — 54-55
World, Climate — 56-57
World, Vegetation — 58-59
World, Population — 60-61
World, Environments — 62-63
World, Time Zones — 64-65

Reference Maps of the World

North America
North America: Thematic Introduction — 66-69
North America, Political — 70
North America, Physical — 71
Canada — 72-73

United States of America
United States, Political — 74-75
United States, Physical — 76-77
U.S. Thematics — 78-80
Alaska and the Aleutians — 81
Northwestern U.S.A. — 82-83
Southwestern U.S.A. — 84-85
Central U.S.A. — 86-87

Northern Interior U.S.A. — 88-89
Northeastern U.S.A. — 90-91
Southeastern U.S.A. — 92-93
Western Gulf of Mexico Region — 94-95
Mexico and Caribbean Lands — 96-97

South America
South America: Thematic Introduction — 98-101
South America, Political — 102
South America, Physical — 103
Northern South America — 104-105
Southern South America — 106
South America, Cities and Environs — 107

Europe
Europe: Thematic Introduction — 108-111
Europe, Political — 112-113
Europe, Physical — 114-115
Western Europe — 116-117
Eastern Europe — 118-119
Mediterranean Lands — 120-121

Africa
Africa: Thematic Introduction — 122-125
Africa, Political — 126
Africa, Physical — 127
Northern Africa — 128-129
Southern Africa — 130-131

Asia
Asia: Thematic Introduction — 132-135
Asia, Political — 136-137
Asia, Physical — 138-139
Northern Asia — 140-141
Southwestern Asia — 142-143
The Middle East — 144-145
China, Korea, and Japan — 146-147
Southeastern Asia — 148-149

Oceania (including Australia and New Zealand)
Oceania: Thematic Introduction — 150-153
Australia and New Zealand, Political — 154-155
Australia and New Zealand, Physical — 156-157
The Pacific Rim — 158-159

Antarctica — 160

Glossary — 161-162

Index — 163-176

Using the Atlas

Maps and Atlases

Today, satellite images (Figure 1) and aerial photography show us the face of the Earth in precise detail. It is hard to imagine how difficult it once was to ascertain what our planet looked like—even small parts of it. Yet from earliest history we have evidence of humans trying to depict the world through maps and charts.

Figure 1

Twenty-five hundred years ago, on a tiny clay tablet the size of a hand, the Babylonians inscribed the earth as a flat disk (Figure 2) with Babylon at the center. The section of the Cantino map of 1502 (Figure 3) is an example of a portolan chart used by mariners to chart the newly discovered Americas. Handsome and useful maps have been produced by many cultures. The Mexican map (Figure 4) drawn in 1583 marks hills with wavy lines and roads with footprints between parallel lines. The methods and materials used to create these maps were dependent upon the technology available, and their accuracy suffered considerably. The maps in this atlas show the detail and accuracy that cartographers are now able to achieve. They benefit from our ever-increasing technology, including satellite imagery and computer-assisted cartography.

Figure 2

In 1589, Gerardus Mercator used the word "atlas" to describe a collection of maps. Atlases have become a unique and indispensable reference for graphically defining the world and answering the question "Where?" Only on a map can the countries, cities, roads, rivers, and lakes covering a vast area be simultaneously viewed in their relative locations. Routes between places can be traced, trips planned,

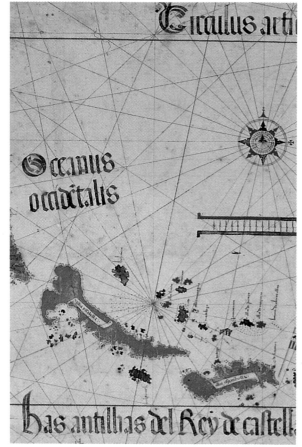

Figure 3

Figure 4

boundaries of neighboring states and countries examined, distances between places measured, the meandering of rivers and streams and the sizes of lakes visualized, and remote places imagined.

Getting the Information

An atlas can be used for many purposes, from planning a trip to finding hot spots in the news and supplementing world knowledge. To realize the potential of an atlas, the user must be able to:

1) Find places on the maps
2) Measure distances
3) Determine directions
4) Understand map symbols

Finding Places

One of the most common and important tasks facilitated by an atlas is finding the location of a place in the world. A river's name in a book, a city mentioned in the news, or a potential vacation spot may prompt your need to know where the place is located. The illustrations and text below explain how to find Lagos, Nigeria.

1) Look up the place-name in the index at the back of the atlas. Lagos, Nigeria can be found in the map on page 128, and it can be located on the map by its latitude and longitude, expressed in degrees: 7 North Latitude, 3 East Longitude (Figure 5).

La Fayette, In., U.S. 40N	87W	**90**
Lafayette, La., U.S. 30N	92W	**95**
Laghouat, Alg. 34N	3 E	**128**
Lagos, Nig. 7N	3 E	**128**
La Grande, Or., U.S. 45N	118W	**82**
LaGrange, Ga., U.S. 33N	85W	**92**
Lahore, Pak. 32N	74 E	**143**
Lahti, Fin. 61N	26 E	**116**

Figure 5

2) Turn to the map of Northern Africa on page 128. Note that the latitude appears in the right and left margins of the map, and the longitude in the upper and lower margins.

3) To find Lagos on the map, place your left index finger on the left margin at 7 degrees (between 5 and 10); and your right index finger in the top margin at 3 degrees East (between 0 and 5). Move your left finger across the map and your right finger down the map. Your fingers will meet in the area in which Lagos is located (Figure 6).

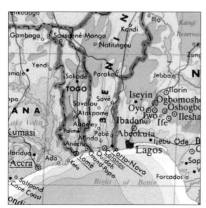

Figure 6

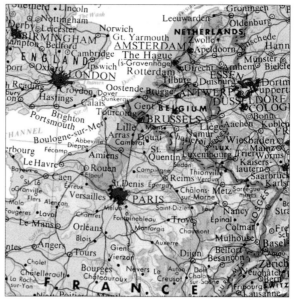

Figure 7

Measuring Distances

In planning trips, determining the distances between two places is essential, and an atlas can help in travel preparation. For instance, to determine the approximate distance between Paris, France and Amsterdam, Netherlands, follow these three steps:

1) Lay a slip of paper on the map on page 117 so that its edge touches the two cities. Adjust the paper so only one corner touches Paris. Mark the paper directly at the spot where Amsterdam is located (Figure 7).

2) Place the paper along the scale of miles beneath the map. Position the corner at 0 and line up the edge of the paper along the scale. The pencil mark on the paper indicates Amsterdam is between 250 and 300 miles from Paris (Figure 8).

3) To find the exact distance, make a second pencil mark at the 250-mile point of the scale. Then slide the paper to the left so that this second mark is lined up with 0 on the scale (Figure 9). The Amsterdam mark now falls at the third 10-mile point on the scale. This means that the Paris and Amsterdam are approximately 250 plus 30—or 280—miles apart.

0	50	100	150	200	250	300 miles

0		100	200	300	400	500 kilometers

Figure 8

0	50	100	150	200	250	300 miles

0		100	200	300	400	500 kilometers

Figure 9

Determining Directions

Most of the maps in the atlas are drawn so that when oriented for normal reading, north is at the top of the map, south is at the bottom, west is at the left, and east is at the right. Most maps have a series of lines drawn across them—the lines of latitude and longitude. Lines of latitude, or parallels of latitude, are drawn east and west. Lines of longitude, or meridians of longitude, are drawn north and south (Figure 10, at bottom of page).

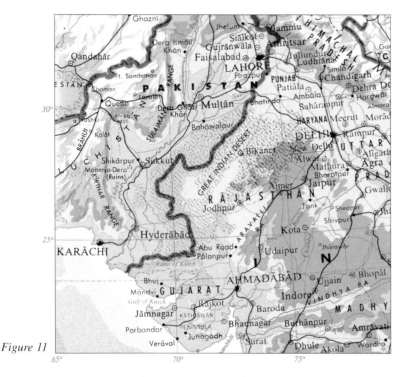

Figure 11

Parallels and meridians appear as either curved or straight lines. For example, in the section of the map of Southwestern Asia (Figure 11), from page 143, the parallels of latitude appear as curved lines. The meridians of longitude are curved vertical lines.

Latitude and longitude lines help locate places on maps. Parallels of latitude are numbered in degrees north and south of the Equator. Meridians of longitude are numbered in degrees east and west of a line called the Prime Meridian, running through Greenwich, England, near London. Any place on Earth can be located by the latitude and longitude lines running through it.

To determine directions or locations on the map, you must use the parallels and meridians. For example, suppose you want to know which is farther north, Karachi, Pakistan or Delhi, India. The map in Figure 11 shows that Karachi is south of the 25° parallel of latitude and that Delhi is north of it. Therefore Delhi is farther north than Karachi. By looking at the meridians of longitude, you can determine which city is farther east. Karachi is approximately 2° east of the 65° meridian, and Delhi is about 2° east of the 75° meridian. Delhi is farther east than Karachi.

Understanding Map Symbols

In a very real sense, every map is a symbol representing the world or part of it. It is a reduced representation of the Earth: each of the world's features —cities, rivers, etc.—is represented by a symbol. Map symbols may take the form of points, such as dots or squares (often used for cities, capital cities, or points of interest) or lines (roads, railroads, rivers). Symbols may also occupy an area, showing extent of coverage (terrain, forests, deserts). They seldom look like the feature they represent and therefore must be identified and interpreted. For instance, some of the maps in this atlas define political units by a colored line depicting their boundaries. Neither the colors nor the boundary lines are actually found on the surface of the Earth, but because countries and states are such important political components of the world, strong symbols are used to represent them. The Legend on page 51 of this atlas identifies the symbols used on the maps.

Figure 10

The Answer Section

Questions and Answers

North America	8-9
South America	10-11
Europe	12-13
Africa	14-15
Asia	16-17
Oceania (including Australia and New Zealand)	18
World	19

World Superlatives, Facts, and Rankings

The Universe and Solar System	20-21
The Earth	22-23
Continents and Islands	24-25
Mountains, Volcanoes, and Earthquakes	26-27
Oceans and Lakes	28-29
Rivers	30-31
Climate and Weather	32-33
Population	34-35
The World's Most Populous Cities	36-38
Countries and Flags	39-50

Questions and Answers

North America

Q What is the difference between "Central America" and "Middle America"?

A The term "Central America" refers to the North American countries which lie south of Mexico and north of Colombia: Belize, Guatemala, Honduras, El Salvador, Nicaragua, Costa Rica, and Panama. The Caribbean islands are not considered part of Central America. "Middle America" is comprised of Central America as well as Mexico and all of the Caribbean islands.

Q What is the largest U.S. city east of Reno, Nevada and west of Chicago?

Los Angeles, California

A Surprisingly, the answer is Los Angeles. Although Los Angeles is located on the Pacific Coast, it actually lies slightly farther east than Reno. The coast, which forms the western edge of the U.S., curves dramatically eastward below Cape Mendocino in northern California. San Diego, at the southern end of California's coast, is approximately as far east as the eastern borders of Washington and Oregon. *(Refer to map on pages 74-75.)*

Q Which is the southernmost U.S. state? The northernmost? The westernmost? The easternmost?

A Hawaii is the southernmost state; Alaska is both the westernmost and the northernmost. The question of which state is the easternmost is a bit problematic. Generally, Maine is considered to be the easternmost, since it extends farther east than any other state along the Atlantic seaboard. However, Alaska is technically the easternmost state, since the Aleutian Islands cross the 180° longitude line which divides the globe into eastern and western hemispheres. These islands sit at the eastern edge of the eastern hemisphere.

Q How many national flags have flown over Texas?

A Six. Spain (1682-1821), France (1685-1686), Mexico (1821-1836), the Republic of Texas (1836-1845), the United States (1845-1861), the Confederate States of America (from 1861 until the state was re-admitted to the Union in 1870), and the United States again (1870 through the present). Texas is the only U.S. state to have existed as an independent country.

Q What is the oldest city in the United States to be founded by Europeans?

A St. Augustine, Florida. Spanish explorer Juan Ponce de León, searching for the Fountain of Youth, landed nearby and claimed the area for Spain in 1513. The French established a colony on the site in 1564, but it was destroyed in 1565 by the Spanish, who then founded the present city. The oldest U.S. state capital is Santa Fe, New Mexico, which was founded in 1609, also by the Spanish.

Q What is Papiamento?

A Papiamento is a language which blends Dutch, Spanish, Portuguese, English, and Indian words. It is the principal language of Aruba and other islands in the Dutch Caribbean, and is spoken by an estimated 200,000 people.

Q If you were on a ship sailing from the Atlantic Ocean to the Pacific Ocean, in which direction would you be traveling as you passed through the Panama Canal?

A Southeast. The Pacific lies west of the Atlantic, and it would seem that a ship passing through the canal from the Atlantic would be sailing west. However, because of the twisting shape of the Isthmus of Panama, the canal's Pacific end lies south and east of its Atlantic end. *(Refer to inset map on page 96.)*

Q Into what body of water does the Colorado River empty?

A Currently, it doesn't empty into any body of water. Until recently, the river flowed into the Gulf of California. As the populations of water-poor Arizona and California have soared, more and more water has been drawn from the river for farms, industry, and homes. Today the Colorado is barely a trickle when it crosses the border into Mexico, and it disappears in the desert before it reaches the Gulf of California.

Q What is Canada's smallest province? Its largest?

A Prince Edward Island is Canada's smallest province, at 2,185 square miles (5,660 sq km). Canada's largest province is Quebec, which covers 594,860 square miles (1,540,680 sq km). The newly created territory of Nunavut represents the country's largest administrative division: It spreads over an area of 733,594 square miles (1,900,000 sq km), much of which lies within the Arctic Circle. If Nuvavut were an independent country, it would be larger than all but 15 of the world's countries.

Q What is the Continental Divide?

A An imaginary line running down the backbone of North America. Except for those which empty into the Great Basin and other basins, rivers to the west of this line flow into the Pacific Ocean, including its bays and gulfs; rivers to the east flow into the Atlantic or Arctic oceans, including their bays and gulfs. From northwest Canada south to New Mexico, the Divide runs along the crest of the Rocky Mountains, and in northern Mexico it follows the ridge of the Sierra Madre Occidental. All continents except frozen Antarctica have "divides."

Q Is Niagara Falls the highest waterfall in the world?

A Not even close. Niagara Falls' maximum drop of 167 feet (51 m) is surpassed by at least 22 waterfalls in North America alone. The highest waterfall in the world is Angel Falls in Venezuela, which spills 3,212 feet (979 m) from a flat mountain plateau. However, Niagara Falls ranks first in a different category: more than 210,000 cubic feet of water cascade over its edge each second, an amount nearly double that of any other waterfall.

Niagara Falls actually consists of two separate waterfalls: American Falls, at left, and Canadian (Horseshoe) Falls.

Q **What did ships do before the Panama Canal was built?**

A Before the canal opened, ships traveling between New York and San Francisco would sail 13,000 miles (21,000 km) around the entire continent of South America. When the canal opened in 1914, this journey was shortened to 5,200 miles (8,400 km). However, the canal is now too narrow for many of today's largest ocean-going vessels, so they must once again sail around South America to reach their destination. A project to widen the canal began in 1992.

Gatun Lake, Panama Canal

Q **What is the largest inland body of water in Central America?**

A Lake Nicaragua, which has a surface area of 3,150 square miles (8,158 sq km). Its only outlet is the San Juan River, which flows into the Caribbean Sea. Lying in a lowland region called the Nicaragua Depression, the lake was once part of the sea but became separated when the land began to rise. The freshwater lake is home to many species of fish usually found only in salt water, including sharks, tuna, and swordfish.

Q **Why does Minnesota have so many lakes?**

A During the height of the most recent Ice Age, glaciers moved southward from the Arctic regions to cover Canada and much of the northern U.S., including Minnesota. As they advanced, the glaciers scoured the landscape, gouging out countless depressions. When the Earth's climate grew warmer, the glaciers began to melt and retreat, and the depressions filled with melt-water to become lakes. Although Minnesota bills itself as the "Land of 10,000 Lakes," it actually has more than 15,000 lakes. Other areas of the world which experienced extreme glaciation, including parts of Europe and Siberia, also contain many lakes.

Q **What is the most popular U.S. national park?**

A Great Smoky Mountains National Park. Covering over 521,500 acres (211,200 hectares) in eastern Tennessee, the park receives approximately 9.1 million visitors each year. Arizona's Grand Canyon National Park has the second-highest visitor count: it receives around 4.6 million people annually.

Q **What two U.S. states share borders with the most other states?**

A Missouri and Tennessee, which each border eight other states. Missouri borders Iowa, Illinois, Kentucky, Tennessee, Arkansas, Oklahoma, Kansas, and Nebraska. Tennessee borders Kentucky, Virginia, North Carolina, Georgia, Alabama, Mississippi, Arkansas, and Missouri.

Q **How many U.S. states border only one other state?**

A One: Maine, which borders only New Hampshire. Two states, Alaska and Hawaii, border no others.

Q **What is the one place in North America where you can see both the Atlantic Ocean and the Pacific Ocean?**

A Irazú, a volcano in central Costa Rica. From its summit, both the Atlantic and Pacific oceans can be seen on a clear day.

Q **Where is the Yucatan Peninsula?**

A This thumb of land juts off of southeastern Mexico, separating the Gulf of Mexico from the Caribbean Sea. Yucatan was the center of the Maya civilization from about the first century B.C. through the tenth century A.D. Extensive Mayan ruins can be found at Chichén Itzá, Kabah, Mayapán, Tulum, and Uxmal. Near the town of Chicxulub at the northern tip of the peninsula, there is evidence of an enormous crater which is thought to be the point of impact of a meteorite 65 million years ago. The impact would have sent so much dust into the atmosphere that the sun's rays would have been blocked for months or perhaps years, lowering temperatures globally and possibly causing the extinction of the dinosaurs.

Q **What is the oldest capital city in the Americas?**

A Mexico City. The city originated as Tenochtitlán, the capital of the Aztecs, founded in the mid-1300s. By the early 1500s, the city had a population of perhaps 150,000, which was not only greater than any other city in the Americas but also greater than any European city at the time. In 1521, after a three-month siege, Spanish invaders under Hernán Cortés captured Tenochtitlán, razed the entire city, and founded Mexico City upon its ruins.

Q **What is the most densely populated country in North America?**

A El Salvador, which has a density of 650 people per square mile (251 per sq km). The U.S. ranks eighth, with 69 people per square mile (27 per sq km). Canada, the continent's largest country, is by far the least densely populated: it averages only 7.3 people per square mile (2.8 per sq km).

Q **What is the largest island in Caribbean Sea?**

A Cuba, the world's 15th-largest island. It has a land area of 42,800 square miles (110,800 sq km). The second-largest Caribbean island is Hispaniola, which covers 29,400 square miles (76,200 sq km) and contains the countries of Haiti and the Dominican Republic. Jamaica, measuring 4,200 square miles (11,000 sq km), is the third-largest Caribbean island.

Q **How many U.S. states have volcanoes that have been active in this century?**

A Four. Alaska has the most: 34 of its volcanoes, most of which are located on the Alaska Peninsula and the Aleutian Islands, have erupted since 1900. The other states with documented eruptions in this century are: Hawaii (3), Washington (1), and California (1).

Caldera and lava lake of Kilauea, on the island of Hawaii

Q **What is the only Caribbean island with large oil reserves?**

A Trinidad. The island's economy is based on oil, which accounts for about 80% of its exports. As a result of oil wealth, Trinidadians enjoy a higher standard of living than the people of most other Caribbean countries.

Q **Which U.S. state has the highest average elevation?**

A Colorado, with an average elevation of 6,800 feet (2,074 m) above sea level. However, the four highest peaks in the U.S. are found not in Colorado but in Alaska.

Questions and Answers

South America

What is Latin America?

The term "Latin America" designates the parts of North and South America which were settled by Spanish and Portuguese colonists and still retain a Hispanic character. These include Mexico, Cuba, Puerto Rico, the Dominican Republic, some of the smaller islands in the West Indies, all of Central America except for Belize, and all of South America except for Guyana, Suriname, and French Guiana.

If you flew due south from Chicago, which South American country would you fly over first?

You wouldn't fly over any South American countries. A straight line drawn south from Chicago passes through the Gulf of Mexico, Central America, and the Pacific Ocean. Point Parinas, Peru, the westernmost point of mainland South America, is about 500 miles (800 km) east of this line. The Galapagos Islands, which belong to Ecuador, lie about 75 miles (120 km) west of the line.

What percentage of the world's coffee beans come from South America?

South America currently produces approximately 45% of the world's coffee beans. Brazil leads the continent, producing just under one-quarter of the world total. Another 16% are grown in Colombia. Coffee plants require hot, moist climates, and they yield the most flavorful beans when cultivated at elevations between 3,000 and 6,000 feet (900 and 1800 m). South America's principal coffee-growing regions are found in the Brazilian and Guiana Highlands, and in the valleys and foothills of the Andes.

Giant Galapagos turtle

What scientist made the Galapagos Islands famous?

Charles Darwin, who visited the islands during his 1831-1836 expedition on the H.M.S. *Beagle*. Darwin's observations of how various animal species had adapted to life on the islands contributed to his ground-breaking theory of evolution, which he presented in the 1859 book *On the Origin of Species*.

Where are the Falkland Islands?

In the Atlantic Ocean, about 275 miles (440 km) off the east coast of Argentina. The Falklands are a dependency of the United Kingdom, and nearly all of the residents are English-speakers of British descent. Argentina, which has asserted claims to the Falklands since 1816, invaded and occupied the islands in 1982. The U.K. sent a large task force that defeated the Argentineans in a war lasting less than a month.

What South American country is the longest when measured from north to south?

Brazil. The country measures 2,725 miles (4,395 km) north to south, which is the approximate distance from New York City to Reno, Nevada. The second-longest country is Chile, with a length of 2,647 miles (4,270 km). In contrast to its great length, Chile measures only 235 miles (380 km) east to west at its widest point.

What was discovered in Venezuela's Lake Maracaibo in 1914?

Oil. Maracaibo sits above one of the world's largest oil fields, and today the lake's surface is a thicket of oil derricks. Wealth from oil exportation has helped to make Venezuela one of the richest countries in Latin America.

What is Patagonia?

Patagonia is a wind-swept plateau region occupying the southern third of South America, east of the Andes. The plateau receives little precipitation, and its only vegetation is scrubby grasses and thorny desert shrubs. The name "Patagonia" probably comes from the Grand Patagon, a dog-headed monster in a European romance called *Primaleon of Greece*. In 1592, the crew members of the ship *Desire* were attacked by a war-party of Tehuelche Indians wearing dog masks.

What South American city is the world's highest national capital?

La Paz, Bolivia. The city sprawls across the floor of a deep canyon high in the Andes, at an elevation of 12,000 feet (19,350 km)—approximately the same height as the summit of Japan's Mt. Fuji. The canyon walls protect the city from the bitterly cold winds that whip across the surrounding plateau. Visitors from lower elevations often suffer from altitude sickness for several days until their bodies adjust to the thin, oxygen-poor air.

What is the southernmost city in the world?

Ushuaia, Argentina, on the island of Tierra del Fuego. This city of 29,452 people lies at 54°48' south latitude, less than 700 miles (1,100 km) from Antarctica. The world's southernmost city with a population greater than 100,000 is Punta Arenas, Chile, located 150 miles (240 km) northwest of Ushuaia.

How many South American countries are named for famous people or cities?

Three. Bolivia was named for Simón Bolívar, the revolutionary who helped to liberate much of northern South America from Spanish rule. Colombia takes its name from the explorer Christopher Columbus, who "discovered" South America in 1498 and sailed along the coast of present-day Colombia in 1502. The name "Venezuela" is Spanish for "Little Venice." When European explorers reached Lake Maracaibo in 1499, they found villages built on pilings over the shallow waters, which reminded them of Venice, Italy.

Why is South America sometimes referred to as "the hollow continent"?

South America earned this nickname because most of its people live on or near the coasts; the interior is sparsely populated. Sixteen of the 20 largest metropolitan areas lie within 200 miles (320 km) of the coast. The continent's uneven population distribution has both a historical and a geographical explanation. Beginning in the 16th century, European colonists settled in the coastal regions from which raw materials were shipped back to Europe. The Amazon rain forest—hot, humid, and nearly impenetrable in places—has discouraged settlement of the northern half of the continent, and the Andes present a formidable barrier to eastward expansion from the Pacific coast. *(Refer to population map on page 99.)*

Q How many of South America's 20 longest rivers empty into the Pacific Ocean?

A None. South America's continental divide runs along the crest of the Andes at the continent's western edge. In most places the divide lies within 200 miles (320 km) of the Pacific coast. Rivers originating west of the divide have only a short distance to travel before reaching the Pacific. Rivers flowing east from the divide have nearly the whole expanse of the continent to cross before emptying into the Atlantic.

Q What South American city was the capital of the Inca empire?

Cathedral and rooftops in Cusco

A Cusco, Peru. The city was built by the Incas in the fourteenth century and served as their capital for 200 years until it was destroyed by Francisco Pizarro in 1533. Today, Cusco thrives as a major tourist attraction. Many of its houses and buildings are constructed on foundations of stone first cut by the Incas. Lying about 50 miles (80 km) northwest of Cusco is Machu Picchu, a well-preserved mountaintop Inca city, which was rediscovered in 1911.

Q What stretch of ocean off the South American coast is considered one of the most treacherous to ships?

A The Drake Passage. Approximately 500 miles (1,800 km) wide, this strait separates Cape Horn—at the southern tip of South America—from the South Shetland Islands which lie just north of Antarctica. First traversed in 1615, the passage was part of a major trade route between the Atlantic and Pacific oceans until 1914, when the Panama Canal opened. Frigid temperatures, rough waters, and high winds make the passage treacherous for all vessels but especially for the sailing ships of centuries past. Because the passage is so perilous, many ships avoid it by cutting through the Strait of Magellan to the north. However, this strait has its own dangers: it is narrow and twisting, and has been the site of numerous major shipwrecks.

Q Where is the Land of Fire?

A At the southern tip of South America. Tierra del Fuego, Spanish for "Land of Fire," is a group of islands lying south of the Strait of Magellan. When Portuguese explorer Ferdinand Magellan arrived in 1520, he named the islands after observing the native inhabitants carrying torches. The largest island, also called Tierra del Fuego, accounts for two-thirds of the land area of the island group. The eastern third of the islands belong to Argentina, and the rest belong to Chile.

Q What are the Nazca Lines?

A The Nazca Lines are gigantic drawings that were etched into Peru's desert floor by the Nazca people between 500 B.C. and A.D. 500. Scattered across 200 square miles (520 sq km), they form the world's largest display of art. The drawings fall into two categories: animal motifs and geometric patterns of crisscrossing straight lines. They were made by scraping away the top layer of red gravel to reveal the yellow sand below it. Archaeologists still disagree about the purpose of the Nazca Lines, but some theories hold that the lines formed ancient highways or were used as a giant calendar.

Q What is "El Niño"?

A El Niño is a seasonal ocean current that flows south along the Pacific coast of South America. The current takes its name—which is Spanish for "the Child"—from its usual arrival during the Christmas season. In normal years, when El Niño reaches northern Peru, southeasterly trade winds push its warm surface waters westward across the Pacific, away from the coast. Every four or five years, these trade winds weaken, allowing El Niño to travel farther south along the coast, raising local water temperatures by several degrees. This warmer water kills plankton and fish, crippling the fishing industry. Increased evaporation leads to excessive rainfall over parts of South America. The change in El Niño's normal flow pattern affects other ocean currents which often leads to dramatic climatic changes around the world.

Q How many of the Earth's species are found in the Amazon rain forest?

A Most of the Amazon basin has not been fully explored, and therefore most of its plant and animal species have not yet been catalogued. However, scientists estimate that the Amazon rain forest, which covers less than 5% of the Earth's total land area, contains almost one half of the planet's animal and plant species. One in ten of the most common medicines we use today comes from rain forest plants, and scientists believe that cures for many diseases, such as cancer, might be derived from plant species not yet discovered.

Q Where in South America could you find places in which no rainfall has ever been recorded?

A The Atacama Desert in northern Chile. This barren land of sand, rocks, borax lakes and saline deposits is one of the driest regions in the world. In parts of the desert, no rainfall has ever been recorded, and the city of Arica, at the northern edge, endured more than 14 consecutive years of drought from October 1903 through January 1918.

Q What South American possession lies farthest from the mainland?

A Easter Island, situated 2,300 miles (3,700 km) west of Chile in the Pacific Ocean. This small volcanic island was discovered on Easter Sunday in 1722, and was annexed by Chile in 1888. Although it belongs to Chile, geographically Easter Island is considered to be part of Oceania, not South America. It is best known for its strange monuments: scattered over the island are more than 600 huge stone faces, the earliest dating back more than 1,500 years.

Ancient statues, Easter Island

Q Where are the pampas?

A These flat, grassy plains—which are much like the prairies of North America—are found in the temperate regions of southern South America, east of the Andes. The largest such plain, known simply as the Pampa, covers much of central and northern Argentina, and extends into Uruguay. Since the 1550s, when European colonists introduced cattle to the Pampa, livestock raising has been a thriving industry. For many people, gauchos, or Argentinean cowboys, are the enduring symbol of the Pampa, although in the last century farming has superseded cattle ranching in economic importance.

Questions and Answers

Europe

Q Where is the Black Forest?

A In southwestern Germany, between the Rhine and Neckar rivers. The Black Forest, or *Schwarzwald* in German, is a mountainous region that takes its name from the dark coniferous trees that cover its slopes. Its fertile valleys provide good pastureland and produce grapes for wine, and its trees supply the lumber and woodworking industries, as well as toy and cuckoo clock manufacturers. The region's scenic beauty, winter sports facilities, and mineral springs attract many tourists each year.

Q How many national capitals are located on the Danube River?

A Four. The capital cities of Bratislava (Slovakia), Budapest (Hungary), Belgrade (Yugoslavia), and Vienna (Austria) are all found along the banks of the Danube. Five other capitals are located on tributaries of the Danube: Bucharest (Romania), Sofia (Bulgaria), Ljubljana (Slovenia), Zagreb (Croatia), and Sarajevo (Bosnia & Herzegovina).

Old Town of Zagreb, Croatia

Q What is killing the forests of Northern Europe?

A Acid rain. In the atmosphere, airborne pollutants—especially sulfur and nitrogen dioxides from automobile and industrial emissions—adhere to water droplets, and then fall back to Earth as acidified rain, snow, or hail. This precipitation poisons plant and animal life, erodes buildings, and contaminates soil and drinking water. As a result of acid rain, as many as one-half of the trees in Germany's Black Forest and Switzerland's central alpine region are dead or dying. At least 4,000 lakes in Sweden are so acidic that no fish survive in them. To combat acid rain, the countries of the European Union recently agreed to significantly reduce nitrogen oxide and sulfur dioxide emissions.

Q What independent countries were once part of the U.S.S.R.?

A When the Union of Soviet Socialist Republics (U.S.S.R.) broke up in 1991, its 15 republics all became independent countries: Armenia, Azerbaijan, Belarus, Estonia, Georgia, Kazakhstan, Krygyzstan, Latvia, Lithuania, Moldova, Russia, Tajikistan, Turkmenistan, Ukraine, and Uzbekistan.

Q How many times has the name of St. Petersburg, Russia, changed in this century?

A Three times. St. Petersburg was founded in 1703 by Peter the Great. In 1914, its name was changed to Petrograd, Russian for "Peter's City," and then in 1924 it was changed again, this time to Leningrad, in honor of Vladimir Lenin, the founder of Russian Communism. In 1991, following the collapse of Communist rule, the city name was changed back to St. Petersburg. Older citizens joke about being born in St. Petersburg, attending school in Petrograd, working in Leningrad, and growing old in St. Petersburg—all while living in the same place.

Q What independent countries were once part of Yugoslavia?

A Prior to 1991, Yugoslavia was comprised of six republics: Bosnia and Herzegovina, Croatia, Macedonia, Montenegro, Serbia, and Slovenia. In 1991-92, four of the six republics—Croatia, Slovenia, Macedonia, and Bosnia and Herzegovina—declared their independence. Yugoslavia now comprises only two republics, Serbia and Montenegro.

Q What is the Chunnel?

A "Chunnel" is a nickname for the English Channel Tunnel, which connects England and France via rail under the English Channel. There are actually three separate tunnels: two for trains and a parallel service tunnel. The tunnels run for 31 miles between Coquelles, France, and Folkestone, England, at an average depth of 150 feet (46 m) below the seafloor. Work on the tunnels began in 1987, and the first trains crossed under the Channel in 1994.

Q Where is "Europe's Grand Canyon"?

A Along the Verdon River in the Provence region of southeastern France. The Verdon has carved a deep, narrow gorge, known as the Grand Cañon du Verdon, through the limestone plateau between the town of Castellane and the artificial Lac de Ste-Croix. The gorge stretches for 13 miles (21 km) and reaches a depth of 3,170 feet (965 m). It is considered one of the natural wonders of Europe.

Q What is the only volcano on the European mainland that has erupted in the 20th century?

A Mt. Vesuvius (Vesuvio), located in southern Italy nine miles (15 km) east of Naples. It has been active through much of the century, with significant eruptions in 1906, 1929, and 1944. Two thousand years ago, most Romans did not recognize Vesuvius as a volcano, and numerous farming communities thrived on the fertile land around its base. Then, in August of A.D. 79, the volcano exploded in a mighty eruption, burying the cities of Pompeii, Herculaneum, and Stabiae under cinders, ash, and mud, and killing more than 3,500 people.

Q How many European countries fall partially within the Arctic Circle?

A Four: Finland, Norway, Russia, and Sweden. Technically, a fifth country could be added to this list: Iceland's mainland ends just short of the Arctic Circle, but one of the country's islands, Grimsey, straddles the line, its northern half sitting within the Circle.

The historic Henningsvaer Port in the Lofoten Islands of Norway, north of the Arctic Circle

Q Where is Waterloo, site of Napoleon's famous defeat?

A Today, Waterloo is a suburb of Brussels, Belgium, although at the time of the battle—June 18, 1815—it lay 12 miles (19 km) away from the city, which was then much smaller. At Waterloo, the troops of French emperor Napoleon I were defeated by British forces under the command of the Duke of Wellington and Prussian forces led by Gebhard Blücher. The French defeat ended the Napoleonic Wars, which had begun in 1803.

Q Is Venice, Italy, really sinking?

A Yes, although at a much slower rate than earlier in the century. The city, which dates back to the 4th century A.D., is built on 118 small islands in a lagoon at the top of the Adriatic Sea. Its buildings sit on foundations of wooden pilings driven deep into the underlying sand, silt and clay. Originally the buildings were safely above high tide level, but over the course of 15 centuries, natural compaction of the sub-soil caused the city to sink more than 30 inches (76 cm). Earlier this century, groundwater was pumped out of the subsoil to satisfy water needs on the mainland. This proved disastrous for Venice: the city quickly sank another five inches (13 cm) at a time when the sea level was rising by four inches (10 cm). The pumping was stopped, and Venice's sinking has slowed to its earlier "natural" rate. Unfortunately, the foundations of many buildings have been severely damaged by high water.

Gondola and canal, Venice

Q Which independent European countries are smaller than Rhode Island, the smallest U.S. state?

A Seven independent European countries cover a smaller area than Rhode Island's 1,545 square miles (4,002 sq km): Vatican City, Monaco, San Marino, Liechtenstein, Malta, Andorra, and Luxembourg.

Q How many official languages are recognized in Switzerland?

A Four: German, French, Italian, and Romansch. German is the most widely spoken language: 65% of the Swiss speak a dialect known as *Schwyzerdütsch*, or Swiss German. French is spoken by 18% of the population, Italian by 10%, and Romansch by only 1%.

Q Why Is Ukraine called "the breadbasket of Europe"?

A Ukraine's topography—flat plains, or "steppes," cover most of the country—and extremely fertile soils combine to make it one of the world's most outstanding agricultural areas. In 1994, the country produced almost 36 million tons (33 metric tons) of grain. Major crops include wheat, rye, barley, corn, potatoes, sunflower seeds, sugar beets, and cotton. Ukraine also has thriving dairy and livestock industries, as well as many food-processing plants.

Q If the Caspian Sea is a *sea*, then how can it be the world's largest *lake*?

A Actually, it is both a sea *and* a lake. The word "sea" is used most often to designate specific regions of the oceans that are more or less surrounded by land; however, it can also apply to inland bodies of water, especially if they are large and/or salty. The Caspian Sea is both large and salty, so it is called a sea. "Lake" is a general term for inland bodies of water of substantial size. The Caspian Sea lies inland and has a surface area of 143,240 square miles (370,990 sq km), so it is also considered to be a lake. Other "sea-lakes" in the world include the Aral Sea, the Dead Sea, the Sea of Galilee, and California's Salton Sea.

Q Where is Transylvania?

A In northwestern Romania. The region is bounded by the Carpathian Mountains in the north and east, the Transylvanian Alps in the south, and by Romania's borders with Hungary and Yugoslavia in the west. A high plateau, averaging 1,000 to 1,600 feet (300 to 500 m) in elevation, covers much of Transylvania. In Bram Stoker's 1897 novel *Dracula*, Transylvania is the home of the blood-sucking Count. Stoker based the story on local vampire legends, many of which persist today: in some parts of eastern Europe, peasants still wear garlic necklaces and hang garlic wreaths from their doors to ward off vampire spirits.

Q What countries contain parts of the Carpathian Mountains?

A Five: the Czech Republic, Slovakia, Poland, Ukraine, and Romania. Curving for more than 900 miles (1,450 km) along the north and east sides of the Danube plain in central and eastern Europe, the Carpathians roughly form a half-circle connecting the Alps and the Balkans. The mountain system consists of two main parts: the Northern Carpathians, which include the Beskid and the Tatra ranges, and the Southern Carpathians, also called the Transylvanian Alps. The Carpathians' highest peak is Gerlachovský štít in Slovakia, which rises to 8,711 feet (2,655 m).

Q Where is Lapland?

A In northern Scandinavia. Lapland is home to the Lapps, a nomadic people who have traditionally engaged in hunting, fishing, and reindeer-herding. When the Finns arrived in the southern part of present-day Finland 2,000 years ago, they found the Lapps already settled there. Over the years, the Lapps have been pushed north, and their territory has expanded to cover parts of northern Norway, Sweden, Finland, and northwestern Russia. Today, there are approximately 42,000 Lapps, most of whom work in a variety of farming, construction, and service fields. The Finnish government has made many efforts to protect the Lapps' language, called Sami, and culture.

Q What European country has a shorter coastline than any other maritime country in the world?

A Monaco, whose Mediterranean coastline is a mere three-and-a-half miles (5.6 km) long. Another European country, Bosnia and Herzegovina, ranks second in this category: its coast on the Adriatic Sea between Croatia and Yugoslavia is only 13 miles (21 km) long. In third place is Slovenia, whose Adriatic coast is 29 miles (47 km) long.

Harbor and coastline, Monaco

Q What European city is the largest city in the world north of the Arctic Circle?

A Murmansk, Russia, a city of 472,900 people located on the Kola Gulf of the Barents Sea. Although Murmansk lies approximately 150 miles north of the Arctic Circle, its harbor remains ice-free throughout the year due to the moderating effect of a warm ocean current called the North Atlantic Drift. While there are thousands of cities and towns north of the Arctic Circle, there are none at all south of the Antarctic Circle at the opposite end of the world.

Questions and Answers

Africa

What is the East African Rift System?

This term refers to a series of rift valleys running through East Africa from Mozambique to the southern end of the Red Sea. These valleys are part of the Great Rift Valley, a 4,000-mile (6,430-km)-long depression that also includes the Red Sea, the Dead Sea, and the rest of the Jordan Valley. The East African Rift System marks the line along which geological forces are splitting East Africa off from the rest of the continent. Eventually, everything east of the Rift System—including all or part of present-day Mozambique, Tanzania, Rwanda, Burundi, Uganda, Kenya, Ethiopia, Djibouti, and Somalia—will be a huge island off of Africa's eastern coast. Madagascar was attached to the African mainland before similar forces split it off into an island 175 million years ago.

What is the Serengeti?

Located in northern Tanzania, east of Lake Victoria and west of Kilimanjaro, the Serengeti is a vast plain of grassland, acacia bushes, forest, and rocky outcrops.

Giraffes on the Serengeti

Serengeti National Park, established in 1951, covers an area of the plain about the size of Connecticut. The park is home to one of the last great concentrations of African wildlife, including antelope, buffalo, cheetahs, elephants, gazelles, giraffes, hyenas, leopards, lions, black rhinoceroses, wildebeests and zebras. Tourists from all over the world visit the park to observe the wildlife and to witness the large-scale animal migrations that occur in May and June.

How has the Aswan High Dam affected the Nile Valley ?

Before the dam was built in 1971, floodwaters inundated the Nile Valley each fall, depositing fresh, fertile silt across the valley floor. This annual replenishment of the soil helped agriculture to thrive in the valley for thousands of years. The dam ended the annual floods, and now much of the Nile's water-borne silt settles to the bottom of Lake Nassar, the enormous artificial lake behind the dam. Water evaporating from the lake's surface has increased the regional humidity, which has accelerated the decay of many of the valley's great tombs and monuments. On the positive side, the dam supplies more than 25% of Egypt's hydro-electric power, and desert irrigation projects using water from Lake Nassar have created 900,000 new acres of arable land.

What is remarkable about the delta of the Okavango River?

It is the largest inland delta in the world. The Okavango originates in the mountains of central Angola and flows 1,000 miles (1,600 km) to the northwest corner of Botswana, where it spills over the Gomare fault and fans out into a swampy delta covering 4,000 square miles (10,350 sq km). Meandering through a myriad of shallow channels, the waters of the Okavango quickly evaporate. The small amount that eventually emerges from the southeastern end of the delta represents less than 5% of the river's pre-delta flow.

What African country was previously known as Upper Volta?

Burkina Faso. The Volta River's three upper branches —the Volta Blanche (White Volta), Volta Rouge (Red Volta), and Volta Noire (Black Volta)—all originate within the country, hence the earlier name. Burkina Faso, the Mossi-dialect name adopted in 1984, translates roughly as "Country of Honest Men."

What are the most important crops grown in Africa?

Africa is the world's leading producer of cocoa beans (55% of the world total) and cassava roots (45% of the world total). It is also a major producer of grain and millet sorghum (27%), coffee (20%), peanuts (20%), palm oil (14%), tea (12%), and olive oil (12%).

Woman in sorghum fields, Bema

What object found along the banks of the Orange River in 1867 changed the course of South African history?

A 21-carat diamond. The discovery of this gem near Hopetown precipitated a huge diamond rush, and thousands of people from all over the continent and the world raced to southern Africa. The town of Kimberley, site of the famous open mine known as the Big Hole, became the diamond capital of the world. Between 1871 and 1914, more than 14 million carats of diamonds were removed from the mine, which eventually reached a depth of 4,000 feet (1,220 m) and a width of one mile (1.6 km).

What is Cabinda?

A coastal province of Angola that lies north of the Congo River and is separated from the rest of the country by a 19-mile (31-km)-wide corridor belonging to the Democratic Republic of the Congo. Most of Cabinda's is covered by tropical forest. Offshore lie rich oil fields which produce one million barrels annually.

What African country was founded in 1847 by freed American slaves?

Liberia, whose name comes from the Latin word *liber*, meaning "free." It is the only country in sub-Saharan Africa that has never been ruled by a colonial power. Liberia's capital city, Monrovia, was named for James Monroe, the fifth U.S. president.

What two African countries border only a single other country?

Lesotho and The Gambia. South Africa surrounds Lesotho, and The Gambia is bordered in the north, east, and south by Senegal: to its west lies the Atlantic Ocean.

What is the Ngorongoro Crater?

Located in northern Tanzania, Ngorongoro is the crater of a volcano that has been extinct for several million years. It has a diameter of 9 miles (14.5 km) and its walls rise about 2,000 feet (610 m) above its floor. The crater supports an abundance of wildlife, including wildebeests, elephants, rhinoceroses, hippopotamuses, lions, leopards, and flamingoes. In 1956 Ngorongoro was established as a conservation area, but its ecological balance is threatened by growing numbers of tourists and the large cattle herds of the nomadic Masai people.

Why is it difficult to say how large Lake Chad is?

The lake's size fluctuates dramatically throughout the year. Numerous rivers and streams flow into Lake Chad, but it has no outlet. During the summer rainy season, floodwaters swell the lake to 10,000 square miles (25,900 sq km) and occasionally to twice that size. Even at its maximum size the lake is extremely shallow; its greatest depth is only 25 feet (8 m). By the end of the following spring, evaporation has shrunk the lake by 60%, to about 4,000 square miles (10,360 sq km). In recent decades, Lake Chad's cyclical fluctuations have been greatly affected by recurring droughts, which have reduced the flow of water into the lake and accelerated evaporation. Its volume has dropped by 80% since 1970.

What is significant about the location of Khartoum, Sudan?

Khartoum, the capital of Sudan, is located at the point where the White Nile and Blue Nile rivers meet to form the Nile. Capitalizing on its strategic location, the city has become Sudan's commercial center and transportation hub. It is built on a curving strip of land that resembles the trunk of an elephant: the name "Khartoum" comes from the Arabic *Ras-al-hartum*, which means "end of the elephant's trunk."

What is Africa's newest country?

Eritrea, which officially became independent in 1993. An Italian colony from 1890 to 1941, Eritrea was captured by the British during World War II. In 1952, the United Nations awarded Eritrea to Ethiopia under the condition that it be ruled as a self-governing territory. Ethiopia violated this agreement by annexing Eritrea in 1962, touching off a civil war which lasted more than 30 years. Eritrea formally declared its independence in May 1993, two years after defeating Ethiopia's Marxist regime.

What is the Sahel?

The Sahel is a semiarid region that separates the Sahara Desert from the tropical savanna and rain forests of central Africa. It stretches halfway across the continent, from Mauritania in the west to Chad in the east, in a band averaging more than 1,000 miles (1,600 km) in width. Most of the Sahel is semiarid savanna, with low grasses in the north and tall grasses in the south. Annual precipitation varies from 4 inches to 24 inches (100 to 600 mm). The 8-month dry season makes farming difficult, and the region has experienced several severe droughts in this century.

Woman returning from well in the Sahel

In what country would you find Africa's northernmost point?

Tunisia. The northernmost point is Cape Ben Sekka, which lies just north of the continent's northernmost town, Bechater. Parts of five European countries—Greece, Italy, Malta, Portugal, and Spain—lie farther south than Cape Ben Sekka. From the tip of the cape, Africa stretches southward approximately 5,000 miles (8,000 km) to its southernmost point, Cape Agulhas in South Africa.

How has the Sahara Desert changed in the last 5,000 years?

Scientists believe that 5,000 years ago the climate of the Sahara was more temperate and far less arid than it is today. Much of the region was grassland. Around 3000 B.C. global climate patterns began to shift, and the region entered an arid period which continues today. The desert currently covers 3,500,000 square miles (9,100,000 sq km), an area nearly as large as the United States, and its size is increasing. In recent decades, recurring droughts and overgrazing in the Sahel region have contributed to the Sahara's southward expansion.

What is the traditional mode of transportation in the Sahara Desert?

The camel, or more specifically, the one-humped dromedary, which was domesticated at least 3,000 years ago. Dromedaries are extremely well-suited to desert conditions. They have the ability to store water in their hump, and can tolerate water losses equal to one-fourth of their body weight. Their heavy-lidded eyes and closeable nostrils offer protection in sandstorms. Today, as the Saharan road system expands, truck convoys are replacing camel caravans, although trucks require frequent refueling, often overheat in the desert sun, and grind to a halt when sand clogs their engines.

Camel eating leaves

Which African country can boast the greatest known deposits, variety, and output of minerals in the world?

South Africa. It has the world's largest known deposits of chromite, gold, manganese, platinum, and vanadium. The country leads the world in production of gold, chromite, vanadium, and the platinum group metals: platinum, palladium, iridium, rhodium, and ruthenium. It is also one of the leading producers of manganese, antimony, and gem and industrial diamonds.

Where is the Horn of Africa?

This term refers to the horn-shaped area of eastern Africa that juts into the Indian Ocean. Somalia and Ethiopia occupy most of the horn. The cape of Gees Gwardafuy and the city of Caluula sit at the northeastern tip of the horn, marking the entrance to the Gulf of Aden, which connects the Arabian Sea and the Red Sea.

What is the Valley of the Kings?

This narrow valley, across the Nile River from the city of Luxor, contains the tombs of the pharaohs who ruled Egypt during the New Kingdom period, 1550 B.C. to 1200 B.C. The tombs are carved deep into the sandstone walls of the valley; most have five to fifteen rooms. Among the pharaohs buried in the valley are Ramses II, Ramses VI, and Seti I. Upon their death, the pharaohs were mummified and then entombed with all of the material things that they might need in the afterlife, including gold, jeweled ornaments, furniture, clothing, and food. Most of the tombs were soon looted by robbers, who removed all items of value. However, in 1922 the tomb of Tutankhamen—"King Tut"—was discovered with most of its riches untouched.

Questions and Answers

Asia

Q What natural features form the physical boundary between Europe and Asia?

A Europe and Asia share the same huge landmass, which is known as Eurasia. The imaginary line dividing this landmass into two continents runs through the Ural Mountains, the Ural River, the Caspian Sea, the Caucasus mountains, the Black Sea, the Bosporus strait, the Sea of Marmara, and the Dardanelles strait.

Q How many countries lie partially within Europe and partially within Asia?

A Four: Azerbaijan, which is traversed by the Caucasus Mountains; Kazakhstan, whose far western lands lie west of the Ural River; Russia, which is split by the Ural Mountains, and Turkey, which includes a small area on the northwestern side of the Sea of Marmara.

Q Why was the Great Wall of China built?

A To defend China against invasion by the Huns and other enemies. Defensive walls were built in China as early as the 6th century B.C. In 214 B.C., under Emperor Shih Huang-ti, the existing walls were connected to form a single continuous wall with watchtowers. This wall was extended during the Han Dynasty (202 B.C. – A.D. 220) and the Sui Dynasty (A.D. 581 – 618). Seven hundred years later the wall had mostly crumbled, and in the late 1400s, under the Ming Emperors, it was completely rebuilt. The portions of the wall that remain today are those that were constructed during this most recent period.

The Great Wall winding through a hilly region in northern China

Q How has the Aral Sea changed in recent decades?

A It has shrunk by about 40% since 1960. The sea once covered nearly 25,000 square miles (64,720 sq km) and was the fourth-largest inland body of water in the world. Today it covers only about 13,000 square miles (33,600 sq km), and the former port city of Muynak lies 30 miles (48 km) inland. The sea's shrinkage can be blamed on cotton farming in the surrounding desert. Soviet-era efforts to establish a profitable cotton industry led to the creation of an extensive network of irrigation canals. These huge canals drain large amounts of water from the Syr Darya and Amu Darya, the only two rivers that empty into the sea.

Q What is the Ring of Fire?

A "Ring of Fire" designates the narrow band of active volcanoes encircling the Pacific Ocean basin. Of the approximately 1,500 volcanoes in the world that have been active within the last 10,000 years, more than two-thirds are part of the Ring. Over half of the Ring's active volcanoes are found in its Asian portion, which passes through Russia's Kamchatka Peninsula, the Kuril Islands, Japan, and the Philippines. The Ring of Fire's most recent major volcanic event was the 1991 eruption of Pinatubo on the Philippine island of Luzon, which prompted the evacuation of 250,000 people.

Q What part of Asia is called Indochina?

A "Indochina" refers to the southeastern Asian peninsula situated south of China and east of India. Countries located on the peninsula are Cambodia, Laos, Myanmar (Burma), Thailand, Vietnam, and the western portion of Malaysia. The eastern part of the Indochinese peninsula, including Cambodia, Laos, and Vietnam, was formerly known as French Indochina because of France's strong colonial presence there.

Q The Khyber Pass links which two countries?

A Afghanistan and Pakistan. Approximately 33 miles (53 km) long and reaching a maximum elevation of about 3,500 feet (1,067 m), the pass cuts through the Safed Koh mountains just south of the Kabul River, connecting the high plateau of Afghanistan with the Indus Valley. It has been used for centuries as a caravan route and as an invasion route into India. Today it is also traversed by a paved highway and, in Pakistan, by a railroad. In the 1980s several million refugees fleeing Afghanistan's civil war crossed into Pakistan via the pass.

Q What Persian Gulf country is a federation of seven Arab sheikdoms?

A United Arab Emirates, formed in 1971 through the unification of the sheikdoms of Abu Dhabi, Ajman, Dubai, Fujeirah, Sharjah, and Umm al-Qawain. Ras al-Khaimah joined the federation in 1972. Underdeveloped a few decades ago, the U.A.E. has been transformed by oil wealth into a modern and affluent country.

Q What Asian country contains, or is bordered by, six of the world's ten highest mountains?

A Nepal. Within Nepal or along its borders with China and India are found the following peaks: Mt. Everest (highest in the world), Kanchenjunga (3rd), Makalu (4th), Dhawalāgiri (5th), Annapurna (7th), and Xixabangma Feng (9th). Nanda Devi (10th) lies only 50 miles (80 km) northwest of Nepal's western border.

Q Where is the Empty Quarter?

A This hostile desert is found in the southern third of the Arabian Peninsula. Called *Ar Rub' Al-Khālī*, or "the Empty Quarter" in Arabic, it covers 250,000 square miles (647,000 sq km) and is the world's largest continuous sand body. Few people live in the Empty Quarter, and much of the region has never been explored.

Q What Asian volcanic eruption has been called the loudest natural explosion in recorded history?

A The 1883 eruption of Krakatau (Krakatoa), an island volcano between Sumatra and Java. Krakatau exploded three times on August 26 and 27, 1883, shooting tremendous amounts of gas and ash 50 miles (80 km) into the atmosphere. The explosions were so violent that they were heard nearly 3,000 miles (4,653 km) away on Rodrigues Island in the western Indian Ocean. Krakatau collapsed into itself, and when the explosions were over most of the island was submerged under 900 feet of water. Tsunamis up to 130 feet (40 m) high slammed the coasts of Sumatra and Java, washing away hundreds of villages and killing more than 36,000 people.

Q **At their closest point, how far apart are Asia and North America?**

A At the narrowest point of the Bering Strait, Asia and North America are separated by only 56 miles (90 km). Russia's Big Diomede (Ratmanov) Island and the United States' Little Diomede Island, which lie in the middle of the strait, are only 2.5 miles (4 km) apart.

Q **Where is the Fertile Crescent?**

A This term refers to a crescent-shaped area of fertile land in the Middle East which begins in the south with Egypt's Nile Valley, runs north along the eastern coast of the Mediterranean Sea, then turns southeast through Mesopotamia, the land between the Tigris and Euphrates rivers, and ends at the head of the Persian Gulf. The Fertile Crescent was the birthplace of some of the world's oldest civilizations, including the Sumerians, Babylonians, and Assyrians.

Q **What country was Pakistan part of before it became independent?**

A India. Conflicts between Hindus and Muslims in British India led to the creation of Pakistan as a separate Muslim state in 1947. Originally, Pakistan included the two main centers of Muslim population, which lay in northwest and east India. The two areas, West Pakistan and East Pakistan, were separated by 1,000 miles (1,600 km). In 1971, East Pakistan declared its independence and changed its name to Bangladesh. The name "Pakistan" comes from the Urdu words *pakh*, meaning "pure," and *stan*, meaning "land."

Q **What was Sri Lanka called before 1972?**

A Ceylon, which is the name the British had given to the island when they claimed it in 1796. The island became independent in 1948, and in 1972 was renamed Sri Lanka, which in the Sinhala language means "Resplendent Land."

The Taj Mahal

Q **What is India's most famous tomb?**

A The Taj Mahal, located in the city of Agra. Often described as one of the world's most beautiful buildings, it was built by the Mogul emperor Shah Jahan to honor the memory of his wife, Mumtaz-i-Mahal. Construction began in 1631 and was completed in 1648.

Q **What two seas are linked by the Suez Canal?**

A The Red Sea and the Mediterranean Sea. Before the 101-mile (163-km) canal was built in the mid-1800s, ships traveling between Europe and the Far East had to sail all the way around the southern tip of Africa. Depending on the origin and destination of the ship, the canal could shorten its trip dramatically. For example, a ship sailing from London to Bombay would have to travel almost 11,000 miles (17,700 km) around the African continent. Using the Suez Canal, the trip could be shortened to 6,300 miles (10,140 km), a distance reduction of over 40%.

Q **Which independent Asian country has the highest population density?**

A The tiny republic of Singapore, with 11,874 people per square mile (4,593 per sq km). Singapore's 2,921,000 people occupy an island measuring only 26 miles east-to-west and 14 miles north-to-south. Mongolia has the lowest density: 4.1 people per square mile (1.6 per sq km). Mongolia's land area is 2,458 times larger than Singapore's, but it holds only 2,462,000 people

Q **How long is Japan, from north to south?**

A The islands of Japan stretch approximately 1,900 miles (3,060 km) from Hokkaido in the north to the Sakishima Archipelago in the south. This is approximately equal to the distance between New York City and Denver.

Landscape on Hokkaido, Japan's northernmost island

Q **What region is known as the "Roof of the World"?**

A Tibet, the high plateau region which lies north of the Himalayas. Covering 471,000 square miles (1,220,000 sq km), and with an average elevation of 15,000 feet (4,600 m), the Tibetan Plateau is the largest and highest plateau in the world. Much of Tibet is uninhabited; the region's fewer than two million people are concentrated in the valleys of the Brahmaputra (Yarlung) River and its tributaries.

Q **Which Asian country leads the world in number of earthquake-related deaths recorded in this century?**

A China, where 48 deadly earthquakes have killed an estimated 967,420 people since 1900. During the same period Iran has lost 147,293 people in 57 earthquakes, and in Japan 32 earthquakes have killed 123,462 people.

Q **What cities mark the endpoints of the Trans-Siberian Railway?**

A The longest railway line in the world, the Trans-Siberian Railway stretches 5,764 miles (9,297 km) between Moscow in the west and the Pacific Coast port city of Nakhodka (near Vladivostok) in the east. The eight-day journey between the two cities includes stops in 92 Russian cities and towns.

Q **How many people live on the Indonesian island of Java?**

A Java is home to approximately 118 million people. It is the world's most populous island, although it is only the 13th-largest in area. By contrast, the island of Cuba is four-fifths the size of Java, but its population is only one-eleventh as large.

Q **What was the name of Ho Chi Minh City, Vietnam, prior to 1975?**

A Saigon. When the city fell to North Vietnamese forces in 1975, it was renamed for Ho Chi Minh, founder of the Indochina Communist Party and president of North Vietnam from 1945 until his death in 1969.

Questions and Answers

Oceania (including Australia and New Zealand)

What is Oceania?

The name "Oceania" refers to the scattered islands of a vast area of the Pacific Ocean, from Palau in the west to Easter Island in the east, and from the Midway Islands in the north to New Zealand in the south. The three main island groups of Oceania are Melanesia, Micronesia, and Polynesia. The continent of Australia and the islands of New Zealand are sometimes considered part of Oceania.

What is the Outback?

This nickname refers to Australia's vast, largely uninhabited interior. Over the years, the Outback's harsh beauty and its remoteness from the rest of Australia have made it popular with adventurous explorers and travelers. Through depictions in literature, art, and film, the region has become an integral part of Australia's identity. However, it is difficult to characterize the Outback, for its boundaries are undefined and its landscape varies from hot deserts to lush wilderness.

Eucalyptus tree in the Outback, Northern Territory

Why is Australia sometimes referred to as "the Land Down Under"?

This nickname originated with the British, who began colonizing Australia in the late 1700s. Because of its extreme southern location in relation to Britain, Australia was considered "Down." The "Under" part of the phrase refers to the continent's position "under" the Eurasian landmass. But while people from the Northern Hemisphere think of Australia as "Down Under," Australians do not.

How much of Australia is arid or semiarid?

More than two-thirds of the continent is considered to be arid or semiarid. The arid areas comprise several large deserts, including the Great Victoria Desert, the Gibson Desert, the Great Sandy Desert, and the Simpson Desert.

What distinction does Wellington, New Zealand have among national capitals of independent countries?

Located at 41°18' south latitude, Wellington is the world's southernmost national capital. In second place is Canberra, Australia, which lies at 35°17' south latitude.

What is unusual about how the island of Nauru was formed?

Nauru, the world's smallest republic, began as a coral atoll. Over the millennia, accumulated bird droppings filled in the central lagoon and created an 8-square-mile (21-sq-km) island whose highest point rises 210 feet (64 m) above sea level. The droppings are a rich source of phosphate, which is used in making fertilizers. Phosphate mining has long been Nauru's economic mainstay, but the resource will soon be exhausted.

What are the principal islands of New Zealand?

Two islands, North Island and South Island, account for more than 98% of New Zealand's total land area. The country also includes Stewart Island, the Chatham Islands, the Antipodes Islands, the Auckland Islands, and hundreds of tiny islets.

What is Ayers Rock?

Ayers Rock, now called by its Aboriginal name, Uluru, is a huge, red, oval-shaped rock outcropping that rises 2,831 feet (863 m) above the plains of central Australia. One of the largest monoliths in the world, Uluru is actually the summit of a massive sandstone hill, most of which is hidden underground. Aborigines consider Uluru sacred and incorporate numerous places around it into their ceremonial life.

What is the ratio of sheep to humans in Australia and New Zealand?

Because both countries are major wool, mutton, and lamb producers, Australia and New Zealand each have a high ratio of sheep to humans. In Australia, there are 132 million sheep, or seven sheep for each human in the country. In New Zealand, the ratio is even greater: the country's 50 million sheep translate into 14 sheep for each human.

How many of Oceania's countries have become independent since 1975?

Eight. Papua New Guinea became independent in 1975, the Solomon Islands and Tuvalu in 1978, Kiribati in 1979, Vanuatu in 1980, the Marshall Islands and the Federated States of Micronesia in 1986, and Palau (Belau) in 1994.

What is the Great Barrier Reef?

This vast coral reef system is the longest in the world, stretching 1,181 miles (1,900 km) along Australia's northeast coast. It is composed of reefs, shoals, and hundreds of islands. Popular with divers, the Great Barrier Reef is home to a myriad of aquatic creatures.

On what island is Robert Louis Stevenson buried?

Stevenson, author of *Dr. Jekyll and Mr. Hyde*, *Kidnapped*, and *Treasure Island*, is buried on the island of Upolu in Western Samoa. Born in Edinburgh, Scotland in 1850, Stevenson sailed to the South Pacific in 1888 and settled permanently in Samoa in 1890. He died there in 1894.

Where does Sydney rank among Australia's most populous cities?

Harbor and skyline of Sydney

Measured by actual city population, Sydney is not even ranked in the top hundred: only 13,501 people live within its tiny city limits. Brisbane is Australia's largest city, with 751,115 people. The Sydney metropolitan area, however, is by far the largest in Australia, with 3,538,749 people.

What is Australia's only island state?

Tasmania, which lies about 150 miles (240 km) south of the Australian mainland. Measuring 26,200 square miles (67,800 sq km) in area, it is the smallest of Australia's six states and accounts for less than 1% of the country's area. Originally part of New South Wales, Tasmania became a separate colony in 1825 and a state in 1901. Hobart, its capital, is home to 45% of the state's population.

World

Which country has the most time zones?

Russia, with ten. The United States and Canada are tied for second place with six times zones each. Interestingly, China, the world's third largest country, has only one time zone, although the sun rises and sets almost four hours earlier at the country's eastern edge than at its western edge. Many other countries, including Nepal, Norway, and Algeria, have also adopted a single time zone to simplify daily life. *(Refer to World Time Zones map on pages 64-65.)*

Through how many continents does the International Dateline pass?

Only one: Antarctica. The Dateline runs through the Pacific Ocean, between the North and South poles. Its jagged course approximately follows the 180° longitude line, although in places it veers as much as 750 miles (1,200 km) east or west of this line.

Which of the world's rivers flows through, or along the border of, the most countries?

The Danube. The second-longest river in Europe (after the Volga), the Danube originates in southwestern Germany and flows through or borders eight countries: Germany, Austria, Slovakia, Hungary, Croatia, Yugoslavia, Romania, and Bulgaria. The Danube's drainage basin spreads over a total of 15 countries.

What is the longest mountain system in the world?

The Andes, which stretch for almost 4,500 miles (7,200 km) along the western edge of South America from Venezuela in the north to Tierra del Fuego in the south. The second-longest system is the Rocky Mountains, the major mountain system of North America. The Rockies extend for 2,500 miles (4,000 km) from northern Canada south to northern New Mexico.

What are Pangaea and Panthalassa?

Scientists believe that all of the landmasses of the world were once joined together in a single supercontinent. Given the name Pangaea, Greek for "all land," this supercontinent was surrounded by a vast universal ocean called Panthalassa, meaning "all seas." Between 225 and 190 million years ago, shifting of the Earth's crustal plates caused Pangaea to break up into northern and southern landmasses, referred to as Laurasia and Gondwanaland. As the plates continued to move, these two landmasses eventually split up into the six land-masses that exist today.

What is the one man-made structure that can be seen from space, with an unaided eye?

The Great Wall of China. To astronauts orbiting hundreds of miles above the Earth, the 4,000-mile (6,500-km)-long Great Wall—the largest structure ever built by human hands—appears as nothing more than a fine line meandering across the hills and plains of northern China. It was once thought that the wall would be visible from the moon, but during a 1969 lunar mission, astronaut Alan Bean found this to be untrue.

Which continent has the highest population density?

Asia, which has a density of 198 people per square mile (76 per square km). Excluding Antarctica, which is uninhabited, the lowest continental density is found in Australia, where there are only 6 people per square mile (2.4 per sq km).

Which continent has the most countries?

Africa, which has 53 independent countries and eight dependencies: Ascension, British Indian Ocean Territory, Mayotte, Reunion, St. Helena, Spanish North Africa, Tristan da Cunha, and Western Sahara. Asia ranks second, with 47 independent countries and one semi-independent country (Bhutan, which is internally self-governing but under the protection of India). Antarctica has no countries, and the entire continent of Australia is covered by the country of the same name.

What country borders the most other countries?

Russia and the People's Republic of China share the honor of being the most "neighborly" countries in the world—both have common boundaries with 14 other countries. Russia borders Finland, Norway, Estonia, Latvia, Belarus, Lithuania, Poland, Ukraine, Georgia, Azerbaijan, Kazakhstan, China, Mongolia, and North Korea. China borders Kazakhstan, Kyrgyzstan, Tajikistan, Afghanistan, Pakistan, India, Nepal, Bhutan, Myanmar, Laos, Vietnam, North Korea, Russia, and Mongolia.

What were the Seven Wonders of the Ancient World?

The Colossus of Rhodes (in modern-day Greece), the Hanging Gardens of Babylon (Iraq), the Pyramids and the Sphinx of Egypt, the Temple of Artemis at Ephesus (Turkey), the Statue of Zeus at Olympia (Greece), the Mausoleum at Halicarnassus (Turkey), and the Pharos of Alexandria (Egypt). Of these seven wonders, only the Pyramids and the Sphinx remain standing today.

People and pyramids at Khufu, Giza Plateau, Cairo

Where would you be if you were at 0° latitude, 0° longitude?

The point where 0° latitude, the Equator, intersects 0° longitude, the Prime Meridian, is located in the Atlantic Ocean off the western coast of Africa, 380 miles (610 km) south of Ghana and 670 miles (1,080 km) west of Gabon.

What are the official languages of the United Nations?

There are more than 2,000 known languages in the world, but official business of the United Nations is conducted in only the following six, which are among the most widely spoken: Mandarin Chinese, English, Arabic, Spanish, Russian, and French.

The Universe and Solar System

The Milky Way Galaxy

Our star, the Sun, is one of 200 billion stars banded together in the enormous gravitational spiral nebula called the Milky Way Galaxy, which is but one of millions of known galaxies in the universe.

The Milky Way is huge; it would take light — which travels at 186,000 miles per second — 100,000 years to go from one end of the galaxy to the other. In addition to the billions of stars, Earth shares the Milky Way with eight other known planets.

Statistical Data for the Milky Way Galaxy

Diameter: 100,000 light-years

Mass: About 200 billion suns

Distance between spiral arms: 6,500 light years

Thickness of galactic disk: 1,300 light-years

Satellite galaxies: 2 (visible only in the southern sky)

Sun

The Sun's diameter — more than 865,000 miles — is 109 times greater than that of the Earth. Even so, the Sun is actually a fairly small star. Somewhere in the vastness of the universe astronomers have located a star that is 3,500 times larger than the Sun.

Diameter: 865,000 miles (1,392,000 km)
Mass: 333,000 times that of the Earth
Surface temperature: 10,300° F (5,700° C)
Central temperature: 27 million° F (15 million° C)
Composition: 70% hydrogen, 27% helium
Spin (at equator): 26 days, 21 hours

Mercury

Distance from the Sun: 35,985,000 miles (57,909,000 km), or 39% that of the Earth
Diameter: 3,031 miles (4,878 km), or 38% that of the Earth
Average surface temperature: 340° F (171° C)
Atmosphere: Extremely thin, contains helium and hydrogen
Length of day: 58 days, 15 hours, 30 minutes
Length of year: 87.97 days
Satellites: None

Venus

Distance from the Sun: 67,241,000 miles (108,209,000 km), or 72% that of the Earth
Diameter: 7,521 miles (12,104 km), or 95% that of the Earth
Surface temperature: 867° F (464° C)
Surface pressure: 90 times that of the Earth, equivalent to the pressure at a water depth of 3,000 feet (900 meters)
Atmosphere: 96% carbon dioxide
Length of day: 243 days, 14 minutes. The planet spins opposite to the rotation of the Earth.
Length of year: 224.7 days
Satellites: None

Earth

Distance from the Sun: 92,960,000 miles (149,598,000 km)
Diameter: 7,926 miles (12,756 km)
Average surface temperature: 58° F (14° C)
Surface pressure: 1 atmosphere
Atmosphere: 78% nitrogen, 21% oxygen
Length of day: 23 hours, 56 minutes and 4 seconds
Length of year: 365.25 days
Satellites: 1

The Moon

The Moon is the Earth's only natural satellite. About 2,160 miles (3,746 km) across, the Moon is an airless, waterless world just one-fourth the size of the Earth. It circles the planet once every 27 days at an average distance of about 238,000 miles (384,000 km).

Jupiter

By any measure, Jupiter is the solar system's giant. To equal Jupiter's bulk would take 318 Earths. Over 1,300 Earth-sized balls could fit within this enormous planet.

Distance from the Sun: 483,631,000 miles (778,292,000 km), or 5.2 times that of the Earth
Diameter: 88,700 miles (142,800 km), or 11.3 times that of the Earth
Temperature at cloud tops: –234° F (–148° C)

Mars

Distance from the Sun: 141,642,000 miles (227,940,000 km), about 1.5 times that of the Earth
Diameter: 4,222 miles (6,794 km), or 53% that of the Earth
Average surface temperature: –13° F (–25° C)
Surface pressure: 0.7% (1/150 th) that of the Earth
Atmosphere: 95% carbon dioxide, 2.7% nitrogen
Length of day: 24 hours, 37 minutes
Length of year: 1 year, 321.73 days
Satellites: 2

Spatial Relationships of the Sun and the Planets

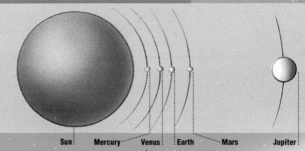

Sun   Mercury   Venus   Earth   Mars   Jupiter   Saturn

Atmosphere: 90% hydrogen, 10% helium
Length of day: 9 hours, 56 minutes
Length of year: 11 years, 314.96 days
Satellites: 16

Uranus

Distance from the Sun: 1,786,521,000 miles (2,874,993,000 km), or 19.2 times that of the Earth
Diameter: 31,700 miles (51,100 km), or four times that of the Earth
Temperature at cloud tops: –351° F (–213° C)
Atmosphere: 85% hydrogen, 15% helium
Length of day: 16 hours, 48 minutes. The planet spins opposite to the rotation of the Earth.
Length of year: 84 years, 3.65 days
Satellites: 15

Pluto

Distance from the Sun: 3,666,347,000 miles (5,900,140,000 km), or 39.4 times that of the Earth
Diameter: 1,416 miles (2,280 km), or 18% that of the Earth
Surface temperature: –369° F (–223° C)
Atmosphere: Extremely thin, contains methane
Length of day: 6 days, 9 hours, 17 minutes. The planet spins opposite to the rotation of the Earth.
Length of year:
248 years, 182 days
Satellites: 1

Neptune

Distance from the Sun:
2,798,989,000 miles
(4,504,328,000 km) or 30.1 times that of the Earth
Diameter: 30,200 miles (48,600 km), or 3.8 times that of the Earth
Temperature at cloud tops:
–357° F (–216° C)
Atmosphere: 85% hydrogen, 15% helium
Length of day: 16 hours, 3 minutes
Length of year: 164 years, 288.54 days
Satellites: 8

Saturn

Distance from the Sun: 888,210,000 miles (1,429,370,000 km), or 9.6 times that of the Earth
Diameter: 75,000 miles (120,700 km), or 9.4 times that of the Earth
Temperature at cloud tops: –288° F (–178° C)
Atmosphere: 94% hydrogen, 5% helium
Length of day: 10 hours, 41 minutes
Length of year: 29 years, 167.25 days
Satellites: 17

Uranus

Neptune

Pluto

The Earth

History of the Earth

Estimated age of the Earth:
At least 4.6 billion (4,600,000,000) years.

Formation of the Earth:
It is generally thought that the Earth was formed from a cloud of gas and dust (A) revolving around the early Sun. Gravitational forces pulled the cloud's particles together into an ever denser mass (B), with heavier particles sinking to the center. Heat from radioactive elements caused the materials of the embryonic Earth to melt and gradually settle into core and mantle layers. As the surface cooled, a crust formed. Volcanic activity released vast amounts of steam, carbon dioxide and other gases from the Earth's interior. The steam condensed into water to form the oceans, and the gases, prevented by gravity from escaping, formed the beginnings of the atmosphere (C).

The calm appearance of our planet today (D) belies the intense heat of its interior and the violent tectonic forces which are constantly reshaping its surface.

A

B

C

D

Periods in Earth's history

Earth's history is divided into different **eras**, which are subdivided into **periods**.

The most recent periods are themselves subdivided into **epochs**. The main divisions and subdivisions are shown below.

	Began	Ended	
	(million years ago)		
Precambrian Era			
Archean Period	3,800	2,500	Start of life
Proterozoic Period	2,500	590	Life in the seas
Paleozoic Era			
Cambrian Period	590	500	Sea life
Ordovician Period	505	438	First fishes
Silurian Period	438	408	First land plants
Devonian Period	408	360	Amphibians
Carboniferous Period	360	286	First reptiles
Permian Period	286	248	Spread of reptiles
Mesozoic Era			
Triassic Period	248	213	Reptiles and early mammals
Jurassic Period	213	144	Dinosaurs
Cretaceous Period	144	65	Dinosaurs, dying out at the end
Cenozoic Era			
Tertiary Period			
Paleocene	65	55	Large mammals
Eocene	55	38	Primates begin
Oligocene	38	25	Development of primates
Miocene	25	5	Modern-type animals
Pliocene	5	2	Australopithecus ape, ancestor to the human race
Quaternary Period			
Pleistocene	2	0.01	Ice ages; true humans
Holocene	0.01	Present	Modern humans

Source: *Atlas of the Universe* by Patrick Moore, Reed International Books Limited, 1994.

Internal Structure of the Earth

In its simplest form, the Earth is composed of a crust, a mantle with an upper and lower layer, and a core, which has an inner region.

Temperatures in the Earth increase with depth, as is observed in a deep mine shaft or bore-hole, but the prediction of temperatures within the Earth is made difficult by the fact that different rocks conduct heat at different rates: rock salt, for example, has 10 times the heat conductivity of coal. Also, estimates have to take into account the abundance of heat-generating atoms in a rock. Radioactive atoms are concentrated toward the Earth's surface, so the planet has, in effect, a thermal blanket to keep it warm. The temperature at the center of the Earth is believed to be approximately 5,400° F (3,000° C).

Upper Mantle
415 miles
(667 km) thick

Molten Outer Core
1,405 miles
(2,265 km) thick

Solid Inner Core
1,520 miles
(2,440 km)
in diameter

Lower Mantle
1,365 miles
(2,200 km) thick

Solid Crust
0–19 miles
(0–33 km) thick

Atmosphere

Chemical composition of the Earth:

The chemical composition of the Earth varies from crust to core. The upper crust of continents, called sial, is mainly granite, rich in aluminum and silicon. Oceanic crust, or sima, is largely basalt, made of magnesium and silicon. The mantle is composed of rocks that are rich in magnesium and iron silicates, whereas the core, it is believed, is made of iron and nickel oxides.

- Sial
- Sima
- Upper Mantle
- Lower Mantle
- Outer Core
- Inner Core

A. Silicon
B. Aluminum
C. Iron
D. Calcium
E. Magnesium
F. Nickel
G. Other

Sial (upper crust of continents)

Sima (oceanic crust)

Mantle

Core

Measurements of the Earth

Equatorial circumference of the Earth: 24,901.45 miles (40,066.43 km)

Polar circumference of the Earth: 24,855.33 miles (39,992.22 km)

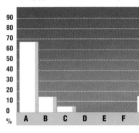

Equatorial diameter of the Earth: 7,926.38 miles (12,753.54 km)

Polar diameter of the Earth: 7,899.80 miles (12,710.77 km)

Equatorial radius of the Earth: 3,963.19 miles (6,376.77 km)

Polar radius of the Earth: 3,949.90 miles (6,355.38 km)

Estimated weight of the Earth:

6,600,000,000,000,000,000,000,000 tons, or 6,600 billion billion tons (5,940 billion billion metric tons)

Total surface area of the Earth: 197,000,000 square miles (510,230,000 sq km)

Total land area of the Earth (including inland water and Antarctica): 57,900,000 square miles (150,100,000 sq km)

Total ocean area of the Earth: 139,200,000 square miles (360,528,000 sq km), or 70% of the Earth's surface area

Total area of the Earth's surface covered with water (oceans and all inland water): 147,750,000 square miles (382,672,500 sq km), or 75% of the Earth's surface area

Types of water: 97% of the Earth's water is salt water; 3% is fresh water

Life on Earth

Number of plant species on Earth: About 350,000

Number of animal species on Earth: More than one million

Estimated total human population of the Earth: 5,628,000,000

Movements of the Earth

Mean distance of the Earth from the Sun: About 93 million miles (149.6 million km)

Period in which the Earth makes one complete orbit around the Sun: 365 days, 5 hours, 48 minutes, and 46 seconds

Speed of the Earth as it orbits the Sun: 66,700 miles (107,320 km) per hour

Period in which the Earth makes one complete rotation on its axis: 23 hours, 56 minutes and 4 seconds

Equatorial speed at which the Earth rotates on its axis: More than 1,000 miles (1,600 km) per hour

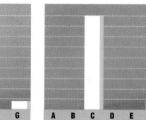

The Shape of the Earth

Comparing the Earth's equatorial and polar dimensions reveals that our planet is actually not a perfect sphere but rather an oblate spheroid, flattened at the poles and bulging at the equator. This is the result of a combination of gravitational and centrifugal forces.

An even more precise term for the Earth's shape is "geoid" — the actual shape of sea level, which is lumpy, with variations away from spheroid of up to 260 feet (80 m). This lumpiness reflects major variations in density in the Earth's outer layers.

The Seasons
(Northern Hemisphere)

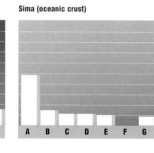

Summer Solstice
Noon sun is directly overhead at 23 1/2° N. Longest day of year.

Vernal Equinox
Noon sun is directly overhead at the equator, on its apparent migration North. Day and night are equal.

Autumnal Equinox
Noon sun is directly overhead at the equator, on its apparent migration South. Day and night are equal.

Winter Solstice
Noon sun is directly overhead at 23 1/2° S. Shortest day of year.

Continents and Islands

The word "continents" designates the largest continuous masses of land in the world.

For reasons that are mainly historical, seven continents are generally recognized: Africa, Antarctica, Asia, Australia, Europe, North America, and South America. Since Asia and Europe actually share the same land mass, they are sometimes identified as a single continent, Eurasia.

The lands of the central and south Pacific, including Australia, New Zealand, Micronesia, Melanesia, and Polynesia, are sometimes grouped together as Oceania.

The Continents

Africa

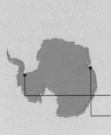

Area in square miles (sq km):
11,700,000 (30,300,000)
Estimated population (Jan. 1, 1995):
697,600,000
Population per square mile (sq km):
60 (23)
Mean elevation in feet (meters):
1,900 (580)
Highest elevation in feet (meters):
Kilimanjaro, Tanzania, 19,340 (5,895)
Lowest elevation in feet (meters):
Lac Assal, Djibouti, 515 (157) below sea level

Antarctica

Area in square miles (sq km):
5,400,000 (14,000,000)
Estimated population (Jan. 1, 1995):
Uninhabited
Population per square mile (sq km):
0 (0)
Mean elevation in feet (meters):
6,000 (1,830)
Highest elevation in feet (meters):
Vinson Massif, 16,066 (4,897)
Lowest elevation in feet (meters):
Deep Lake, 184 (56) below sea level

Asia

Area in square miles (sq km):
17,300,000 (44,900,000)
Estimated population (Jan. 1, 1995):
3,422,700,000
Population per square mile (sq km):
198 (76)
Mean elevation in feet (meters):
3,000 (910)
Highest elevation in feet (meters):
Mt. Everest, China (Tibet)–Nepal, 29,028 (8,848)
Lowest elevation in feet (meters):
Dead Sea, Israel–Jordan, 1,339 (408) below sea level

Australia

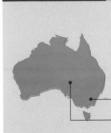

Area in square miles (sq km):
2,966,155 (7,682,300)
Estimated population (Jan. 1, 1995):
18,205,000
Population per square mile (sq km):
6.1 (2.4)
Mean elevation in feet (meters):
1,000 (305)
Highest elevation in feet (meters):
Mt. Kosciuszko, New South Wales, 7,313 (2,229)
Lake Eyre, South Australia, 52 (16) below sea level

Europe

Area in square miles (sq km):
3,800,000 (9,900,000)
Estimated population (Jan. 1, 1995):
712,100,000
Population per square mile (sq km):
187 (72)
Mean elevation in feet (meters):
980 (300)
Highest elevation in feet (meters):
Gora El'brus, Russia, 18,510 (5,642)
Lowest elevation in feet (meters):
Caspian Sea, Asia-Europe, 92 (28) below sea level

North America

Area in square miles (sq km):
9,500,000 (24,700,000)
Estimated population (Jan. 1, 1995):
453,300,000
Population per square mile (sq km):
48 (18)
Mean elevation in feet (meters):
2,000 (610)
Highest elevation in feet (meters):
Mt. McKinley, Alaska, U.S., 20,320 (6,194)
Lowest elevation in feet (meters):
Death Valley, California, U.S.,
282 (86) below sea level

Oceania *(incl. Australia)*

Area in square miles (sq km):
3,300,000 (8,500,000)
Estimated population (Jan. 1, 1995):
28,400,000
Population per square mile (sq km):
8.6 (3.3)
Mean elevation in feet (meters):
0 (0)
Highest elevation in feet (meters):
Mt. Wilhelm, Papua New Guinea, 14,793 (4,509)
Lowest elevation in feet (meters):
Lake Eyre, South Australia, 52 (16) below sea level

South America

Area in square miles (sq km):
6,900,000 (17,800,000)
Estimated population (Jan. 1, 1995):
313,900,000
Population per square mile (sq km):
45 (18)
Mean elevation in feet (meters):
1,800 (550)
Highest elevation in feet (meters):
Cerro Aconcagua, Argentina, 22,831 (6,959)
Lowest elevation in feet (meters):
Salinas Chicas, Argentina, 138 (42) below sea level

World

Area in square miles (sq km):
57,900,000 (150,100,000)
Estimated population (Jan. 1, 1995):
5,628,000,000
Population per square mile (sq km):
97 (37)
Mean elevation in feet (meters):
0 (0)
Highest elevation in feet (meters):
Mt. Everest, China (Tibet)–Nepal, 29,028 (8,848)
Lowest elevation in feet (meters):
Dead Sea, Israel–Jordan,
1,339 (408) below sea level

Largest Islands

Rank	Name	Area square miles	square km
1	Greenland, North America	840,000	2,175,600
2	New Guinea, Asia-Oceania	309,000	800,000
3	Borneo (Kalimantan), Asia	287,300	744,100
4	Madagascar, Africa	226,500	587,000
5	Baffin Island, Canada	195,928	507,451
6	Sumatra (Sumatera), Indonesia	182,860	473,606
7	Honshū, Japan	89,176	230,966
8	Great Britain, United Kingdom	88,795	229,978
9	Victoria Island, Canada	83,897	217,291
10	Ellesmere Island, Canada	75,767	196,236
11	Celebes (Sulawesi), Indonesia	73,057	189,216
12	South Island, New Zealand	57,708	149,463
13	Java (Jawa), Indonesia	51,038	132,187
14	North Island, New Zealand	44,332	114,821
15	Cuba, North America	42,800	110,800
16	Newfoundland, Canada	42,031	108,860
17	Luzon, Philippines	40,420	104,688
18	Iceland, Europe	39,800	103,000
19	Mindanao, Philippines	36,537	94,630
20	Ireland, Europe	32,600	84,400
21	Hokkaidō, Japan	32,245	83,515
22	Sakhalin, Russia	29,500	76,400
23	Hispaniola, North America	29,400	76,200
24	Banks Island, Canada	27,038	70,028
25	Tasmania, Australia	26,200	67,800
26	Sri Lanka, Asia	24,900	64,600
27	Devon Island, Canada	21,331	55,247
28	Berkner Island, Antarctica	20,005	51,829
29	Alexander Island, Antarctica	19,165	49,652
30	Tierra del Fuego, South America	18,600	48,200
31	Novaya Zemlya, north island, Russia	18,436	47,764
32	Kyūshū, Japan	17,129	44,363
33	Melville Island, Canada	16,274	42,149
34	Southampton Island, Canada	15,913	41,214
35	Axel Heiberg, Canada	15,498	40,151
36	Spitsbergen, Norway	15,260	39,523
37	New Britain, Papua New Guinea	14,093	36,500
38	Taiwan, Asia	13,900	36,000
39	Hainan Dao, China	13,100	34,000
40	Prince of Wales Island, Canada	12,872	33,339
41	Novaya Zemlya, south island, Russia	12,633	32,730
42	Vancouver Island, Canada	12,079	31,285
43	Sicily, Italy	9,926	25,709
44	Somerset Island, Canada	9,570	24,700
45	Sardinia, Italy	9,301	24,090
46	Bathurst Island, Canada	7,600	19,684
47	Shikoku, Japan	7,258	18,799
48	Ceram (Seram), Indonesia	7,191	18,625
49	North East Land, Norway	6,350	16,446
50	New Caledonia, Oceania	6,252	16,192
51	Prince Patrick Island, Canada	5,986	15,509
52	Timor, Indonesia	5,743	14,874
53	Sumbawa, Indonesia	5,549	14,377
54	Ostrov Oktyabr'skoy Revolyutsii, Russia	5,511	14,279
55	Flores, Indonesia	5,502	14,250
56	Samar, Philippines	5,100	13,080
57	King William Island, Canada	4,961	12,853
58	Negros, Philippines	4,907	12,710
59	Thurston Island, Antarctica	4,854	12,576
60	Palawan, Philippines	4,550	11,785

Islands, Islands, Everywhere

Four islands—Hokkaidō, Honshū, Kyūshū, and Shikoku—
constitute 98% of Japan's total land area, but the country is actually
comprised of more than 3,000 islands. Similarly, two islands—
Great Britain and Ireland—make up 93% of the total land area of
the British Isles, but the island group also includes more than 5,000
smaller islands.

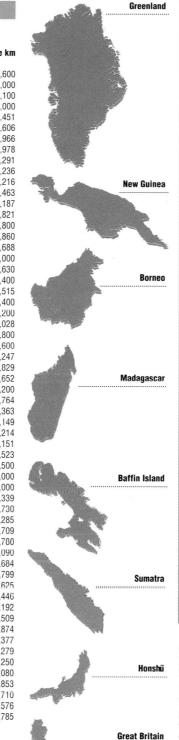

Greenland

New Guinea

Borneo

Madagascar

Baffin Island

Sumatra

Honshū

Great Britain

Victoria Island

Ellesmere Island

Major World Island Groups

Aleutian Islands (Pacific Ocean)

Alexander Archipelago (Pacific Ocean)

Azores (Atlantic Ocean)

Bahamas (Atlantic Ocean)

Balearic Islands (Mediterranean Sea)

Bismarck Archipelago (Pacific Ocean)

British Isles (Atlantic Ocean)

Cape Verde Islands (Atlantic Ocean)

Dodecanese (Mediterranean Sea)

Faroe Islands (Atlantic Ocean)

Falkland Islands (Atlantic Ocean)

Fiji Islands (Pacific Ocean)

Galapagos Islands (Pacific Ocean)

Greater Sunda Islands (Indian/Pacific Oceans)

Hawaiian Islands (Pacific Ocean)

Ionian Islands (Mediterranean Sea)

Islas Canarias (Atlantic Ocean)

Japan (Pacific Ocean)

Kikládhes (Mediterranean Sea)

Kuril Islands (Pacific Ocean)

Lesser Sunda Islands (Indian Ocean)

Moluccas (Pacific Ocean)

Nansei Shotō (Pacific Ocean)

New Hebrides (Atlantic Ocean)

New Siberian Islands (Arctic Ocean)

Novaya Zemlya (Arctic Ocean)

Philippine Islands (Pacific Ocean)

Severnaya Zemlya (Arctic Ocean)

Solomon Islands (Pacific Ocean)

Spitsbergen (Arctic Ocean)

West Indies (Atlantic Ocean)

Contrasting Population Densities

Some islands are among
the most densely populated
places on Earth, while
others are among the least
densely populated. This
fact is dramatically
illustrated by
the following
comparison of
five islands:

| Manhattan, N.Y., U.S., (pop. 1,488,000) | 67,636/ sq mile (26,105/ sq km) |

| Singapore Island, Singapore (pop. 2,921,000) | 11,874/ sq mile (4,593/ sq km) |

| Long Island, N.Y., U.S. (pop. 6,863,000) | 4,984/ sq mile (1,925/ sq km) |

Population per square mile (sq km)

| Baffin Island, Canada (pop. 8,800) | 0.04/ sq mile (0.02/ sq km) |

| Greenland (pop. 57,000) | 0.07/ sq mile (0.03/ sq km) |

Mountains, Volcanoes, and Earthquakes

The Tallest Mountain in the World

With its peak reaching 29,028 feet (8,848 m) above sea level, Mt. Everest ranks as the *highest* mountain in the world, but not the *tallest*. That title goes to Mauna Kea, one of the five volcanic mountains that make up the island of Hawaii. From its base on the floor of the Pacific Ocean, Mauna Kea rises 33,476 feet (10,210 m)—more than six miles—although only the top 13,796 feet (4,205 m) are above sea level.

Seafloor Atop Mt. Everest

When Sir Edmund Percival Hillary and Tenzing Norgay reached the summit of Mt. Everest in 1953, they probably did not realize they were standing on the seafloor.

The Himalayan mountain system was formed through the process of plate tectonics. Ocean once separated India and Asia, but 180 million years ago the Indo-Australian crustal plate, on which India sits, began a northward migration and eventually collided with the Eurasian plate. The seafloor between the two landmasses crumpled and was slowly thrust upward. Rock layers that once lay at the bottom of the ocean now crown the peaks of the highest mountains in the world.

Principal Mountain Systems and Ranges of the World

Alaska Range (North America)
Alps (Europe)
Altai (Asia)
Andes (South America)
Appennino (Europe)
Atlas Mountains (Africa)
Appalachian Mountains (North America)
Brooks Range (North America)
Carpathian Mountains (Europe)
Cascade Range (North America)
Caucasus (Europe/Asia)
Coast Mountains (North America)
Coast Ranges (North America)
Great Dividing Range (Australia)
Greater Khingan Range (Asia)
Himalayas (Asia)
Hindu Kush (Asia)
Karakoram Range (Asia)
Kunlun Shan (Asia)
Madre Occidental, Sierra (North America)
Madre Oriental, Sierra (North America)
Nevada, Sierra (North America)
Pamirs (Asia)
Pyrenees (Europe)
Rocky Mountains (North America)
Sayan Khrebet (Asia)
Southern Alps (New Zealand)
Tien Shan (Asia)
Urals (Europe)
Zagros Mountains (Asia)

Principal Mountains of the World

Δ = Highest mountain in range, region, country, or state named

Location	Feet	Meters
Africa		
Kilimanjaro, Δ Tanzania (Δ Africa)	19,340	5,895
Kirinyaga (Mount Kenya), Δ Kenya	17,058	5,199
Margherita Peak, Δ Uganda-Δ Dem. Rep. of the Congo	16,763	5,109
Ras Dashen Terara, Δ Ethiopia	15,158	4,620
Meru, Mount, Tanzania	14,978	4,565
Karisimbi, Volcan, Δ Rwanda-Dem. Rep. of the Congo	14,787	4,507
Elgon, Mount, Kenya-Uganda	14,178	4,321
Toubkal, Jebel, Δ Morocco (Δ Atlas Mts.)	13,665	4,165
Cameroon Mountain, Δ Cameroon	13,451	4,100
Antarctica		
Vinson Massif, Δ Antarctica	16,066	4,897
Kirkpatrick, Mount	14,856	4,528
Markham, Mount	14,049	4,282
Jackson, Mount	13,747	4,190
Sidley, Mount	13,717	4,181
Wade, Mount	13,396	4,083
Asia		
Everest, Mount, Δ China-Δ Nepal (Δ Tibet; Δ Himalayas; Δ Asia; Δ World)	29,028	8,848
K2 (Qogir Feng), China-Δ Pakistan (Δ Kashmir; Δ Karakoram Range)	28,250	8,611
Kanchenjunga, Δ India-Nepal	28,208	8,598
Makalu, China-Nepal	27,825	8,481
Dhawalāgiri, Nepal	26,810	8,172
Nanga Parbat, Pakistan	26,660	8,126
Annapurna, Nepal	26,504	8,078
Gasherbrum, China-Pakistan	26,470	8,068
Xixabangma Feng, China	26,286	8,012
Nanda Devi, India	25,645	7,817
Kamet, China-India	25,447	7,756
Namjagbarwa Feng, China	25,446	7,756
Muztag, China (Δ Kunlun Shan)	25,338	7,723
Tirich Mir, Pakistan (Δ Hindu Kush)	25,230	7,690
Gongga Shan, China	24,790	7,556
Kula Kangri, Δ Bhutan	24,784	7,554
Kommunizma, Pik, Δ Tajikistan (Δ Pamir)	24,590	7,495
Nowshak, Δ Afghanistan-Pakistan	24,557	7,485
Pobedy, Pik, China-Russia	24,406	7,439
Chomo Lhari, Bhutan-China	23,997	7,314
Muztag, China	23,891	7,282
Lenina, Pik, Δ Kyrgyzstan-Tajikistan	23,406	7,134
Api, Nepal	23,399	7,132
Kangrinboqê Feng, China	22,028	6,714
Hkakabo Razi, Δ Myanmar	19,296	5,881
Damavand, Qolleh-ye, Δ Iran	18,386	5,604
Agri Dagi (Mount Ararat), Δ Turkey	16,854	5,137
Fuladi, Kuh-e, Afghanistan	16,847	5,135
Jaya, Puncak, Δ Indonesia (Δ New Guinea)	16,503	5,030
Klyuchevskaya, Vulkan, Russia (Δ Poluostrov Kamchatka)	15,584	4,750
Trikora, Puncak, Indonesia	15,584	4,750
Belukha, Gora, Kazakhstan-Russia	14,783	4,506
Turgen, Mount, Mongolia	14,311	4,362
Kinabalu, Gunong, Δ Malaysia (Δ Borneo)	13,455	4,101
Yü Shan, Δ Taiwan	13,114	3,997
Erciyes Dağı, Turkey	12,851	3,917
Kerinci, Gunung, Indonesia (Δ Sumatra)	12,467	3,800
Fuji San, Δ Japan (Δ Honshu)	12,388	3,776
Rinjani, Gunung, Indonesia (Δ Lombok)	12,224	3,726
Semeru, Gunung, Indonesia (Δ Java)	12,060	3,676
Hadūr Shu'ayb, Jabal an-, Δ Yemen (Δ Arabian Peninsula)	12,008	3,660
Australia / Oceania		
Wilhelm, Mt., Δ Papua New Guinea	14,793	4,509
Giluwe, Mt., Papua New Guinea	14,330	4,368
Bangeta, Mt., Papua New Guinea	13,520	4,121
Victoria, Mt., Papua New Guinea (Δ Owen Stanley Range)	13,238	4,035
Aoraki (Mt. Cook), Δ New Zealand (Δ South Island)	12,316	3,754
Europe		
El'brus, Gora, Δ Russia (Δ Caucasus; Δ Europe)	18,510	5,642
Dykhtau, Mt., Russia	17,073	5,204
Blanc, Mont (Monte Bianco) Δ France-Δ Italy (Δ Alps)	15,771	4,807

Location	Feet	Meters
Dufourspitze, Italy-Δ Switzerland	15,203	4,634
Weisshorn, Switzerland	14,783	4,506
Matterhorn, Italy-Switzerland	14,692	4,478
Finsteraarhorn, Switzerland	14,022	4,274
Jungfrau, Switzerland	13,642	4,158
Écrins, Barre des, France	13,458	4,102
Viso, Monte, Italy (Δ Cottian Alps)	12,602	3,841
Grossglockner, Δ Austria	12,461	3,798
Teide, Pico de, Δ Spain (Δ Canary Is.)	12,188	3,715
North America		
McKinley, Mt., Δ Alaska (Δ United States; Δ North America)	20,320	6,194
Logan, Mt., Δ Canada (Δ Yukon; Δ St. Elias Mts.)	19,551	5,959
Orizaba, Pico de, Δ Mexico	18,406	5,610
St. Elias, Mt., Alaska-Canada	18,008	5,489
Popocatépetl, Volcán, Mexico	17,930	5,465
Foraker, Mt., Alaska	17,400	5,304
Iztaccíhuatl, Mexico	17,159	5,230
Lucania, Mt., Canada	17,147	5,226
Fairweather, Mt., Alaska-Canada (Δ British Columbia)	15,300	4,663
Whitney, Mt., Δ California	14,494	4,418
Elbert, Mt., Δ Colorado (Δ Rocky Mts.)	14,433	4,399
Massive, Mt., Colorado	14,421	4,396
Harvard, Mt., Colorado	14,420	4,395
Rainier, Mt., Δ Washington (Δ Cascade Range)	14,410	4,392
Williamson, Mt., California	14,370	4,380
La Plata Pk., Colorado	14,361	4,377
Blanca Pk., Colorado (Δ Sangre de Cristo Mts.)	14,345	4,372
Uncompahgre Pk., Colorado (Δ San Juan Mts.)	14,309	4,361
Grays Pk., Colorado (Δ Front Range)	14,270	4,349
Evans, Mt., Colorado	14,264	4,348
Longs Pk., Colorado	14,255	4,345
Wrangell, Mt., Alaska	14,163	4,317
Shasta, Mt., California	14,162	4,317
Pikes Pk., Colorado	14,110	4,301
Colima, Nevado de, Mexico	13,991	4,240
Tajumulco, Volcán, Δ Guatemala (Δ Central America)	13,845	4,220
Gannett Pk., Δ Wyoming	13,804	4,207
Mauna Kea, Δ Hawaii	13,796	4,205
Grand Teton, Wyoming	13,770	4,197
Mauna Loa, Hawaii	13,679	4,169
Kings Pk., Δ Utah	13,528	4,123
Cloud Pk., Wyoming (Δ Bighorn Mts.)	13,167	4,013
Waddington, Mt., Canada (Δ Coast Mts.)	13,163	4,012
Wheeler Pk., Δ New Mexico	13,161	4,011
Boundary Pk., Δ Nevada	13,140	4,005
Robson, Mt., Canada (Δ Canadian Rockies)	12,972	3,954
Granite Pk., Δ Montana	12,799	3,901
Borah Pk., Δ Idaho	12,662	3,859
Humphreys Pk., Δ Arizona	12,633	3,851
Chirripó, Volcán, Δ Costa Rica	12,530	3,819
Columbia, Mt., Canada (Δ Alberta)	12,294	3,747
Adams, Mt., Washington	12,276	3,742
Gunnbjørn Fjeld, Δ Greenland	12,139	3,700
South America		
Aconcagua, Cerro, Δ Argentina (Δ Andes; Δ South America)	22,831	6,959
Ojos del Salado, Nevado, Argentina-Δ Chile	22,615	6,893
Bonete, Cerro, Argentina	22,546	6,872
Huascarán, Nevado, Δ Peru	22,133	6,746
Llullaillaco, Volcán, Argentina-Chile	22,110	6,739
Yerupaja, Nevado, Peru	21,765	6,634
Tupungato, Cerro, Argentina-Chile	21,555	6,570
Sajama, Nevado, Bolivia	21,463	6,542
Illampu, Nevado, Bolivia	21,066	6,421
Illimani, Nevado, Bolivia	20,741	6,322
Chimborazo, Δ Ecuador	20,702	6,310
Antofalla, Volcán, Argentina	20,013	6,100
Cotopaxi, Ecuador	19,347	5,897
Misti, Volcán, Peru	19,101	5,822
Huila, Nevado de, Colombia (Δ Cordillera Central)	18,865	5,750
Bolívar, Pico, Δ Venezuela	16,427	5,007

Notable Volcanic Eruptions

Year	Volcano Name, Location	Comments
ca. 4895 B.C.	Crater Lake, Oregon, U.S.	Collapse forms caldera that now contains Crater Lake.
ca. 4350 B.C.	Kikai, Ryukyu Islands, Japan	Japan's largest known eruption.
ca. 1628 B.C.	Santorini (Thira), Greece	Eruption devastates late Minoan civilization.
79 A.D.	Vesuvius (Vesuvio), Italy	Roman towns of Pompeii and Herculaneum are buried.
ca. 180	Taupo, New Zealand	Area measuring 6,200 square miles (16,000 sq km) is devastated.
ca. 260	Ilopango, El Salvador	Thousands killed, with major impact on Mayan civilization.
915	Towada, Honshu, Japan	Japan's largest historic eruption.
ca. 1000	Baitoushan, China/Korea	Largest known eruption on Asian mainland.
1259	Unknown	Evidence from polar ice cores suggests that a huge eruption, possibly the largest of the millennium, occurred in this year.
1586	Kelut, Java	Explosions in crater lake; mudflows kill 10,000.
1631	Vesuvius (Vesuvio), Italy	Eruption kills 4,000.
ca. 1660	Long Island, Papua New Guinea	"The time of darkness" in tribal legends on Papua New Guinea.
1672	Merapi, Java	Pyroclastic flows and mudflows kill 3,000.
1711	Awu, Sangihe Islands, Indonesia	Pyroclastic flows kill 3,000.
1760	Makian, Halmahera, Indonesia	Eruption kills 2,000; island evacuated for seven years.
1772	Papandayan, Java	Debris avalanche causes 2,957 fatalities.
1783	Lakagigar, Iceland	Largest historic lava flows; 9,350 deaths.
1790	Kilauea, Hawaii	Hawaii's last large explosive eruption.
1792	Unzen, Kyushu, Japan	Tsunami and debris avalanche kill 14,500.
1815	Tambora, Indonesia	History's most explosive eruption; 92,000 deaths.
1822	Galunggung, Java	Pyroclastic flows and mudflows kill 4,011.
1856	Awu, Sangihe Islands, Indonesia	Pyroclastic flows kill 2,806.
1883	Krakatau, Indonesia	Caldera collapse; 36,417 people killed, most by tsunami.
1888	Ritter Island, Papua New Guinea	3,000 killed, most by tsunami created by debris avalanche.
1902	Mont Pelee, West Indies	Town of St. Pierre destroyed; 28,000 people killed.
1902	Santa Maria, Guatemala	5,000 killed as 10 villages are buried by volcanic debris.
1912	Novarupta (Katmai), Alaska	Largest 20th-century eruption.
1914	Lassen, California, U.S.	California's last historic eruption.
1919	Kelut, Java	Mudflows devastate 104 villages and kill 5,110 people.
1930	Merapi, Java	1,369 people are killed as 42 villages are totally or partially destroyed.
1943	Parícutin, Mexico	Fissure in cornfield erupts, building cinder cone 1,500 feet (460 m) high within two years. One of the few volcano births ever witnessed.
1951	Lamington, Papua New Guinea	Pyroclastic flows kill 2,942.
1963	Surtsey, Iceland	Submarine eruption builds new island.
1977	Nyiragongo, Dem. Rep. of the Congo	One of the shortest major eruptions and fastest lava flows ever recorded.
1980	St. Helens, Washington, U.S.	Lateral blast; 230-square-mile (600 sq km) area devastated.
1982	El Chichón, Mexico	Pyroclastic surges kill 1,877.
1985	Ruiz, Colombia	Mudflows kill 23,080.
1991	Pinatubo, Luzon, Philippines	Major eruption in densely populated area prompts evacuation of 250,000 people; fatalities number fewer than 800. Enormous amount of gas released into stratosphere lowers global temperatures for more than a year.
1993	Juan de Fuca Ridge, off the coast of Oregon, U.S.	Deep submarine rift eruptions account for three-fourths of all lava produced; this is one of the very few such eruptions that have been well-documented.

Eruption of Mt. St. Helens in 1980

Sources: Smithsonian Institution Global Volcanism Program; Volcanoes of the World, *Second Edition, by Tom Simkin and Lee Siebert, Geoscience Press and Smithsonian Institution, 1994.*

Significant Earthquakes through History

Year	Estimated Magnitude	Number of Deaths	Place
365		50,000	Knossos, Crete
844		50,000	Damascus, Syria; Antioch, Turkey
856		150,000	Dāmghān, Kashan, Qumis, Iran
893		150,000	Caucasus region
894		180,000	western India
1042		50,000	Palmyra, Baalbek, Syria
1138		230,000	Aleppo, Gansana, Syria
1139	6.8	300,000	Gäncä, Kiapas, Azerbaijan
1201		50,000	upper Egypt to Syria
1290	6.7	100,000	eastern China
1556		820,000	Shanxi Province, China
1662		300,000	China
1667	6.9	80,000	Caucusus region, northern Iran
1668		50,000	Shandong Province, China
1693		93,000	Sicily, Italy
1727		77,000	Tabrīz, Iran
1731		100,000	Beijing, China
1739		50,000	China
1755		62,000	Morocco, Portugal, Spain
1780	6.7	100,000	Tabrīz, Iran
1868	7.7	70,000	Ecuador, Colombia
1908	7.5	83,000	Calabria, Messina, Italy
1920	8.5	200,000	Gansu and Shanxi provinces, China

Year	Estimated Magnitude	Number of Deaths	Place
1923	8.2	142,807	Tokyo, Yokohama, Japan
1927	8.3	200,000	Gansu and Qinghai provinces, China
1932	7.6	70,000	Gansu Province, China
1970	7.8	66,794	northern Peru
1976	7.8	242,000	Tangshan, China
1990	7.7	50,000	northwestern Iran

Some Significant U.S. Earthquakes

Year	Estimated Magnitude	Number of Deaths	Place
1811–12	8.6, 8.4, 8.7	<10	New Madrid, Missouri (series)
1886	7.0	60	Charleston, South Carolina
1906	8.3	3,000	San Francisco, California
1933	6.3	115	Long Beach, California
1946	7.4	5 ‡	Alaska
1964	8.4	125	Anchorage, Alaska
1971	6.8	65	San Fernando, California
1989	7.1	62	San Francisco Bay Area, California
1994	6.8	58	Northridge, California

‡ A tsunami generated by this earthquake struck Hilo, Hawaii, killing 159 people.
Sources: Lowell S. Whiteside, National Geophysical Data Center; Catalog of Significant Earthquakes 2150 B.C.—1991 A.D. by Paula K. Dunbar, Patricia A. Lockridge, and Lowell S. Whiteside, National Geophysical Data Center, National Oceanic and Atmospheric Administration.

Oceans and Lakes

Oceans, Seas, Gulfs, and Bays

	Area sq. miles	Area sq. km.	Volume of water cubic miles	Volume of water cubic km.	Mean depth feet	Mean depth meters	Greatest known depth feet	Greatest known depth meters	
Pacific Ocean	63,800,000	165,200,000	169,650,000	707,100,000	12,987	3,957	35,810	10,922	Mariana Trench
Atlantic Ocean	31,800,000	82,400,000	79,199,000	330,100,000	11,821	3,602	28,232	8,611	Puerto Rico Trench
Indian Ocean	28,900,000	74,900,000	68,282,000	284,600,000	12,261	3,736	23,812	7,258	Weber Basin
Arctic Ocean	5,400,000	14,000,000	4,007,000	16,700,000	3,712	1,131	17,897	5,453	Lat. 77° 45'N, long. 175°W
Coral Sea	1,850,000	4,791,000	2,752,000	11,470,000	7,857	2,394	30,079	9,165	
Arabian Sea	1,492,000	3,864,000	2,416,000	10,070,000	8,973	2,734	19,029	5,803	
South China Sea	1,331,000	3,447,000	943,000	3,929,000	3,741	1,140	18,241	5,563	
Caribbean Sea	1,063,000	2,753,000	1,646,000	6,860,000	8,175	2,491	25,197	7,685	Off Cayman Islands
Mediterranean Sea	967,000	2,505,000	901,000	3,754,000	4,916	1,498	16,470	5,023	Off Cape Matapan, Greece
Bering Sea	876,000	2,269,000	911,000	3,796,000	5,382	1,640	25,194	7,684	Off Buldir Island
Bengal, Bay of	839,000	2,173,000	1,357,000	5,616,000	8,484	2,585	17,251	5,261	
Okhotsk, Sea of	619,000	1,603,000	316,000	1,317,000	2,694	821	1,029	3,374	Lat. 146° 10'E, long. 46° 50'N
Norwegian Sea	597,000	1,546,000	578,000	2,408,000	5,717	1,742	13,189	4,022	
Mexico, Gulf of	596,000	1,544,000	560,000	2,332,000	8,205	2,500	14,370	4,382	Sigsbee Deep
Hudson Bay	475,000	1,230,000	22,000	92,000	328	100	850	259	Near entrance
Greenland Sea	465,000	1,204,000	417,000	1,740,000	4,739	1,444	15,899	4,849	
Japan, Sea of	413,000	1,070,000	391,000	1,630,000	5,037	1,535	12,041	3,669	
Arafura Sea	400,000	1,037,000	49,000	204,000	646	197	12,077	3,680	
East Siberian Sea	357,000	926,000	14,000	61,000	216	66	508	155	
Kara Sea	349,000	903,000	24,000	101,000	371	113	2,034	620	
East China Sea	290,000	752,000	63,000	263,000	1,145	349	7,778	2,370	
Banda Sea	268,000	695,000	511,000	2,129,000	10,056	3,064	24,418	7,440	
Baffin Bay	263,000	681,000	142,000	593,000	2,825	861	7,010	2,136	
Laptev Sea	262,000	678,000	87,000	363,000	1,772	540	9,780	2,980	
Timor Sea	237,000	615,000	60,000	250,000	1,332	406	10,863	3,310	
Andaman Sea	232,000	602,000	158,000	660,000	3,597	1,096	13,777	4,198	
Chukchi Sea	228,000	590,000	11,000	45,000	252	77	525	160	
North Sea	214,000	554,000	12,000	52,000	315	96	2,655	809	
Java Sea	185,000	480,000	5,000	22,000	147	45	292	89	
Beaufort Sea	184,000	476,000	115,000	478,000	3,295	1,004	12,245	3,731	
Red Sea	174,000	450,000	60,000	251,000	1,831	558	8,648	2,635	
Baltic Sea	173,000	448,000	5,000	20,000	157	48	1,506	459	
Celebes Sea	168,000	435,000	380,000	1,586,000	11,962	3,645	19,173	5,842	
Black Sea	166,000	431,000	133,000	555,000	3,839	1,170	7,256	2,211	
Yellow Sea	161,000	417,000	4,000	17,000	131	40	344	105	
Sulu Sea	134,000	348,000	133,000	553,000	5,221	1,591	18,300	5,576	
Molucca Sea	112,000	291,000	133,000	554,000	6,242	1,902	16,311	4,970	
Ceram Sea	72,000	187,000	54,000	227,000	3,968	1,209	17,456	5,319	
Flores Sea	47,000	121,000	53,000	222,000	6,003	1,829	16,813	5,123	
Bali Sea	46,000	119,000	12,000	49,000	1,349	411	4,253	1,296	
Savu Sea	41,000	105,000	43,000	178,000	5,582	1,701	11,060	3,370	
White Sea	35,000	91,000	1,000	4,400	161	49	1,083	330	
Azov, Sea of	15,000	40,000	100	400	29	9	46	14	
Marmara, Sea of	4,000	11,000	1,000	4,000	1,171	357	4,138	1,261	

Source: Atlas of World Water Balance, USSR National Committee for the International Water Decade and UNESCO, 1977.

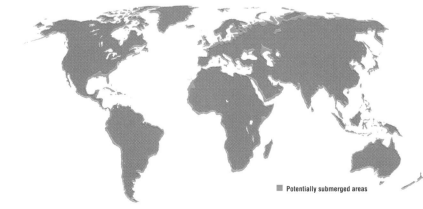

■ Potentially submerged areas

Fluctuating Sea Level

Changes in the Earth's climate have a dramatic effect on the sea level. Only 20,000 years ago, at the height of the most recent ice age, a vast amount of the Earth's water was locked up in ice sheets and glaciers, and the sea level was 330 feet (100 meters) lower than it is today. As the climate warmed slowly, the ice began to melt and the oceans began to rise.

Today there is still a tremendous amount of ice on the Earth. More than nine-tenths of it resides in the enormous ice cap which covers Antarctica. Measuring about 5.4 million square miles (14 million sq km) in surface area, the ice cap is on average one mile (1.6 km) thick but in some places is nearly three miles (4.8 km) thick. If it were to melt, the oceans would rise another 200 feet (60 m), and more than half of the world's population would have to relocate.

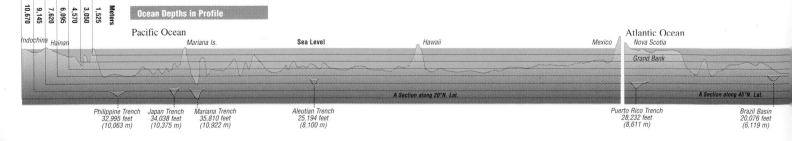

Ocean Depths in Profile

Feet	Meters
5,000	1,525
10,000	3,050
15,000	4,570
20,000	6,095
25,000	7,620
30,000	9,145
35,000	10,670

Pacific Ocean   Mariana Is.   Sea Level   Hawaii   Mexico   Atlantic Ocean   Nova Scotia

Indochina   Hainan

Grand Bank

A Section along 20°N. Lat.   *A Section along 45°N. Lat.*

Philippine Trench 32,995 feet (10,063 m)   Japan Trench 34,038 feet (10,375 m)   Mariana Trench 35,810 feet (10,922 m)   Aleutian Trench 25,194 feet (8,100 m)   Puerto Rico Trench 28,232 feet (8,611 m)   Brazil Basin 20,076 feet (6,119 m)

Deepest Lakes

Lake	Greatest depth feet	meters
1 Baikal, Lake, Russia	5,315	1,621
2 Tanganyika, Lake, Africa	4,800	1,464
3 Caspian Sea, Asia-Europe	3,363	1,025
4 Nyasa, Lake (Lake Malawi), Malawi-Mozambique-Tanzania	2,317	706
5 Issyk-Kul', Lake, Kyrgyzstan	2,303	702
6 Great Slave Lake, NWT, Canada	2,015	614
7 Matana, Lake, Indonesia	1,936	590
8 Crater Lake, Oregon, U.S.	1,932	589
9 Toba, Lake (Danau Toba), Indonesia	1,736	529
10 Sarez, Lake, Tajikistan	1,657	505
11 Tahoe, Lake, California-Nevada, U.S.	1,645	502
12 Kivu, Lake, Rwanda-Dem. Rep. of the Congo	1,628	496
13 Chelan, Lake, Washington, U.S.	1,605	489
14 Quesnel Lake, BC, Canada	1,560	476
15 Adams Lake, BC, Canada	1,500	457

Lakes with the Greatest Volume of Water

Lake	Volume of water cubic mi	cubic km
1 Caspian Sea, Asia-Europe	18,900	78,200
2 Baikal, Lake, Russia	5,500	23,000
3 Tanganyika, Lake, Africa	4,500	18,900
4 Superior, Lake, Canada-U.S.	2,900	12,200
5 Nyasa, Lake (Lake Malawi), Malawi-Mozambique-Tanzania	1,900	7,725
6 Michigan, Lake, U.S.	1,200	4,910
7 Huron, Lake, Canada-U.S.	860	3,580
8 Victoria, Lake, Kenya-Tanzania-Uganda	650	2,700
9 Issyk-Kul', Lake, Kyrgyzstan	415	1,730
10 Ontario, Lake, Canada-U.S.	410	1,710
11 Great Slave Lake, Canada	260	1,070
12 Aral Sea, Kazakhstan-Uzbekistan	250	1,020
13 Great Bear Lake, Canada	240	1,010
14 Ladozhskoye, Ozero, Russia	220	908
15 Titicaca, Lago, Bolivia-Peru	170	710

Sources for volume and depth information: Atlas of World Water Balance, USSR National Committee for the International Water Decade and UNESCO, 1977; Principal Rivers and Lakes of the World, National Oceanic and Atmospheric Administration, 1982.

Principal Lakes

Lake	Area sq mi	sq km
1 Caspian Sea, Asia-Europe	143,240	370,990
2 Superior, Lake, Canada-U.S.	31,700	82,100
3 Victoria, Lake, Kenya-Tanzania-Uganda	26,820	69,463
4 Aral Sea, Kazakhstan-Uzbekistan	24,700	64,100
5 Huron, Lake, Canada-U.S.	23,000	60,000
6 Michigan, Lake, U.S.	22,300	57,800
7 Tanganyika, Lake, Africa	12,350	31,986
8 Baikal, Lake, Russia	12,200	31,500
9 Great Bear Lake, Canada	12,095	31,326
10 Nyasa, Lake (Lake Malawi), Malawi-Mozambique-Tanzania	11,150	28,878
11 Great Slave Lake, Canada	11,030	28,568
12 Erie, Lake, Canada-U.S.	9,910	25,667
13 Winnipeg, Lake, Canada	9,416	24,387
14 Ontario, Lake, Canada-U.S.	7,540	19,529
15 Balqash koli (Lake Balkhash), Kazakhstan	7,100	18,300
16 Ladozhskoye, Ozero, Russia	6,833	17,700
17 Chad, Lake (Lac Tchad), Cameroon-Chad-Nigeria	6,300	16,300
18 Onezhskoye, Ozero, Russia	3,753	9,720
19 Eyre, Lake, Australia	3,700	9,500
20 Titicaca, Lago, Bolivia-Peru	3,200	8,300
21 Nicaragua, Lago de, Nicaragua	3,150	8,158
22 Mai-Ndombe, Lac, Dem. Rep. of the Congo	3,100	8,000
23 Athabasca, Lake, Canada	3,064	7,935
24 Reindeer Lake, Canada	2,568	6,650
25 Tônlé Sap, Cambodia	2,500	6,500
26 Rudolf, Lake, Ethiopia-Kenya	2,473	6,405
27 Issyk-Kul', Ozero, Kyrgyzstan	2,425	6,280
28 Torrens, Lake, Australia	2,300	5,900
29 Albert, Lake, Uganda-Dem. Rep. of the Congo	2,160	5,594
30 Vänern, Sweden	2,156	5,584
31 Nettilling Lake, Canada	2,140	5,542
32 Winnipegosis, Lake, Canada	2,075	5,374
33 Bangweulu, Lake, Zambia	1,930	4,999
34 Nipigon, Lake, Canada	1,872	4,848
35 Orumiyeh, Daryacheh-ye, Iran	1,815	4,701
36 Manitoba, Lake, Canada	1,785	4,624
37 Woods, Lake of the, Canada-U.S.	1,727	4,472
38 Kyoga, Lake, Uganda	1,710	4,429

Lake Baikal

Caspian Sea · **Lake Superior** · **Lake Victoria** · **Aral Sea**

Lake Huron · **Lake Michigan** · **Lake Tanganyika**

Lake Baikal · **Great Bear Lake** · **Lake Nyasa (Malawi)**

Russia's Great Lake

On a map of the world, Lake Baikal is easy to overlook — a thin blue crescent adrift in the vastness of Siberia. But its inconspicuousness is deceptive, for Baikal is one of the greatest bodies of fresh water on Earth.

Although lakes generally have a life span of less than one million years, Baikal has existed for perhaps as long as 25 million years, which makes it the world's oldest body of fresh water. It formed in a rift that tectonic forces had begun to tear open in the Earth's crust. As the rift grew, so did Baikal. Today the lake is 395 miles (636 km) long and an average of 30 miles (48 km) wide. Only seven lakes in the world have a greater surface area.

Baikal is the world's deepest lake. Its maximum depth is 5,315 feet (1,621 m) — slightly over a mile, and roughly equal to the greatest depth of the Grand Canyon. The lake bottom lies 4,250 feet (1,295 m) below sea level and two-and-a-third miles (3.75 km) below the peaks of the surounding mountains. The crustal rift which Baikal occupies is the planet's deepest land depression, extending to a depth of more than five-and-a-half miles (9 km). The lake sits atop at least four miles (6.4 km) of sediment, the accumulation of 25 million years.

More than 300 rivers empty into Baikal, but only one, the Angara, flows out of it. Despite having only 38% of the surface area of North America's Lake Superior, Baikal contains more water than all five of the Great Lakes combined. Its volume of 5,500 cubic miles (23,000 cubic km) is greater than that of any other freshwater lake in the world and represents approximately one-fifth of all of the Earth's unfrozen fresh water.

Mediterranean Sea · Indian Ocean · Arctic Ocean · Pacific Ocean

France · Gibraltar · Malta · Israel · Sea Level · Sumba · North Pole · 65°N 65°S · South Pole

A Section along 10°N. Lat.

Rivers

World's Longest Rivers

Rank	River	Length Miles	Length Kilometers	Rank	River	Length Miles	Length Kilometers
1	Nile, Africa	4,145	6,671	36	Murray, Australia	1,566	2,520
2	Amazon (Amazonas)-Ucayali, South America	4,000	6,400	37	Ganges, Asia	1,560	2,511
3	Yangtze (Chang), Asia	3,900	6,300	38	Pilcomayo, South America	1,550	2,494
4	Mississippi-Missouri, North America	3,740	6,019	39	Euphrates, Asia	1,510	2,430
5	Huang (Yellow), Asia	3,395	5,464	40	Ural, Asia	1,509	2,428
6	Ob'-Irtysh, Asia	3,362	5,410	41	Arkansas, North America	1,459	2,348
7	Río de la Plata-Paraná, South America	3,030	4,876	42	Colorado, North America (U.S.-Mexico)	1,450	2,334
8	Congo, Africa	2,900	4,700	43	Aldan, Asia	1,412	2,273
9	Paraná, South America	2,800	4,500	44	Syr Darya, Asia	1,370	2,205
10	Amur-Argun, Asia	2,761	4,444	45	Dnieper, Europe	1,350	2,200
11	Lena, Asia	2,700	4,400	46	Araguaia, South America	1,350	2,200
12	Mackenzie, North America	2,635	4,241	47	Cassai (Kasai), Africa	1,338	2,153
13	Mekong, Asia	2,600	4,200	48	Tarim, Asia	1,328	2,137
14	Niger, Africa	2,600	4,200	49	Kolyma, Asia	1,323	2,129
15	Yenisey, Asia	2,543	4,092	50	Orange, Africa	1,300	2,100
16	Missouri-Red Rock, North America	2,533	4,076	51	Negro, South America	1,300	2,100
17	Mississippi, North America	2,348	3,779	52	Ayeyarwady (Irrawaddy), Asia	1,300	2,100
18	Murray-Darling, Australia	2,330	3,750	53	Red, North America	1,270	2,044
19	Missouri, North America	2,315	3,726	54	Juruá, South America	1,250	2,012
20	Volga, Europe	2,194	3,531	55	Columbia, North America	1,240	2,000
21	Madeira, South America	2,013	3,240	56	Xingu, South America	1,230	1,979
22	São Francisco, South America	1,988	3,199	57	Ucayali, South America	1,220	1,963
23	Grande, Rio (Río Bravo), North America	1,885	3,034	58	Saskatchewan-Bow, North America	1,205	1,939
24	Purús, South America	1,860	2,993	59	Peace, North America	1,195	1,923
25	Indus, Asia	1,800	2,900	60	Tigris, Asia	1,180	1,899
26	Danube, Europe	1,776	2,858	61	Don, Europe	1,162	1,870
27	Brahmaputra, Asia	1,770	2,849	62	Songhua, Asia	1,140	1,835
28	Yukon, North America	1,770	2,849	63	Pechora, Europe	1,124	1,809
29	Salween (Nu), Asia	1,750	2,816	64	Kama, Europe	1,122	1,805
30	Zambezi, Africa	1,700	2,700	65	Limpopo, Africa	1,120	1,800
31	Vilyuy, Asia	1,647	2,650	66	Angara, Asia	1,105	1,779
32	Tocantins, South America	1,640	2,639	67	Snake, North America	1,038	1,670
33	Orinoco, South America	1,615	2,600	68	Uruguay, South America	1,025	1,650
34	Paraguay, South America	1,610	2,591	69	Churchill, North America	1,000	1,600
35	Amu Darya, Asia	1,578	2,540	70	Marañón, South America	995	1,592

The World's Greatest River

Although the Nile is slightly longer, the Amazon surpasses all other rivers in volume, size of drainage basin, and in nearly every other important category. If any river is to be called the greatest in the world, surely it is the Amazon.

It has been estimated that one-fifth of all of the flowing water on Earth is carried by the Amazon. From its 150-mile (240-km)-wide mouth, the river discharges 6,180,000 cubic feet (174,900 cubic m) of water per second — four-and-a-half times as much as the Congo, ten times as much as the Mississippi, and fifty-six times as much as the Nile. The Amazon's tremendous outflow turns the waters of the Atlantic from salty to brackish for more than 100 miles (160 km) offshore.

Covering more than one-third of the entire continent of South America, the Amazon's vast drainage basin measures 2,669,000 square miles (6,915,000 sq km) and is nearly twice as large as that of the second-ranked Congo. The Amazon begins its 4,000-mile (6,400-km) journey to the Atlantic from high up in the Andes, only 100 miles (160 km) from the Pacific. Along its course it receives the waters of more than 1,000 tributaries, which rise principally from the Andes, the Guiana Highlands, and the Brazilian Highlands. Seven of the tributaries are more than 1,000 miles (1,600 km) long, and one, the Madeira, is more than 2,000 miles (3,200 km) long.

The depth of the Amazon throughout most of its Brazilian segment exceeds 150 feet (45 m). Depths of more than 300 feet (90 m) have been recorded at points near the mouth. The largest ocean-going vessels can sail as far inland as Manaus, 1,000 miles (1,600 km) from the mouth. Freighters and small passenger vessels can navigate to Iquitos, 2,300 miles (3,700 km) from the mouth, even during times of low water.

Drainage basin of the Amazon River

Rivers with the Greatest Volume of Water

Rank	River Name	Flow of water per second at mouth cubic feet	Flow of water per second at mouth cubic meters	Rank	River Name	Flow of water per second at mouth cubic feet	Flow of water per second at mouth cubic meters
1	Amazon (Amazonas), South America	6,180,000	174,900	18	Para-Tocantins, South America (joins Amazon at mouth)	360,000	10,200
2	Congo, Africa	1,377,000	39,000	19	Salween, Asia	353,000	10,000
3	Negro, South America (tributary of Amazon)	1,236,000	35,000	20	Cassai (Kasai), Africa (trib. of Congo)	351,000	9,900
4	Orinoco, South America	890,000	25,200	21	Mackenzie, North America	343,000	9,700
5	Río de la Plata-Paraná, South America	809,000	22,900	22	Volga, Europe	271,000	7,700
6	Yangtze (Chang), Asia;	770,000	21,800	23	Ohio, North America (trib. of Mississippi)	257,000	7,300
	Madeira, South America (trib. of Amazon)	770,000	21,800	24	Yukon, North America	240,000	6,800
7	Missouri, North America (trib. of Mississippi)	763,000	21,600	25	Indus, Asia	235,000	6,600
8	Mississippi, North America*	640,300	18,100	26	Danube, Europe	227,000	6,400
9	Yenisey, Asia	636,000	18,000	27	Niger, Africa	215,000	6,100
10	Brahmaputra, Asia	575,000	16,300	28	Atchafalaya, North America	181,000	5,100
11	Lena, Asia	569,000	16,100	29	Paraguay, South America	155,000	4,400
12	Zambezi, Africa	565,000	16,000	30	Ob'-Katun, Asia	147,000	4,200
13	Mekong, Asia	500,000	14,100	31	São Francisco, South America	120,000	3,400
14	Saint Lawrence, North America	460,000	13,000	32	Tunguska, Asia	118,000	3,350
15	Ayeyarwady (Irrawaddy), Asia	447,000	12,600	33	Huang (Yellow), Asia	116,000	3,300
16	Ob'-Irtysh, Asia; Ganges, Asia	441,000	12,500	34	Nile, Africa	110,000	3,100
17	Amur, Asia	390,000	11,000				

*Approximately one-third of the Mississippi's water is diverted above Baton Rouge, Louisiana, and reaches the Gulf of Mexico via the Atchafalaya River.

Principal Rivers of the Continents

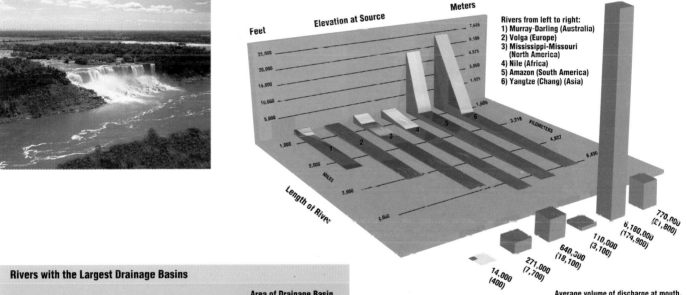

Rivers from left to right:
1) Murray-Darling (Australia)
2) Volga (Europe)
3) Mississippi-Missouri (North America)
4) Nile (Africa)
5) Amazon (South America)
6) Yangtze (Chang) (Asia)

Average volume of discharge at mouth, in cubic feet (cubic meters) per second

Rivers with the Largest Drainage Basins

Rank	River	Area of Drainage Basin Square Miles	Area of Drainage Basin Square Kilometers
1	Amazon (Amazonas), South America	2,669,000	6,915,000
2	Congo, Africa	1,474,500	3,820,000
3	Mississippi-Missouri, North America	1,243,000	3,220,000
4	Río de la Plata-Paraná, South America	1,197,000	3,100,000
5	Ob'-Irtysh, Asia	1,154,000	2,990,000
6	Nile, Africa	1,108,000	2,870,000
7	Yenisey-Angara, Asia	1,011,000	2,618,500
8	Lena, Asia	961,000	2,490,000
9	Niger, Africa	807,000	2,090,000
10	Amur-Argun, Asia	792,000	2,051,300
11	Yangtze (Chang), Asia	705,000	1,826,000
12	Volga, Europe	525,000	1,360,000
13	Zambezi, Africa	513,500	1,330,000
14	St. Lawrence, North America	503,000	1,302,800
15	Huang (Yellow), Asia	486,000	1,258,700

Sources for volume and drainage basin information: Atlas of World Water Balance, USSR National Committee for the International Hydrological Decade and UNESCO, 1977; Principal Rivers and Lakes of the World, National Oceanic and Atmospheric Administration, 1982.

Climate and Weather

Temperature Extremes by Continent

Africa
Highest recorded temperature
Al 'Azīzīyah, Libya, September 13, 1922:
136° F (58° C),
Lowest recorded temperature
Ifrane, Morocco, February 11, 1935:
-11° F (-24° C)

Antarctica
Highest recorded temperature
Vanda Station, January 5, 1974:
59° F (15° C)
Lowest recorded temperature
Vostok, July 21, 1983:
-129° F (-89° C)

Asia
Highest recorded temperature
Tirat Zevi, Israel, June 21, 1942:
129° F (54° C)
Lowest recorded temperature
Oymyakon and Verkhoyansk,
Russia, February 5 and 7, 1892,
and February 6, 1933: -90° F (-68° C)

Australia / Oceania
Highest recorded temperature
Cloncurry, Queensland, January 16, 1889:
128° F (53° C)
Lowest recorded temperature
Charlottes Pass, New South Wales,
June 14, 1945, and July 22, 1947: -8° F (-22° C)

Europe
Highest recorded temperature
Sevilla, Spain, August 4, 1881:
122° F (50° C)
Lowest recorded temperature
Ust' Ščugor, Russia, (date not known):
-67° F (-55° C)

North America
Highest recorded temperature
Death Valley, California, United States,
July 10, 1913: 134° F (57° C)
Lowest recorded temperature
Northice, Greenland, January 9, 1954:
-87° F (-66° C)

South America
Highest recorded temperature
Rivadavia, Argentina, December 11, 1905:
120° F (49° C)
Lowest recorded temperature
Sarmiento, Argentina, June 1, 1907:
-27° F (-33° C)

World
Highest recorded temperature
Al 'Azīzīyah, Libya, September 13, 1922:
136° F (58° C)
Lowest recorded temperature
Vostok, Antarctica, July 21, 1983:
-129° F (-89° C)

World Temperature Extremes

Highest mean annual temperature Dalol, Ethiopia, 94° F (34° C)
Lowest mean annual temperature Plateau Station, Antarctica: -70° F (-57° C)

Greatest difference between highest and lowest recorded temperatures
Verkhoyansk, Russia. The highest temperature ever recorded there is 93.5° F (34.2° C); the lowest is -89.7° F (−67.6° C)
— a difference of 183° F (102° C).

Highest temperature ever recorded at the South Pole 7.5° F (-14° C) on December 27, 1978

Most consecutive days with temperatures of 100° F (38° C) or above Marble Bar, Australia, 162 days: October 30, 1923 to April 7, 1924

Greatest rise in temperature within a 12-hour period
Granville, North Dakota, on February 21, 1918. The temperature rose 83° F (46° C), from -33° F (-36° C)
in early morning to +50° F (10° C) in late afternoon

Greatest drop in temperature within a 12-hour period
Fairfield, Montana, on December 24, 1924. The temperature dropped 84° F (46° C), from 63° F (17° C)
at noon to -21° F (-29° C) by midnight

Temperature Ranges for 14 Major Cities around the World

City	Mean Temperature	
	Coldest Winter Month	Hottest Summer Month
Buenos Aires, Argentina	Aug: 51.3° F (10.7° C)	Jan: 75.0° F (23.9° C)
Kolkata (Calcutta), India	Jan: 67.5° F (19.7° C)	May: 88.5° F (31.4° C)
London, England	Feb: 39.4° F (4.1° C)	Jul: 63.9° F (17.7° C)
Los Angeles, U.S.	Jan: 56.3° F (13.5° C)	Jul: 74.1° F (23.4° C)
Manila, Philippines	Jan: 77.7° F (25.4° C)	May: 84.9° F (29.4° C)
Mexico City, Mexico	Jan: 54.1° F (12.3° C)	May: 64.9° F (18.3° C)
Moscow, Russia	Feb: 14.5° F (-9.7° C)	Jul: 65.8° F (18.8° C)

City	Mean Temperature	
	Coldest Winter Month	Hottest Summer Month
Mumbai (Bombay), India	Jan: 74.3° F (23.5° C)	May: 85.5° F (29.7° C)
New York City, U.S.	Jan: 32.9° F (0.5° C)	Jul: 77.0° F (25.0° C)
Osaka, Japan	Jan: 40.6° F (4.8° C)	Aug: 82.2° F (27.9° C)
Rio de Janeiro, Brazil	Jul: 70.2 ° F (21.2° C)	Jan: 79.9° F (26.6° C)
São Paulo, Brazil	Jul: 58.8° F (14.9° C)	Jan: 71.1° F (21.7° C)
Scoul, South Korea	Jan: 23.2° F (-4.9° C)	Aug: 77.7° F (25.4° C)
Tokyo, Japan	Jan: 39.6° F (4.2° C)	Aug: 79.3° F (26.3° C)

Precipitation

Greatest local average annual rainfall
Mt. Waialeale, Kauai, Hawaii,
460 inches (1,168 cm)

Lowest local average annual rainfall
Arica, Chile, .03 inches (.08 cm)

Greatest rainfall in 12 months
Cherrapunji, India, August 1860 to August 1861:
1,042 inches (2,647 cm)

Greatest rainfall in one month
Cherrapunji, India, July 1861: 366 inches (930 cm)

Greatest rainfall in 24 hours
Cilaos, Reunion, March 15 and 16, 1952:
74 inches (188 cm)

Greatest rainfall in 12 hours
Belouve, Reunion, February 28 and 29, 1964:
53 inches (135 cm)

Most thunderstorms annually
Kampala, Uganda, averages 242 days per
year with thunderstorms

Between 1916 and 1920, Bogor, Indonesia,
averaged 322 days per year with thunderstorms

Longest dry period
Arica, Chile, October, 1903
to January, 1918 — over 14 years

Largest hailstone ever recorded
Coffeyville, Kansas, U.S., September 3, 1970:
circumference 17.5 inches (44.5 cm)
diameter 5.6 inches (14 cm),
weight 1.67 pounds (758 grams)

Heaviest hailstone ever recorded
Kazakhstan, 1959: 4.18 pounds (1.9 kilograms)

North America's greatest snowfall in one season
Rainier Paradise Ranger Station, Washington,
U.S., 1971–1972: 1,122 inches (2,850 cm)

North America's greatest snowfall in one storm
Mt. Shasta Ski Bowl, California, U.S.,
February 13 to 19, 1959: 189 inches (480 cm)

North America's greatest snowfall in 24 hours
Silver Lake, Colorado, U.S., April 14 and 15, 1921:
76 inches (192.5 cm)

N. America's greatest depth of snowfall on the ground
Tamarack, California, U.S., March 11, 1911:
451 inches (1,145.5 cm)

Foggiest place on the U.S. West Coast
Cape Disappointment, Washington,
averages 2,552 hours of fog per year

Foggiest place on the U.S. East Coast
Mistake Island, Maine, averages
1,580 hours of fog per year

Wind

Highest 24-hour mean surface wind speed
Mt. Washington, New Hampshire, U.S.,
April 11 and 12, 1934: 128 mph (206 kph)

Highest 5-minute mean surface wind speed
Mt. Washington, New Hampshire, U.S.,
April 12, 1934: 188 mph (303 kph)

Highest surface wind peak gust:
Mt. Washington, New Hampshire, U.S.,
April 12, 1934: 231 mph (372 kph)

Windiest U.S. Cities

Chicago is sometimes called "The Windy City."
It earned this nickname because of long-winded politicians,
not because it has the strongest gales.

The windiest cities in the U.S. are as follows:

Cities	Average wind speed	
	mph	kph
Great Falls, Montana	13.1	21.0
Oklahoma City, Oklahoma	13.0	20.9
Boston, Massachusetts	12.9	20.7
Cheyenne, Wyoming	12.8	20.6
Wichita, Kansas	12.7	20.4

Chicago ranks 16th, with a 10.4 mph (16.7 kph) average.

Deadliest Hurricanes in the U.S. since 1890

Rank	Place	Year	Number of Deaths
1	Texas (Galveston)	1900	>6,000
2	Louisiana	1893	2,000
3	Florida (Lake Okeechobee)	1928	1,836
4	South Carolina, Georgia	1893	>1,000
5	Florida (Keys)	1919	>600
6	New England	1938	600
7	Florida (Keys)	1935	408
8	Southwest Louisiana, north Texas— "Hurricane Audrey"	1957	390
	Northeast U.S.	1944	390
9	Louisiana (Grand Isle)	1909	350
10	Louisiana (New Orleans)	1915	275

Tornadoes in the U.S., 1950—1993

Rank	State	Total Number of Tornadoes	Yearly Average	Total Number of Deaths
1	Texas	5,303	120	471
2	Oklahoma	2,259	51	217
3	Kansas	2,068	47	199
4	Florida	1,932	44	81
5	Nebraska	1,618	37	51
	U.S. Total	33,120	753	4,045

Deadliest Floods in the U.S. since 1900

Rank	Place	Year	Number of Deaths
1	Ohio River and tributaries	1913	467
2	Mississippi Valley	1927	313
3	Black Hills, South Dakota	1972	237
4	Texas rivers	1921	215
5	Northeastern U.S., following Hurricane Dianne	1955	187
6	Texas rivers	1913	177
7	James River basin, Virginia	1969	153
8	Big Thompson Canyon, Colorado	1976	139
9	Ohio and Lower Mississippi river basins	1937	137
10	Buffalo Creek, West Virginia	1972	125

Population

During the first two million years of our species' existence, human population grew at a very slow rate, and probably never exceeded 10 million. With the development of agriculture circa 8000 B.C., the growth rate began to rise sharply: by the year A.D. 1, the world population stood at approximately 250 million.

By 1650 the population had doubled to 550 million, and within only 200 years it doubled again, reaching almost 1.2 billion by 1850. Each subsequent doubling has taken only about half as long as the previous one: 100 years to reach 2.5 billion, and 40 years to reach 5.2 billion.

Experts have estimated that today's world population of 5.6 billion represents 5.5% of all of the people who have ever lived on Earth.*

* Population Today, *Population Reference Bureau,* February 1995

World Population

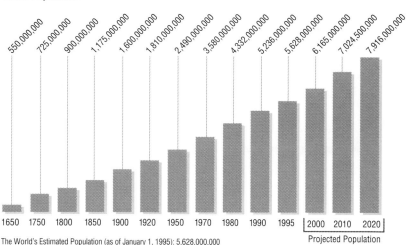

The World's Estimated Population (as of January 1, 1995): 5,628,000,000
Population Density: 97 people per square mile (37 people per square kilometer)

Historical Populations of the Continents and the World

Year	Africa	Asia	Australia	Europe	North America	Oceania, incl. Australia	South America	World
1650	100,000,000	335,000,000	<1,000,000	100,000,000	5,000,000	2,000,000	8,000,000	550,000,000
1750	95,000,000	476,000,000	<1,000,000	140,000,000	5,000,000	2,000,000	7,000,000	725,000,000
1800	90,000,000	593,000,000	<1,000,000	190,000,000	13,000,000	2,000,000	12,000,000	900,000,000
1850	95,000,000	754,000,000	<1,000,000	265,000,000	39,000,000	2,000,000	20,000,000	1,175,000,000
1900	118,000,000	932,000,000	4,000,000	400,000,000	106,000,000	6,000,000	38,000,000	1,600,000,000
1920	140,000,000	1,000,000,000	6,000,000	453,000,000	147,000,000	9,000,000	61,000,000	1,810,000,000
1950	199,000,000	1,418,000,000	8,000,000	530,000,000	219,000,000	13,000,000	111,000,000	2,490,000,000
1970	346,900,000	2,086,200,000	12,460,000	623,700,000	316,600,000	19,200,000	187,400,000	3,580,000,000
1980	463,800,000	2,581,000,000	14,510,000	660,000,000	365,000,000	22,700,000	239,000,000	4,332,000,000
1990	648,300,000	3,156,100,000	16,950,000	688,000,000	423,600,000	26,300,000	293,700,000	5,236,000,000

Figures for years prior to 1970 are rounded to the nearest million. Figures in italics represent rough estimates.

The 50 Most Populous Countries

Rank	Country	Population	Rank	Country	Population	Rank	Country	Population
1	China	1,196,980,000	18	United Kingdom	58,430,000	35	Algeria	27,965,000
2	India	909,150,000	19	Egypt	58,100,000	36	Morocco	26,890,000
3	United States	262,530,000	20	France	58,010,000	37	Sudan	25,840,000
4	Indonesia	193,680,000	21	Italy	57,330,000	38	Korea, North	23,265,000
5	Brazil	159,690,000	22	Ethiopia	55,070,000	39	Peru	23,095,000
6	Russia	150,500,000	23	Ukraine	52,140,000	40	Uzbekistan	22,860,000
7	Pakistan	129,630,000	24	Myanmar	44,675,000	41	Romania	22,745,000
8	Japan	125,360,000	25	Korea, South	44,655,000	42	Venezuela	21,395,000
9	Bangladesh	119,370,000	26	South Africa	44,500,000	43	Nepal	21,295,000
10	Nigeria	97,300,000	27	Dem. Rep. of the Congo	43,365,000	44	Taiwan	21,150,000
11	Mexico	93,860,000	28	Spain	39,260,000	45	Iraq	20,250,000
12	Germany	81,710,000	29	Poland	38,730,000	46	Afghanistan	19,715,000
13	Vietnam	73,760,000	30	Colombia	34,870,000	47	Malaysia	19,505,000
14	Philippines	67,910,000	31	Argentina	34,083,000	48	Uganda	18,270,000
15	Iran	63,810,000	32	Kenya	28,380,000	49	Sri Lanka	18,240,000
16	Turkey	62,030,000	33	Tanzania	28,350,000	50	Australia	18,205,000
17	Thailand	59,870,000	34	Canada	28,285,000			

Most Densely Populated Countries

Rank	Country (Population)	Population per Square Mile	Kilometer
1	Monaco (31,000)	44,286	16,316
2	Singapore (2,921,000)	11,874	4,593
3	Vatican City (1,000)	5,000	2,500
4	Malta (368,000)	3,016	1,165
5	Maldives (251,000)	2,183	842
6	Bangladesh (119,370,000)	2,147	829
7	Guernsey (64,000)	2,133	821
8	Bahrain (563,000)	2,109	815
9	Jersey (86,000)	1,911	741
10	Barbados (261,000)	1,572	607
11	Taiwan (21,150,000)	1,522	587
12	Mauritius (1,121,000)	1,423	550
13	Nauru (10,000)	1,235	476
14	Korea, South (44,655,000)	1,168	451
15	Puerto Rico (3,625,000)	1,031	398

Least Densely Populated Countries

Rank	Country (Population)	Population per Square Mile	Kilometer
1	Greenland (57,000)	0.07	0.03
2	Mongolia (2,462,000)	4.1	1.6
3	Namibia (1,623,000)	5.1	2.0
4	Mauritania (2,228,000)	5.6	2.2
5	Australia (18,205,000)	6.1	2.4
6	Botswana (1,438,000)	6.4	2.5
7	Iceland (265,000), Suriname (426,000)	6.7	2.6
8	Canada (28,285,000)	7.3	2.8
9	Libya (5,148,000)	7.6	2.9
10	Guyana (726,000)	8.7	3.4
11	Gabon (1,035,000)	10.1	3.9
12	Chad (6,396,000)	12.9	5.0
13	Central African Republic (3,177,000)	13.0	5.1
14	Bolivia (6,790,000)	16.0	6.2
15	Kazakhstan (17,025,000)	16.3	6.3

Most Highly Urbanized Countries

Country	Urban pop. as a % of total pop.
Vatican City	100%
Singapore	100%
Monaco	100%
Belgium	96%
Kuwait	96%
San Marino	92%
Israel (excl. Occupied Areas)	92%
Venezuela	91%
Iceland	91%
Qatar	90%
Uruguay	89%
Netherlands	89%
United Kingdom	89%
Malta	87%
Argentina	86%

Least Urbanized Countries

Country	Urban pop. as a % of total pop.
Bhutan	5%
Burundi	5%
Rwanda	6%
Nepal	11%
Oman	11%
Uganda	11%
Ethiopia	12%
Cambodia (Kampuchea)	12%
Malawi	12%
Burkina Faso	15%
Eritrea	15%
Grenada	15%
Solomon Islands	15%
Bangladesh	16%
Northern Mariana Islands	16%

Fastest-Growing and Slowest-Growing Countries

A country's rate of natural increase is determined by subtracting the number of deaths from the number of births for a given period. Immigration and emigration are not included in this formulation.

The highest rate of natural increase among major countries today is Syria's 3.74%. At this rate, Syria's 1995 population of 14,100,000 will double in 19 years and triple in 30 years.

In Hungary and Ukraine deaths currently outnumber births, and the two countries share the same negative rate of natural increase, -0.026%, the lowest in the world.

When all of the countries of the world are compared, pronounced regional patterns become apparent. Of the 35 fastest-growing countries, 30 are found in either Africa or the Middle East. Of the 45 slowest-growing countries, 42 are found in Europe.

World's Largest Metropolitan Areas

Rank	Name	Population
1	Tokyo-Yokohama, Japan	30,300,000
2	New York City, U.S.	18,087,000
3	São Paulo, Brazil	16,925,000
4	Osaka-Kobe-Kyoto, Japan	16,900,000
5	Seoul, South Korea	15,850,000
6	Los Angeles, U.S.	14,531,000
7	Mexico City, Mexico	14,100,000
8	Moscow, Russia	13,150,000
9	Mumbai (Bombay), India	12,596,000
10	London, England	11,100,000
11	Rio de Janeiro, Brazil	11,050,000
12	Kolkata (Calcutta), India	11,022,000
13	Buenos Aires, Argentina	11,000,000
14	Paris, France	10,275,000
15	Jakarta, Indonesia	10,200,000

The World's Most Populous Cities

The following table lists the most populous cities of the world by continent and in descending order of population. It includes all cities with central city populations of 500,000 or greater. Cities with populations of less than 500,000 but with metropolitan area populations of 1,000,000 or greater have also been included in the table.

The city populations listed are the latest available census figures or official estimates. For a few cities, only unofficial estimates are available. The year in which the census was taken or to which the estimate refers is provided in parentheses preceding the city population. When comparing populations it is important to keep in mind that some figures are more current than others.

Figures in parentheses represent metropolitan area populations — the combined populations of the cities and their suburbs.

The sequence of information in each listing is as follows: city name, country name (metropolitan area population) (date of census or estimate) city population.

The Most Populous City in the World, through History

With more than 30 million people, Japan's Tokyo-Yokohama agglomeration ranks as the most populous metropolitan area in the world today. New York City held this title from the mid-1920's through the mid-1960's. But what city was the most populous in the world five hundred years ago? Five *thousand* years ago?

The following time line represents one expert's attempt to name the cities that have reigned as the most populous in the world since 3200 B.C. The time line begins with Memphis, the capital of ancient Egypt, which was possibly the first city in the world to attain a population of 20,000.

Listed after each city name is the name of the political entity to which the city belonged during the time that it was the most populous city in the world. The name of the modern political entity in which the city, its ruins, or its site is located, where this entity differs from the historic political entity, is listed in parentheses.

For the purpose of this time line, the word "city" is used in the general sense to denote a city, metropolitan area, or urban agglomeration.

It is important to note that reliable census figures are not available for most of the 5,200 years covered by this time line. Therefore the time line is somewhat subjective and conjectural.

Africa

Cairo (Al Qāhirah),
Egypt (9,300,000) ('86) 6,068,695
Kinshasa, Dem. Rep. of the Congo ('86) . 3,000,000
Alexandria (Al Iskandarīyah),
Egypt (3,350,000) ('86) 2,926,859
Casablanca (Dar-el-Beida),
Morocco (2,475,000) ('82) 2,139,204
Abidjan, Cote d'Ivoire ('88) 1,929,079
Addis Ababa, Ethiopia (1,990,000) ('90) . 1,912,500
Giza (Al Jīzah), Egypt ('86) 1,883,189
Algiers (El Djazaïr),
Algeria (2,547,983)('87) 1,507,241
Nairobi, Kenya ('90) 1,505,000
Dakar, Senegal ('88) 1,490,450
Luanda, Angola ('89) 1,459,900
Antananarivo, Madagascar ('88) 1,250,000
Lagos, Nigeria (3,800,000) ('87) 1,213,000
Ibadan, Nigeria ('87) 1,144,000
Dar es Salaam, Tanzania ('85) 1,096,000
Maputo, Mozambique ('89) 1,069,727
Lusaka, Zambia ('90) 982,362
Accra, Ghana (1,390,000) ('87) 949,113
Cape Town,
South Africa (1,900,000) ('91) 854,616
Conakry, Guinea ('86) 800,000
Kampala, Uganda ('91) 773,463
Durban, South Africa (1,740,000) ('91) . . . 715,669
Shubrā al Khaymah, Egypt ('86) 714,594
Johannesburg,
South Africa (4,000,000) ('91) 712,507
Douala, Cameroon ('87) 712,251
Brazzaville, Congo ('89) 693,712
Harare, Zimbabwe (955,000) ('83) 681,000
Bamako, Mali ('87) 658,275
Oran, Algeria ('87) 628,558
Mogadishu (Muqdisho), Somalia ('84) . . . 600,000
Bangui, Central African Republic ('89) . . . 596,800
Tunis, Tunisia (1,225,000) ('84) 596,654
Soweto, South Africa ('91) 596,632
Tripoli (Tarābulus),
Libya (960,000) ('88) 591,062
Ogbomosho, Nigeria ('87) 582,900
Lubumbashi, Dem. Rep. of the Congo ('84) 564,830
Yaoundé, Cameroon ('87) 560,785
Kano, Nigeria ('87) 538,300
Mombasa, Kenya ('90) 537,000
Cotonou, Benin ('92) 533,212
Omdurman (Umm Durmān),
Sudan ('83) 526,192
Pretoria, South Africa (1,100,000) ('91) . . 525,583
Rabat, Morocco (980,000) ('82) 518,616
Lomé, Togo ('87) 500,000
N'Djamena, Chad ('88) 500,000
Khartoum (Al Khartūm),
Sudan (1,450,000) ('83) 473,597

Asia

Seoul (Sŏul),
South Korea (15,850,000) ('90) 10,627,790
Mumbai (Bombay), India (12,596,243) ('91) 9,925,891
Jakarta, Indonesia (10,200,000) ('90) . . . 8,227,746
Tōkyō, Japan (30,300,000) ('90) 8,163,573
Shanghai, China (9,300,000) ('88) 7,220,000
Delhi, India (8,419,084) ('91) 7,206,704
Beijing (Peking),
China (7,320,000) ('88) 6,710,000
İstanbul, Turkey (7,550,000) ('90) 6,620,241
Tehrān, Iran (7,550,000) ('86) 6,042,584

Bangkok (Krung Thep),
Thailand (7,060,000) ('91) 5,620,591
Tianjin (Tientsin), China ('88) 4,950,000
Karāchi, Pakistan (5,300,000) ('81) 4,901,627
Kolkata (Calcutta), India (11,021,918) ('91). 4,399,819
Shenyang (Mukden), China ('88) 3,910,000
Chennai (Madras), India (5,421,985) ('91) 3,841,396
Baghdād, Iraq ('87) 3,841,268
Pusan, South Korea (3,800,000) ('90) . . . 3,797,566
Dhaka (Dacca),
Bangladesh (6,537,308) ('91) 3,637,892
Wuhan, China ('88) 3,570,000
Yokohama, Japan ('90) 3,220,331
Guangzhou (Canton), China ('88) 3,100,000
Hyderābād, India (4,344,437) ('91) 3,043,896
Ahmadābād, India (3,312,216) ('91) 2,876,710
Ho Chi Minh City (Saigon),
Vietnam (3,300,000) ('89) 2,796,229
Harbin, China ('88) 2,710,000
Lahore, Pakistan (3,025,000) ('81) 2,707,215
T'aipei, Taiwan (6,130,000) ('92) 2,706,453
Singapore, Singapore (3,025,000) ('90) . . 2,690,100
Bangalore, India (4,130,288) ('91) 2,660,088
Ōsaka, Japan (16,900,000) ('90) 2,623,801
Ankara, Turkey (2,650,000) ('90) 2,559,471
Rangoon (Yangon),
Myanmar (2,650,000) ('83) 2,513,023
Chongqing (Chungking), China ('88) 2,502,000
Surabaya, Indonesia ('90) 2,473,272
Nanjing (Nanking), China ('88) 2,390,000
P'yŏngyang, North Korea ('81) 2,355,000
Dalian (Dairen), China ('88) 2,280,000
Taegu, South Korea ('90) 2,228,834
Xi'an (Sian), China ('88) 2,210,000
Nagoya, Japan (4,800,000) ('90) 2,154,793
Tashkent,
Uzbekistan (2,325,000) ('91) 2,113,300
Bandung, Indonesia (2,220,000) ('90) . . . 2,058,122
Chengdu (Chengtu), China ('88) 1,884,000
Kānpur, India (2,029,889) ('91) 1,874,409
Changchun, China ('88) 1,822,000
Inch'ŏn, South Korea ('90) 1,818,293
İzmir, Turkey (1,900,000) ('90) 1,757,414
Medan, Indonesia ('90) 1,730,052
Taiyuan, China ('88) 1,700,000
Sapporo, Japan (1,900,000) ('90) 1,671,742
Quezon City, Philippines ('90) 1,666,766
Nāgpur, India (1,664,006) ('91) 1,624,752
Lucknow, India (1,669,204) ('91) 1,619,115
Manila, Philippines (9,650,000) ('90) . . . 1,598,918
Aleppo, Syria (1,640,000) ('94) 1,591,400
Pune, India (2,493,987) ('91) 1,566,651
Chittagong, Bangladesh (2,342,662) ('91) 1,566,070
Damascus (Dimashq),
Syria (2,230,000) ('94) 1,549,932
Jinan (Tsinan), China ('88) 1,546,000
Xinjiulong (New Kowloon),
China ('86) 1,526,910
Sūrat, India (1,518,950) ('91) 1,498,817
Kōbe, Japan ('90) 1,477,410
Mashhad, Iran ('86) 1,463,508
Kyōto, Japan ('90) 1,461,103
Jaipur, India (1,518,235) ('91) 1,458,483
Novosibirsk, Russia (1,600,000) ('91) . . . 1,446,300
Kābul, Afghanistan ('88) 1,424,400
Kaohsiung, Taiwan (1,845,000) ('92) 1,401,239
Anshan, China ('88) 1,330,000
Kunming, China ('88) 1,310,000
Jiddah, Saudi Arabia ('80) 1,300,000
Qingdao (Tsingtao), China ('88) 1,300,000
Lanzhou (Lanchow), China ('88) 1,297,000
Hangzhou (Hangchow), China ('88) 1,290,000

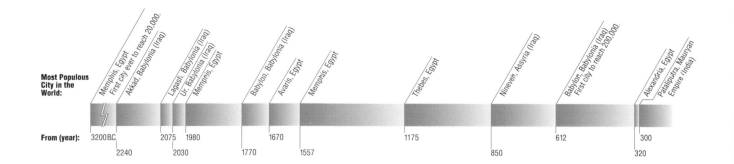

Most Populous City in the World:	Memphis, Egypt First city ever to reach 20,000	Akkad, Babylonia (Iraq)	Lagash, Babylonia (Iraq)	Ur, Babylonia (Iraq) Memphis, Egypt	Babylon, Babylonia (Iraq)	Avaris, Egypt	Memphis, Egypt	Thebes, Egypt	Nineveh, Assyria (Iraq)	Babylon, Babylonia (Iraq) First city to reach 200,000	Alexandria, Egypt	Pataliputra, Mauryan Empire (India)
From (year):	3200 B.C.	2240	2075 / 1980 / 2030		1670 / 1770	1557		1175	850	612	300 / 320	

Fushun (Funan), China ('88) 1,290,000
Tbilisi, Georgia (1,460,000) ('91) 1,279,000
Hong Kong, China (4,770,000) ('91) 1,250,993
Riyadh (Ar-Riyād), Saudi Arabia ('80) . . . 1,250,000
Semarang, Indonesia ('90) 1,249,230
Fukuoka, Japan (1,750,000) ('90) 1,237,062
Changsha, China ('88) 1,230,000
Shijiazhuang, China ('88) 1,220,000
Jilin (Kirin), China ('88) 1,200,000
Yerevan, Armenia (1,315,000) ('89) 1,199,000
Qiqihar (Tsitsihar), China ('88) 1,180,000
Kawasaki, Japan ('90) 1,173,603
Omsk, Russia (1,190,000) ('91) 1,166,800
Almaty, Kazakhstan (1,190,000) ('91) . . . 1,156,200
Zhengzhou (Chengchow), China ('88) . . . 1,150,000
Chelyabinsk, Russia (1,325,000) ('91) . . . 1,148,300
Kwangju, South Korea ('90) 1,144,695
Palembang, Indonesia ('90) 1,144,047
Baotou (Paotow), China ('88) 1,130,000
Faisalabad (Lyallpur), Pakistan ('81) . . . 1,104,209
Indore, India (1,109,056) ('91) 1,091,674
Nanchang, China ('88) 1,090,000
Hiroshima, Japan (1,575,000) ('90) 1,085,705
Baku (Bakı),
  Azerbaijan (2,020,000) ('91) 1,080,500
Tangshan, China ('88) 1,080,000
Bhopāl, India ('91) 1,062,771
Taejŏn, South Korea ('90) 1,062,084
Ürümqi, China ('88) 1,060,000
Ludhiāna, India ('91) 1,042,740
Vadodara, India (1,126,824) ('91) 1,031,346
Guiyang (Kweiyang), China ('88) 1,030,000
Kitakyūshū, Japan (1,525,000) ('90) 1,026,455
Kalyān, India ('91) 1,014,557
Esfahān, Iran (1,175,000) ('86) 986,753
Tabriz, Iran ('86) 971,482
Hāora, India ('91) 950,435
Ujungpandang (Makasar),
  Indonesia ('90) 944,372
Madurai, India (1,085,914) ('91) 940,989

'Ammān, Jordan (1,625,000) ('89) 936,300
Vārānasi (Benares), India (1,030,863) ('91) 929,270
Krasnoyarsk, Russia ('91) 924,400
Kuala Lumpur, Malaysia (1,475,000) ('80) . 919,610
Sendai, Japan (1,175,000) ('90) 918,398
Patna, India (1,099,647) ('91) 917,243
Adana, Turkey ('90) 916,150
Fuzhou, China ('88) 910,000
Hanoi, Vietnam (1,275,000) ('89) 905,939
Āgra, India (948,063) ('91) 891,790
Wuxi (Wuhsi), China ('88) 880,000
Handan, China ('88) 870,000
Xuzhou (Süchow), China ('88) 860,000
Benxi (Penhsi), China ('88) 860,000
Shīrāz, Iran ('86) 848,289
Zibo (Zhangdian), China ('88) 840,000
Yichun, China ('88) 840,000
Bursa, Turkey ('90) 834,576

Chiba, Japan ('90) 829,455
Coimbatore, India (1,100,746) ('91) 816,321
Datong, China ('88) 810,000
Sakai, Japan ('90) 807,765
Thāna, India ('91) 803,369
Allahābād, India (844,546) ('91) 792,858
T'aichung, Taiwan ('92) 785,182
Jiulong (Kowloon), China ('86) 774,781
Caloocan, Philippines ('90) 761,011
Luoyang (Loyang), China ('88) 760,000
Meerut, India (849,799) ('91) 753,778
Vishākhapatnam, India (1,057,118) ('91) . . 752,037
Jabalpur, India (888,916) ('91) 741,927
Suzhou (Soochow), China ('88) 740,000
Hefei, China ('88) 740,000
Nanning, China ('88) 720,000
Jinzhou (Chinchou), China ('88) 710,000
Amritsar, India ('91) 708,835
Hyderābād, Pakistan (800,000) ('81) 702,539
Vijayawāda, India (845,756) ('91) 701,827
Fuxin, China ('88) 700,000
Jixi, China ('88) 700,000
Huainan, China ('88) 700,000
Multān, Pakistan (732,070) ('81) 696,316
Malang, Indonesia ('90) 695,089
T'ainan, Taiwan ('92) 692,116
Gwalior, India (717,780) ('91) 690,765
Ulsan, South Korea ('90) 682,978
Liuzhou, China ('88) 680,000
Hohhot, China ('88) 670,000
Bucheon, South Korea ('90) 667,777
Jodhpur, India ('91) 666,279
Nāshik, India (725,341) ('91) 656,925
Mudanjiang, China ('88) 650,000
Hubli-Dhārwār, India ('91) 648,298
Vladivostok, Russia ('91) 648,000
Suwŏn, South Korea ('90) 644,968
Hims, Syria ('94) 644,204
Irkutsk, Russia ('91) 640,500
Daqing, China ('88) 640,000
Bishkek, Kyrgyzstan ('91) 631,300
Phnom Penh, Cambodia ('90) 620,000
Xining (Sining), China ('88) 620,000
Farīdābad, India ('91) 617,717
Al Basrah, Iraq ('85) 616,700
Khabarovsk, Russia ('91) 613,300
Colombo, Sri Lanka (2,050,000) ('89) 612,000
Cebu, Philippines (825,000) ('90) 610,417
Qaraghandy, Kazakhstan ('91) 608,600
Barnaul, Russia (673,000) ('91) 606,800
Solāpur, India (620,846) ('91) 604,215
Gaziantep, Turkey ('90) 603,434
Novokuznetsk, Russia ('91) 601,900
Khulna, Bangladesh (966,096) ('91) 601,051
Gujrānwāla, Pakistan (658,753) ('81) 600,993
Ranchi, India (614,795) ('91) 599,306
Srīnagar, India (606,002) ('81) 594,775
Okayama, Japan ('90) 593,730
Hegang, China ('86) 588,300
Bareilly, India (617,350) ('91) 587,211
Guwāhāti, India ('91) 584,342
Dushanbe, Tajikistan ('91) 582,400
Ahvāz, Iran ('86) 579,826
Dandong, China ('86) 579,800
Kumamoto, Japan ('90) 579,306
Ulan Bator, Mongolia ('91) 575,000
Aurangābād, India (592,709) ('91) 573,272
Al-Mawsil, Iraq ('85) 570,926
Ningbo, China ('88) 570,000
Kochi, India (1,140,605) ('91) 564,589
Bākhtarān (Kermānshāh), Iran ('86) 560,514
Shantou (Swatow), China ('88) 560,000
Rājkot, India (654,490) ('91) 559,407

Mecca (Makkah), Saudi Arabia ('80) 550,000
Qom, Iran ('86) 543,139
Sŏngnam, South Korea ('90) 540,764
T'aipeihsien, Taiwan ('91) 538,954
Kota, India ('91) 537,371
Kagoshima, Japan ('90) 536,752
Hamamatsu, Japan ('90) 534,620
Funabashi, Japan ('90) 533,270
Mandalay, Myanmar ('83) 532,949
Sagamihara, Japan ('90) 531,542
Jerusalem (Yerushalayim) (Al-Quds),
  Israel (560,000) ('91) 524,500
Trivandrum, India (826,225) ('91) 524,006
Changzhou (Changchow), China ('86) 522,700
Davao, Philippines ('90) 521,525
Kemerovo, Russia ('91) 520,700
Higashiōsaka, Japan ('90) 518,319

Chŏnju, South Korea ('90) 517,104
Pimpri-Chinchwad, India ('91) 517,083
Quanwan (Tsuen Wan), China ('86) 514,241
Konya, Turkey ('90) 513,346
Jalandhar, India ('91) 509,510
Beirut (Bayrūt), Lebanon (1,675,000) ('82) . 509,000
Peshāwar, Pakistan (566,248) ('81) 506,896
Tomsk, Russia ('91) 505,600
Gorakhpur, India ('91) 505,566
Chandīgarh, India (575,829) ('91) 504,094
Surakarta, Indonesia (590,000) ('90) 503,827
Zhangjiakou (Kalgan), China ('88) 500,000
Rāwalpindi, Pakistan (1,040,000) ('81) . . . 457,091
Tel Aviv-Yafo, Israel (1,735,000) ('91) 339,400
Kuwait (Al-Kuwayt),
  Kuwait (1,375,000) ('85) 44,335

Australia and Oceania

Brisbane, Australia (1,334,017) ('91) 751,115
Perth, Australia (1,143,249) ('91) 80,517
Melbourne, Australia (3,022,439) ('91) 60,476
Adelaide, Australia (1,023,597) ('91) 14,843
Sydney, Australia (3,538,749) ('91) 13,501

Europe

Moscow (Moskva),
  Russia (10,150,000) ('91) 8,801,500
London, England, U.K. (11,100,000) ('81) 6,574,009
Saint Petersburg (Leningrad),
  Russia (5,525,000) ('91) 4,466,800
Berlin, Germany (4,150,000) ('91) 3,433,695
Madrid, Spain (4,650,000) ('88) 3,102,846
Rome (Roma), Italy (3,175,000) ('91) 2,693,383
Kiev (Kyyiv), Ukraine (3,250,000) ('91) . . . 2,635,000
Paris, France (10,275,000) ('90) 2,152,423
Bucharest (Bucureşti),
  Romania (2,300,000) ('92) 2,064,474
Budapest, Hungary (2,515,000) ('90) 2,016,774
Barcelona, Spain (4,040,000) ('88) 1,714,355
Hamburg, Germany (2,385,000) ('91) 1,652,363

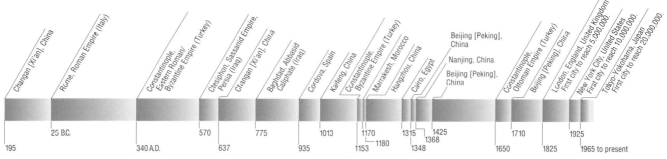

Source: Four Thousand Years of Urban Growth *by Tertius Chandler, Edwin Mellen Press, 1987.*

Warsaw (Warszawa), Poland (2,312,000) ('93)	1,644,500
Minsk, Belarus (1,694,000) ('91)	1,633,600
Kharkiv (Kharkov), Ukraine (2,050,000) ('91)	1,622,800
Vienna (Wien), Austria (1,900,000) ('91)	1,539,848
Nizhniy Novgorod (Gorky), Russia (2,025,000) ('91)	1,445,000
Yekaterinburg, Russia (1,620,000) ('91)	1,375,400
Milan (Milano), Italy (3,750,000) ('91)	1,371,008
Samara (Kuybyshev), Russia (1,505,000) ('91)	1,257,300
Munich (München), Germany (1,900,000) ('91)	1,229,026
Prague (Praha), Czech Republic (1,328,000) ('91)	1,212,010
Dnipropetrovs'k, Ukraine (1,600,000) ('91)	1,189,300
Sofia (Sofiya), Bulgaria (1,205,000) ('89)	1,136,875
Belgrade (Beograd), Yugoslavia (1,554,826) ('91)	1,136,786
Donets'k, Ukraine (2,125,000) ('91)	1,121,300
Perm', Russia (1,180,000) ('91)	1,110,400
Kazan', Russia (1,165,000) ('91)	1,107,300
Odesa, Ukraine (1,185,000) ('91)	1,100,700
Ufa, Russia (1,118,000) ('91)	1,097,000
Rostov-na-Donu, Russia (1,165,000) ('91)	1,027,600
Naples (Napoli), Italy (2,875,000) ('91)	1,024,601
Birmingham, England, U.K. (2,675,000) ('81)	1,013,995
Volgograd (Stalingrad), Russia (1,360,000) ('91)	1,007,300
Turin (Torino), Italy (1,550,000) ('91)	961,916
Cologne, Germany (1,810,000) ('91)	953,551
Łódź, Poland (950,000) ('93)	938,400
Saratov, Russia (1,155,000) ('91)	911,100
Rīga, Latvia (1,005,000) ('91)	910,200
Voronezh, Russia ('91)	900,000
Zaporizhzhya, Ukraine ('91)	896,600
Lisbon (Lisboa), Portugal (2,250,000) ('81)	807,167
L'viv (L'vov), Ukraine ('91)	802,200
Marseille, France (1,225,000) ('90)	800,550
Athens (Athínai), Greece (3,096,775) ('91)	748,110
Kraków, Poland (823,000) ('93)	744,000
València, Spain (1,270,000) ('88)	743,933
Kryvyy Rih, Ukraine ('91)	724,000
Amsterdam, Netherlands (1,875,000) ('92)	713,407
Zagreb, Croatia ('87)	697,925
Palermo, Italy ('91)	697,162
Glasgow, Scotland, U.K. (1,800,000) ('90)	689,210
Chişinău (Kishinev), Moldova ('91)	676,700
Genoa (Genova), Italy (805,000) ('91)	675,639
Stockholm, Sweden (1,491,726) ('91)	674,452
Sevilla, Spain (945,000) ('88)	663,132
Tol'yatti, Russia ('91)	654,700
Ul'yanovsk, Russia ('91)	648,300
Izhevsk, Russia ('91)	646,800
Frankfurt (Frankfurt am Main), Germany (1,935,000) ('91)	644,865
Wrocław (Breslau), Poland ('93)	640,700
Yaroslavl', Russia ('91)	638,100
Krasnodar, Russia ('91)	631,200
Essen, Germany (5,050,000) ('91)	626,973
Dortmund, Germany ('91)	599,055
Vilnius, Lithuania ('92)	596,900
Rotterdam, Netherlands (1,120,000) ('92)	589,707
Poznań, Poland (666,000) ('93)	582,900
Zaragoza, Spain ('88)	582,239
Stuttgart, Germany (2,005,000) ('91)	579,988
Düsseldorf, Germany (1,225,000) ('91)	575,794
Málaga, Spain ('88)	574,456
Orenburg, Russia ('91)	556,500
Bremen, Germany (790,000) ('91)	551,219
Penza, Russia ('91)	551,100
Tula, Russia (640,000) ('91)	543,600
Liverpool, England, U.K. (1,525,000) ('81)	538,809
Duisburg, Germany ('91)	535,447
Ryazan', Russia ('91)	527,200
Mariupol' (Zhdanov), Ukraine ('91)	521,800
Hannover, Germany (1,000,000) ('91)	513,010
Astrakhan', Russia ('91)	511,900
Mykolayiv, Ukraine ('91)	511,600
Leipzig, Germany (720,000) ('91)	511,079
Naberezhnyye Chelny, Russia ('91)	510,100
Luhans'k, Ukraine (650,000) ('91)	503,900
Gomel', Belarus ('91)	503,300
Dublin, Ireland (1,140,000) ('86)	502,749
Helsinki (Helsingfors), Finland (1,045,000) ('93)	501,514
Nürnberg, Germany (1,065,000) ('91)	493,692
Antwerp, Belgium (1,140,000) ('91)	467,518
Copenhagen (København), Denmark (1,670,000) ('92)	464,566
Leeds, England, U.K. (1,540,000) ('81)	445,242
Manchester, England, U.K. (2,775,000) ('81)	437,612
Lyon, France (1,335,000) ('90)	415,487
Katowice, Poland (2,770,000) ('93)	359,900
Porto, Portugal (1,225,000) ('81)	327,368
Mannheim, Germany (1,525,000) ('91)	310,411
Newcastle upon Tyne, England, U.K. (1,300,000) ('81)	199,064
Lille, France (1,050,000) ('90)	172,142
Brussels (Bruxelles), Belgium (2,385,000) ('91)	136,424

North America

Mexico City (Ciudad de México), Mexico (14,100,000) ('90)	8,235,744
New York, N.Y., U.S. (18,087,251) ('90)	7,322,564
Los Angeles, Ca., U.S. (14,531,529) ('90)	3,485,398
Chicago, Il., U.S. (8,065,633) ('90)	2,783,726
Santo Domingo, Dominican Republic ('90)	2,411,900
Havana (La Habana), Cuba (2,210,000) ('91)	2,119,059
Guadalajara, Mexico (2,325,000) ('90)	1,650,042
Houston, Tx., U.S. (3,711,043) ('90)	1,630,553
Philadelphia, Pa., U.S. (5,899,345) ('90)	1,585,577
Nezahualcóyotl, Mexico ('90)	1,255,456
Ecatepec, Mexico ('90)	1,218,135
San Diego, Ca., U.S. (2,949,000) ('90)	1,110,549
Monterrey, Mexico (2,015,000) ('90)	1,068,996
Guatemala, Guatemala (1,400,000) ('89)	1,057,210
Detroit, Mi., U.S. (4,665,236) ('90)	1,027,974
Montréal, P.Q., Canada (3,127,242) ('91)	1,017,666
Puebla, Mexico (1,200,000) ('90)	1,007,170
Dallas, Tx., U.S. (3,885,415) ('90)	1,006,877
Phoenix, Az., U.S. (2,122,101) ('90)	983,403
San Antonio, Tx., U.S. (1,302,099) ('90)	935,933
Naucalpan de Juárez, Mexico ('90)	845,960
Port-au-Prince, Haiti (880,000) ('87)	797,000
Ciudad Juárez, Mexico ('90)	789,522
San Jose, Ca., U.S. (1,497,577) ('90)	782,248
León, Mexico ('90)	758,279
Baltimore, Md., U.S. (2,382,172) ('90)	736,014
Indianapolis, In., U.S. (1,249,822) ('90)	731,327
San Francisco, Ca., U.S. (6,253,311) ('90)	723,959
Calgary, Ab., Canada (754,033) ('91)	710,677

Tlalnepantla, Mexico ('90)	702,270
Tijuana, Mexico ('90)	698,752
Managua, Nicaragua ('85)	682,000
Zapopan, Mexico ('90)	668,323
Toronto, On., Canada (3,893,046) ('91)	635,395
Jacksonville, Fl., U.S. (906,727) ('90)	635,230
Columbus, Oh., U.S. (1,377,419) ('90)	632,910
Milwaukee, Wi., U.S. (1,607,183) ('90)	628,088
Winnipeg, Mb., Canada (652,354) ('91)	616,790
Edmonton, Ab., Canada (839,924) ('91)	616,741
Memphis, Tn., U.S. (981,747) ('90)	610,337
Washington, D.C., U.S. (3,923,574) ('90)	606,900
Kingston, Jamaica (890,000) ('91)	587,798
Tegucigalpa, Honduras ('88)	576,661
Boston, Ma., U.S. (4,171,643) ('90)	574,283
North York, On., Canada ('91)	562,564
Guadalupe, Mexico ('90)	535,332
Scarborough, On., Canada ('91)	524,598
Mérida, Mexico ('90)	523,422
Seattle, Wa., U.S. (2,559,164) ('90)	516,259
Chihuahua, Mexico ('90)	516,153
Acapulco de Juárez, Mexico ('90)	515,374
El Paso, Tx., U.S. (1,211,300) ('90)	515,342
Cleveland, Oh., U.S. (2,759,823) ('90)	505,616
New Orleans, La., U.S. (1,238,816) ('90)	496,938
Vancouver, B.C., Canada (1,602,502) ('91)	471,844
Denver, Co., U.S. (1,848,319) ('90)	467,610
Fort Worth, Tx., U.S. (1,332,053) ('90)	447,619
Portland, Or., U.S. (1,477,895) ('90)	437,319
Kansas City, Mo., U.S. (1,566,280) ('90)	435,146
San Juan, Puerto Rico (1,877,000) ('90)	426,832
Saint Louis, Mo., U.S. (2,444,099) ('90)	396,685
Charlotte, N.C., U.S. (1,162,093) ('90)	395,934
Atlanta, Ga., U.S. (2,833,511) ('90)	394,017
Oakland, Ca., U.S. (2,082,914) ('90)	372,242
Pittsburgh, Pa., U.S. (2,242,798) ('90)	369,879
Sacramento, Ca., U.S. (1,481,102) ('90)	369,365
Minneapolis, Mn., U.S. (2,464,124) ('90)	368,383
Cincinnati, Oh., U.S. (1,744,124) ('90)	364,040
Miami, Fl., U.S. (3,192,582) ('90)	358,548
Buffalo, N.Y., U.S. (1,189,288) ('90)	328,123
Tampa, Fl., U.S. (2,067,959) ('90)	280,015
San José, Costa Rica (1,355,000) ('88)	278,600
Newark, N.J., U.S. (1,824,321) ('90)	275,221
Anaheim, Ca., U.S. (2,410,556) ('90)	266,406
Norfolk, Va., U.S. (1,396,107) ('90)	261,229
Rochester, N.Y., U.S. (1,002,410) ('90)	231,636
Riverside, Ca., U.S. (2,588,793) ('90)	226,505
Orlando, Fl., U.S. (1,072,748) ('90)	164,693
Providence, R.I., U.S. (1,141,510) ('90)	160,728
Salt Lake City, Ut., U.S. (1,072,227) ('90)	159,936
Fort Lauderdale, Fl., U.S. (1,255,488) ('90)	149,377
Hartford, Ct., U.S. (1,085,837) ('90)	139,739

South America

São Paulo, Brazil (16,925,000) ('91)	9,393,753
Rio de Janeiro, Brazil (11,050,000) ('91)	5,473,909
Bogotá (Santa Fe de Bogotá), Colombia (4,260,000) ('85)	3,982,941
Buenos Aires, Argentina (11,000,000) ('91)	2,960,976
Salvador, Brazil (2,340,000) ('91)	2,070,296
Caracas, Venezuela (4,000,000) ('90)	1,824,654
Belo Horizonte, Brazil (3,340,000) ('91)	1,529,566
Brasília, Brazil ('91)	1,513,470
Guayaquil, Ecuador ('90)	1,508,444
Medellín, Colombia (2,095,000) ('85)	1,468,089
Cali, Colombia (1,400,000) ('85)	1,350,565
Recife, Brazil (2,880,000) ('91)	1,296,995
Montevideo, Uruguay (1,550,000) ('85)	1,251,647
Maracaibo, Venezuela ('90)	1,249,670
Porto Alegre, Brazil (2,850,000) ('91)	1,247,352
Córdoba, Argentina (1,260,000) ('91)	1,148,305
San Justo, Argentina ('91)	1,111,811
Quito, Ecuador (1,300,000) ('90)	1,100,847
Manaus, Brazil ('91)	1,005,634
Goiânia, Brazil (1,130,000) ('91)	912,136
Valencia, Venezuela ('90)	903,621
Barranquilla, Colombia (1,140,000) ('85)	899,781
Rosario, Argentina (1,190,000) ('91)	894,645
Curitiba, Brazil (1,815,000) ('91)	841,882
Belém, Brazil (1,355,000) ('91)	765,476
Campinas, Brazil (1,290,000) ('91)	759,032
Fortaleza, Brazil (2,040,000) ('91)	743,335
La Paz, Bolivia (1,120,000) ('92)	713,378
Santa Cruz de la Sierra, Bolivia ('92)	697,278
General Sarmiento (San Miguel), Argentina ('91)	646,891
Morón, Argentina ('91)	641,541
Barquisimeto, Venezuela ('90)	625,450
Lomas de Zamora, Argentina ('91)	572,769
Osasco, Brazil ('91)	566,949
Nova Iguaçu, Brazil ('91)	562,062
Teresina, Brazil (665,000) ('91)	556,073
Maceió, Brazil ('91)	554,727
São Bernardo do Campo, Brazil ('91)	550,030
Guarulhos, Brazil ('91)	546,417
Cartagena, Colombia ('85)	531,426
La Plata, Argentina ('91)	520,449
Mar del Plata, Argentina ('91)	519,707
Santo André, Brazil ('91)	518,272
Campo Grande, Brazil ('91)	516,403
Quilmes, Argentina ('91)	509,445
Asunción, Paraguay (700,000) ('92)	502,426
Santos, Brazil (1,165,000) ('91)	415,554
Lima, Perú (4,608,010) ('81)	371,122
Santiago, Chile (4,100,000) ('82)	232,667

Countries and Flags

This 12-page section presents basic information about each of the world's countries, along with an illustration of each country's flag. A total of 198 countries are listed: the world's 191 fully independent countries, and 7 internally independent countries which are under the protection of other countries in matters of defense and foreign affairs. Colonies and other dependent political entities are not listed.

The categories of information provided for each country are as follows.

Flag: In many countries two or more versions of the national flag exist. For example, there is often a "civil" version which the average person flies, and a "state" version which is flown only at government buildings and government functions. A common difference between the two is the inclusion of a coat of arms on the state version. The flag versions shown here are the ones that each country has chosen to fly at the United Nations.

Country name: The short form of the English translation of the official country name.

Official name: The long form of the English translation of the official country name.

Population: The population figures listed are 1995 estimates based on U.S. census bureau figures and other available information.

Area: Figures provided represent total land area and all inland water. They are based on official data or U.N. data.

Population density: The number of people per square mile and square kilometer, calculated by dividing the country's population figure by its area figure.

Capital: The city that serves as the official seat of government. Population figures follow the capital name. These figures are based upon the latest official data.

AFGHANISTAN
Official Name: Islamic State of Afghanistan
Population: 19,715,000
Area: 251,826 sq mi (652,225 sq km)
Density: 78/sq mi (30/sq km)
Capital: Kābul, 1,424,400

ALGERIA
Official Name: Democratic and Popular Republic of Algeria
Population: 27,965,000
Area: 919,595 sq mi (2,381,741 sq km)
Density: 30/sq mi (12/sq km)
Capital: Algiers (El Djazaïr),1,507,241

ANGUILLA
Official Name: Anguilla
Population: 7,100
Area: 35 sq mi (91 sq km)
Density: 203/sq mi (78/sq km)
Capital: The Valley, 1,042

ALBANIA
Official Name: Republic of Albania
Population: 3,394,000
Area: 11,100 sq mi (28,748 sq km)
Density: 306/sq mi (118/sq km)
Capital: Tiranë, 238,100

ANDORRA
Official Name: Principality of Andorra
Population: 59,000
Area: 175 sq mi (453 sq km)
Density: 337/sq mi (130/sq km)
Capital: Andorra, 20,437

ANTIGUA AND BARBUDA
Official Name: Antigua and Barbuda
Population: 67,000
Area: 171 sq mi (442 sq km)
Density: 392/sq mi (152/sq km)
Capital: St. John's, 24,359

ANGOLA
Official Name: Republic of Angola
Population: 10,690,000
Area: 481,354 sq mi (1,246,700 sq km)
Density: 22/sq mi (8.6/sq km)
Capital: Luanda, 1,459,900

Countries
and Flags
continued

BAHAMAS
Official Name: Commonwealth of the
Bahamas
Population: 275,000
Area: 5,382 sq mi (13,939 sq km)
Pop. Density: 51/sq mi (20/sq km)
Capital: Nassau, 141,000

BELIZE
Official Name: Belize
Population: 212,000
Area: 8,866 sq mi (22,963 sq km)
Pop. Density: 24/sq mi (9.2/sq km)
Capital: Belmopan, 5,256

ARGENTINA
Official Name: Argentine Republic
Population: 34,083,000
Area: 1,073,519 sq mi (2,780,400 sq km)
Pop. Density: 32/sq mi (12/sq km)
Capital: Buenos Aires (de facto), 2,960,976,
and Viedma (future), 40,452

BAHRAIN
Official Name: State of Bahrain
Population: 563,000
Area: 267 sq mi (691 sq km)
Pop. Density: 2,109/sq mi (815/sq km)
Capital: Al Manāmah, 82,700

BENIN
Official Name: Republic of Benin
Population: 5,433,000
Area: 43,475 sq mi (112,600 sq km)
Pop. Density: 125/sq mi (48/sq km)
Capital: Porto-Novo (designated), 164,000,
and Cotonou (de facto), 533,212

ARMENIA
Official Name: Republic of Armenia
Population: 3,794,000
Area: 11,506 sq mi (29,800 sq km)
Pop. Density: 330/sq mi (127/sq km)
Capital: Yerevan, 1,199,000

BANGLADESH
Official Name: People's Republic of
Bangladesh
Population: 119,370,000
Area: 55,598 sq mi (143,998 sq km)
Pop. Density: 2,147/sq mi (829/sq km)
Capital: Dhaka (Dacca), 3,637,892

BHUTAN
Official Name: Kingdom of Bhutan
Population: 1,758,000
Area: 17,954 sq mi (46,500 sq km)
Pop. Density: 98/sq mi (38/sq km)
Capital: Thimphu, 12,000

AUSTRALIA
Official Name: Commonwealth of Australia
Population: 18,205,000
Area: 2,966,155 sq mi (7,682,300 sq km)
Pop. Density: 6.1/sq mi (2.4/sq km)
Capital: Canberra, 276,162

BARBADOS
Official Name: Barbados
Population: 261,000
Area: 166 sq mi (430 sq km)
Pop. Density: 1,572/sq mi (607/sq km)
Capital: Bridgetown, 5,928

BOLIVIA
Official Name: Republic of Bolivia
Population: 6,790,000
Area: 424,165 sq mi (1,098,581 sq km)
Pop. Density: 16/sq mi (6.2/sq km)
Capital: La Paz (seat of government),
713,378, and Sucre (legal capital), 131,769

AUSTRIA
Official Name: Republic of Austria
Population: 7,932,000
Area: 32,377 sq mi (83,856 sq km)
Pop. Density: 245/sq mi (95/sq km)
Capital: Vienna (Wien), 1,539,848

BELARUS
Official Name: Republic of Belarus
Population: 10,425,000
Area: 80,155 sq mi (207,600 sq km)
Pop. Density: 130/sq mi (50/sq km)
Capital: Minsk, 1,633,600

BOSNIA AND HERZEGOVINA
Official Name: Republic of Bosnia and
Herzegovina
Population: 4,481,000
Area: 19,741 sq mi (51,129 sq km)
Pop. Density: 227/sq mi (88/sq km)
Capital: Sarajevo, 341,200

AZERBAIJAN
Official Name: Azerbaijani Republic
Population: 7,491,000
Area: 33,436 sq mi (86,600 sq km)
Pop. Density: 224/sq mi (87/sq km)
Capital: Baku (Bakı), 1,080,500

BELGIUM
Official Name: Kingdom of Belgium
Population: 10,075,000
Area: 11,783 sq mi (30,518 sq km)
Pop. Density: 855/sq mi (330/sq km)
Capital: Brussels (Bruxelles), 136,424

BOTSWANA
Official Name: Republic of Botswana
Population: 1,438,000
Area: 224,711 sq mi (582,000 sq km)
Pop. Density: 6.4/sq mi (2.5/sq km)
Capital: Gaborone, 133,468

BRAZIL
Official Name: Federative Republic of Brazil
Population: 159,690,000
Area: 3,286,500 sq mi (8,511,996 sq km)
Pop. Density: 49/sq mi (19/sq km)
Capital: Brasília, 1,513,470

CAMEROON
Official Name: Republic of Cameroon
Population: 13,330,000
Area: 183,568 sq mi (475,440 sq km)
Pop. Density: 73/sq mi (28/sq km)
Capital: Yaoundé, 560,785

CHINA
Official Name: People's Republic of China
Population: 1,196,980,000
Area: 3,689,631 sq mi (9,556,100 sq km)
Pop. Density: 324/sq mi (125/sq km)
Capital: Beijing (Peking), 6,710,000

BRUNEI
Official Name: Negara Brunei Darussalam
Population: 289,000
Area: 2,226 sq mi (5,765 sq km)
Pop. Density: 130/sq mi (50/sq km)
Capital: Bandar Seri Begawan, 22,777

CANADA
Official Name: Canada
Population: 28,285,000
Area: 3,849,674 sq mi (9,970,610 sq km)
Pop. Density: 7.3/sq mi (2.8/sq km)
Capital: Ottawa, 313,987

COLOMBIA
Official Name: Republic of Colombia
Population: 34,870,000
Area: 440,831 sq mi (1,141,748 sq km)
Pop. Density: 79/sq mi (31/sq km)
Capital: Santa Fe de Bogotá (Bogotá),
3,982,941

BULGARIA
Official Name: Republic of Bulgaria
Population: 8,787,000
Area: 42,855 sq mi (110,994 sq km)
Pop. Density: 205/sq mi (79/sq km)
Capital: Sofia (Sofiya), 1,136,875

CAPE VERDE
Official Name: Republic of Cape Verde
Population: 429,000
Area: 1,557 sq mi (4,033 sq km)
Pop. Density: 276/sq mi (106/sq km)
Capital: Praia, 61,644

COMOROS
Official Name: Federal Islamic Republic of
the Comoros
Population: 540,000
Area: 863 sq mi (2,235 sq km)
Pop. Density: 626/sq mi (242/sq km)
Capital: Moroni, 23,432

BURKINA FASO
Official Name: Burkina Faso
Population: 10,275,000
Area: 105,792 sq mi (274,000 sq km)
Pop. Density: 97/sq mi (38/sq km)
Capital: Ouagadougou, 441,514

CENTRAL AFRICAN REPUBLIC
Official Name: Central African Republic
Population: 3,177,000
Area: 240,535 sq mi (622,984 sq km)
Pop. Density: 13/sq mi (5.1/sq km)
Capital: Bangui, 596,800

CONGO
Official Name: Republic of the Congo
Population: 2,474,000
Area: 132,047 sq mi (342,000 sq km)
Pop. Density: 19/sq mi (7.2/sq km)
Capital: Brazzaville, 693,712

BURUNDI
Official Name: Republic of Burundi
Population: 6,192,000
Area: 10,745 sq mi (27,830 sq km)
Pop. Density: 576/sq mi (222/sq km)
Capital: Bujumbura, 226,628

CHAD
Official Name: Republic of Chad
Population: 6,396,000
Area: 495,755 sq mi (1,284,000 sq km)
Pop. Density: 13/sq mi (5/sq km)
Capital: N'Djamena, 500,000

CONGO, DEMOCRATIC REPUBLIC OF THE
Official Name: Democratic Republic
of the Congo
Population: 43,365,000
Area: 905,355 sq mi (2,344,858 sq km)
Pop. Density: 48/sq mi (18/sq km)
Capital: Kinshasa, 3,000,000

CAMBODIA
Official Name: Kingdom of Cambodia
Population: 9,713,000
Area: 69,898 sq mi (181,035 sq km)
Pop. Density: 139/sq mi (54/sq km)
Capital: Phnom Penh (Phnum Pénh), 620,000

CHILE
Official Name: Republic of Chile
Population: 14,050,000
Area: 292,135 sq mi (756,626 sq km)
Pop. Density: 48/sq mi (19/sq km)
Capital: Santiago, 232,667

COSTA RICA
Official Name: Republic of Costa Rica
Population: 3,379,000
Area: 19,730 sq mi (51,100 sq km)
Pop. Density: 171/sq mi (66/sq km)
Capital: San José, 278,600

Countries
and Flags
continued

CZECH REPUBLIC
Official Name: Czech Republic
Population: 10,430,000
Area: 30,450 sq mi (78,864 sq km)
Pop. Density: 343/sq mi (132/sq km)
Capital: Prague (Praha), 1,212,010

EGYPT
Official Name: Arab Republic of Egypt
Population: 58,100,000
Area: 386,662 sq mi (1,001,449 sq km)
Pop. Density: 150/sq mi (58/sq km)
Capital: Cairo (Al Qāhirah), 6,068,695

COTE D'IVOIRE
Official Name: Republic of Cote d'Ivoire
Population: 14,540,000
Area: 124,518 sq mi (322,500 sq km)
Pop. Density: 117/sq mi (45/sq km)
Capital: Abidjan (de facto), 1,929,079, and
  Yamoussoukro (future), 106,786

DENMARK
Official Name: Kingdom of Denmark
Population: 5,207,000
Area: 16,639 sq mi (43,094 sq km)
Pop. Density: 313 sq mi (121/sq km)
Capital: Copenhagen (København), 464,566

EL SALVADOR
Official Name: Republic of El Salvador
Population: 5,280,000
Area: 8,124 sq mi (21,041 sq km)
Pop. Density: 650/sq mi (251/sq km)
Capital: San Salvador, 462,652

CROATIA
Official Name: Republic of Croatia
Population: 4,801,000
Area: 21,829 sq mi (56,538 sq km)
Pop. Density: 220/sq mi (85/sq km)
Capital: Zagreb, 697,925

DJIBOUTI
Official Name: Republic of Djibouti
Population: 557,000
Area: 8,958 sq mi (23,200 sq km)
Pop. Density: 62/sq mi (24/sq km)
Capital: Djibouti, 329,337

EQUATORIAL GUINEA
Official Name: Republic of Equatorial Guinea
Population: 394,000
Area: 10,831 sq mi (28,051 sq km)
Pop. Density: 36/sq mi (14/sq km)
Capital: Malabo, 31,630

CUBA
Official Name: Republic of Cuba
Population: 11,560,000
Area: 42,804 sq mi (110,861 sq km)
Pop. Density: 270/sq mi (104/sq km)
Capital: Havana (La Habana), 2,119,059

DOMINICA
Official Name: Commonwealth of Dominica
Population: 89,000
Area: 305 sq mi (790 sq km)
Pop. Density: 292/sq mi (113/sq km)
Capital: Roseau, 9,348

ERITREA
Official Name: State of Eritrea
Population: 3,458,000
Area: 36,170 sq mi (93,679 sq km)
Pop. Density: 96/sq mi (37/sq km)
Capital: Asmera, 358,100

CYPRUS
Official Name: Republic of Cyprus
Population: 551,000
Area: 2,276 sq mi (5,896 sq km)
Pop. Density: 242/sq mi (93/sq km)
Capital: Nicosia (Levkosía), 48,221

DOMINICAN REPUBLIC
Official Name: Dominican Republic
Population: 7,896,000
Area: 18,704 sq mi (48,442 sq km)
Pop. Density: 422/sq mi (163/sq km)
Capital: Santo Domingo, 2,411,900

ESTONIA
Official Name: Republic of Estonia
Population: 1,515,000
Area: 17,413 sq mi (45,100 sq km)
Pop. Density: 87/sq mi (34/sq km)
Capital: Tallinn, 481,500

CYPRUS, NORTH
Official Name: Turkish Republic of
  Northern Cyprus
Population: 182,000
Area: 1,295 sq mi (3,355 sq km)
Pop. Density: 141/sq mi (54/sq km)
Capital: Nicosia (Lefkoşa), 37,400

ECUADOR
Official Name: Republic of Ecuador
Population: 11,015,000
Area: 105,037 sq mi (272,045 sq km)
Pop. Density: 105/sq mi (40/sq km)
Capital: Quito, 1,100,847

ETHIOPIA
Official Name: Ethiopia
Population: 55,070,000
Area: 446,953 sq mi (1,157,603 sq km)
Pop. Density: 123/sq mi (48/sq km)
Capital: Addis Ababa (Adis Abeba), 1,912,500

FIJI
Official Name: Republic of Fiji
Population: 775,000
Area: 7,056 sq mi (18,274 sq km)
Pop. Density: 110/sq mi (42/sq km)
Capital: Suva, 69,665

FINLAND
Official Name: Republic of Finland
Population: 5,098,000
Area: 130,559 sq mi (338,145 sq km)
Pop. Density: 39/sq mi (15/sq km)
Capital: Helsinki (Helsingfors), 501,514

FRANCE
Official Name: French Republic
Population: 58,010,000
Area: 211,208 sq mi (547,026 sq km)
Pop. Density: 275/sq mi (106/sq km)
Capital: Paris, 2,152,423

GABON
Official Name: Gabonese Republic
Population: 1,035,000
Area: 103,347 sq mi (267,667 sq km)
Pop. Density: 10/sq mi (3.9/sq km)
Capital: Libreville, 235,700

THE GAMBIA
Official Name: Republic of the Gambia
Population: 1,082,000
Area: 4,127 sq mi (10,689 sq km)
Pop. Density: 262/sq mi (101/sq km)
Capital: Banjul, 44,188

GEORGIA
Official Name: Republic of Georgia
Population: 5,704,000
Area: 26,911 sq mi (69,700 sq km)
Pop. Density: 212/sq mi (82/sq km)
Capital: Tbilisi, 1,279,000

GERMANY
Official Name: Federal Republic of Germany
Population: 81,710,000
Area: 137,822 sq mi (356,955 sq km)
Pop. Density: 593/sq mi (229/sq km)
Capital: Berlin, 3,433,695

GHANA
Official Name: Republic of Ghana
Population: 17,210,000
Area: 92,098 sq mi (238,533 sq km)
Pop. Density: 187/sq mi (72/sq km)
Capital: Accra, 949,113

GREECE
Official Name: Hellenic Republic
Population: 10,475,000
Area: 50,949 sq mi (131,957 sq km)
Pop. Density: 206/sq mi (79/sq km)
Capital: Athens (Athínai), 748,110

GREENLAND
Official Name: Greenland
Population: 57,000
Area: 840,004 sq mi (2,175,600 sq km)
Pop. Density: 0.1/sq mi (0.03/sq km)
Capital: Godthåb (Nuuk), 12,217

GRENADA
Official Name: Grenada
Population: 92,000
Area: 133 sq mi (344 sq km)
Pop. Density: 692/sq mi (267/sq km)
Capital: St. George's, 4,439

GUATEMALA
Official Name: Republic of Guatemala
Population: 10,420,000
Area: 42,042 sq mi (108,889 sq km)
Pop. Density: 248/sq mi (96/sq km)
Capital: Guatemala, 1,057,210

GUINEA
Official Name: Republic of Guinea
Population: 6,469,000
Area: 94,926 sq mi (245,857 sq km)
Pop. Density: 68/sq mi (26/sq km)
Capital: Conakry, 800,000

GUINEA-BISSAU
Official Name: Republic of Guinea-Bissau
Population: 1,111,000
Area: 13,948 sq mi (36,125 sq km)
Pop. Density: 80/sq mi (31/sq km)
Capital: Bissau, 125,000

GUYANA
Official Name: Co-operative Republic of Guyana
Population: 726,000
Area: 83,000 sq mi (214,969 sq km)
Pop. Density: 8.7/sq mi (3.4/sq km)
Capital: Georgetown, 78,500

HAITI
Official Name: Republic of Haiti
Population: 7,069,000
Area: 10,714 sq mi (27,750 sq km)
Pop. Density: 660/sq mi (255/sq km)
Capital: Port-au-Prince, 797,000

HONDURAS
Official Name: Republic of Honduras
Population: 5,822,000
Area: 43,277 sq mi (112,088 sq km)
Pop. Density: 135/sq mi (52/sq km)
Capital: Tegucigalpa, 576,661

HUNGARY
Official Name: Republic of Hungary
Population: 10,270,000
Area: 35,919 sq mi (93,030 sq km)
Pop. Density: 286/sq mi (110/sq km)
Capital: Budapest, 2,016,774

Countries and Flags
continued

IRELAND
Official Name: Ireland
Population: 3,546,000
Area: 27,137 sq mi (70,285 sq km)
Pop. Density: 131/sq mi (50/sq km)
Capital: Dublin (Baile Átha Cliath), 502,749

KAZAKHSTAN
Official Name: Republic of Kazakhstan
Population: 17,025,000
Area: 1,049,156 sq mi (2,717,300 sq km)
Pop. Density: 16/sq mi (6.3/sq km)
Capital: Astana, 286,000

ICELAND
Official Name: Republic of Iceland
Population: 265,000
Area: 39,769 sq mi (103,000 sq km)
Pop. Density: 6.7/sq mi (2.6/sq km)
Capital: Reykjavik, 100,850

ISRAEL
Official Name: State of Israel
Population: 5,059,000
Area: 8,019 sq mi (20,770 sq km)
Pop. Density: 631/sq mi (244/sq km)
Capital: Jerusalem (Yerushalayim), 524,500

KENYA
Official Name: Republic of Kenya
Population: 28,380,000
Area: 224,961 sq mi (582,646 sq km)
Pop. Density: 126/sq mi (49/sq km)
Capital: Nairobi, 1,505,000

INDIA
Official Name: Republic of India
Population: 909,150,000
Area: 1,237,062 sq mi (3,203,975 sq km)
Pop. Density: 735/sq mi (284/sq km)
Capital: New Delhi, 301,297

ITALY
Official Name: Italian Republic
Population: 57,330,000
Area: 116,324 sq mi (301,277 sq km)
Pop. Density: 493/sq mi (190/sq km)
Capital: Rome (Roma), 2,693,383

KIRIBATI
Official Name: Republic of Kiribati
Population: 79,000
Area: 313 sq mi (811 sq km)
Pop. Density: 252/sq mi (97/sq km)
Capital: Bairiki, 2,226

INDONESIA
Official Name: Republic of Indonesia
Population: 193,680,000
Area: 752,410 sq mi (1,948,732 sq km)
Pop. Density: 257/sq mi (99/sq km)
Capital: Jakarta, 8,227,746

JAMAICA
Official Name: Jamaica
Population: 2,568,000
Area: 4,244 sq mi (10,991 sq km)
Pop. Density: 605/sq mi (234/sq km)
Capital: Kingston, 587,798

KOREA, NORTH
Official Name: Democratic People's Republic
of Korea
Population: 23,265,000
Area: 46,540 sq mi (120,538 sq km)
Pop. Density: 500/sq mi (193/sq km)
Capital: P'yŏngyang, 2,355,000

IRAN
Official Name: Islamic Republic of Iran
Population: 63,810,000
Area: 632,457 sq mi (1,638,057 sq km)
Pop. Density: 101/sq mi (39/sq km)
Capital: Tehrän, 6,042,584

JAPAN
Official Name: Japan
Population: 125,360,000
Area: 145,870 sq mi (377,801 sq km)
Pop. Density: 859/sq mi (332/sq km)
Capital: Tōkyō, 8,163,573

KOREA, SOUTH
Official Name: Republic of Korea
Population: 44,655,000
Area: 38,230 sq mi (99,016 sq km)
Pop. Density: 1,168/sq mi (451/sq km)
Capital: Seoul (Sŏul), 10,627,790

IRAQ
Official Name: Republic of Iraq
Population: 20,250,000
Area: 169,235 sq mi (438,317 sq km)
Pop. Density: 120/sq mi (46/sq km)
Capital: Baghdäd, 3,841,268

JORDAN
Official Name: Hashemite Kingdom of
Jordan
Population: 4,028,000
Area: 35,135 sq mi (91,000 sq km)
Pop. Density: 115/sq mi (44/sq km)
Capital: 'Ammän, 936,300

KUWAIT
Official Name: State of Kuwait
Population: 1,866,000
Area: 6,880 sq mi (17,818 sq km)
Pop. Density: 271/sq mi (105/sq km)
Capital: Kuwait (Al Kuwayt), 44,335

KYRGYZSTAN
Official Name: Kyrgyz Republic
Population: 4,541,000
Area: 76,641 sq mi (198,500 sq km)
Pop. Density: 59/sq mi (23/sq km)
Capital: Bishkek, 631,300

LIBYA
Official Name: Socialist People's Libyan
  Arab Jamahiriya
Population: 5,148,000
Area: 679,362 sq mi (1,759,540 sq km)
Pop. Density: 7.6/sq mi (2.9/sq km)
Capital: Tripoli (Ṭarābulus), 591,062

MALAWI
Official Name: Republic of Malawi
Population: 8,984,000
Area: 45,747 sq mi (118,484 sq km)
Pop. Density: 196/sq mi (76/sq km)
Capital: Lilongwe, 223,318

LAOS
Official Name: Lao People's Democratic
  Republic
Population: 4,768,000
Area: 91,429 sq mi (236,800 sq km)
Pop. Density: 52/sq mi (20/sq km)
Capital: Viangchan (Vientiane), 377,409

LIECHTENSTEIN
Official Name: Principality of Liechtenstein
Population: 30,000
Area: 62 sq mi (160 sq km)
Pop. Density: 484/sq mi (188/sq km)
Capital: Vaduz, 4,887

MALAYSIA
Official Name: Malaysia
Population: 19,505,000
Area: 127,320 sq mi (329,758 sq km)
Pop. Density: 153/sq mi (59/sq km)
Capital: Kuala Lumpur, 919,610

LATVIA
Official Name: Republic of Latvia
Population: 2,532,000
Area: 24,595 sq mi (63,700 sq km)
Pop. Density: 103/sq mi (40/sq km)
Capital: Rīga, 910,200

LITHUANIA
Official Name: Republic of Lithuania
Population: 3,757,000
Area: 25,212 sq mi (65,300 sq km)
Pop. Density: 149/sq mi (58/sq km)
Capital: Vilnius, 596,900

MALDIVES
Official Name: Republic of Maldives
Population: 251,000
Area: 115 sq mi (298 sq km)
Pop. Density: 2,183/sq mi (842/sq km)
Capital: Male', 55,130

LEBANON
Official Name: Republic of Lebanon
Population: 3,660,000
Area: 4,015 sq mi (10,400 sq km)
Pop. Density: 912/sq mi (352/sq km)
Capital: Beirut (Bayrūt), 509,000

LUXEMBOURG
Official Name: Grand Duchy of Luxembourg
Population: 396,000
Area: 998 sq mi (2,586 sq km)
Pop. Density: 397/sq mi (153/sq km)
Capital: Luxembourg, 75,377

MALI
Official Name: Republic of Mali
Population: 9,585,000
Area: 482,077 sq mi (1,240,574 sq km)
Pop. Density: 20/sq mi (7.7/sq km)
Capital: Bamako, 658,275

LESOTHO
Official Name: Kingdom of Lesotho
Population: 1,967,000
Area: 11,720 sq mi (30,355 sq km)
Pop. Density: 168/sq mi (65/sq km)
Capital: Maseru, 109,382

MACEDONIA
Official Name: Republic of Macedonia
Population: 2,102,000
Area: 9,928 sq mi (25,713 sq km)
Pop. Density: 212/sq mi (82/sq km)
Capital: Skopje, 444,900

MALTA
Official Name: Republic of Malta
Population: 368,000
Area: 122 sq mi (316 sq km)
Pop. Density: 3,016/sq mi (1,165/sq km)
Capital: Valletta, 9,199

LIBERIA
Official Name: Republic of Liberia
Population: 2,771,000
Area: 38,250 sq mi (99,067 sq km)
Pop. Density: 72/sq mi (28/sq km)
Capital: Monrovia, 465,000

MADAGASCAR
Official Name: Republic of Madagascar
Population: 13,645,000
Area: 226,658 sq mi (587,041 sq km)
Pop. Density: 60/sq mi (23/sq km)
Capital: Antananarivo, 1,250,000

MARSHALL ISLANDS
Official Name: Republic of the Marshall
  Islands
Population: 55,000
Area: 70 sq mi (181 sq km)
Pop. Density: 786/sq mi (304/sq km)
Capital: Majuro (island)

Countries and Flags
continued

MONACO
Official Name: Principality of Monaco
Population: 31,000
Area: 0.7 sq mi (1.9 sq km)
Pop. Density: 44,286/sq mi (16,316/sq km)
Capital: Monaco, 31,000

NAURU
Official Name: Republic of Nauru
Population: 10,000
Area: 8.1 sq mi (21 sq km)
Pop. Density: 1,235/sq mi (476/sq km)
Capital: Yaren District

MAURITANIA
Official Name: Islamic Republic of
Mauritania
Population: 2,228,000
Area: 395,956 sq mi (1,025,520 sq km)
Pop. Density: 5.6/sq mi (2.2/sq km)
Capital: Nouakchott, 285,000

MONGOLIA
Official Name: Mongolia
Population: 2,462,000
Area: 604,829 sq mi (1,566,500 sq km)
Pop. Density: 4.1/sq mi (1.6/sq km)
Capital: Ulan Bator (Ulaanbaatar), 575,000

NEPAL
Official Name: Kingdom of Nepal
Population: 21,295,000
Area: 56,827 sq mi (147,181 sq km)
Pop. Density: 375/sq mi (145/sq km)
Capital: Kathmandu, 421,258

MAURITIUS
Official Name: Republic of Mauritius
Population: 1,121,000
Area: 788 sq mi (2,040 sq km)
Pop. Density: 1,423/sq mi (550/sq km)
Capital: Port Louis, 141,870

MOROCCO
Official Name: Kingdom of Morocco
Population: 26,890,000
Area: 172,414 sq mi (446,550 sq km)
Pop. Density: 156/sq mi (60/sq km)
Capital: Rabat, 518,616

NETHERLANDS
Official Name: Kingdom of the Netherlands
Population: 15,425,000
Area: 16,164 sq mi (41,864 sq km)
Pop. Density: 954/sq mi (368/sq km)
Capital: Amsterdam (designated), 713,407,
and The Hague ('s-Gravenhage) (seat of
government), 445,287

MEXICO
Official Name: United Mexican States
Population: 93,860,000
Area: 759,534 sq mi (1,967,183 sq km)
Pop. Density: 124/sq mi (48/sq km)
Capital: Mexico City (Ciudad de México),
8,235,744

MOZAMBIQUE
Official Name: Republic of Mozambique
Population: 17,860,000
Area: 308,642 sq mi (799,380 sq km)
Pop. Density: 58/sq mi (22/sq km)
Capital: Maputo, 1,069,727

NEW ZEALAND
Official Name: New Zealand
Population: 3,558,000
Area: 104,454 sq mi (270,534 sq km)
Pop. Density: 34/sq mi (13/sq km)
Capital: Wellington, 150,301

MICRONESIA, FEDERATED STATES OF
Official Name: Federated States of
Micronesia
Population: 122,000
Area: 271 sq mi (702 sq km)
Pop. Density: 450/sq mi (174/sq km)
Capital: Palikir, 5,047

MYANMAR
Official Name: Union of Myanmar
Population: 44,675,000
Area: 261,228 sq mi (676,577 sq km)
Pop. Density: 171/sq mi (66/sq km)
Capital: Rangoon (Yangon), 2,513,023

NICARAGUA
Official Name: Republic of Nicaragua
Population: 4,438,000
Area: 50,054 sq mi (129,640 sq km)
Pop. Density: 89/sq mi (34/sq km)
Capital: Managua, 682,000

MOLDOVA
Official Name: Republic of Moldova
Population: 4,377,000
Area: 13,012 sq mi (33,700 sq km)
Pop. Density: 336/sq mi (130/sq km)
Capital: Chişinău (Kishinev), 676,700

NAMIBIA
Official Name: Republic of Namibia
Population: 1,623,000
Area: 318,253 sq mi (824,272 sq km)
Pop. Density: 5.1/sq mi (2.0/sq km)
Capital: Windhoek, 114,500

NIGER
Official Name: Republic of Niger
Population: 9,125,000
Area: 489,191 sq mi (1,267,000 sq km)
Pop. Density: 19/sq mi (7.2/sq km)
Capital: Niamey, 392,165

NIGERIA
Official Name: Federal Republic of Nigeria
Population: 97,300,000
Area: 356,669 sq mi (923,768 sq km)
Pop. Density: 273/sq mi (105/sq km)
Capital: Abuja, 250,000

PALAU
Official Name: Republic of Palau
Population: 17,000
Area: 196 sq mi (508 sq km)
Pop. Density: 87/sq mi (33/sq km)
Capital: Koror (de facto), 9,018, and
Melekeok (future)

POLAND
Official Name: Republic of Poland
Population: 38,730,000
Area: 121,196 sq mi (313,895 sq km)
Pop. Density: 320/sq mi (123/sq km)
Capital: Warsaw (Warszawa), 1,644,500

NIUE
Official Name: Niue
Population: 1,900
Area: 100 sq mi (259 sq km)
Pop. Density: 19/sq mi (7.3/sq km)
Capital: Alofi, 706

PANAMA
Official Name: Republic of Panama
Population: 2,654,000
Area: 29,157 sq mi (75,517 sq km)
Pop. Density: 91/sq mi (35/sq km)
Capital: Panamá, 411,549

PORTUGAL
Official Name: Portuguese Republic
Population: 9,907,000
Area: 35,516 sq mi (91,985 sq km)
Pop. Density: 279/sq mi (108/sq km)
Capital: Lisbon (Lisboa), 807,167

NORTHERN MARIANA ISLANDS
Official Name: Commonwealth of the
Northern Mariana Islands
Population: 51,000
Area: 184 sq mi (477 sq km)
Pop. Density: 277/sq mi (107/sq km)
Capital: Saipan (island)

PAPUA NEW GUINEA
Official Name: Independent State of Papua
New Guinea
Population: 4,057,000
Area: 178,704 sq mi (462,840 sq km)
Pop. Density: 23/sq mi (8.8/sq km)
Capital: Port Moresby, 193,242

PUERTO RICO
Official Name: Commonwealth of Puerto Rico
Population: 3,625,000
Area: 3,515 sq mi (9,104 sq km)
Pop. Density: 1,031/sq mi (398/sq km)
Capital: San Juan, 426,832

NORWAY
Official Name: Kingdom of Norway
Population: 4,339,000
Area: 149,412 sq mi (386,975 sq km)
Pop. Density: 29/sq mi (11/sq km)
Capital: Oslo, 470,204

PARAGUAY
Official Name: Republic of Paraguay
Population: 4,400,000
Area: 157,048 sq mi (406,752 sq km)
Pop. Density: 28/sq mi (11/sq km)
Capital: Asunción, 502,426

QATAR
Official Name: State of Qatar
Population: 519,000
Area: 4,412 sq mi (11,427 sq km)
Pop. Density: 118/sq mi (45/sq km)
Capital: Ad Dawḩah (Doha), 217,294

OMAN
Official Name: Sultanate of Oman
Population: 2,089,000
Area: 82,030 sq mi (212,457 sq km)
Pop. Density: 25/sq mi (9.8/sq km)
Capital: Muscat (Masqat), 30,000

PERU
Official Name: Republic of Peru
Population: 23,095,000
Area: 496,225 sq mi (1,285,216 sq km)
Pop. Density: 47/sq mi (18/sq km)
Capital: Lima, 371,122

ROMANIA
Official Name: Romania
Population: 22,745,000
Area: 91,699 sq mi (237,500 sq km)
Pop. Density: 248/sq mi (96/sq km)
Capital: Bucharest (Bucureşti), 2,064,474

PAKISTAN
Official Name: Islamic Republic of Pakistan
Population: 129,630,000
Area: 339,732 sq mi (879,902 sq km)
Pop. Density: 382/sq mi (147/sq km)
Capital: Islāmābād, 204,364

PHILIPPINES
Official Name: Republic of the Philippines
Population: 67,910,000
Area: 115,831 sq mi (300,000 sq km)
Pop. Density: 586/sq mi (226/sq km)
Capital: Manila, 1,598,918

RUSSIA
Official Name: Russian Federation
Population: 150,500,000
Area: 6,592,849 sq mi (17,075,400 sq km)
Pop. Density: 23/sq mi (8.8/sq km)
Capital: Moscow (Moskva), 8,801,500

Countries and Flags
continued

SAN MARINO
Official Name: Republic of San Marino
Population: 24,000
Area: 24 sq mi (61 sq km)
Pop. Density: 1,000/sq mi (393/sq km)
Capital: San Marino, 2,794

SINGAPORE
Official Name: Republic of Singapore
Population: 2,921,000
Area: 246 sq mi (636 sq km)
Pop. Density: 11,874/sq mi (4,593/sq km)
Capital: Singapore, 2,921,000

RWANDA
Official Name: Republic of Rwanda
Population: 7,343,000
Area: 10,169 sq mi (26,338 sq km)
Pop. Density: 722/sq mi (279/sq km)
Capital: Kigali, 232,733

SAO TOME AND PRINCIPE
Official Name: Democratic Republic of Sao Tome and Principe
Population: 127,000
Area: 372 sq mi (964 sq km)
Pop. Density: 341/sq mi (132/sq km)
Capital: São Tomé, 5,245

SLOVAKIA
Official Name: Slovak Republic
Population: 5,353,000
Area: 18,933 sq mi (49,035 sq km)
Pop. Density: 283/sq mi (109/sq km)
Capital: Bratislava, 441,453

ST. KITTS AND NEVIS
Official Name: Federation of St. Kitts and Nevis
Population: 42,000
Area: 104 sq mi (269 sq km)
Pop. Density: 404/sq mi (156/sq km)
Capital: Basseterre, 14,725

SAUDI ARABIA
Official Name: Kingdom of Saudi Arabia
Population: 18,190,000
Area: 830,000 sq mi (2,149,690 sq km)
Pop. Density: 22/sq mi (8.5/sq km)
Capital: Riyadh (Ar Riyād), 1,250,000

SLOVENIA
Official Name: Republic of Slovenia
Population: 1,993,000
Area: 7,820 sq mi (20,253 sq km)
Pop. Density: 255/sq mi (98/sq km)
Capital: Ljubljana, 233,200

ST. LUCIA
Official Name: St. Lucia
Population: 138,000
Area: 238 sq mi (616 sq km)
Pop. Density: 580/sq mi (224/sq km)
Capital: Castries, 11,147

SENEGAL
Official Name: Republic of Senegal
Population: 8,862,000
Area: 75,951 sq mi (196,712 sq km)
Pop. Density: 117/sq mi (45/sq km)
Capital: Dakar, 1,490,450

SOLOMON ISLANDS
Official Name: Solomon Islands
Population: 393,000
Area: 10,954 sq mi (28,370 sq km)
Pop. Density: 36/sq mi (14/sq km)
Capital: Honiara, 30,413

ST. VINCENT AND THE GRENADINES
Official Name: St. Vincent and the Grenadines
Population: 110,000
Area: 150 sq mi (388 sq km)
Pop. Density: 733/sq mi (284/sq km)
Capital: Kingstown, 15,466

SEYCHELLES
Official Name: Republic of Seychelles
Population: 75,000
Area: 175 sq mi (453 sq km)
Pop. Density: 429/sq mi (166/sq km)
Capital: Victoria, 23,000

SOMALIA
Official Name: Somalia
Population: 7,187,000
Area: 246,201 sq mi (637,657 sq km)
Pop. Density: 29/sq mi (11/sq km)
Capital: Mogadishu (Muqdisho), 600,000

SAMOA
Official Name: Independent State of Samoa
Population: 172,000
Area: 1,093 sq mi (2,831 sq km)
Pop. Density: 157/sq mi (61/sq km)
Capital: Apia, 34,126

SIERRA LEONE
Official Name: Republic of Sierra Leone
Population: 4,690,000
Area: 27,925 sq mi (72,325 sq km)
Pop. Density: 168/sq mi (65/sq km)
Capital: Freetown, 469,776

SOUTH AFRICA
Official Name: Republic of South Africa
Population: 44,500,000
Area: 471,010 sq mi (1,219,909 sq km)
Pop. Density: 94/sq mi (36/sq km)
Capital: Pretoria (administrative), 525,583, Cape Town (legislative), 854,616, and Bloemfontein (judicial), 126,867

SPAIN
Official Name: Kingdom of Spain
Population: 39,260,000
Area: 194,885 sq mi (504,750 sq km)
Pop. Density: 201/sq mi (78/sq km)
Capital: Madrid, 3,102,846

SWITZERLAND
Official Name: Swiss Confederation
Population: 7,244,000
Area: 15,943 sq mi (41,293 sq km)
Pop. Density: 454/sq mi (175/sq km)
Capital: Bern (Berne), 136,338

TOGO
Official Name: Republic of Togo
Population: 4,332,000
Area: 21,925 sq mi (56,785 sq km)
Pop. Density: 198/sq mi (76/sq km)
Capital: Lomé, 500,000

SRI LANKA
Official Name: Democratic Socialist Republic
   of Sri Lanka
Population: 18,240,000
Area: 24,962 sq mi (64,652 sq km)
Pop. Density: 731/sq mi (282/sq km)
Capital: Colombo (designated), 612,000, and
   Sri Jayawardenepura (seat of government),
   108,000

SYRIA
Official Name: Syrian Arab Republic
Population: 14,100,000
Area: 71,498 sq mi (185,180 sq km)
Pop. Density: 197/sq mi (76/sq km)
Capital: Damascus (Dimashq), 1,549,932

TONGA
Official Name: Kingdom of Tonga
Population: 110,000
Area: 288 sq mi (747 sq km)
Pop. Density: 382/sq mi (147/sq km)
Capital: Nuku'alofa, 21,265

SUDAN
Official Name: Republic of the Sudan
Population: 25,840,000
Area: 967,500 sq mi (2,505,813 sq km)
Pop. Density: 27/sq mi (10/sq km)
Capital: Khartoum (Al Kharṭum), 473,597

TAIWAN
Official Name: Republic of China
Population: 21,150,000
Area: 13,900 sq mi (36,002 sq km)
Pop. Density: 1,522/sq mi (587/sq km)
Capital: T'aipei, 2,706,453

TRINIDAD AND TOBAGO
Official Name: Republic of Trinidad and
   Tobago
Population: 1,281,000
Area: 1,980 sq mi (5,128 sq km)
Pop. Density: 647/sq mi (250/sq km)
Capital: Port of Spain, 50,878

SURINAME
Official Name: Republic of Suriname
Population: 426,000
Area: 63,251 sq mi (163,820 sq km)
Pop. Density: 6.7/sq mi (2.6/sq km)
Capital: Paramaribo, 241,000

TAJIKISTAN
Official Name: Republic of Tajikistan
Population: 6,073,000
Area: 55,251 sq mi (143,100 sq km)
Pop. Density: 110/sq mi (42/sq km)
Capital: Dushanbe, 582,400

TUNISIA
Official Name: Republic of Tunisia
Population: 8,806,000
Area: 63,170 sq mi (163,610 sq km)
Pop. Density: 139/sq mi (54/sq km)
Capital: Tunis, 596,654

SWAZILAND
Official Name: Kingdom of Swaziland
Population: 889,000
Area: 6,704 sq mi (17,364 sq km)
Pop. Density: 133/sq mi (51/sq km)
Capital: Mbabane (administrative), 38,290,
   and Lobamba (legislative)

TANZANIA
Official Name: United Republic of Tanzania
Population: 28,350,000
Area: 341,217 sq mi (883,749 sq km)
Pop. Density: 83/sq mi (32/sq km)
Capital: Dar es Salaam (de facto), 1,096,000,
   and Dodoma (legislative), 85,000

TURKEY
Official Name: Republic of Turkey
Population: 62,030,000
Area: 300,948 sq mi (779,452 sq km)
Pop. Density: 206/sq mi (80/sq km)
Capital: Ankara, 2,559,471

SWEDEN
Official Name: Kingdom of Sweden
Population: 8,981,000
Area: 173,732 sq mi (449,964 sq km)
Pop. Density: 52/sq mi (20/sq km)
Capital: Stockholm, 674,452

THAILAND
Official Name: Kingdom of Thailand
Population: 59,870,000
Area: 198,115 sq mi (513,115 sq km)
Pop. Density: 302/sq mi (117/sq km)
Capital: Bangkok (Krung Thep), 5,620,591

TURKMENISTAN
Official Name: Turkmenistan
Population: 4,035,000
Area: 188,456 sq mi (488,100 sq km)
Pop. Density: 21/sq mi (8.3/sq km)
Capital: Ashgabat, 412,200

Countries and Flags
continued

UNITED STATES
Official Name: United States of America
Population: 262,530,000
Area: 3,787,425 sq mi (9,809,431 sq km)
Pop. Density: 69/sq mi (27/sq km)
Capital: Washington, D.C., 606,900

VIETNAM
Official Name: Socialist Republic of Vietnam
Population: 73,760,000
Area: 127,428 sq mi (330,036 sq km)
Pop. Density: 579/sq mi (223/sq km)
Capital: Hanoi, 905,939

TUVALU
Official Name: Tuvalu
Population: 10,000
Area: 10 sq mi (26 sq km)
Pop. Density: 1,000/sq mi (385/sq km)
Capital: Funafuti, 2,191

URUGUAY
Official Name: Oriental Republic of Uruguay
Population: 3,317,000
Area: 68,500 sq mi (177,414 sq km)
Pop. Density: 48/sq mi (19/sq km)
Capital: Montevideo, 1,251,647

YEMEN
Official Name: Republic of Yemen
Population: 12,910,000
Area: 203,850 sq mi (527,968 sq km)
Pop. Density: 63/sq mi (24/sq km)
Capital: San'ā', 427,150

UGANDA
Official Name: Republic of Uganda
Population: 18,270,000
Area: 93,104 sq mi (241,139 sq km)
Pop. Density: 196/sq mi (76/sq km)
Capital: Kampala, 773,463

UZBEKISTAN
Official Name: Republic of Uzbekistan
Population: 22,860,000
Area: 172,742 sq mi (447,400 sq km)
Pop. Density: 132/sq mi (51/sq km)
Capital: Tashkent, 2,113,300

YUGOSLAVIA
Official Name: Socialist Federal Republic of Yugoslavia
Population: 10,765,000
Area: 39,449 sq mi (102,173 sq km)
Pop. Density: 273/sq mi (105/sq km)
Capital: Belgrade (Beograd), 1,136,786

UKRAINE
Official Name: Ukraine
Population: 52,140,000
Area: 233,090 sq mi (603,700 sq km)
Pop. Density: 224/sq mi (86/sq km)
Capital: Kiev (Kyyiv), 2,635,000

VANUATU
Official Name: Republic of Vanuatu
Population: 161,000
Area: 4,707 sq mi (12,190 sq km)
Pop. Density: 34/sq mi (13/sq km)
Capital: Port Vila, 18,905

ZAMBIA
Official Name: Republic of the Zambia
Population: 8,809,000
Area: 290,587 sq mi (752,618 sq km)
Pop. Density: 30/sq mi (12/sq km)
Capital: Lusaka, 982,362

UNITED ARAB EMIRATES
Official Name: United Arab Emirates
Population: 2,855,000
Area: 32,278 sq mi (83,600 sq km)
Pop. Density: 88/sq mi (34/sq km)
Capital: Abū Ẓaby (Abu Dhabi), 242,975

VATICAN CITY
Official Name: State of the Vatican City
Population: 1,000
Area: 0.2 sq mi (0.4 sq km)
Pop. Density: 5,000/sq mi (2,500/sq km)
Capital: Vatican City, 1,000

ZIMBABWE
Official Name: Republic of Zimbabwe
Population: 11,075,000
Area: 150,872 sq mi (390,757 sq km)
Pop. Density: 73/sq mi (28/sq km)
Capital: Harare (Salisbury), 681,000

UNITED KINGDOM
Official Name: United Kingdom of Great Britain and Northern Ireland
Population: 58,430,000
Area: 94,249 sq mi (244,101 sq km)
Pop. Density: 620/sq mi (239/sq km)
Capital: London, 6,574,009

VENEZUELA
Official Name: Republic of Venezuela
Population: 21,395,000
Area: 352,145 sq mi (912,050 sq km)
Pop. Density: 61/sq mi (23/sq km)
Capital: Caracas, 1,822,465

Legend

Continental and regional coverage of the world's land areas is provided by the following section of physical-political reference maps. The section falls into a continental arrangement: North America, South America, Europe, Africa, Asia, and Oceania. Introducing each regional reference map section are several basic thematic maps.

To aid the reader in understanding the relative sizes of continents and of some of the countries and regions, uniform scales for comparable areas were used as far as possible. Most of the world is covered by a series of regional maps at scales of 1:16,000,000 and 1:12,000,000. Maps at 1:10,000,000 provide even greater detail for parts of Europe. The United States and parts of South America are mapped at 1:4,000,000.

Many of the symbols used are self-explanatory. A complete legend below provides a key to the symbols on the reference maps in the atlas.

The color tints on the maps depict the varying elevations and depths of land areas and bodies of water. The Relief legend that accompanies each map shows the specific elevation or depth that each color tint represents.

The surface configuration is represented by hill-shading, which gives the three-dimensional impression of landforms. This terrain representation is superimposed on the layer tints to convey a realistic and readily visualized impression of the surface. The combination of altitudinal tints and hill-shading best shows elevation, relief, steepness of slope, and ruggedness of terrain.

If the world used one alphabet and language, no particular difficulty would arise in understanding place-names. However, some of the people of the world, the Chinese and the Japanese, for example, use non-alphabetic languages. Their symbols are transliterated into the Roman alphabet. In this atlas, a "local-name" policy generally was used for naming cities, towns, and all local topographic and water features. However, for a few major cities the Anglicized name was preferred and the local name given in parentheses: for instance, Moscow (Moskva), Vienna (Wien), Bangkok (Krung Thep). In countries where more than one official language is used, a name appears in the dominant local language. The generic parts of local names for topographic and water features are self-explanatory in many cases because of the associated map symbols or type styles. A complete list of foreign generic names is given in the Glossary.

Physical-Political Reference Map Legend

Cultural Features

Political Boundaries

▬▬▬ --- (over water)	International (Demarcated, Undemarcated, and Administrative)
▬ ▬ ▬ ▬	Disputed de facto
— - — - —	Claim Boundary
▬ ▬ ▬ ▬	Indefinite or Undefined
▬▬▬ (over water)	Secondary, State, Provincial, etc.
⬚	Parks, Indian Reservations
⬚	City Limits 🖤 Urbanized Areas
▫	Neighborhoods, Sections of City

Populated Places

⊙	1,000,000 and over
◎	250,000 to 1,000,000
⊙	100,000 to 250,000
•	25,000 to 100,000
○	0 to 25,000
TŌKYŌ	National Capitals
Boise	Secondary Capitals

Note: On maps at 1:20,000,000 and smaller the town symbols do not follow the specific population classification shown above. On all maps, type size indicates the relative importance of the city.

Transportation

———	Railroads
———	Railroads On 1:1,000,000 scale maps
- - - - -	Railroad Ferries
	Roads
Major	On 1:1,000,000 scale maps
Other	
Major	On 1:4,000,000 scale maps
Other	
———	On other scale maps
· · · · · ·	Caravan Routes
✈	Airports

Other Cultural Features

⌣	Dams
+++++++	Pipelines
▲	Points of Interest
∴	Ruins

Land Features

△	Peaks, Spot Heights
=	Passes
░░░	Sand
	Contours

Water Features

Lakes and Reservoirs

⬭	Fresh Water
⬭	Fresh Water: Intermittent
⬭	Salt Water
⬭	Salt Water: Intermittent

Other Water Features

⬭	Salt Basins, Flats
	Swamps
	Ice Caps and Glaciers
	Rivers
	Intermittent Rivers
	Aqueducts and Canals
=====	Ship Channels
⌣	Falls
╫╫╫	Rapids
♪	Springs
△	Water Depths
	Fishing Banks
⬭	Sand Bars
⌒⌒⌒	Reefs

Note: Country populations used throughout the atlas are 1995 estimates based on U.S. Census Bureau figures and other available information. City populations reflect the latest available official data.

180° 1 165° 2 150° 3 135° 4 120° 5 105° 6 90° 7 75° 8 60° 9 45° 10 30° 11 15° 12 0°

A

90°

ARCTIC OCEAN

75°

Beaufort Sea

VICTORIA ISLAND

Baffin Bay

GREENLAND
(Den.)

B

UNITED
STATES
Arctic Circle

Yellowknife

BAFFIN ISLAND

Godthåb

Reykjavík

ICELAND
FAROE
ISLAND
(Den.)

Mount
McKinley
6194
Anchorage

60°

Hudson
Bay

Juneau

C

Bering Sea

Gulf of
Alaska

CANADA

NEWFOUNDLAND

IRELAND

UNI
KING
LON

ALEUTIAN ISLANDS

45°

Vancouver

Winnipeg

St. Lawrence
Montréal

Seattle

NORTH AMERICA

Toronto

DETROIT

CHICAGO

NEW YORK

ATLANTIC OCEAN

PORTUGAL

SPA

D

PACIFIC

SAN FRANCISCO

UNITED STATES

Denver

St.
Louis

Washington

Appalachian Mountains

AÇORES AZORES
(Port.)

LOS ANGELES

Phoenix

Atlanta

BERMUDA
(U.K.)

ARQUIPÉLAGO
DA MADEIRA
(Port.)

Casablanca

30°

OCEAN

Houston

New
Orleans

BAHAMAS

Monterrey

Gulf of Mexico

Miami

ISLAS CANARIAS
CANARY ISLANDS
(Sp.)

MOROCCO

MIDWAY ISLANDS
(U.S.)

Tropic of Cancer

La Habana

WESTERN
SAHARA

E

HAWAIIAN ISLANDS

Honolulu

MEXICO

CIUDAD
DE MEXICO

Guadalajara

CUBA

BELIZE

HAITI DOMINICAN
REPUBLIC

JAMAICA

PUERTO RICO (U.S.)

CAPE VERDE

SENEGAL

MAURI-
TANIA

S

A

15°

P
O
L
Y
N
E
S
I
A

GUATEMALA

HONDURAS

Caribbean Sea

GUADELOUPE (Fr.)

MARTINIQUE (Fr.)

THE GAMBIA
GUINEA-BISSAU

GUINEA

EL SALVADOR

NICARAGUA

TRINIDAD AND
TOBAGO

SIERRA
LEONE

COT
IVOIR

CLIPPERTON
(Fr.)

COSTA
RICA

Panamá

Caracas

LIBERIA

F

PANAMA

VENEZUELA

Santa Fe de Bogotá

GUYANA

SURI-
NAME

FRENCH
GUIANA

COLOMBIA

Quito

0°

Equator

ARCHIPIÉLAGO DE COLÓN
GALAPAGOS ISLANDS
(Ec.)

ECUADOR

Manaus

Amazon

Belém

Equator

TOKELAU ISLANDS
(N.Z.)

ÎLES MARQUISES

Fortaleza

G

WALLIS
AND
FUTUNA
(Fr.)

SAMOA AM.
SAMOA

P
E
R
U

B   R   A   Z   I   L

Recife

Lima

SOUTH AMERICA

Salvador

ATLANTIC OCEAN

15°

FIJI

La Paz

Brasília

NIUE
(N.Z.)

COOK
ISLANDS
(N.Z.)

FRENCH
POLYNESIA

BOLIVIA

H

TONGA

Tropic of Capricorn

PITCAIRN
(U.K.)

P
A
R
A
G
U
A
Y

SÃO PAULO

RIO DE JANEIRO

30°

ISLA DE PASCUA
EASTER ISLAND
(Chile)

Antofagasta

Asunción

Pôrto Alegre

CHILE

Córdoba

URUGUAY

I

International Date Line

Santiago

Co. Aconcagua
6959

BUENOS AIRES

Montevideo

ARGENTINA

PACIFIC

CHATHAM ISLAND
(N.Z.)

45°

OCEAN

J

FALKLAND ISLANDS
(U.K.)

Punta Arenas

SOUTH GEORGIA
(Falk. Is.)

60°

CABO DE HORNOS
CAPE HORN

SOUTH ORKNEY
ISLANDS
(B.A.T.)

K

Antarctic Circle

Bellingshausen Sea

Weddell Sea

75°

Ross Sea

L

Vinson Massif
4897

A   N   T   A   R

90°

180° 1 165° 2 150° 3 135° 4 120° 5 105° 6 90° 7 75° 8 60° 9 45° 10 30° 11 15° 12 0°

Robinson Projection

WORLD TERRAIN

Arctic Ocean

QUEEN ELIZABETH ISLANDS

GREENLAND

Arctic Circle

RUSSIA UNITED STATES

ICELAND

BAFFIN ISLAND

C A N A D A

N O R T H

A M E R I C A

PORTUGAL

Chicago

New York

Atlantic

MOR

UNITED STATES

APPALACHIAN MOUNTAINS

GREAT BASIN

Los Angeles

Pacific

Ocean

WESTERN SAHARA

MAURI-TANIA

Tropic of Cancer

Mexico City

WEST INDIES

GUINEA

Ocean

Equator

VENEZUELA

COLOMBIA

ARCHIPIÉLAGO DE COLÓN GALÁPAGOS ISLANDS

Amazon

S O U T H

Equator

B R A Z I L

Pacific

A M E R I C A

BOLIVIA

Ocean

Tropic of Capricorn

PARAGUAY

Rio de Janeiro

Atlantic

IS CANARIAS

URUGUAY

Buenos Aires

PAMPA

Ocean

Antarctic Circle

A

Terrain

Land Elevations in Profile

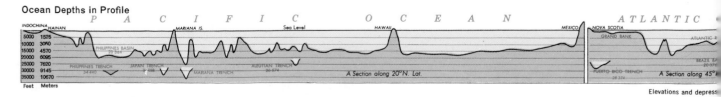

| | OCEANIA | NORTH AMERICA | SOUTH AMERICA | AFRICA |

LOS ANDES

ATLAS

30000	9145	NEW ZEALAND	ALASKA RANGE	SIERRA NEVADA	ROCKY MTS.	Pico de	Aconcagua (Vol.) 22 831		
25000	7620				Pikes Peak	Orizaba	Chimborazo Nev. Illimani	Jebel Toubkal	Ras Dashen Terra
20000	6095	HAWAII	Mt. McKinley	CASCADE RANGE Mt. Whitney	14 110	18 406	20 702 20 741	13 665	15 158
15000	4570	Aoraki Mauna Kea (Vol.)	20 320	Mt. Rainier 14 410 14 494		Irazú (Vol.) Mt.	Pico da Bandeira	Cameroon Mtn.	
		12 316 13 796				11 200 Mitchell	PLATEAU OF BOLIVIA 9 482	IS CANARIAS 13 451	
10000	3050	TAHITI		GREAT BASIN		Pico Duarte		Pico de Teide	
5000	1525					6 684 10 417		12 188	
Feet	Meters		7 352						

Ocean Depths in Profile

| | P A C I F I C | O C E A N | A T L A N T I C |

INDOCHINA HAINAN			MARIANA IS.	Sea Level	HAWAII	MEXICO	NOVA SCOTIA	
5000	1525						GRAND BANK	ATLANTIC B
10000	3050	PHILIPPINES BASIN 20 384						
15000	4570		JAPAN TRENCH					
20000	6095						BRAZIL 20 076	
25000	7620	PHILIPPINES TRENCH 34 440		ALEUTIAN TRENCH 26 574			PUERTO RICO TRENCH	
30000	9145		JAPAN TRENCH 27 598				28 374	
35000	10670		MARIANA TRENCH	A Section along 20°N. Lat.			A Section along 45°

Feet Meters

Elevations and depress

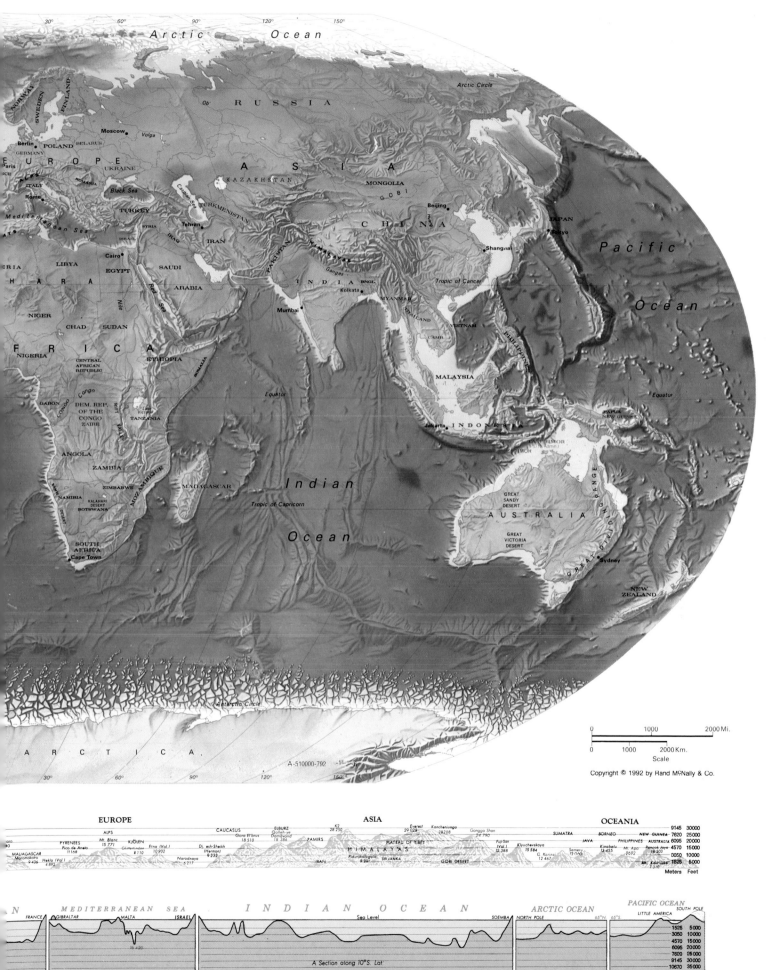

Arctic Ocean

Arctic Circle

RUSSIA
Ob
30° 60° 90° 120° 150°

NORWAY
SWEDEN
FINLAND
Berlin
POLAND
BELARUS
GERMANY
Paris
EUROPE
UKRAINE
Moscow
Volga
ITALY
ROMANIA
Rome
Black Sea
Caspian Sea
KAZAKHSTAN
MONGOLIA
ASIA
GOBI
Beijing
JAPAN
Tokyo
Mediterranean Sea
TURKEY
TURKMENISTAN
Tehran
SYRIA
ISRAEL
IRAQ
IRAN
PAKISTAN
HIMALAYAS
CHINA
Shanghai
Pacific
Cairo
LIBYA
EGYPT
SAUDI
ARABIA
Red Sea
Nile
INDIA
Ganges
Kolkata
Tropic of Cancer
BNGL.
MYANMAR
THAILAND
VIETNAM
Ocean
SAHARA
NIGER
CHAD
SUDAN
AFRICA
NIGERIA
CENTRAL
AFRICAN
REPUBLIC
ETHIOPIA
SOMALIA
Mumbai
CAMB.
PHILIPPINES
MALAYSIA
GABON
Congo
DEM. REP.
OF THE
CONGO
ZAIRE
LAKE
VICTORIA
TANZANIA
RIFT VALLEY
Equator
Jakarta
INDONESIA
PAPUA
NEW GUINEA
Equator
ANGOLA
ZAMBIA
MADAGASCAR
Indian
TIMOR
TIMOR
ZIMBABWE
MOZAMBIQUE
Tropic of Capricorn
GREAT
SANDY
DESERT
GREAT DIVIDING RANGE
NAMIBIA
KALAHARI
DESERT
BOTSWANA
AUSTRALIA
Ocean
GREAT
VICTORIA
DESERT
SOUTH
AFRICA
Cape Town
Sydney
NEW
ZEALAND

Antarctic Circle

ANTARCTICA

30° 60° 90° 120° 150°

A-510000-792

Scale
0 1000 2000 Mi.
0 1000 2000 Km.

Copyright © 1992 by Rand McNally & Co.

EUROPE
ASIA
OCEANIA

ALPS
CAUCASUS
ELBURZ
K2
28,250
Everest
29,028
Kanchenjunga
28,208
Gongga Shan
24,790
SUMATRA
BORNEO
NEW GUINEA
7620
25000
9145
30000
PYRENEES
Mt. Blanc
15,771
KJÖLEN
Gora Elbrus
18,510
Qolleh-ye
Damavand
18,386
PAMIRS
PLATEAU OF TIBET
Fuji-San
(Vol.)
12,388
Klyuchevskaya
15,584
JAVA
Kinabalu
13,455
PHILIPPINES
AUSTRALIA
Puncak Jaya
16,503
6095
20000
Pico de Aneto
11,168
Glittertinden
8,110
Etna (Vol.)
10,902
Dj. esh-Sheikh
(Hermon)
9,232
HIMALAYAS
MADAGASCAR
Maromokotro
9,436
Hekla (Vol.)
4,892
Norodnaya
6,217
Piduratalagala
8,281
SRI LANKA
C. Karinci
12,467
Semeru
(Vol.)
12,060
3050
10000
IRAN
GOBI DESERT
Mt. Kosciuko
1525
5000
7,310
Meters Feet

N
MEDITERRANEAN SEA
INDIAN OCEAN
ARCTIC OCEAN
PACIFIC OCEAN
SOUTH POLE
FRANCE
GIBRALTAR
MALTA
ISRAEL
Sea Level
SOEMBA
NORTH POLE
65°N. 65°S.
LITTLE AMERICA
1525
5000
3050
10000
10,420
4570
15000
6095
20000
7600
25000
A Section along 10°S. Lat.
9145
30000
10670
35000
Meters Feet

...ven in feet

World Climate

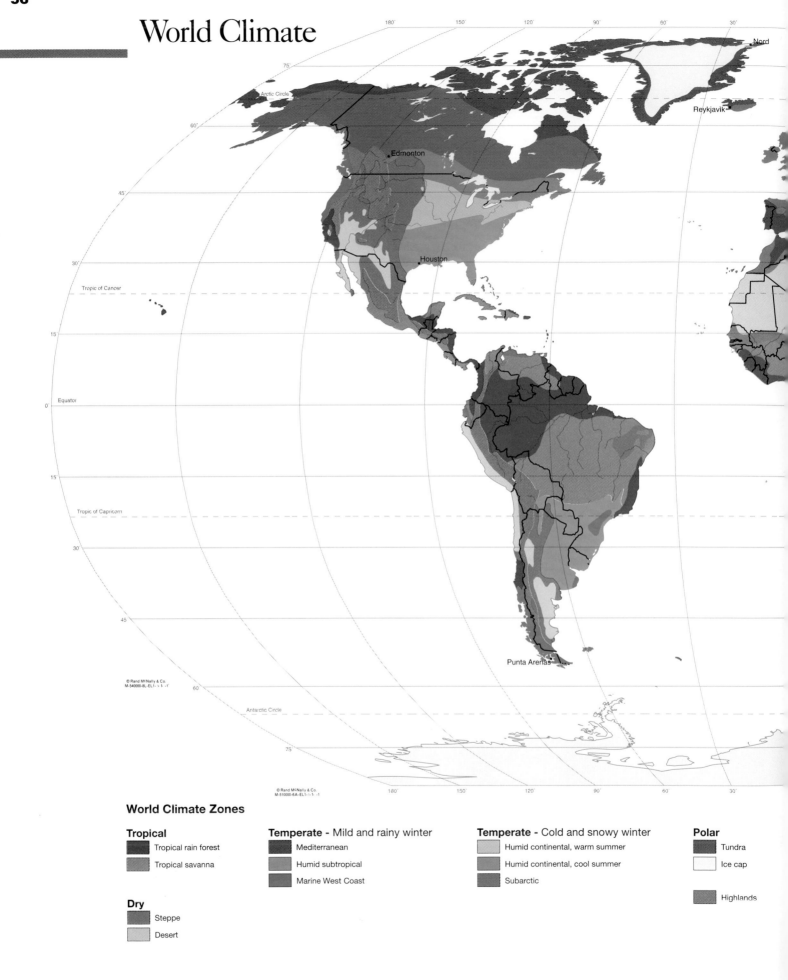

World Climate Zones

Tropical

- Tropical rain forest
- Tropical savanna

Dry

- Steppe
- Desert

Temperate - Mild and rainy winter

- Mediterranean
- Humid subtropical
- Marine West Coast

Temperate - Cold and snowy winter

- Humid continental, warm summer
- Humid continental, cool summer
- Subarctic

Polar

- Tundra
- Ice cap

- Highlands

© Rand McNally & Co.
M-540000-8L-EL1- > 1- -1'

© Rand McNally & Co.
M-510000-6A-EL1-1-1- -1

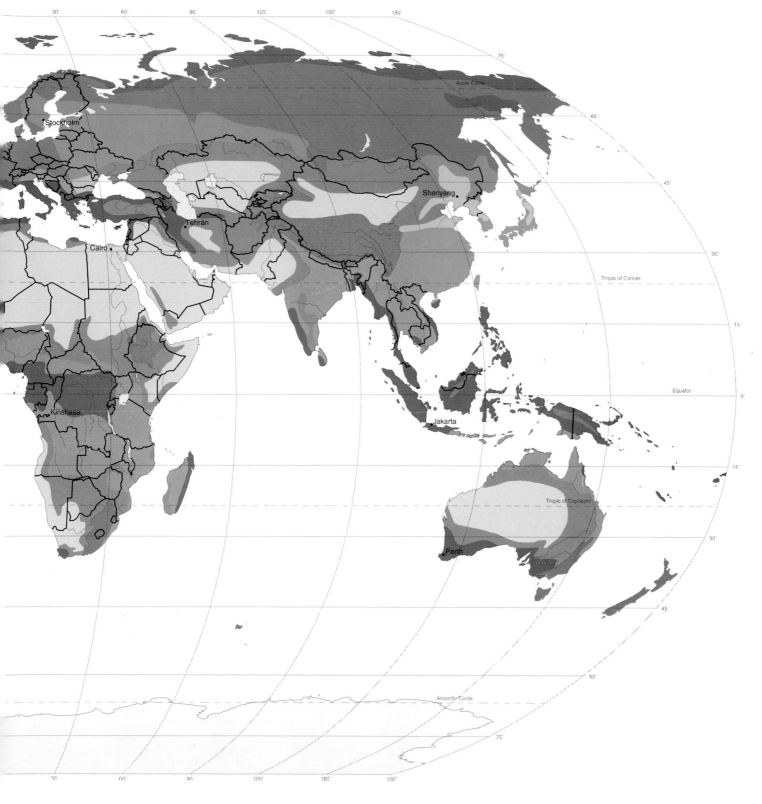

*Tinted areas show
temperature in
degrees Fahrenheit.
Vertical bars show
precipitation in inches.*

Jakarta
Hot and rainy

Kinshasa
Hot with rainy
and dry
seasons

Tehrān
Semiarid

Cairo
Very dry

Perth
Hot, dry
summer / mild,
rainy winter

Houston
Warm, humid
summer /
mild winter

Punta Arenas
Mild and rainy

Shenyang
Warm, humid
summer / cold,
snowy winter

Stockholm
Cool, humid
summer / cold,
snowy winter

Edmonton
Short, cool,
humid summer /
very cold,
snowy winter

Reykjavík
Cold and dry

Nord
Very cold,
perpetual frost

Extensive uplands
Climate varies
with elevation
and latitude

World Vegetation

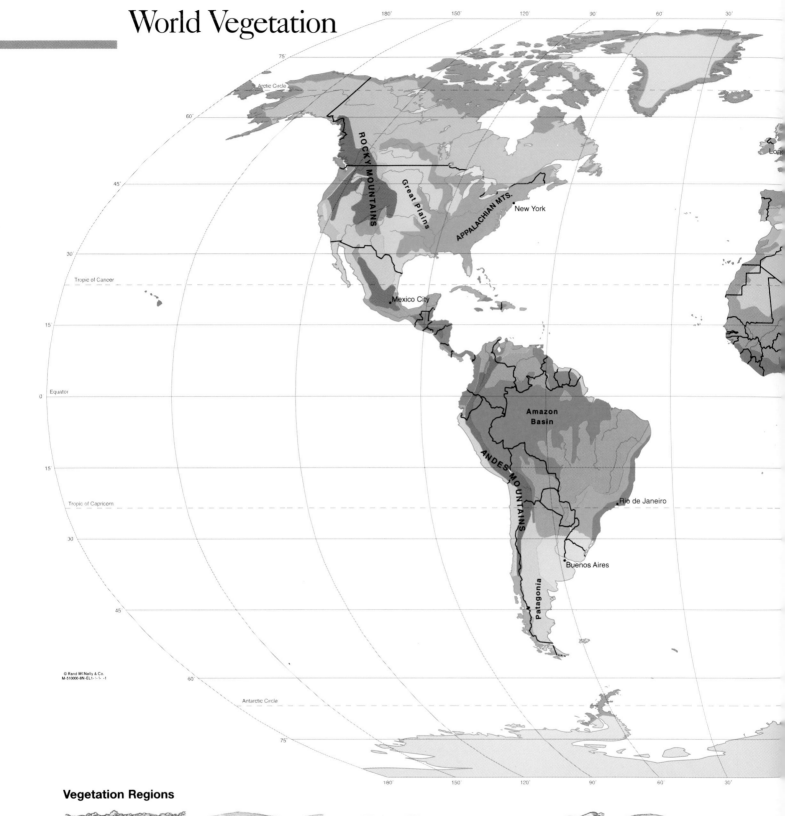

ROCKY MOUNTAINS

Great Plains

APPALACHIAN MTS.

New York

Mexico City

Amazon Basin

ANDES MOUNTAINS

Rio de Janeiro

Buenos Aires

Patagonia

Arctic Circle

Tropic of Cancer

Equator

Tropic of Capricorn

Antarctic Circle

© Rand McNally & Co.
M-510000-8N-EL1-1-1-1--1

Vegetation Regions

Tropical and sub-tropical forests

Savanna

Desert

Mediterranean

Temperate grassland

Temperate forest

Taiga (northern forests)

Tundra (lichen and moss)

Mountain

Polar and high mountain

World Population

Population Density
Inhabitants per sq. km. (mi.)

- Uninhabited
- <1 (2)
- 1-10 (2-25)
- 10-25 (25-60)
- 25-50 (60-125)
- 50-100 (125-250)
- >100 (250)

© Rand McNally & Co.
N-ANS10000-T1- -3-94

Comparative Land Areas (Land and inland water. Numbers indicate thousands of square miles.)

CHINA 3,690	INDIA 1,237	KAZAKHSTAN 1,049 · SAUDI ARABIA 830 · INDONESIA 752 · IRAN 632 · MONGOLIA 605 · PAKISTAN 340 · TURKEY 301 · MYANMAR 261 · ALL OTHERS 2,574

ASIA 17,337

RUSSIA 5,065	RUSSIA 1,527 · UKRAINE 233 · FRANCE 211 · SPAIN · SWEDEN · GERMANY · ALL OTHERS 1,339

EUROPE 3,828

SUDAN 968	ALGERIA 920	DEM. REP. OF THE CONGO 905	LIBYA 679	CHAD 496	NIGER 489	MALI 482	ANGOLA 481	S. AFRICA 471	ETHIOPIA 447	MAURITANIA 396	EGYPT 387	TANZANIA 365	NIGERIA 357	NAMIBIA 318	MOZAMBIQUE 309

AFRICA 11,716

Comparative Populations (Numbers indicate millions of people.)

CHINA 1,197.0	INDIA 909.2	INDONESIA 193.7	PAKISTAN 129.6	JAPAN 125.4	BANGLADESH 119.4	VIET NAM 73.8	PHILIPPINES 67.9

ASIA 3,422.7

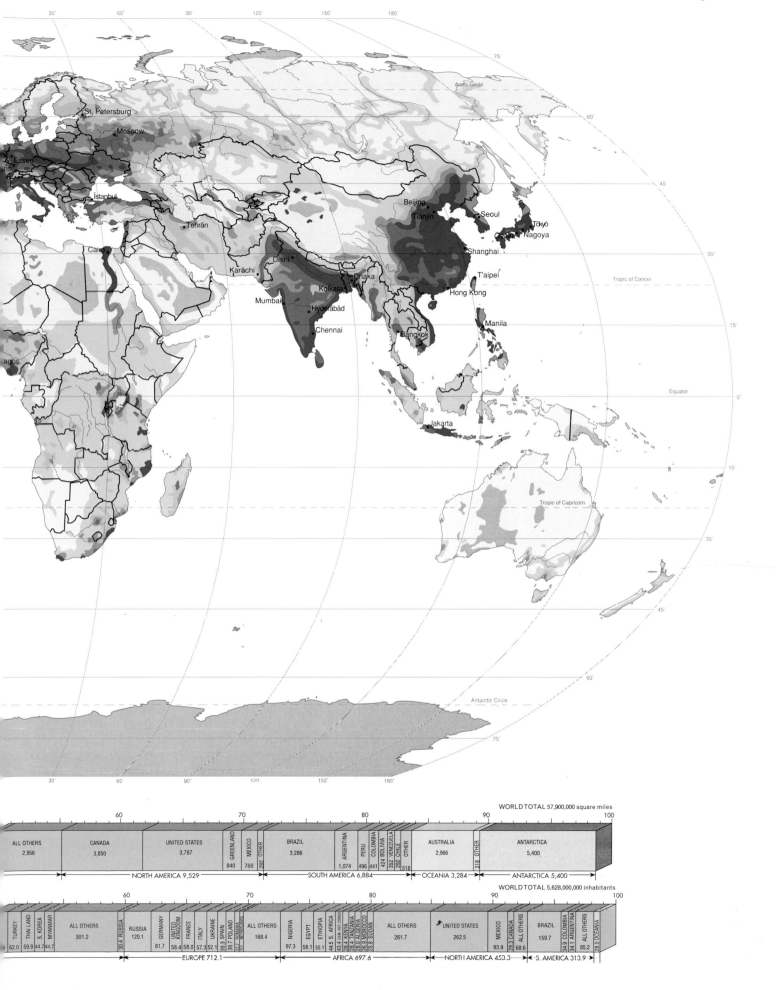

St. Petersburg · Moscow · Essen · İstanbul · Tehrān · Cairo · Karāchi · Delhi · Mumbai · Hyderābād · Chennai · Kolkata · Dhaka · Bangkok · Beijing · Tianjin · Seoul · Tōkyō · Ōsaka · Nagoya · Shanghai · T'aipei · Hong Kong · Manila · Jakarta · Lagos

Arctic Circle · Tropic of Cancer · Equator · Tropic of Capricorn · Antarctic Circle

WORLD TOTAL 57,900,000 square miles

| ALL OTHERS 2,956 | CANADA 3,850 | UNITED STATES 3,787 | GREENLAND 840 | MEXICO 760 | OTHER 292 | BRAZIL 3,286 | ARGENTINA 1,074 | PERU 496 | COLOMBIA 441 | BOLIVIA 424 | VENEZUELA 352 | CHILE 292 | OTHER 518 | AUSTRALIA 2,966 | OTHER 318 | ANTARCTICA 5,400 |

← NORTH AMERICA 9,529 → ← SOUTH AMERICA 6,884 → ← OCEANIA 3,284 → ← ANTARCTICA 5,400 →

WORLD TOTAL 5,628,000,000 inhabitants

| TURKEY 62.0 | THAILAND 59.9 | S. KOREA 44.7 | MYANMAR 44.7 | ALL OTHERS 301.2 | RUSSIA 30.4 | RUSSIA 120.1 | GERMANY 81.7 | UNITED KINGDOM 58.4 | FRANCE 58.0 | ITALY 57.3 | UKRAINE 52.1 | SPAIN 39.3 | POLAND 38.7 | ROMANIA 22.7 | NETHERLANDS 15.4 | ALL OTHERS 168.4 | NIGERIA 97.3 | EGYPT 58.1 | ETHIOPIA 55.1 | S. AFRICA 44.5 | DEM. REP. CONGO 43.4 | KENYA 28.4 | TANZANIA 28.0 | ALGERIA 28.0 | MOROCCO 26.8 | SUDAN 26.8 | ALL OTHERS 261.7 | UNITED STATES 262.5 | MEXICO 93.9 | CANADA 28.3 | ALL OTHERS 68.6 | BRAZIL 159.7 | COLOMBIA 34.9 | ARGENTINA 34.1 | ALL OTHERS 85.2 | OCEANIA 28.0 |

← EUROPE 712.1 → ← AFRICA 697.6 → ← NORTH AMERICA 453.3 → ← S. AMERICA 313.9 →

World Environments

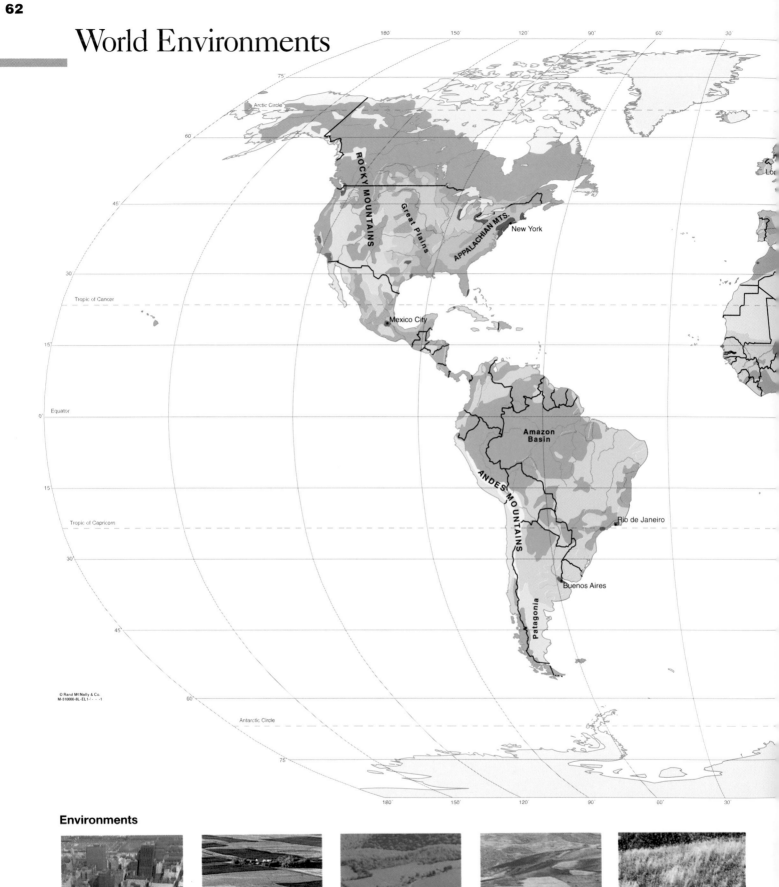

Environments

■ Urban   ■ Cropland   ■ Cropland, woodland   ■ Cropland, grazing land   ■ Grassland, grazing land

Forest, woodland	Swamp, marsh	Tundra	Shrub, sparse grass, wasteland	Barren land

165　180　165　150　135　120　105　90　75　60　45　30

| -11h | -12h | +12h | +11h | +10h | +9h | +8h | +7h | +6h | +5h | +4h | +3h | +2h |

ARCTIC　OCEAN

Greenland
+3h

-12h

Alaska
+9h

+7h

Hudson Bay

Canada

+4h

Newfoundland
+3h 30m

NORTH ATLAN
OCEAN

Bering　Sea

Pribilof
Is.
+10h

Aleutian Is.

+8h

+5h

St. Pierre
and Miquelon
+3h

NORTH　PACIFIC

OCEAN

United States

Azores
+1h

Midway
Is.
+11h

Bermuda

Wake
-12h

+10h

Hawaii

Gulf of
Mexico

Bahamas
Turks and Caicos Is.
Dominican
Rep.
Cuba

Ca
Ver
+1

Johnston
+10h

Mexico

West
Indies
Puerto Rico
Barbados

Marshall
Is.
-12h

Hond.
Guatemala
El Salvador
Costa Rica
Panama

Jamaica Haiti

Neth.
Antilles

Trinidad

Nicaragua

Palmyra
+10h

Kiritimati

Venezuela
Guyana
Suriname
French Guiana

Colombia

Nauru
-12h

Kiribati

Galapagos
Is.

Ecuador

Tuvalu

Peru

Brazil
+3h

Phoenix Is.
+11h

Marquesas
Is.
+9h 30m

Vanuatu

Wallis
Fiji

Samoa
Am. Sam.

Society
Is.

Bolivia

Niue

Gambier Is.
+9h

Paraguay

New
Caledonia

-13h
Tonga

Cook Is.
+10h

Pitcairn
+8h 30m

Easter

+4h

Juan
Fernandez
Is.

Argentina
+3h

Uruguay

Chile

Norfolk
-11h 30m

SOUTH　PACIFIC

OCEAN

SO

New
Zealand
-12h

Chatham Is.
-12h 45m

Falkland
Is.

S. Geor

Auckland
Is.
-12h
Campbell

MONDAY
SUNDAY

S.
Sandwic
Is.

| 11 PM | MIDNIGHT | 1 AM | 2 AM | 3 AM | 4 AM | 5 AM | 6 AM | 7 AM | 8 AM | 9 AM | 10 A |

Time Zones

Standard time zone of even-numbered hours from Greenwich time

`h m` hours, minutes

Standard time zone of odd-numbered hours from Greenwich time

Time varies from the standard time zone by half an hour

Time varies from the standard time zone by other than half an hour

The standard time zone system, fixed by international agreement and by law in each country, is based on a theoretical division of the globe into 24 zones of 15° longitude each. The mid-meridian of each zone fixes the hour for the entire zone. The zero time zone extends 7½° east and 7½° west of the Greenwich meridian, 0° longitude. Since the earth rotates toward the east, time zones to the west of Greenwich are earlier, to the east, later.

Plus and minus hours at the top of the map are added to or subtracted from local time to find Greenwich time. Local standard time can be determined for any area in the world by adding one hour for each time zone counted in an easterly direction from one's own, or by subtracting one hour for each zone counted in a westerly direction. To separate one day from the next, the 180th meridian has been designated as the international date line. On both sides of the line the time of day is the same, but west of the line it is one day later than it is to the east. Countries that adhere to the international zone system adopt the zone applicable to their location. Some countries, however, establish time zones based on political boundaries, or adopt the time zone of a neighboring unit. For all or part of the year some countries also advance their time by one hour, thereby utilizing more daylight hours each day.

North America

North America is the world's third-largest continent, covering an area of 9.5 million square miles (24.7 million sq km). It lies primarily between the Arctic Circle and the Tropic of Cancer, and comes within 500 miles (800 km) of both the North Pole and the Equator. The continent's western flank is dominated by the spectacular Rocky Mountains. Covering vast stretches of the central United States and Canada are the fertile Great Plains, a large part of which is drained by the Mississippi River and its tributaries.

In the north, Hudson Bay is frozen for much of the year. Mexico, located in the continent's southern third, is mostly mountainous and dry, but farther south, the climate is wet. Many of the small Central American countries have volcanoes along the Pacific Coast.

North America at a glance

Land area: 9,500,000 square miles (24,700,000 sq km)

Estimated population (January 1, 1995): 453,300,000

Population density: 48/square mile (18/sq km)

Mean elevation: 2,000 feet (610 m)

Highest point: Mt. McKinley, Alaska, U.S. 20,230 feet (6,194 m)

Lowest point: Death Valley, California, U.S., 282 feet (86 m) below sea level

Longest river: Mississippi-Missouri, 3,740 mi (6,019 km)

Number of countries (incl. dependencies): 38

Largest independent country: Canada, 3,849,674 square miles (9,970,610 sq km)

Smallest independent country: St. Kitts and Nevis, 101 square miles (261 sq km)

Most populous independent country: United States, 262,530,000

Least populous independent country: St. Kitts and Nevis, 44,000

Largest city: Mexico City, pop. 8,235,744 (1990)

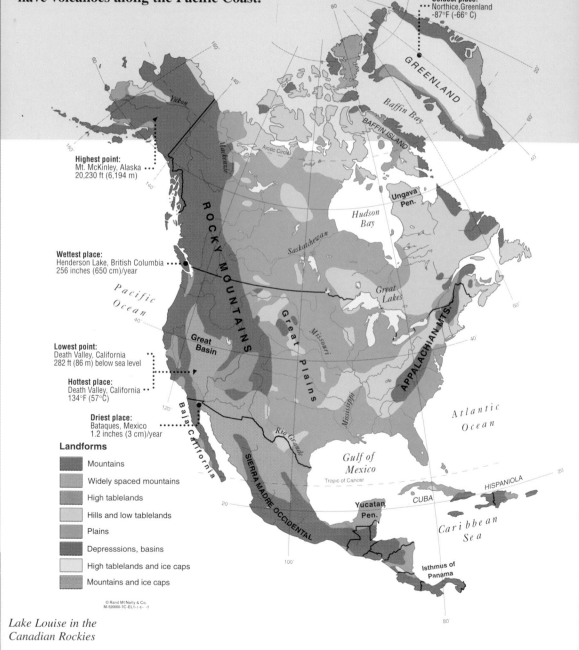

Coldest place: Northice, Greenland -87°F (-66° C)

Highest point: Mt. McKinley, Alaska 20,230 ft (6,194 m)

Wettest place: Henderson Lake, British Columbia 256 inches (650 cm)/year

Lowest point: Death Valley, California 282 ft (86 m) below sea level

Hottest place: Death Valley, California 134°F (57°C)

Driest place: Bataques, Mexico 1.2 inches (3 cm)/year

Landforms

- Mountains
- Widely spaced mountains
- High tablelands
- Hills and low tablelands
- Plains
- Depresssions, basins
- High tablelands and ice caps
- Mountains and ice caps

© Rand McNally & Co.
M-520000-7C-EL1-1-1- -1

Lake Louise in the Canadian Rockies

Climate

North America contains almost every type of climate that can be found in the world. Ice and tundra cover northern Canada and Greenland. Much of the central and eastern parts of the U.S. and Canada are temperate, with great seasonal changes marked by warm summers and cold winters. The Pacific Ocean moderates weather changes along the west coast, where it is cool and wet in the north and warm and dry in the south. Desert and semi-desert cover much of the southwestern U.S. and Mexico. The tropical southern region of the continent and the islands of the Caribbean Sea are hot and rainy.

Belize City
Hot and rainy

Havana
Hot with rainy and dry seasons

Monterrey
Semiarid

Las Vegas
Very dry

Los Angeles
Hot, dry summer / mild, rainy winter

Houston
Warm, humid summer / mild winter

Seattle
Mild and rainy

Tinted areas show temperature in degrees Fahrenheit. Vertical bars show precipitation in inches.

Chicago
Warm, humid summer / cold, snowy winter

Toronto
Cool, humid summer / cold, snowy winter

Edmonton
Short, cool, humid summer / very cold, snowy winter

Barrow
Cold and dry

Nord
Very cold, perpetual frost

Extensive uplands
Climate varies with elevation and latitude

© Rand McNally & Co.
M-520000-6A-EL1-1-1- -1

Population

About 60% of all North Americans live in the United States, the world's third most-populous country. Canada is the continent's largest country, but one of the world's least densely populated; most Canadians live within 100 miles (160 km) of the country's southern border. Mexico, with approximately 20% of North America's inhabitants, has one of the world's largest and fastest growing metropolitan areas, Mexico City, which is home to more than 14 million people.

Canada is populated mostly by descendants of French and British settlers, as well as native Americans, such as the Inuit (Eskimos) of the far north. The United States' populace reflects the country's diverse history of immigration, with European ancestry being the most common. The people of Mexico and Central America trace their origins to Spaniards and native Americans. The population of the Caribbean islands includes many descendants of African slaves and European settlers.

Fastest-Growing Countries

Honduras, 2.88% (annual rate of natural increase)

Belize, 2.87%

Nicaragua, 2.80%

Slowest-Growing Countries

Montserrat, 0.61%

United States, 0.65%

Canada, 0.67%

Inhabitants per sq. km. (mi.)

- Uninhabited
- <1 (2)
- 1-10 (2-25)
- 10-25 (25-60)
- 25-50 (60-125)
- 50-100 (125-250)
- >100 (250)

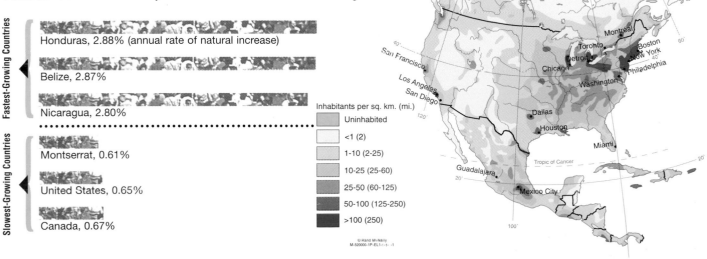

© Rand McNally
M-520000-1P-EL1-1-1- -1

Environments and Land Use

Although only 12% of the continent is suitable for agriculture, North America is the world's leading food producer. Unlike other parts of the world, famine is virtually unknown. Large quantities of food, such as grains from the central U.S. and Canada, are exported worldwide. Sixteen percent of the continent is used for grazing, and the livestock raised on these lands are also an important source of food at home and abroad.

Forests cover one-third of the land, and the timber and paper industries are important to the U.S. and Canada. The continent has an extremely long coastline, and many countries send great fishing fleets to sea. This is especially true of Canada, whose eastern-most provinces are fittingly known as the "Maritime Provinces." However, sharp declines in catches due to over-fishing have put the industry in economic turmoil.

Blue waters, sunny skies, and idyllic beaches draw millions of tourists to the Caribbean each year. While tourism provides income for island countries that have few other assets, the economic gap between the visitors and the people who serve them remains dramatic.

One of the greatest challenges facing North America in the coming decades is a familiar one: coping with a growing population and dwindling resources. Pollution and the environment are divisive issues. Although the United States has begun to clean up its air and water, economic pressures will continue to be an argument for a relaxation of policies. Meanwhile, in Mexico, environmental issues have been pushed aside by concerns about the economy and the exploding population.

GREENLAND

BAFFIN ISLAND

Arctic Circle

Hudson Bay

Ungava Pen.

Edmonton

Pacific Ocean

ROCKY MOUNTAINS

Great Basin

Great Plains

Great Lakes

Montreal

Chicago

New York

APPALACHIAN MTS.

Denver

Los Angeles

Atlantic Ocean

Gulf of Mexico

Tropic of Cancer

Yucatan Pen.

Mexico City

Caribbean Sea

- ■ Urban
- ■ Cropland
- ■ Cropland and woodland
- ■ Cropland and grazing land
- ■ Grassland, grazing land
- ■ Forest, woodland
- ■ Swamp, marsh
- ■ Tundra
- ■ Shrub, sparse grass, wasteland
- ■ Barren land

© Rand McNally & Co.
M-520000-8L-EL1-1-1- -1

| 0 | 200 | 400 | 600 | 800 | 1000 Miles |
| 0 | 300 | 600 | 900 | 1200 | 1500 Kilometers |

Field of corn in the midwestern United States

Urbanization in North America

Seen from the air, large portions of North America still bear the checkerboard imprint left by the people who settled the continent: a vast array of small farms that could be worked by one man and a horse. As industrialization swept through the United States in the second half of the 19th century, many farmers left their farms. Great numbers moved to fast-growing cities such as Chicago and St. Louis. Many small towns saw their populations dwindle.

In the cities, change was continuous. The former farm families were joined by waves of European immigrants. Over the next 100 years, urban populations con- tinued to grow, and cities that had once been separate became part of vast urban megalopolises. An example can be seen in the eastern United States, where a band of urban centers stretches almost continuously from Boston south through New York City to Washington D.C. (see map at right).

After World War II, as the U. S. middle class expanded, large numbers of fami- lies moved out of the city centers into suburban communities of mass-pro- duced, affordable homes. Many of those who remained were economically disad- vantaged. A shrinking tax base meant that cities could not support their infra- structures, and conditions in the inner cities worsened. In the suburbs the opposite was true: vast sums were spent building new roads, houses, and shopping centers.

The same process that transformed the U.S. is now occurring in Mexico. In 1945, 25% of the population was considered urban, but today the figure surpasses 70% (see graph above). Not content to lead lives as subsistence farmers, scores of Mexicans arrive in the cities each day in search of jobs that will enable them to provide a better life for their families.

Sadly, these dreams are often elusive. Most of the people end up in low-paying jobs, with their meager wages going to pay for the food that they once grew themselves. City officials are hard-pressed to provide clean water to their ever-growing populations, let alone electricity, trans- portation and education.

As elsewhere in the world, coping with the pressures of growing popu- lations is one of the greatest challenges facing North Americans today.

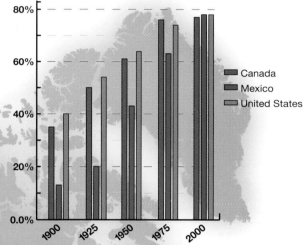

Rising Urban Population
Urban population as a percentage of total population, 1900-2000 (estimated)

Legend:
- Canada
- Mexico
- United States

(The definition of "urban" varies from country to country. In Canada, all towns with more than 1,000 people are considered urban, while in the U.S. and Mexico only towns with more than 2,500 people are defined as urban.)

Urban Centers
- 50,000-99,999 people
- 100,000-500,000 people
- Over 500,000 people

© Rand McNally
M-59XXXVL9F-FI 1-1-1- -1

Mexico City, whose metropolitan area population exceeds 14 million, sprawls toward the distant mountains.

Scale 1:40 000 000; one inch to 630 miles. Lambert's Azimuthal Equal Area Projection
Elevations and depressions are given in feet

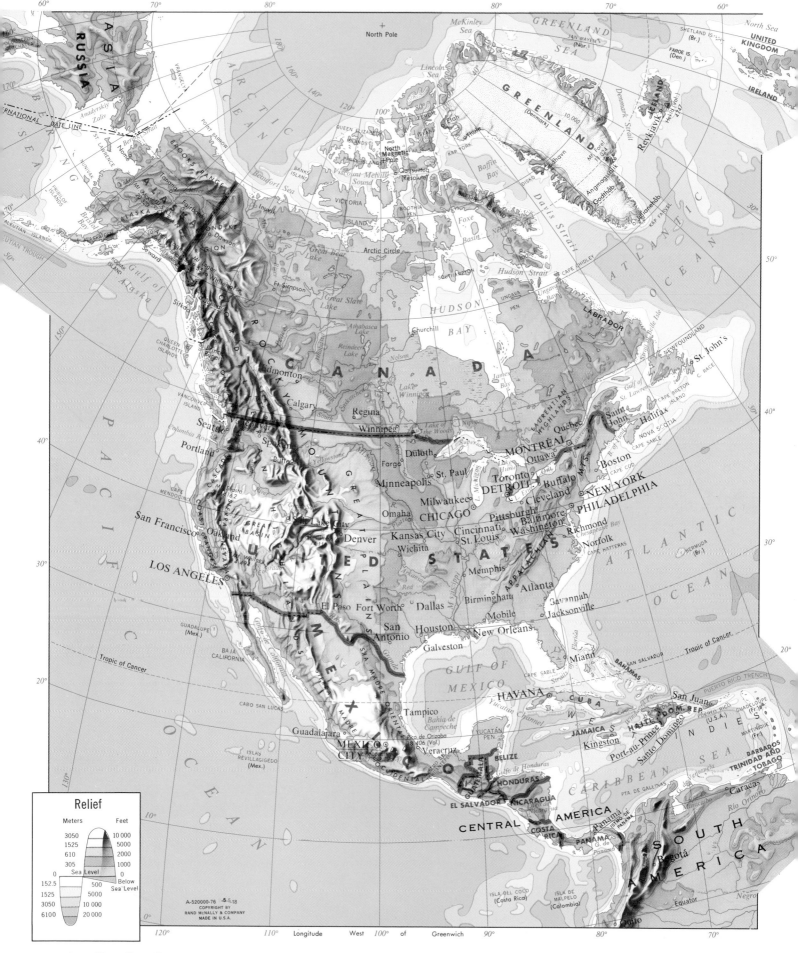

Relief

Meters	Feet
3050	10 000
1525	5000
610	2000
305	1000
0 Sea Level	0 Sea Level
152.5	500 Below Sea Level
1525	5000
3050	10 000
6100	20 000

A-520000-76   -5-2-18
COPYRIGHT BY
RAND McNALLY & COMPANY
MADE IN U.S.A.

200   400   600   800   1000 Miles
400   800   1200   1600 Kilometers

Scale 1:40 000 000; one inch to 630 miles. Lambert's Azimuthal Equal Area Projection
Elevations and depressions are given in feet

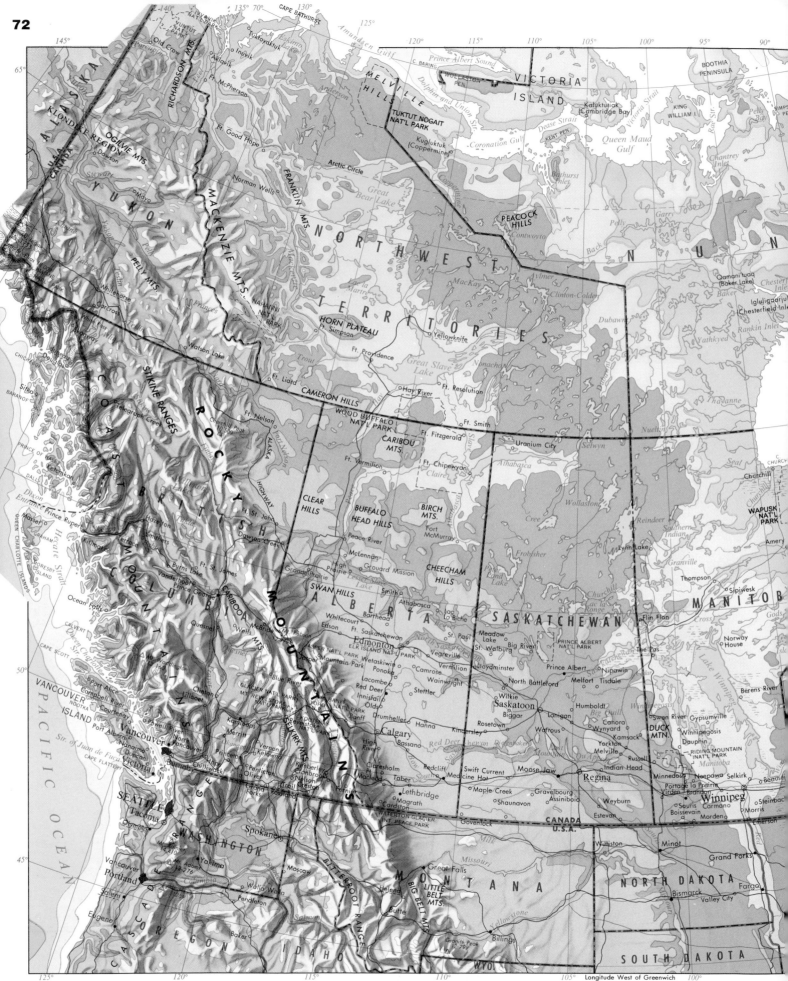

Scale 1: 12 000 000; one inch to 190 miles. Conic Projection
Elevations and depressions are given in feet

Scale 1:12 000 000; one inch to 190 miles. Polyconic Projection
Elevations and depressions are given in feet

Scale 1:12 000 000; one inch to 190 miles. Polyconic Projection
Elevations and depressions are given in feet

Relief

Meters		Feet
3050		10 000
1525		5000
610		2000
305		1000
152.5		500
Sea Level		Sea Level
152.5		500
		Below Sea Level
152.5		500
1525		5 000
3050		10 000
6100		20 000

0   25 50 75 100   200   300   400   500 Miles
100   200   400   600   800 Kilometers

Cities and Towns

0 to 50,000   500,000 to 1,000,000

50,000 to 500,000   1,000,000 and over

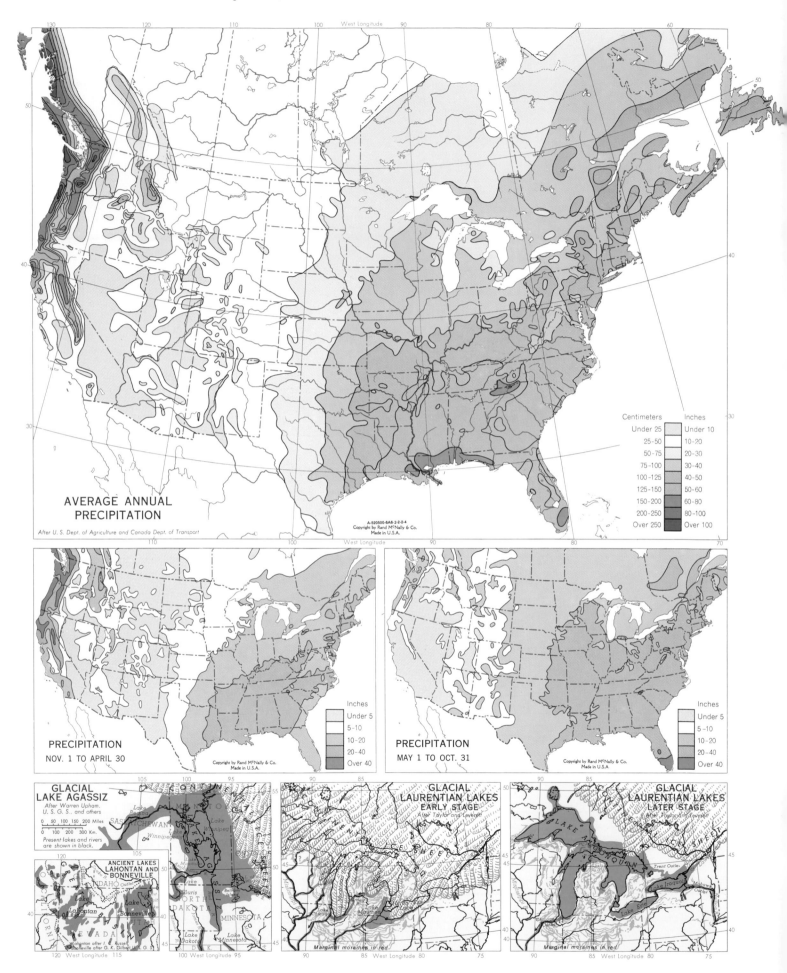

AVERAGE ANNUAL
PRECIPITATION

After U. S. Dept. of Agriculture and Canada Dept. of Transport

A-520500-6A6-2-2-2-4
Copyright by Rand McNally & Co.
Made in U.S.A.

Centimeters	Inches
Under 25	Under 10
25–50	10–20
50–75	20–30
75–100	30–40
100–125	40–50
125–150	50–60
150–200	60–80
200–250	80–100
Over 250	Over 100

PRECIPITATION
NOV. 1 TO APRIL 30

Copyright by Rand McNally & Co.
Made in U.S.A.

Inches
Under 5
5–10
10–20
20–40
Over 40

PRECIPITATION
MAY 1 TO OCT. 31

Copyright by Rand McNally & Co.
Made in U.S.A.

Inches
Under 5
5–10
10–20
20–40
Over 40

GLACIAL
LAKE AGASSIZ
After Warren Upham,
U. S. G. S. and others

0 50 100 150 200 Miles
0 100 200 300 Km.

Present lakes and rivers
are shown in black.

ANCIENT LAKES
LAHONTAN AND
BONNEVILLE

Lahontan after I. Russell
Bonneville after G. K. Gilbert, U.S.G.S.

GLACIAL
LAURENTIAN LAKES
EARLY STAGE
After Taylor and Leverett

Marginal moraines in red

GLACIAL
LAURENTIAN LAKES
LATER STAGE
After Taylor and Leverett

Marginal moraines in red

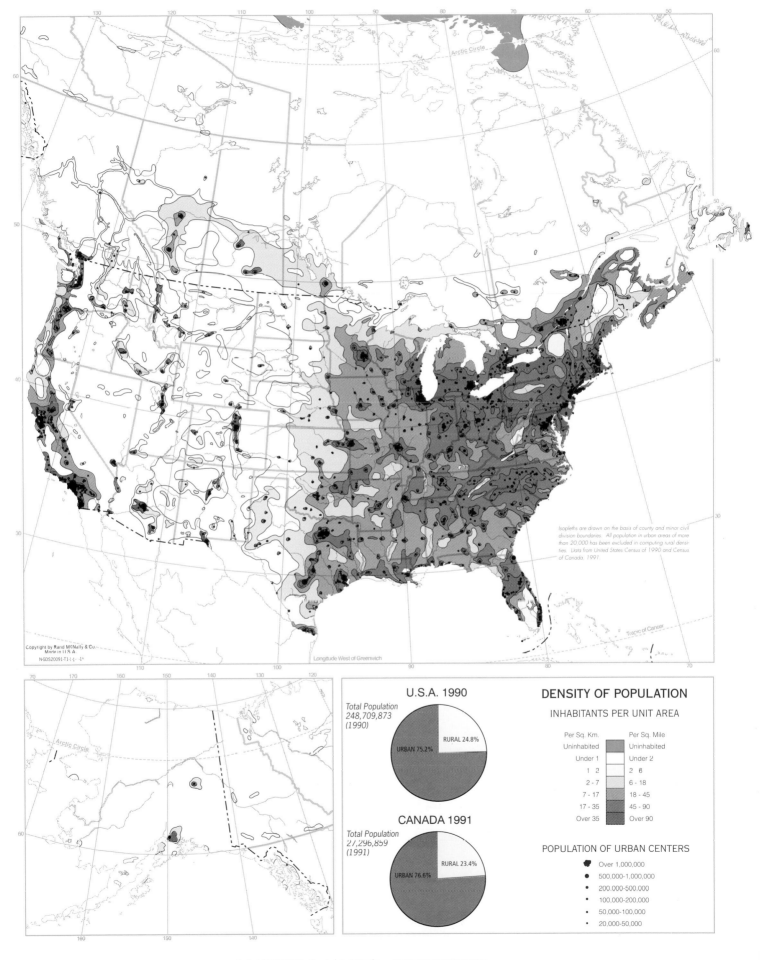

Isopleths are drawn on the basis of county and minor civil division boundaries. All population in urban areas of more than 20,000 has been excluded in computing rural densities. Data from United States Census of 1990 and Census of Canada, 1991.

Copyright by Rand McNally & Co.
Made in U.S.A.
NGDS20091-T1-1-1-1-1A

Longitude West of Greenwich

U.S.A. 1990

Total Population
248,709,873
(1990)

URBAN 75.2%   RURAL 24.8%

CANADA 1991

Total Population
27,296,859
(1991)

URBAN 76.6%   RURAL 23.4%

DENSITY OF POPULATION

INHABITANTS PER UNIT AREA

Per Sq. Km.	Per Sq. Mile
Uninhabited	Uninhabited
Under 1	Under 2
1 - 2	2 - 6
2 - 7	6 - 18
7 - 17	18 - 45
17 - 35	45 - 90
Over 35	Over 90

POPULATION OF URBAN CENTERS

- Over 1,000,000
- 500,000-1,000,000
- 200,000-500,000
- 100,000-200,000
- 50,000-100,000
- 20,000-50,000

Scale 1:29,000,000; One inch to 457 miles.   ALBERS CONIC PROJECTION

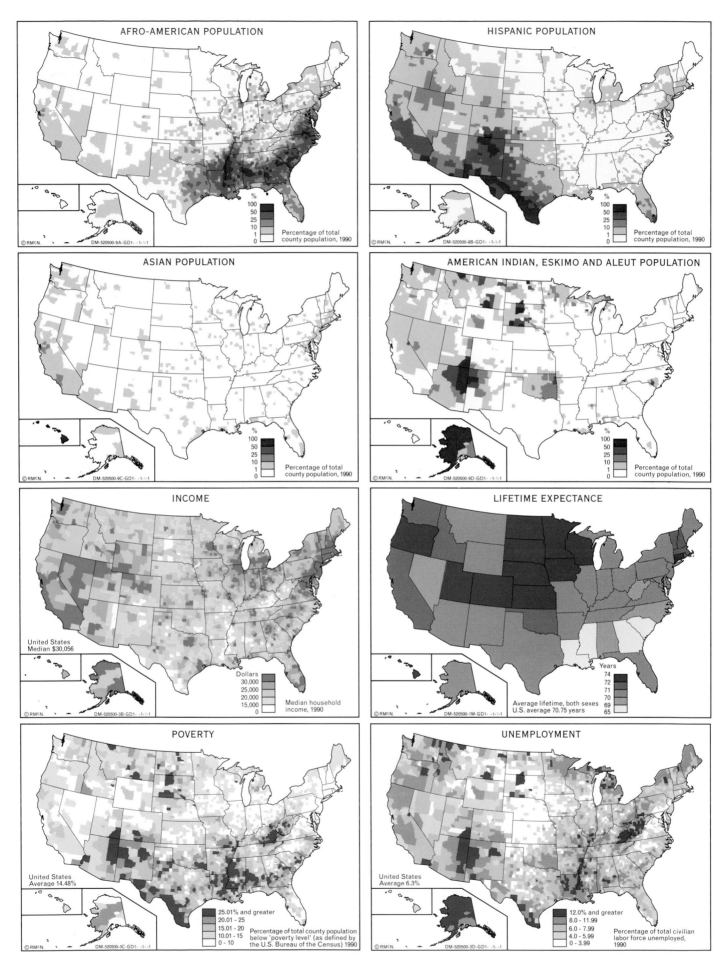

AFRO-AMERICAN POPULATION

%
100
50
25
10
1
0

Percentage of total
county population, 1990

©RM©N. DM-520500-9A-GD1- -1-1-1

HISPANIC POPULATION

%
100
50
25
10
1
0

Percentage of total
county population, 1990

©RM©N. DM-520500-9B-GD1- -1-1-1

ASIAN POPULATION

%
100
50
25
10
1
0

Percentage of total
county population, 1990

©RM©N. DM-520500-9C-GD1- -1-1-1

AMERICAN INDIAN, ESKIMO AND ALEUT POPULATION

%
100
50
25
10
1
0

Percentage of total
county population, 1990

©RM©N. DM-520500-9D-GD1- -1-1-1

INCOME

United States
Median $30,056

Dollars
30,000
25,000
20,000
15,000
0

Median household
income, 1990

©RM©N. DM-520500-3B-GD1- -1-1-1

LIFETIME EXPECTANCE

Years
74
72
71
70
69
65

Average lifetime, both sexes
U.S. average 70.75 years

©RM©N. DM-520500-1M-GD1- -1-1-1

POVERTY

United States
Average 14.48%

25.01% and greater
20.01 - 25
15.01 - 20
10.01 - 15
0 - 10

Percentage of total county population
below 'poverty level' (as defined by
the U.S. Bureau of the Census) 1990

©RM©N. DM-520500-3C-GD1- -1-1-1

UNEMPLOYMENT

United States
Average 6.3%

12.0% and greater
8.0 - 11.99
6.0 - 7.99
4.0 - 5.99
0 - 3.99

Percentage of total civilian
labor force unemployed,
1990

©RM©N. DM-520500-3D-GD1- -1-1-1

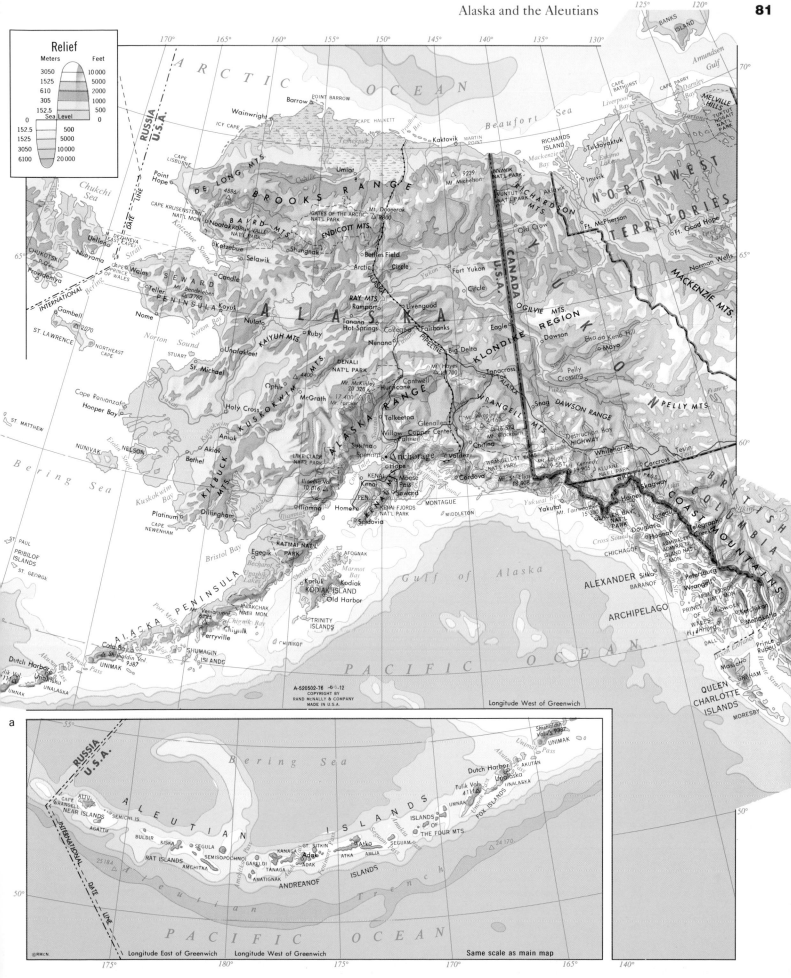

Scale 1: 12 000 000; one inch to 190 miles.   Conic Projection

Elevations and depressions are given in feet

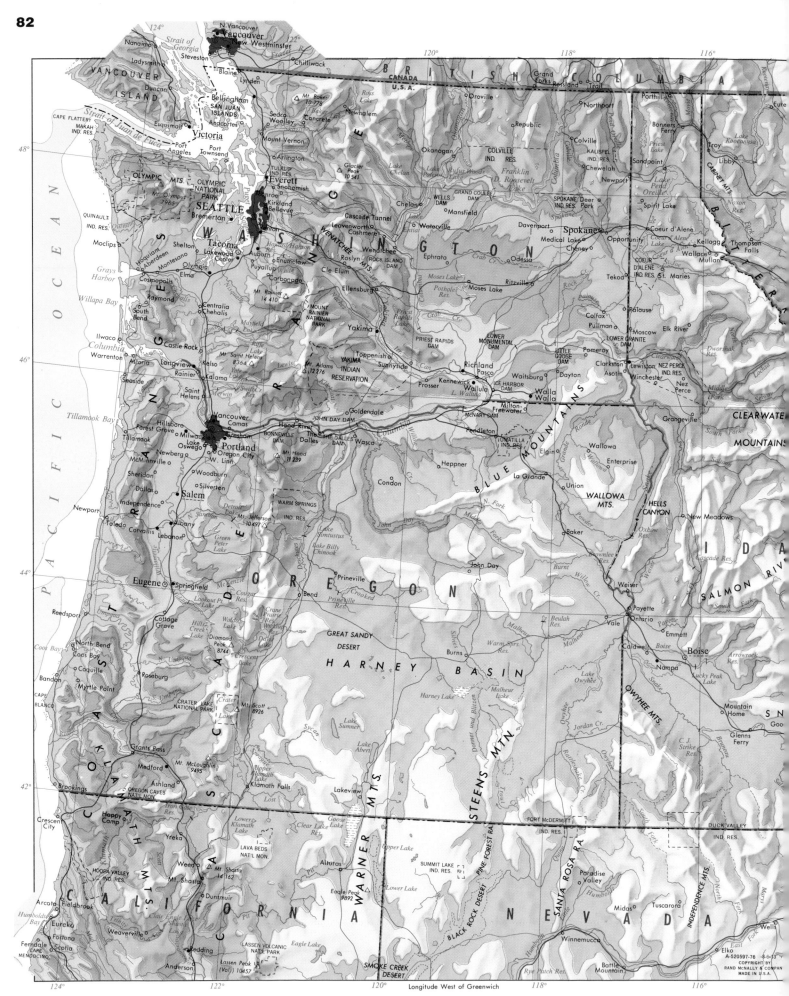

Scale 1: 4,000 000; one inch to 64 miles. Conic Projection
Elevations and depressions are given in feet

Scale 1:4 000 000; one inch to 64 miles. Conic Projection
Elevations and depressions are given in feet

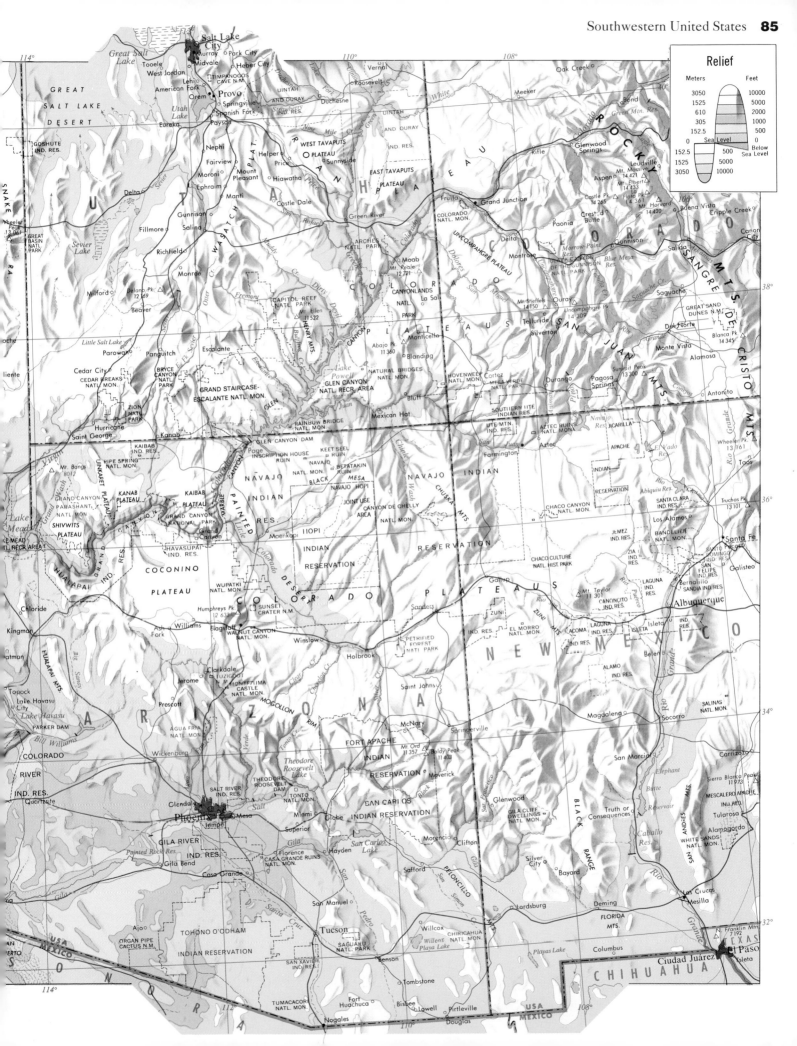

Relief

Meters		Feet
3050		10000
1525		5000
610		2000
305		1000
152.5		500
0	Sea Level	0
152.5		Below Sea Level
	500	
1525	5000	
3050	10000	

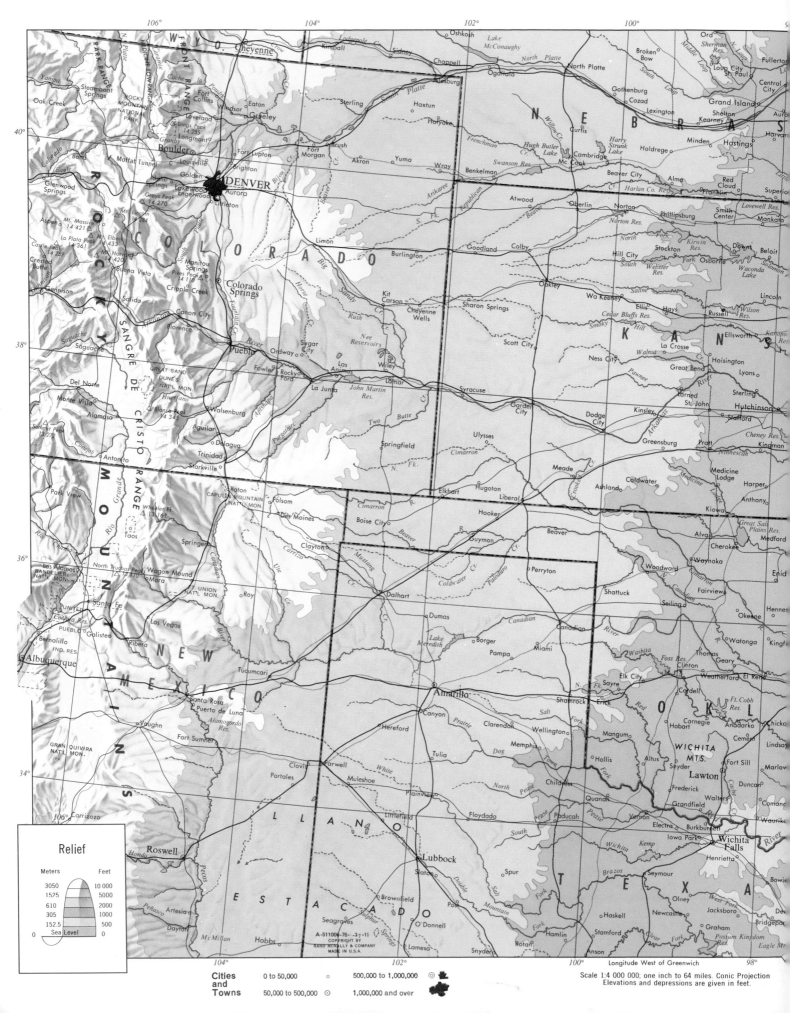

Relief

Meters	Feet
3050	10 000
1525	5000
610	2000
305	1000
152.5	500
0 Sea Level	0

A-511006-76-.1-7-11
COPYRIGHT BY
RAND McNALLY & COMPANY
MADE IN U.S.A.

Cities and **Towns**

0 to 50,000	○	500,000 to 1,000,000	◉
50,000 to 500,000	⊙	1,000,000 and over	

Longitude West of Greenwich

Scale 1:4 000 000; one inch to 64 miles. Conic Projection
Elevations and depressions are given in feet.

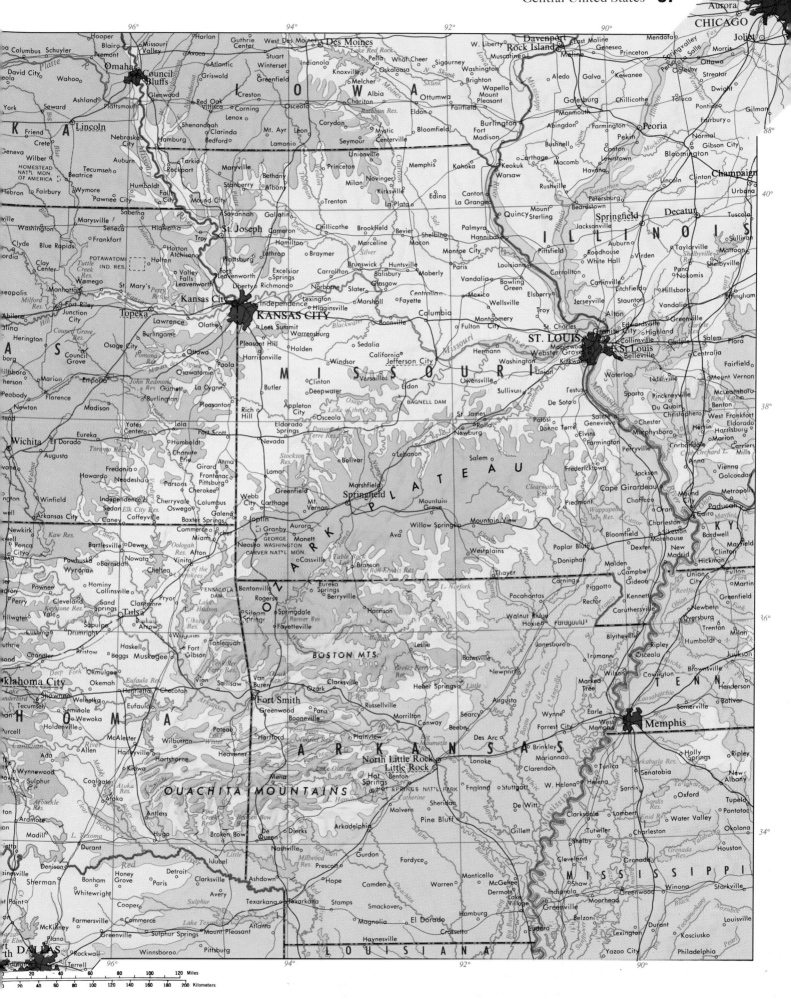

Cities and Towns — 0 to 50,000 ○ — 50,000 to 500,000 ⊙ — 500,000 to 1,000,000 ◎ — 1,000,000 and over

Scale 1:4 000 000; one inch to 64 miles. Conic Projection
Elevations and depressions are given in feet

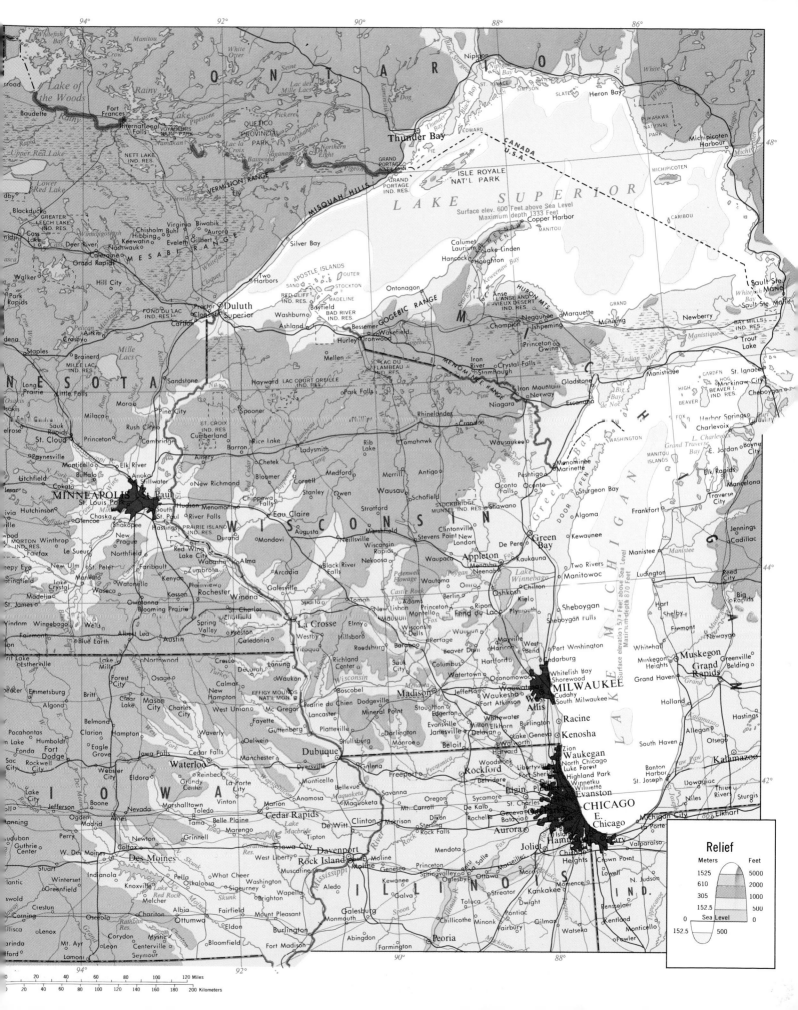

Cities and Towns

0 to 50,000	∘ 500,000 to 1,000,000
50,000 to 500,000	1,000,000 and over

Scale 1:4 000 000; one inch to 64 miles. Conic Projection
Elevations and depressions are given in feet

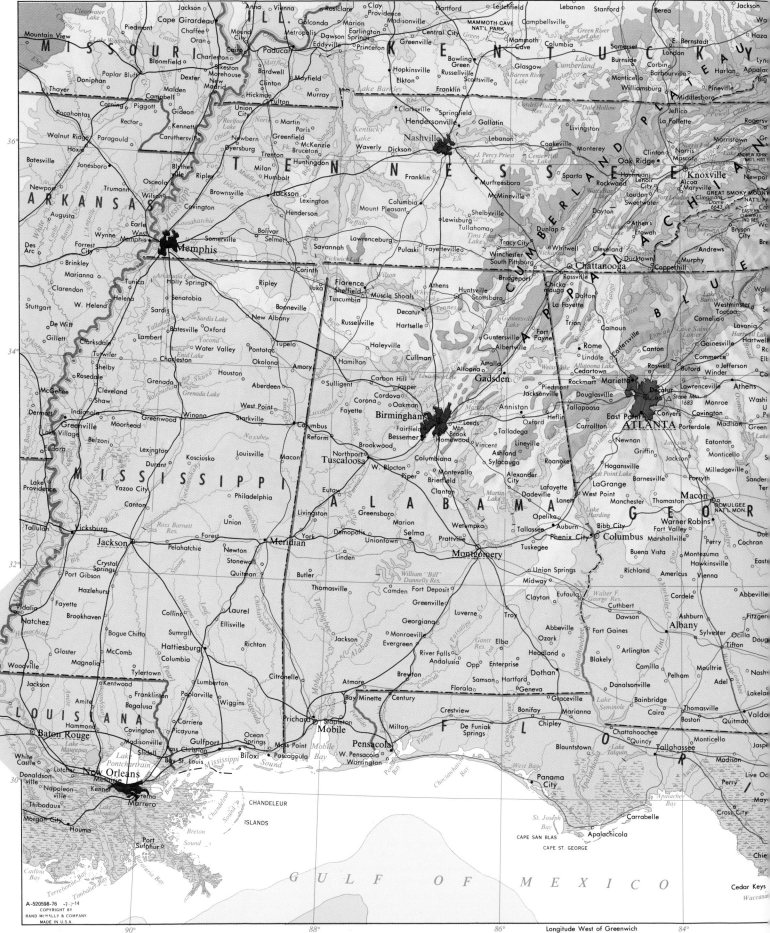

Scale 1:4 000 000; one inch to 64 miles. Conic Projection
Elevations and depressions are given in feet

A-520598-76 -7-7-14
COPYRIGHT BY
RAND McNALLY & COMPANY
MADE IN U.S.A.

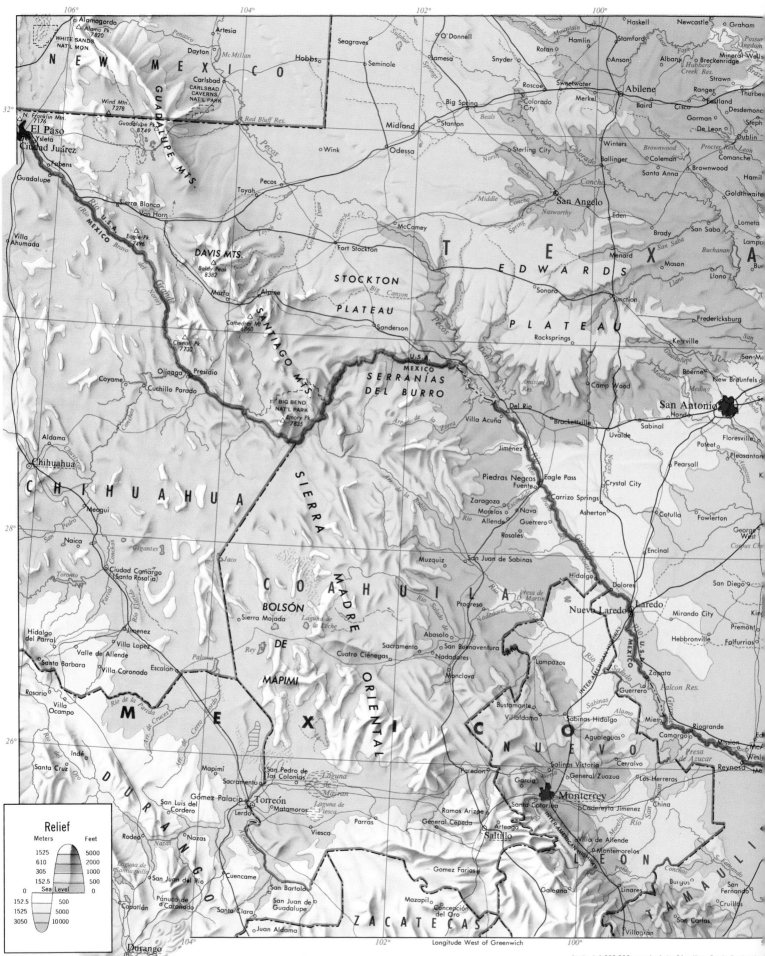

Scale 1:4 000 000; one inch to 64 miles. Conic Projection
Elevations and depressions are given in feet

Scale 1:1 000 000

Cities and Towns	0 to 50,000	500,000 to 1,000,000
	50,000 to 500,000	1,000,000 and over

Scale 1:16 000 000; one inch to 250 miles. Polyconic Projection
Elevations and depressions are given in feet

b

ATLANTIC OCEAN

Arecibo   San Juan
Aguadilla   Bayamón   CABEZAS DE   ST. THOMAS   TORTOLA
PTA. HIGUERO   Utuado   SAN JUAN   (U.S.A.)   (Br.)
                    Fajardo   CULEBRA   Charlotte   ST. JOHN
PUERTO   RICO   Caguas   Amalie   (U.S.A.)
Mayagüez   (U.S.A.)   Humacao   Vieques
            Coamo   Coyey   VIEQUES
CABO ROJO   Ponce   Salinas   Guayama   Christiansted

CARIBBEAN   SEA   SAINT CROIX
                        (U.S.A.)

Scale 1:4 000 000
0 10 20   30   40 Miles
0 10 20 30 40 50 60 Kilometers
©RMCN

c
65°   64°50'
LITTLE
OUTER BRASS   HANS LOLLICK
INNER BRASS   HANS LOLLICK
            PICARA PT   GRASS
STORMY PT.   THATCH CAY   CAY
        ST. THOMAS
        Crown Mt. (U.S.A.)   18°
            1558   Charlotte Amalie   20'
                (St. Thomas) Nadir
WATER
FLAMINGO PT. St. Thomas
            Harbor   Scale 1:500 000
©RMCN

Relief

Meters		Feet
3050		10 000
1525		5000
610		2000
305		1000
152.5		500
Sea Level		0
152.5		500
1525		5000
3050		10 000
6100		20 000

Cities and Towns

0 to 50,000   ○   500,000 to 1,000,000   ◎
50,000 to 500,000   ⊙   1,000,000 and over

0   50   100   200   300   400   500 Miles
0   100   200   300   400   500   600   700   800 Kilometers

Longitude West of Greenwich

South America

Floodplain of the Amazon River, Brazil

With an area of 6.9 million square miles (17.8 million sq km), triangular-shaped South America is fourth among the continents in size. The Andes, which pass through seven of the continent's 13 mainland countries, are the longest mountain chain in the world. The mighty Amazon River carries a greater volume of water than any other river: 46 million gallons per second flow into the Atlantic Ocean. The Amazon basin contains an estimated one-fifth of the world's fresh water and is home to the world's largest rain forest with its countless plant and animal species. Angel Falls, in a remote Venezuelan forest, is the world's highest waterfall, dropping 3,212 feet (979 m), or almost the height of three Empire State Buildings.

One of South America's other great wonders is manmade. High in the Peruvian Andes lie the ruins of the sacred city of Machu Picchu, built centuries ago by the Incas. The city has an exquisite design and was built with remarkable skill. The Inca population, like most of South America's other native peoples, declined rapidly after the arrival of Europeans in the early 16th century.

South America at a glance

Land area: 6,900,000 square miles (17,800,000 sq km)

Estimated population (January 1, 1995): 313,900,000

Population density: 45/square mile (18/sq km)

Mean elevation: 1,800 feet (550 m)

Highest point: Aconcagua, Argentina, 22,831 feet (6,959 m)

Lowest point: Salinas Chicas, Argentina, 138 feet (42 m) below sea level

Longest river: Amazon-Ucayali, 4,000 mi (6,400 km)

Number of countries (incl. dependencies): 15

Largest independent country: Brazil, 3,286,500 square miles (8,511,996 sq km)

Smallest independent country: Suriname, 63,251 square miles (163,820 sq km)

Most populous independent country: Brazil, 159,690,000

Least populous independent country: Suriname, 426,000

Largest city: São Paulo, pop. 9,393,753 (1991)

The Andes, at the western edge of Argentina's Patagonia region.

Wettest place: Quibdó, Colombia 354 inches (899 cm)/year

Driest place: Arica, Chile .03 inches (.08 cm)/year

Hottest place: Rivadavia, Argentina 120°F (49°C)

Highest point: Cerro Aconcagua, Argentina 22,831 ft (6,959 m)

Coldest place: Sarmiento, Argentina -27°F (-33°C)

Lowest point: Salinas Chicas, Argentina 138 ft (42 m) below sea level

Orinoco

Llanos

Guiana Highlands

Equator

Amazon

Amazon Basin

Madeira

São Francisco

Pacific Ocean

ANDES MOUNTAINS

Lago Titicaca

Mato Grosso

Brazilian Highlands

Atlantic Ocean

Gran Chaco

Paraná

Tropic of Capricorn

Paraguay

Pampas

Patagonia

FALKLAND ISLANDS

TIERRA DEL FUEGO

Landforms

- Mountains
- Widely spaced mountains
- High tablelands
- Hills and low tablelands
- Plains
- Depresssions, basins
- High tablelands and ice caps
- Mountains and ice caps

© Rand McNally & Co.
M-540000-7C-EL1-1-1- -1

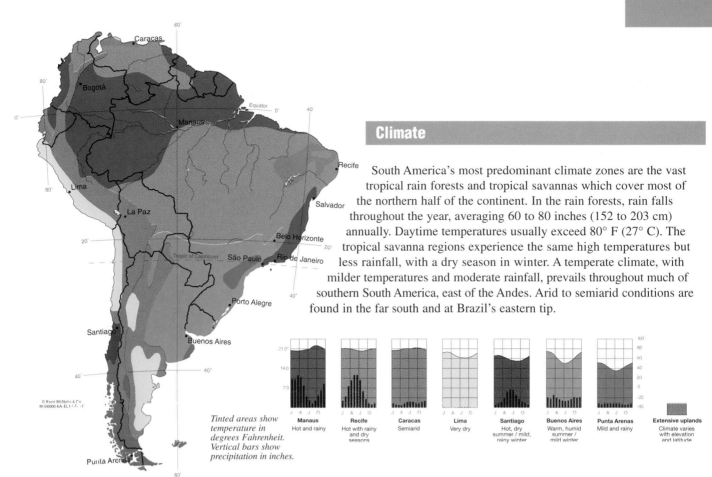

Climate

South America's most predominant climate zones are the vast tropical rain forests and tropical savannas which cover most of the northern half of the continent. In the rain forests, rain falls throughout the year, averaging 60 to 80 inches (152 to 203 cm) annually. Daytime temperatures usually exceed 80° F (27° C). The tropical savanna regions experience the same high temperatures but less rainfall, with a dry season in winter. A temperate climate, with milder temperatures and moderate rainfall, prevails throughout much of southern South America, east of the Andes. Arid to semiarid conditions are found in the far south and at Brazil's eastern tip.

Tinted areas show temperature in degrees Fahrenheit. Vertical bars show precipitation in inches.

Manaus	**Recife**	**Caracas**	**Lima**	**Santiago**	**Buenos Aires**	**Punta Arenas**	**Extensive uplands**
Hot and rainy	Hot with rainy and dry seasons	Semiarid	Very dry	Hot, dry summer / mild, rainy winter	Warm, humid summer / mild winter	Mild and rainy	Climate varies with elevation and latitude

Population

South America is the fourth most-densely populated continent, with 45 people per square mile (18 per sq km). Despite this relatively low figure, the continent is intensely urban because the Andes and the Amazon rain forest render most of it either inaccessible or unsuitable for farming. More than 90% of South America's 314 million people live within 150 miles (240 km) of the coast. São Paulo, Brazil, with a metropolitan population of almost 17 million, is the world's third-largest metropolitan area. Most South Americans are *mestizo*—of mixed European and Indian descent. Spanish is the predominant language, followed by Portuguese. More than 90% of the people are Roman Catholics.

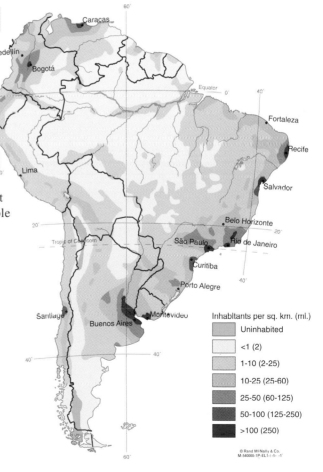

Inhabitants per sq. km. (mi.)

	Uninhabited
	<1 (2)
	1-10 (2-25)
	10-25 (25-60)
	25-50 (60-125)
	50-100 (125-250)
	>100 (250)

© Rand McNally & Co.
M-540000-1P-EL1-1-1- -1'

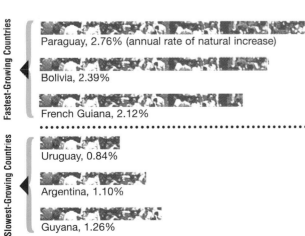

Fastest-Growing Countries

Paraguay, 2.76% (annual rate of natural increase)

Bolivia, 2.39%

French Guiana, 2.12%

Slowest-Growing Countries

Uruguay, 0.84%

Argentina, 1.10%

Guyana, 1.26%

Environments and Land Use

Land suitable for farming is very limited in South America, covering only about 6% of the continent. Small, family-run subsistence farms are common, and typical crops are maize, wheat, and potatoes. Despite the scarcity of arable land, commercial agriculture for export is a major part of the economies of several countries. Ecuador is the world's leading exporter of bananas, while Brazil and Colombia grow almost 40% of the world's coffee beans. Brazil is also a major exporter of sugar. Chile has developed a large trade in produce—such as tomatoes and grapes—that is exported to North America during its winter months (South America's summer months). Production of coca, the basis for illicit drugs, has become a part of the rural economies of Colombia, Bolivia and Peru.

Cattle ranching is centered on the vast, grassy Pampas region, which extends through northern Argentina, Uruguay, and southern Brazil. Sheep, raised both for meat and wool, are important throughout the Andes and southern Argentina. About 25% of the continent is suitable for grazing.

As South America's population grows, pressure builds to clear more land for farming. Much expansion has taken place in the Amazon basin at the cost of millions of acres of rain forest, which are cleared of trees and drained. Balancing the demands of the population with the need to preserve the rain forest is one of the continent's most pressing issues.

Urban

Cropland

Cropland and woodland

Cropland and grazing land

Grassland, grazing land

Forest, woodland

Swamp, marsh

Tundra

Shrub, sparse grass, wasteland

Barren land

© Rand McNally & Co.
M-540000-8L-EL1-1-1--1'

| 0 | 200 | 400 | 600 | 800 | 1000 Miles |

| 0 | 300 | 600 | 900 | 1200 | 1500 Kilometers |

Coffee plantation in the Brazilian highlands

Destruction of the Rain Forest

The Amazonian rain forest contains an abundance and diversity of life that is matched by few places in the world. In fact, it has been estimated that the plant and animal species of Amazonia account for nearly one-half of those found on Earth. New plants and animals are constantly being discovered, and scientists have found in Amazonian plants a treasure trove of new substances, some of which are now being used to produce life-saving medicines. It is thought that cures for many more diseases could be found in the plants yet to be studied.

In recent decades, nearly 10% of the rain forest's original 1.58 million square miles (4.09 million sq km) has been cleared (see map below) for farming, cattle ranching, mining, and commercial logging. The most effective way to clear the land is the "slash-and-burn" method, which has been practiced by indigenous peoples on an insignificant scale for centuries. Today, widespread usage of this method is destroying vast areas of the rain forest, and smoke from the fires is polluting the atmosphere and possibly contributing to global warming. The destruction also imperils the Indians living within the forest; their numbers have shrunk by more than half in this century alone.

The plight of the Amazonian rain forest has raised concern among many South Americans as well as people throughout the world. One of the rain forest's greatest champions was a Brazilian named Chico Mendes who on numerous occasions confronted and drove off workers hired by cattle ranchers to clear areas of the forest. Through his activism, Mendes made some strong enemies, one of whom gunned him down outside his home in 1988.

There are those who argue that, in order to grow economically and support its expanding population, South America must make full use of the lands of the Amazon basin. They point out that many developed countries are guilty of similar environmental exploitation at home.

The irony of the destruction of the Amazonian rain forest is that once the land is cleared of its native plants and trees, it is ill-suited for the demands of crops. After just a few years, the soil's fertility is exhausted. The people who cleared the land soon abandon it, leaving a landscape that has been robbed of its biodiversity.

In recent years, Brazil and other countries have strengthened legislation aimed at protecting the rain forest. However, they lack the resources to effectively enforce the laws, and today destruction of the rain forest continues at an alarming rate.

Extent of Tropical Rain Forest

Deforested areas

Current extent of rain forest

© Rand McNally
M-540000-8A-EL1-1-1- -1

The Juruá River, at left, and a clearwater slough wind through the dense Amazon rain forest near Eirunepé, Brazil.

Scale 1:40 000 000; one inch to 630 miles. Lambert's Azimuthal. Equal Area Projection
Elevations and depressions are given in feet

40,000 SQ MI
AREA

0   300   600
Miles

0 200 400 600 800 1000 Miles
0 400 800 1200 1600 Kilometers

A-540000-26 -4-7-16
COPYRIGHT BY
RAND McNALLY & COMPANY
MADE IN U.S.A.

Relief

Meters		Feet
3050		10 000
1525		5000
610		2000
305		1000
0	Sea Level	0
152.5		500
1525		5000
3050		10 000
6100		20 000

Scale 1:40 000 000; one inch to 630 miles. Lambert's Azimuthal, Equal Area Projection
Elevations and depressions are given in feet

A-540000-76-3-716
COPYRIGHT BY
RAND McNALLY & COMPANY
MADE IN U.S.A.

Longitude West of Greenwich

| 0 | 200 | 400 | 600 | 800 | 1000 Miles |
| 0 | 400 | 800 | 1200 | 1600 Kilometers |

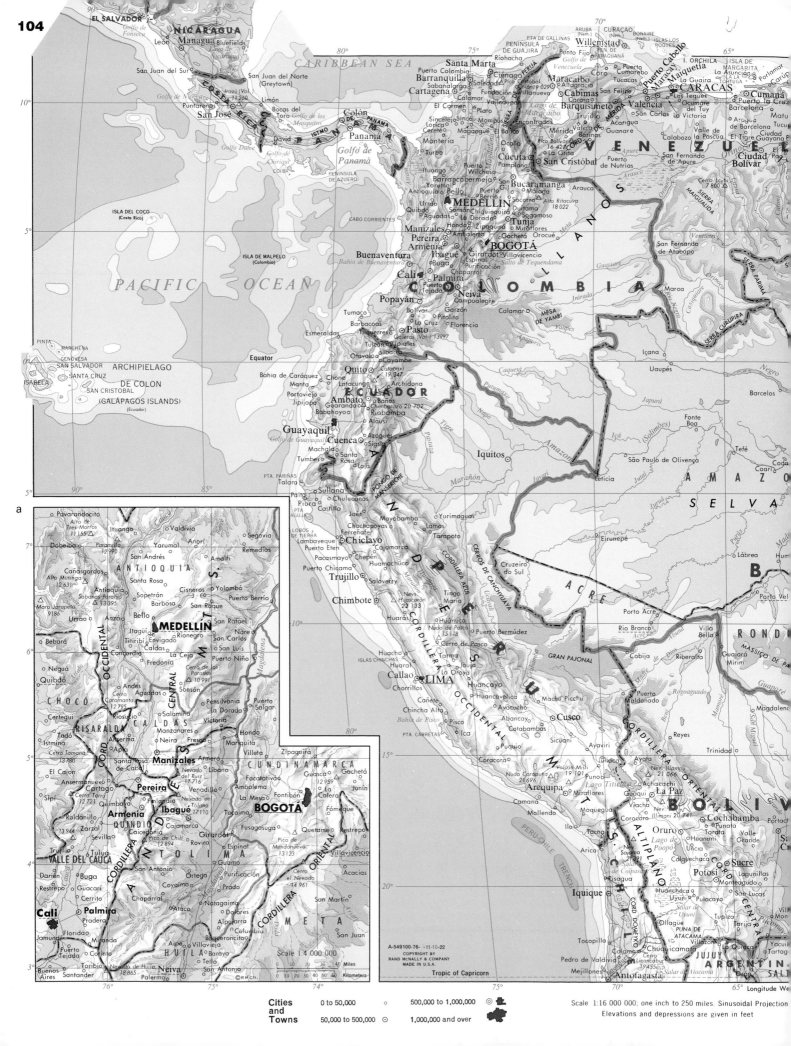

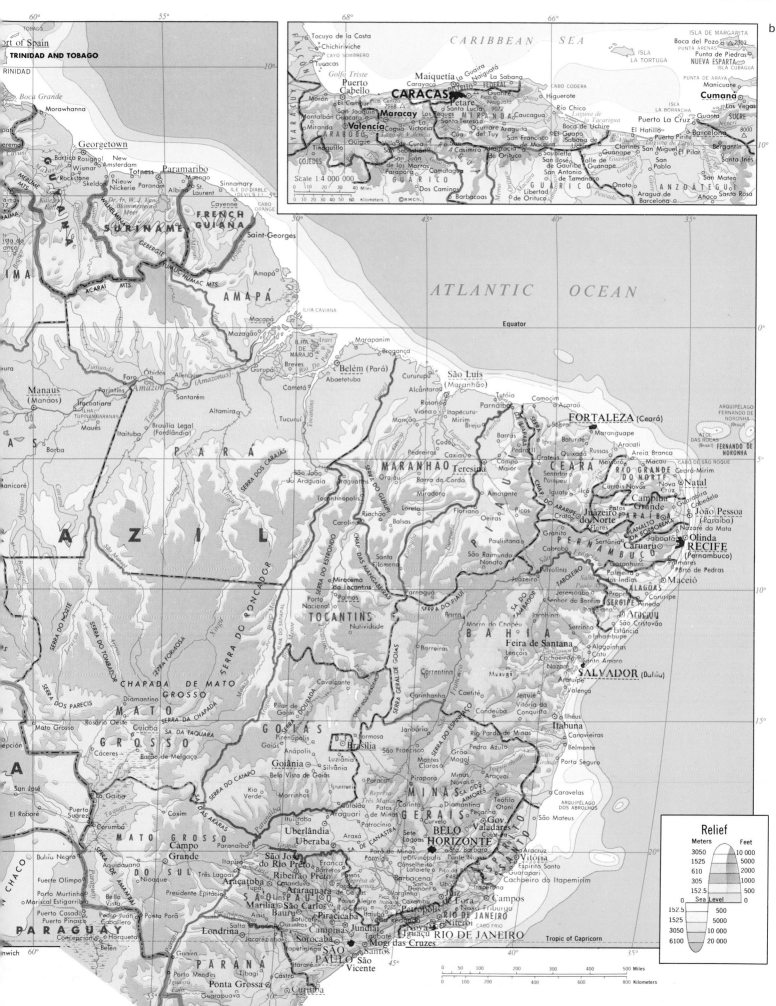

b

CARIBBEAN SEA

Tocuyo de la Costa
Chichiriviche
CAYO SOMBRERO
Tucacas
Golfo Triste
Puerto Cabello
Morón
El Cambur
San Joaquín
Montalbán Guacara
Miranda
Güigue
ARAGUA
Tinaquillo
COJEDES
Scale 1:4 000 000

ISLA DE MARGARITA
Boca del Pozo
Punta Arenas
PUNTA DE PIEDRAS
NUEVA ESPARTA
Punta de Araya
Manicuare
ISLA LA TORTUGA
La Guaira Naiguatá
Maiquetía La Sabana
Carayaca
DISTRITO FEDERAL
CARACAS
Petare
Maracay
Los Teques
Valencia La Victoria
Cagua
Villa de Cura
San Sebastián
San Juan de los Morros
Parapara
GUÁRICO
Dos Caminos
Barbacoas

CABO CODERA
Higuerote
Río Chico
Laguna de la Tacarigua
Boca de Uchire
El Guapo
Sabana de Macaira
San Francisco
Soublette
San José de Guaribe
San Antonio
Valle de Guanape
San Pablo

ISLA LA BORRACHA
Puerto La Cruz
Guanta
Puerto Píritu
Clarines
Píritu Barcelona
San Mateo

ISLA CUBAGUA
Cumaná
SUCRE
Las Vegas
Bergantín
8000
Santa Inés

ARAGUA
MIRANDA
ANZOÁTEGUI
Onoto
Aragua de Barcelona
Anaco
Santa Rosa

TRINIDAD AND TOBAGO
TOBAGO
TRINIDAD
Port of Spain
Boca Grande

Morawhanna
Bartica Rosignol New Amsterdam
Wismar Skeldon
Rockstone
Georgetown
Totness Paramaribo
Nieuw Nickerie Paranam
Albina St. Laurent
Sinnamary
ILE DU DIABLE (DEVIL'S I.)
Cayenne
CABO ORANGE
Saint-Georges

SURINAME
FRENCH GUIANA
Dr. Fr. W.J. Van Blommestein Meer
GEBERGTE
TUMUC-HUMAC MTS.
ACARAÍ MTS.

ATLANTIC OCEAN

Equator

Amapá
AMAPÁ
Macapá
Mazagão
ILHA CAVIANA
ILHA DE MARAJÓ

Manaus (Manaos)
Itacoatiara
Parintins
Óbidos
Alenquer (Amazonas)
Santarém
Brasília Legal (Fordlândia)
Itaituba
Maués
Borba

Breves
Gurupá
Belém (Pará)
Abaetetuba
Cametá
Tucuruí
Altamira

Marapanim
Bragança
Cururupu
São Luís (Maranhão)
Alcântara
Rosário
Viana
Itapecuru-Mirim
Brejo
Codó

Tutóia
Parnaíba
Camocim
Acaraú
FORTALEZA (Ceará)
Maranguape
Baturité
Sobral
Ipu
ARQUIPÉLAGO FERNANDO DE NORONHA (Brazil)
ATOL DAS ROCAS (Brazil)
FERNANDO DE NORONHA

P A R Á
São João do Araguaia
Araguatins
Tocantinópolis

MARANHÃO
Grajaú
Barra do Corda
Teresina
Mirador
Amarante

PIAUÍ
SERRA DA IBIAPABA
Pedro II
Campo Maior
Barras
Pedreiras
Caxias
Crateús
Quixadá
Russas
Aracati
Areia Branca
Macau
Mossoró
Ceará-Mirim
CEARÁ
SERRA DO ARARIPE
Iguatu
Icó
Currais Novos
Nova Cruz
Natal

RIO GRANDE DO NORTE
Campina Grande
Guarabira
Cabedelo
João Pessoa (Paraíba)
PARAÍBA
Patos
Juàzeiro do Norte
Crato
Flores
Sertânia
Caruaru
PLANALTO DA BORBOREMA
Jaboatão
Olinda
RECIFE (Pernambuco)
Palmares
Porto de Pedras
PERNAMBUCO
Granito
Cabrobó
Garanhuns
Senhor do Bonfim
Maceió
ALAGOAS
SERGIPE
Propriá
Penedo
Aracaju

B R A Z I L

SERRA DO NORTE
SERRA DO TOMBADOR
SERRA DOS PARECIS
Manaus
Borba
Manicoré

SERRA DO CACHIMBO
SERRA DO RONCADOR
SERRA DO ESTRONDO
SERRA DO GURUPI
Carolina
Riachão
Balsas
Loreto
Floriano
Oeiras
Picos
São Raimundo Nonato
Paulistana
Juàzeiro
Senhor do Bonfim

TOCANTINS
Miracema do Tocantins
Porto Nacional
Palmas
Natividade
Barreiras

CHAP. DAS MANGABEIRAS
Santa Filomena
Corrente
Parnaguá
Carinhanha

Morro do Chapéu
Jacobina
Serrinha
São Cristóvão
Estância
Inhambupe
Feira de Santana
Santo Amaro
Cachoeira
Nazaré
Alagoinhas

B A H I A
Lençóis
Itaberaba
Muguba
SALVADOR (Bahia)
Valença
Jequié
Caetité
Vitória da Conquista
Condeúba
Itabuna
Ilhéus

CHAPADA DE MATO GROSSO
Diamantino
SERRA DA CHAPADA
SA. DA TAQUARA
M A T O   G R O S S O
Rosário Oeste
Cuiabá
Cáceres
Barão de Melgaço

GOIÁS
Pilar de Goiás
Cavalcante
SERRA DOURADA
SERRA GERAL DE GOIÁS
Goiás
Pirenópolis
Anápolis
Brasília
Formosa
São Francisco
Januária
SERRA DO ESPINHAÇO
Rio Pardo de Minas
Pedra Azul
Araçuaí
Salto Grande
Porto Seguro
Canavieiras
Belmonte

SA. DOS AIMORÉS
Caravelas
ARQUIPÉLAGO DOS ABROLHOS
Mucuri

Luziânia
Silvânia
Bela Vista de Goiás
Goiânia
Paracatu
Unaí
Montes Claros
Pirapora
Diamantina
Teófilo Otoni
Peçanha
São Mateus

SA. DAS ARARAS
Rio Verde
Morrinhos
Ipameri
Catalão
Araguari
Patrocínio
Araxá
SA. DE CANASTRA
Patos de Minas
MINAS GERAIS
Curvelo
Corinto
Sete Lagoas
Gov. Valadares
Aimorés
Colatina
Aracruz
Vitória
ESPÍRITO SANTO
Guarapari
Cachoeiro de Itapemirim

M A T O   G R O S S O   D O   S U L
San José
La Gaiba
Puerto Suárez
Corumbá
Aquidauana
Miranda
Campo Grande
Coxim
Paranaíba
Uberlândia
Uberaba
BELO HORIZONTE
Sta. Bárbara
Divinópolis
Conselheiro Lafaiete
Barbacena
Ponte Nova
Pico do Bandeira 9480
Itaperuna
Campos

PARAGUAY
Buliú Negra
Fuerte Olimpo
Porto Murtinho
Mariscal Estigarribia
Bella Vista
Puerto Casado
Concepción

Bela Vista
Porto Mendes
Guaíra
Belén
Horqueta
Pedro Juan Caballero
Ponta Porã

Bauru
Marília
Assis
Presidente Epitácio
Três Lagoas
SÃO PAULO
Araçatuba
Tupã
Araraquara
São Carlos
Ribeirão Preto
Barretos
Franca
Poços de Caldas
Pouso Alegre
Itajubá
Taubaté
São José do Rio Preto
Catanduva
Botucatu
Piracicaba
Campinas
Jundiaí
Sorocaba
Mogi das Cruzes
Nova Friburgo
Petrópolis
RIO DE JANEIRO
Niterói
CABO FRIO
Juiz de Fora

PARANÁ
Londrina
Jacarézinho
Tibagi
Ponta Grossa
Guarapuava
Castro
SÃO PAULO
São Vicente
Santos
Curitiba

Tropic of Capricorn

Relief	
Meters	Feet
3050	10 000
1525	5000
610	2000
305	1000
152.5	500
0 Sea Level	0
152.5	500
1525	5000
3050	10 000
6100	20 000

0 50 100 200 300 400 500 Miles
0 100 200 400 600 800 Kilometers

Relief

Meters	Feet
3050	10 000
1525	5000
610	2000
305	1000
152.5	500
0 Sea Level	0
152.5	500
1525	5000
3050	10 000
6100	20 000

Sea Level

Below Sea Level

FALKLAND IS.
(ISLAS MALVINAS)
(Br.)
(Claimed by Argentina)

A-549200-76 -11-8-14
COPYRIGHT BY
RAND McNALLY & COMPANY
MADE IN U.S.A.

Longitude West of Greenwich

Scale 1:16 000 000; one inch to 250 miles. Sinusoidal Projection
Elevations and depressions are given in feet

a

BUENOS AIRES

Scale 1:1 000 000

b

RIO DE JANEIRO

Scale 1:1 000 000

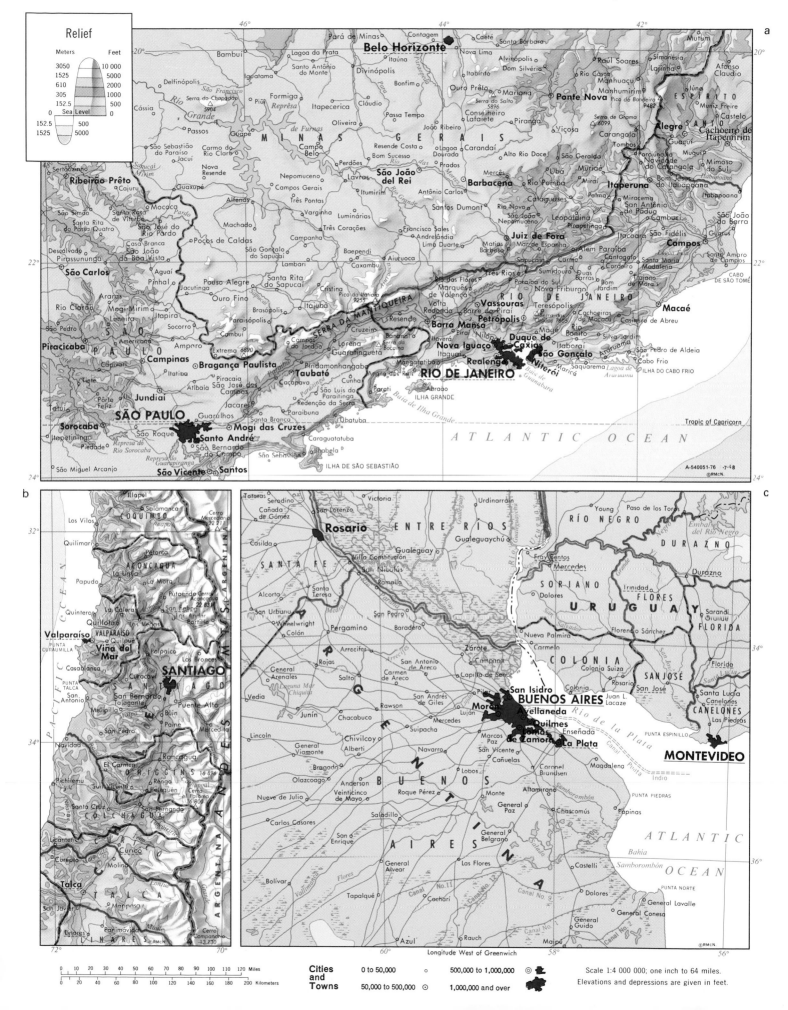

a

b

c

Relief

Meters	Feet
3050	10 000
1525	5000
610	2000
305	1000
152.5	500
0 Sea Level	0
152.5	500
1525	5000

Cities and Towns

0 to 50,000 ○
50,000 to 500,000 ⊙
500,000 to 1,000,000 ◎
1,000,000 and over

Scale 1:4 000 000; one inch to 64 miles.

Elevations and depressions are given in feet.

Europe

Europe is smaller than every other continent except Australia. In a sense, Europe is not really a continent at all, since it is part of the same vast landmass as Asia. Geographers sometimes refer to this landmass as a single continent, Eurasia. Europe occupies only about 18% of the land area of Eurasia.

Europe can be described as an enormous peninsula, stretching from the Ural Mountains, Ural River, and Caspian Sea in the east, to the Atlantic Ocean in the west; and from the Arctic Ocean in the north to the Mediterranean Sea, Black Sea, and Caucasus mountains in the south. The British Isles, Iceland, Corsica, Crete, and thousands of smaller islands that lie off the European mainland are usually considered as part of the continent.

A sweep of mountain ranges, including the Pyrenees, Alps and Carpathians, divides the colder, wetter north from the sun-drenched south.

Europe at a glance

Land area: 3,800,000 square miles (9,900,000 sq km)

Estimated population (January 1, 1995): 712,100,000

Population density: 187/square mile (72/sq km)

Mean elevation: 980 feet (300 m)

Highest point: Gora El' brus, Russia, 18,510 feet (5,642 m)

Lowest point: Caspian Sea, Asia-Europe, 92 feet (28 m) below sea level

Longest river: Volga, 2,194 mi (3,531 km)

Number of countries (incl. dependencies): 49

Largest independent country: Russia (Europe/Asia), 6,592,849 square miles (17,075,400 sq km)

Smallest independent country: Vatican City, 0.2 square miles (0.4 sq km)

Most populous independent country: Russia (Europe/Asia), 150,500,000

Least populous independent country: Vatican City, 1,000

Largest city: Moscow, pop. 8,801,500 (1991)

Coldest place:
Ust'- Shchugor, Russia
-67°F (-55°C)

Driest place:
Astrakhan', Russia
6.4 inches (16 cm)/ye

Lowest point:
Caspian Sea, Asia-Europe
92 ft (28 m) below sea le

Highest point:
Gora El'brus, Russia
18,510 ft (5,642 m)

Wettest place:
Crkvice, Bosnia & Herzegovina
183 inches (465 cm)/year

Hottest place:
Sevilla, Spain
122°F (50°C)

Landforms

	Mountains
	Widely spaced mountains
	High tablelands
	Hills and low tablelands
	Plains
	Depresssions, basins
	High tablelands and ice caps
	Mountains and ice caps

© Rand McNally & Co.
M-550000-7C-EL1-1-1- -1

The Alps tower above a village in the Virgen Tal valley of western Austria.

Climate

Warm, moist air masses flowing in from the Atlantic Ocean give much of Europe a mild climate and abundant precipitation. Cities like London, Paris and Rome all enjoy warmer weather than cities at similar latitudes in North America and Asia. The moderate winds don't reach eastern Europe, where the winters are long and cold and the summers short and cool. The same is true in the northern regions of Scandinavia.

Much of the south enjoys a Mediterranean climate, marked by short, rainy winters and long, dry summers. Indeed, the many beaches and islands found throughout the region are popular with vacationers year-round.

© Rand McNally & Co.
M-550000-6A-EL1-1-1- -1

Tinted areas show temperature in degrees Fahrenheit. Vertical bars show precipitation in inches.

Zaragoza
Semiarid

Athens
Hot, dry summer / mild, rainy winter

Venice
Warm, humid summer / mild winter

Paris
Mild and rainy

Bucharest
Warm, humid summer / cold, snowy winter

Stockholm
Cool, humid summer / cold, snowy winter

Arkhangelsk
Short, cool, humid summer / very cold, snowy winter

Reykjavik
Cold and dry

Extensive uplands
Climate varies with elevation and latitude

Population

With a population of 712 million, Europe is home to 13% of the world's people. Only one continent, Asia, has a larger population. Europe's population density—187 people per square mile (72 per sq km) is also second only to Asia. However, the continent's density varies dramatically from country to country. The Netherlands, for instance, has a density of 954 people per square mile (368 per sq km), making it one of the most densely populated countries in the world. In contrast, Norway has only 29 people per square mile (11 per sq km).

A vast array of ethnic groups and cultures can be found in Europe's relatively small area. Throughout the centuries, this diversity has enriched European culture while also leading to many hostilities. Of the 60 languages spoken, the majority are derived from Latin, Germanic or Slavic roots. Most Europeans are Christian, either Protestant or Roman Catholic.

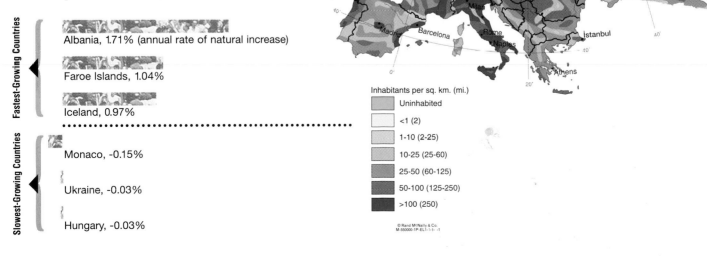

Fastest-Growing Countries

Albania, 1.71% (annual rate of natural increase)

Faroe Islands, 1.04%

Iceland, 0.97%

Slowest-Growing Countries

Monaco, -0.15%

Ukraine, -0.03%

Hungary, -0.03%

Inhabitants per sq. km. (mi.)

Uninhabited
<1 (2)
1-10 (2-25)
10-25 (25-60)
25-50 (60-125)
50-100 (125-250)
>100 (250)

© Rand McNally & Co.
M-550000-1P-EL1-1-1- -1

Environments and Land Use

Given the high population density of Europe, it is not surprising that evidence of human development can be seen in every part of the continent, with the exception of the northern reaches of Scandinavia. In Western Europe, small farms are surrounded by towns, cities and industrial areas. Only in the east, in areas such as the vast rolling steppes of the Ukraine, can large farms and unbroken natural vistas be found.

Harvesting grapes from vineyards in Burgundy, France

The heavily industrialized countries of Western Europe boast rich economies and high standards of living. Switzerland has a per capita Gross Domestic Product (GDP) approaching U.S. $22,000, the highest in the world. The figures are generally much lower in Eastern Europe. One of the continent's poorest countries is the tiny former Communist state of Albania, which has a per capita GDP of only U.S. $998.

Pollution is an unfortunate by-product of the continent's industry. One example is the scenic Rhine River: in the 1980s, large stretches were found to be so polluted that they were devoid of life. These findings sparked a 20-year program to clean up the river. In general, the countries of Eastern Europe suffer from the worst pollution, as economic development has in the past taken precedence over environmental policies.

The vast forests of Scandinavia support a large paper and wood-products economy. Where forests survive in countries farther to the south, they are often used for recreation. Along the Mediterranean, the warm and dry lands support olive and fruit orchards. In many of these areas, agriculture is being supplemented and even replaced by tourism.

Over-fishing has depleted the seas and ocean around Europe. The fleets of countries such as Spain and Great Britain must sail far into the North Atlantic to find the ever-dwindling stocks of fish.

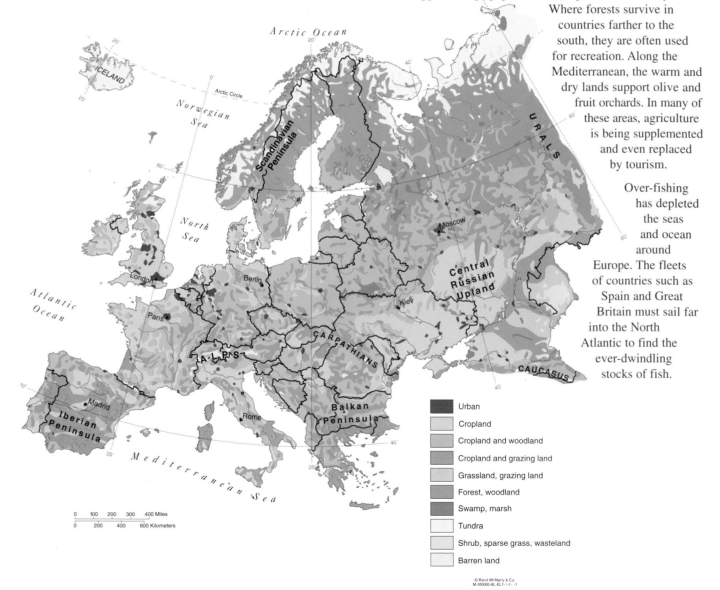

Arctic Ocean

ICELAND

Arctic Circle

Norwegian Sea

Scandinavian Peninsula

North Sea

London

Berlin

Moscow

Kiev

Central Russian Upland

URALS

Atlantic Ocean

Paris

ALPS

CARPATHIANS

CAUCASUS

Madrid

Iberian Peninsula

Rome

Balkan Peninsula

Mediterranean Sea

■	Urban
	Cropland
	Cropland and woodland
	Cropland and grazing land
	Grassland, grazing land
	Forest, woodland
	Swamp, marsh
	Tundra
	Shrub, sparse grass, wasteland
	Barren land

0 100 200 300 400 Miles
0 200 400 600 Kilometers

© Rand McNally & Co.
M-550000-8L-EL1-1-1- -1

Political Changes Since 1989

Much of Europe lay in economic and physical ruin after World War II ended in 1945. Germany's cities and industrial centers had been ravaged by aerial bombardment and assaults by the Allied armies. Many other countries, such as Russia, Poland, Belgium, and the Netherlands suffered gravely from Nazi invasions and occupation.

After 1945, tensions among the victorious Allies grew, specifically between the Western powers—the United States, Great Britain and France—and the Soviet Union. It became clear that the two sides had vastly different visions for post-war Europe. In 1946, former British prime minister Winston Churchill observed that an "Iron Curtain" had gone down across Europe. It was to stay in place for almost 45 years.

Germany and the city of Berlin were divided between the Western Allies and the Soviet Union. West Germany quickly joined the other countries of Western Europe in building a stable, affluent democratic society. East Germany became part of a bloc of Eastern European countries dominated by the Soviet Union. These included Poland, Czechoslovakia, Hungary, Romania, Albania, and Bulgaria (see map at right). The economies in these countries were tightly controlled and personal freedoms were severely limited by the Communist governments in power.

The two blocs faced each other in a tense, generally non-military standoff called "The Cold War," which lasted for four decades. However, in 1985 winds of reform began sweeping through Eastern Europe. In 1989, Hungary relaxed its borders with Austria, setting off a flow of refugees from the east who had been forbidden to travel to the West. Thus began a dizzying period of change: the next two years saw the collapse of the Soviet Union, the reunification of Germany, independence for the former Soviet republics, and freedom from Soviet influence for the former bloc countries.

Although much of the old east seems intent on adopting Western ideals of democracy and freedom, the process is not without problems. Switching from communism to market economies has meant hardship for millions. It has also led to ethnic tensions that resulted in the peaceful break-up of Czechoslovakia and the violent civil wars in the former Yugoslavia.

Still, most countries in the east seem intent on one day becoming a part of the European Union, the political and economic organization that currently has 15 member countries.

East Germany and West Germany reunited in 1990.

In 1991, the Soviet Union broke up into 15 independent states: Russia, Estonia, Latvia, Lithuania, Belarus, Ukraine, Moldova, Georgia, Armenia, Azerbaijan, Kazakstan, Turkmenistan, Kyrgyzstan, Uzbekistan, and Tajikistan.

In 1991-92 the former Yugoslavia broke up when Slovenia, Croatia, Macedonia, and Bosnia and Herzegovina declared their independence, leaving Serbia and Montenegro as the remaining Yugoslav Republics.

In 1993, Czechoslovakia split into two separate countries: the Czech Republic and Slovakia.

Political Change Since 1989

- Former Soviet Union
- Former Czechoslovakia
- Former Yugoslavia
- Former East and West Germany
- Former Soviet-bloc countries

© Rand McNally & Co.
M-550000-2P-EL1-1-1- -1

Berlin Wall memorial

40,000 SQ MI
AREA

0   100   200
Miles

Scale 1: 16 000 000; one inch to 250 miles. Conic Projection
Elevations and depressions are given in feet

Longitude West of Greenwich   Longitude East of Greenwich

0 50 100   200   300   400   500 Miles

0 100 200   400   600   800 Kilometers

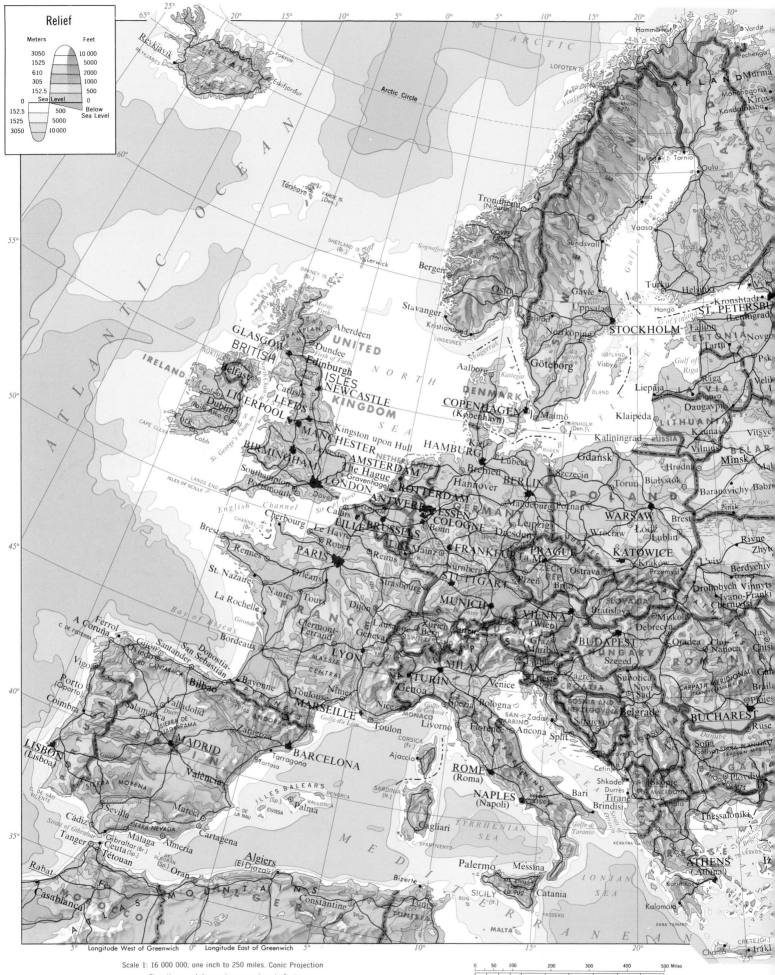

Relief

Meters		Feet
3050		10 000
1525		5000
610		2000
305		1000
152.5		500
0	Sea Level	0
	Sea Level	Below
152.5		500
1525		5000
3050		10 000

Scale 1: 16 000 000; one inch to 250 miles. Conic Projection

Elevations and depressions are given in feet

Longitude West of Greenwich   0°   Longitude East of Greenwich

| 0 | 50 | 100 | 200 | 300 | 400 | 500 Miles |
| 0 | 100 | 200 | 400 | 600 | 800 Kilometers |

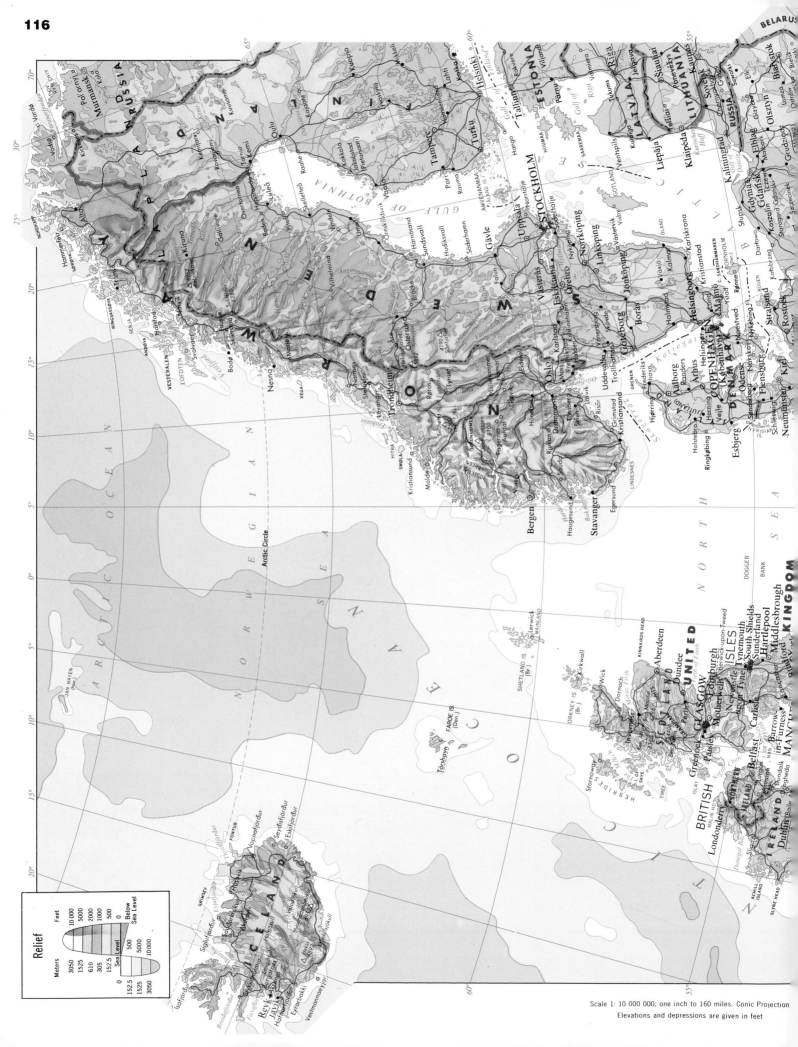

Scale 1: 10 000 000; one inch to 160 miles. Conic Projection

Elevations and depressions are given in feet

Cities and Towns

0 to 50,000	○
50,000 to 500,000	⊙
500,000 to 1,000,000	◉
1,000,000 and over	⬛

Relief

Meters	Feet
3050	10000
1525	5000
610	2000
305	1000
152.5	500
0	Sea Level
	Below Sea Level
Sea Level	0
152.5	500
1525	5000
3050	10000

0   50   100   150   200   250   300 Miles

0   100   200   300   400   500 Kilometers

Scale 1:10 000 000; one inch to 160 miles. Conic Projection
Elevations and depressions are given in feet.

Relief

Meters	Feet
3050	10000
1525	5000
610	2000
305	1000
152.5	500
0 Sea Level	0
	Below
	Sea Level
152.5	500
1525	5000
3050	10000

A-558300-76 T8 1 3
COPYRIGHT BY
RAND McNALLY & COMPANY
MADE IN U.S.A.

Longitude West of Greenwich   0° Longitude East of Greenwich

Scale 1:10 000 000; one inch to 160 miles. Bonne's Projection
Elevations and depressions are given in feet

Africa

The Drakensberg Mountains mark the southern end of the African plateau.

Africa, the second-largest continent, comprises about one-fifth of the world's land area. From the Equator, Africa extends roughly the same distance to the north as it does to the south.

A high plateau covers much of the continent. The edges of the plateau are marked by steep slopes, called escarpments, where the land angles sharply downward onto narrow coastal plains or into the sea. Many of the continent's great rivers plunge over these escarpments in falls or rapids, and therefore cannot be used as transportation routes from the coast into the continent's interior.

Among Africa's most significant mountain systems are the Atlas range in the far north and the Drakensberg range in the far south. A long string of mountain ranges and highlands running north-south through eastern Africa marks the course of the Great Rift Valley.

Africa at a glance

Land area: 11,700,000 square miles (30,300,000 sq km)

Estimated population (January 1, 1995): 697,600,000

Population density: 60/ square mile (23/sq km)

Mean elevation: 1,900 feet (580 m)

Highest point: Kilimanjaro, Tanzania, 19,340 feet (5,895 m)

Lowest point: Lac Assal, Djibouti, 515 feet (157 m) below sea level

Longest river: Nile, 4,145 mi (6,671 km)

Number of countries (incl. dependencies): 61

Largest independent country: Sudan, 967,500 square miles (2,505,813 sq km)

Smallest independent country: Seychelles, 175 square miles (453 sq km)

Most populous independent country: Nigeria, 97,300,000

Least populous independent country: Seychelles, 75,000

Largest city: Cairo, pop. 6,068,695 (1990)

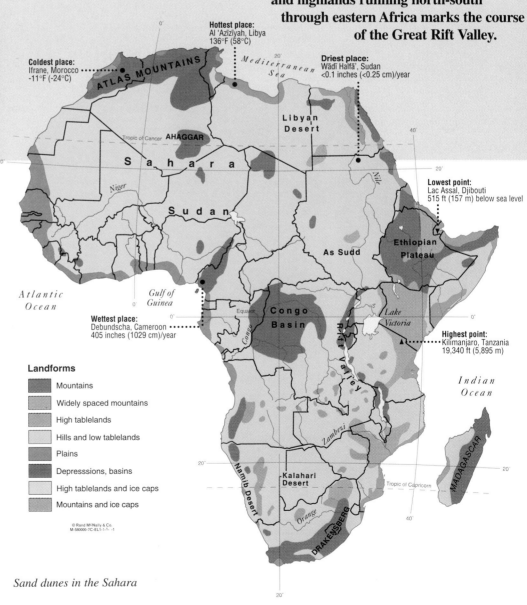

Coldest place:
Ifrane, Morocco
-11°F (-24°C)

Hottest place:
Al 'Azīzīyah, Libya
136°F (58°C)

Driest place:
Wādī Halfā', Sudan
<0.1 inches (<0.25 cm)/year

Lowest point:
Lac Assal, Djibouti
515 ft (157 m) below sea level

Wettest place:
Debundscha, Cameroon
405 inches (1029 cm)/year

Highest point:
Kilimanjaro, Tanzania
19,340 ft (5,895 m)

ATLAS MOUNTAINS
Mediterranean Sea
Tropic of Cancer AHAGGAR
Libyan Desert
Sahara
Niger
Nile
Sudan
As Sudd
Ethiopian Plateau
Atlantic Ocean
Gulf of Guinea
Equator
Congo Basin
Lake Victoria
Great Rift Valley
Indian Ocean
Congo
Zambezi
MADAGASCAR
Namib Desert
Kalahari Desert
Orange
Tropic of Capricorn
DRAKENSBERG

Landforms

- Mountains
- Widely spaced mountains
- High tablelands
- Hills and low tablelands
- Plains
- Depresssions, basins
- High tablelands and ice caps
- Mountains and ice caps

© Rand McNally & Co.
M-580000-7C-EL1-1-1- -1

Sand dunes in the Sahara

Climate

Africa's most prominent climatic region is the vast Sahara desert which spreads over much of the northern half of the continent. The Sahara experiences scorching daytime temperatures, minimal rainfall, and hot, dry, dust-laden winds that blow nearly continuously. South of the Sahara, the climate becomes increasingly humid, moving through zones of semiarid steppe and tropical savanna to the tropical rain forest that stretches across equatorial Africa from the Atlantic Ocean to the Rift Valley.

The climate patterns of northern Africa are repeated in reverse south of the Equator. The rain forest gives way to zones of decreasing humidity, and desert regions cover western South Africa and Namibia. Africa's mildest, most temperate climates are found along its Mediterranean coast, at its southwestern tip, and in eastern South Africa.

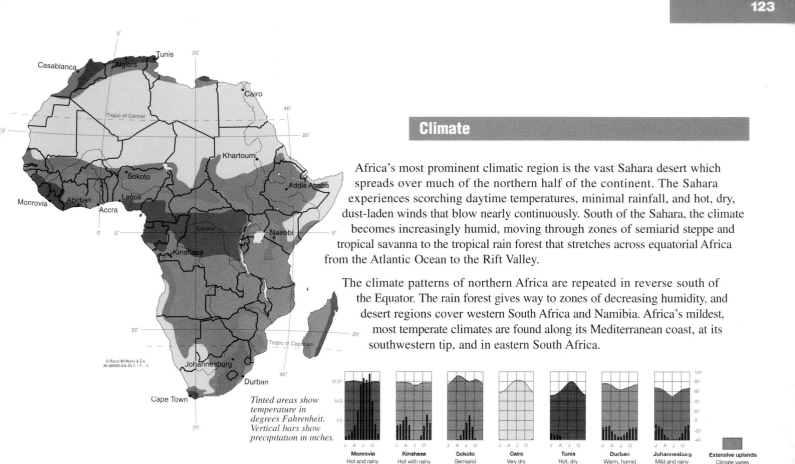

Tinted areas show temperature in degrees Fahrenheit. Vertical bars show precipitation in inches.

Monrovia	Kinshasa	Sokoto	Cairo	Tunis	Durban	Johannesburg	Extensive uplands
Hot and rainy	Hot with rainy and dry seasons	Semiarid	Very dry	Hot, dry summer / mild, rainy winter	Warm, humid summer / mild winter	Mild and rainy	Climate varies with elevation and latitude

Population

Approximately one-eighth of the world's people live in Africa. The population is almost evenly divided between the sub-Saharan countries and those bordering the Mediterranean. Large tracts of the Sahara are uninhabited. Despite recurring famines and warfare, the population is rapidly increasing. Twenty-two African countries have annual growth rates at or above 3%, which means that the number of inhabitants in each can double within 25 years.

The largest concentrations of people are generally found in regions in which one or more of the following conditions exist: moderate temperatures, ample water supply, and arable land. These regions include Egypt's fertile Nile Valley, the northern coast of the Gulf of Guinea, the highlands of East Africa, and the coastal regions of Morocco, Algeria, and Tunisia, north of the Atlas Mountains.

Fastest-Growing Countries

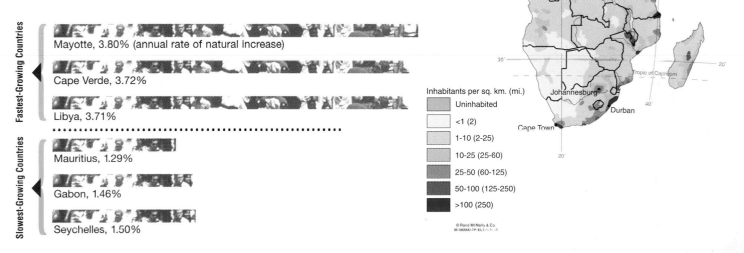

Mayotte, 3.80% (annual rate of natural increase)

Cape Verde, 3.72%

Libya, 3.71%

Slowest-Growing Countries

Mauritius, 1.29%

Gabon, 1.46%

Seychelles, 1.50%

Inhabitants per sq. km. (mi.)

	Uninhabited
	<1 (2)
	1-10 (2-25)
	10-25 (25-60)
	25-50 (60-125)
	50-100 (125-250)
	>100 (250)

© Rand McNally & Co.
M-580000-1P-EL1-1-1- -1

Environments and Land Use

Deserts account for one-third of Africa's land area, and they claim new land every year. Drought, over-farming and over-grazing can quickly turn marginal land, such as that of the Sahel region, into barren wasteland. The huge Sahara desert has itself only existed a short time, in geological terms: cave paintings and other archeological evidence indicate that green pastureland covered the area just a few thousand years ago.

Shepherd with goats in the Sahel

Most Africans are subsistence farmers, growing sorghum, corn, millet, sweet potatoes, and other starchy foods. Commercial farms, most of which date from the colonial period, can be found throughout central and southern Africa, producing cash crops such as coffee, bananas, tobacco and cacao. One-quarter of the continent's land is suitable for grazing, but disease and drought have made raising animals difficult. Although three out of four Africans work in agriculture, Africa is the only continent that is not self-sufficient for food.

The great rain forests that cover much of equatorial Africa produce mahogany, ebony, and other valuable hardwoods. However, only limited areas of the forests are suitable for logging, and the lack of developed road networks makes it difficult and costly to transport the wood.

Vast mineral reserves are spread throughout the continent. Most are unexploited, but notable exceptions include the diamond mines of South Africa and Namibia, the copper mines of Zambia and Democratic Republic of the Congo, and the oil fields of Nigeria, Libya, and Algeria.

The great concentrations of wildlife for which Africa is famous can still be found in places such as Tanzania's Serengeti Plain and Botswana's Kalahari Desert. In many other parts of the continent, however, wildlife is quickly disappearing as humans encroach on habitat and poachers decimate entire species.

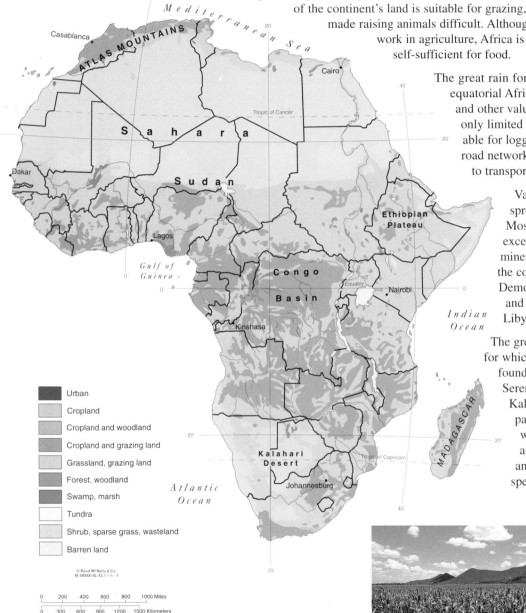

Urban

Cropland

Cropland and woodland

Cropland and grazing land

Grassland, grazing land

Forest, woodland

Swamp, marsh

Tundra

Shrub, sparse grass, wasteland

Barren land

© Rand McNally & Co.
M-580000-8L-EL1-1-1- -1

| 0 | 200 | 400 | 600 | 800 | 1000 Miles |
| 0 | 300 | 600 | 900 | 1200 | 1500 Kilometers |

Field of sorghum in Zimbabwe

Africa: from Colonial Rule to Independence

The origins of Europe's colonization of Africa can be traced back to the 1500s, when a lucrative slave trade developed to supply European settlers in the New World with laborers. Africa became the primary source for slaves: between the mid-1500s and the mid-1800s, 11 million Africans were captured and sold into slavery.

When the slave trade was banned across Europe in the early 1800s, commercial trade with Africa continued. In the second half of the century, competition for Africa's minerals and other raw materials intensified, and between 1880 and 1914, France, Britain, Italy, Portugal, Belgium, Spain, and Germany annexed large areas of Africa. Colonial rule was often characterized by racial prejudice and segregation.

In the late 19th and early 20th centuries, Egypt, Ethiopia, and South Africa began to break free from colonial influence. For most or Africa, however, colonial rule persisted through the mid-1900s, although it faced growing bitterness and nationalist sentiment. As the colonial powers struggled through two world wars, and as their international dominance declined, it became increasingly difficult for them to maintain their empires.

In 1951, Libya gained its independence, following a UN resolution that ended British and French control. Sudan peacefully won independence from Britain and Egypt in 1956. A year later, Britain granted independence to the Gold Coast, which became the new country of Ghana. Guinea separated from France in 1958, followed by all of the other French colonies in 1960. Anti-colonial movements gathered strength across Africa, and by the end of the 1970s, a total of 43 countries had become independent.

The end of colonial rule, however, has not brought peace and prosperity. Many of the newly freed countries were ill-prepared for independence. Their economies were oriented to fit the needs of the now-departed colonists, few transportation networks existed, and dictators and rival despots fought for power in civil wars.

People of the Samburu tribe

Further, most Africans identify themselves primarily with the tribe to which they belong. The political delineations established by the European powers have little meaning and often conflict with traditional tribal boundaries. In some cases, enemy tribes found themselves pushed together in a single country; in others, single tribes were divided among several countries. These conditions have already brought much warfare and hardship. Still, Africa is a land of promise and opportunity. The rich diversity of its people and abundance of its resources should inevitably enable the continent to realize its potential.

Africa in 1950

- Independent
- British
- French
- Portuguese
- Spanish
- Belgian
- Italian
- Other

© Rand McNally & Co.
M-490065-2S-El.1-1-1- -1

Africa Today

- Independent
- Other

1960 Date of independence

© Rand McNally & Co.
M 580000 3S EL1 1 1   1

Ethno-linguistic Groups

Semitic-Hamitic	Bantu	Indo-European	Nilotic	Central/Eastern Sudanese, Bantu
Mande	Central Bantoid	Kanuri	Malay-Polynesian	Indo-European, Semitic-Hamitic
Guinean	Eastern Bantoid	Songhai	Kanuri, Semitic-Hamitic	Central/Eastern Sudanese, Semitic-Hamitic
Hausa	Western Bantoid	Khoisan	Hausa, Western Bantoid	Central/Eastern Sudanese

© Rand McNally & Co.
M-580000-1D-EL1-·-1· -1

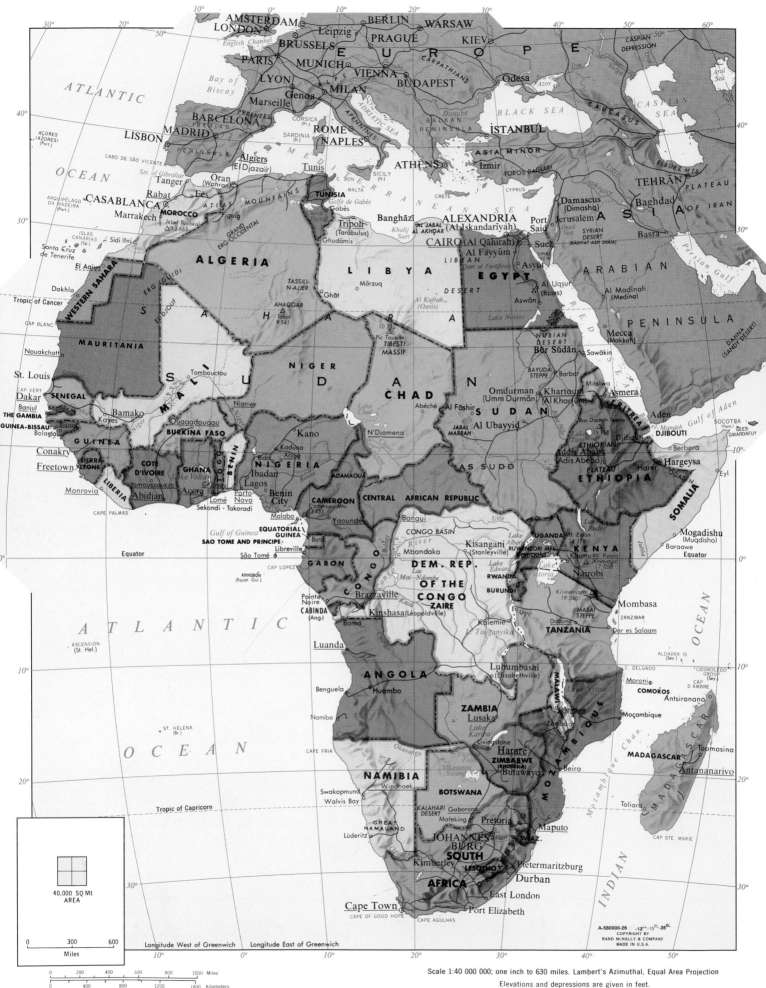

Scale 1:40 000 000; one inch to 630 miles. Lambert's Azimuthal, Equal Area Projection
Elevations and depressions are given in feet.

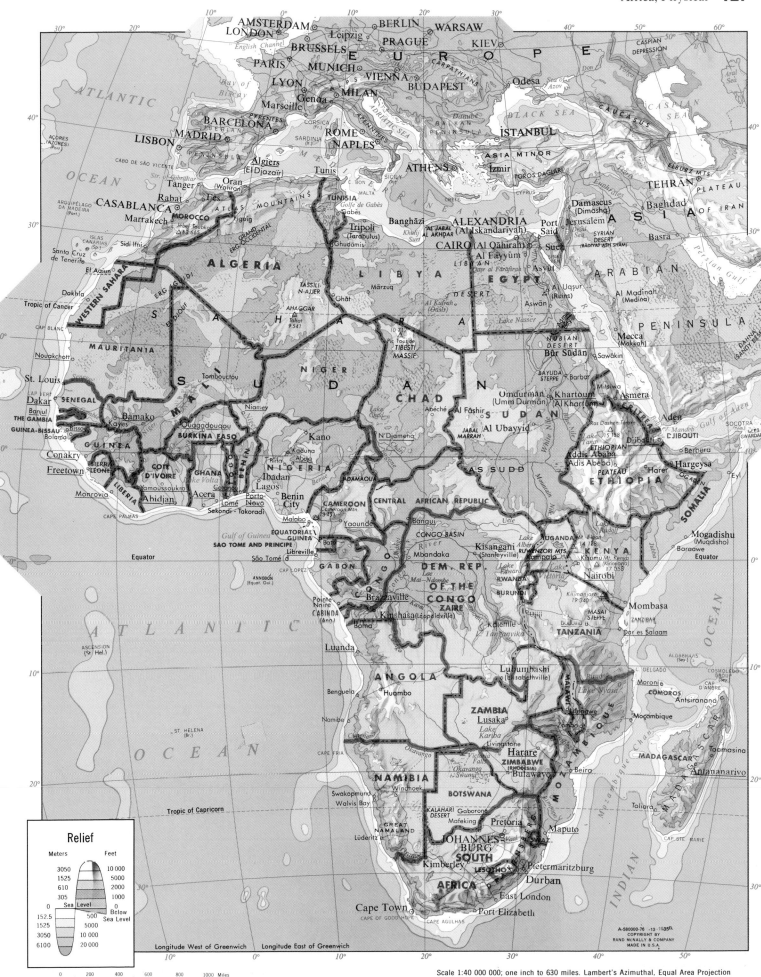

Relief

Meters	Feet
3050	10 000
1525	5000
610	2000
305	1000
0	Sea Level	0
	Below Sea Level
152.5	500
1525	5000
3050	10 000
6100	20 000

Longitude West of Greenwich   Longitude East of Greenwich

Scale 1:40 000 000; one inch to 630 miles. Lambert's Azimuthal, Equal Area Projection
Elevations and depressions are given in feet.

A-580000-76 -13-1635EL
COPYRIGHT BY
RAND McNALLY & COMPANY
MADE IN U.S.A.

0   200   400   600   800   1000 Miles
0   400   800   1200   1600 Kilometers

128

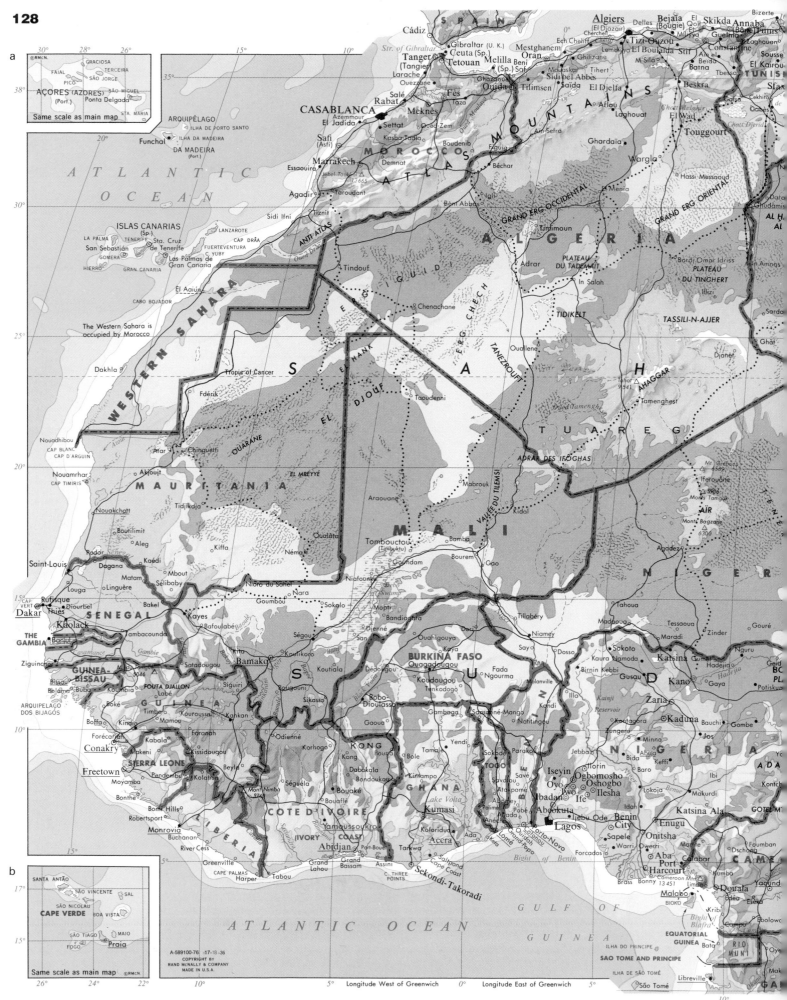

Scale 1:16 000 000; one inch to 250 miles. Sinusoidal Projection
Elevations and depressions are given in feet

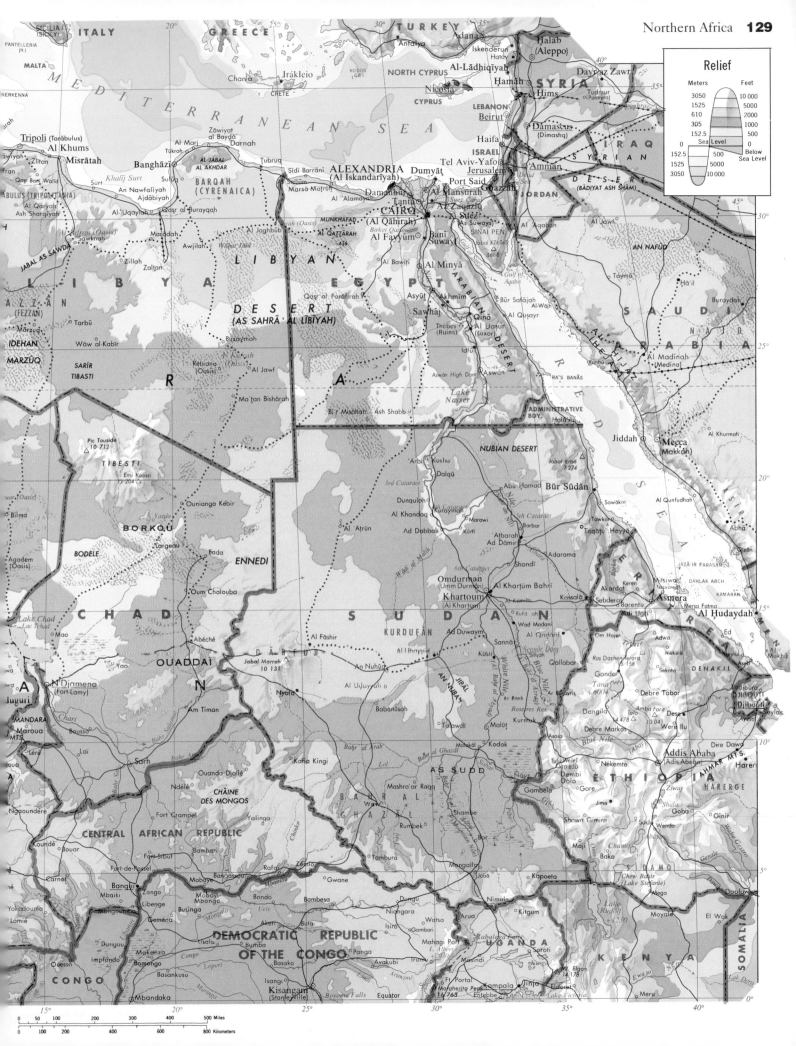

Relief

Meters	Feet
3050	10 000
1525	5000
610	2000
305	1000
152.5	500
0 Sea Level	0
152.5	500 Below
1525	5000 Sea Level
3050	10 000

ITALY
SICILIA (SICILY)
PANTELLERIA (I.)
MALTA
Kerkenna

MEDITERRANEAN SEA

GREECE
Irákleio
Chania
CRETE
RODOS (GR)

TURKEY
Antalya
Adana
Iskenderun
Halab (Aleppo)
Al-Lādhiqīyah
Hatay
Ḥamāh
Dayr az Zawr
Tudmur (Palmyra)
SYRIA
Ḥimṣ
Euphrates
Nicosia
NORTH CYPRUS
CYPRUS
Beirut
LEBANON
Damascus (Dimashq)
SYRIAN
IRAQ

Tripoli (Tarābulus)
Al Khums
Zlitan
Misrātah
Qaṣr Banī Walīd
Banghāzī
Zāwiyat al Bayḍā
Al Marj
Ṭūkrah
Darnah
AL JABAL AL AKHDAR
BARQAH (CYRENAICA)
Tubruq
Sīdī Barrānī
Sallūm
ALEXANDRIA (Al Iskandarīyah)
Dumyāṭ
Port Said
Haifa
Tel Aviv-Yafo
Jerusalem
ISRAEL
Ghazzah
JORDAN
Amman
Al Jawf
Tabūk
SAUDI
Buraydah
Ḥāʾil
AN NAFŪD
ARABIA
NAJD

Surt
Khalīj Surt
An Nawfalīyah
Ajdābiyā
Qaṣr al Burayqah
BULUS (TRIPOLITANIA)
Al Qaryah
Ash Shargīyah
Al ʿUqaylah
Marādah
Awjilah
Sawknah
Zillah
Zaltan
JABAL AS SAWDA
FEZZAN
IDEHAN MARZŪQ
Tarbū
Marzuq
Wāw al-Kabīr
Waḥat Jālū
Siwah (Oasis)
MUNKHAFAḌ AL QAṬṬĀRAH
-436
Al Jaghbūb
Al Fayyūm
Birket Qārūn
Banī Suwayf
Al Minyā
Al Alamayn
Marsā Maṭrūḥ
Al Bawīṭī
CAIRO (Al Qāhirah)
Suez (As Suways)
Az Zaqāzīq
Damanhūr
Tanta
Al Manṣūrah
SINAI PEN
Jabal Kātrīnā 8668
Gulf of Suez
Al ʿAqabah
Gulf of Aqaba
ARABIAN

LIBYAN DESERT (AS SAHRĀ AL LĪBĪYAH)
EGYPT
Qaṣr al Farāfirah
Asyūṭ
Sawhāj
Akhmīm
Qinā
Thebes (Ruins)
Al Uqsur (Luxor)
Idfū
Aswān
Aswān High Dam
RAʾS BANĀS
Bi ʾr Misāḥah
Ash Shabb
Lake Nasser
ADMINISTRATIVE BDY.
Halāʾib
Tāymā
Ḥāʾil
Al Wajh
Al Quṣayr
Yanbuʿ
Al Madīnah (Medina)
AL HIJAZ

SARĪR TIBESTI
Rebiana (Oasis)
Kufrah (Oasis)
Al Jawf
Maʾtan Bishārah
LIBYA
RED SEA
Jiddah
Mecca (Makkah)
Al Khurmah

Pic Toussidé 10 712
TIBESTI
Emi Koussi 11 204
BORKOU
Ounianga Kébir
Largeau
Fada
Yarda
ʿArbi
Koshu
Dalqū
Dunqulah
Abu Ḥamad
Būr Sūdān
NUBIAN DESERT
Jabal Erba 7 274
Al Qunfudhah
Abha
Jizan
JAZĀ IR FARASAN
DAHLAK ARCH.
KAMARAN

Al ʿAṭrūn
3rd Cataract
Al Khandaq
Kuraymah
4th Cataract
5th Cataract
Marawi
Kūrtī
ʿAtbarah
Sawākin
Tawkar
Ṭaqāṭū
Ḥayyā
Mifswa
Tassaw
Akordat
Keren
Asmera
ERITREA

Ounianga
Oum Chalouba
ENNEDI
Al Fāshir
Ad Dabbah
Barbar
Ad Dāmir
Adarama
Shandī
6th Cataract
Omdurman (Umm Durmān)
Al Kharṭūm Baḥri
Khartoum (Al Khartūm)
Kassalā
Sebderat
Barentu
Adi Ugri
Mersa Fatma
Al Ḥudaydah
YEMEN
Mukhā

Lake Chad
Lac Tchad
Mao
CHAD
SUDAN
KURDUFĀN
Ad Duwaym
Rufaʿah
Wad Madanī
Om Hajer
Ed
Abéché
DĀRFŪR
Jabal Marrah 10 131
An Nuhūd
Al Ubayyiḍ
Al Qaḍārif
Sannār
AN NUBA
JIBAL
Kūstī
Sinjah
Sennar Dam
Ar Ruṣayriṣ
Roseires Res.
Gonder
Tana 6004
Debre Tabor
Adwa
Makale
Sekota
DENAKIL
Djibouti
Tadjoura
DJIBOUTI
Ayshā
Zayla

OUADDAĪ
Yao
Nyala
An Nuhūd
Al Ujayyil
Babanūsah
Malūṭ
Kurmuk
Asosa
Dangila
Tala
Amba Farit 13 041
Debre Markos
Dese
Were Ilu
Dire Dawa
Harer
HARERGE

N'Djamena (Fort-Lamy)
MANDARA MTS
Maroua
Bousso
Chari
Am Timan
Bahr Salamat
Talawdī
Matakal
Kodok
Nāṣir
Tullu Welel 10 830
Dembi Dolo
Gore
Gambela
Blue Nile
Abay
Nekemte
ETHIOPIA
Nazret
Addis Ababa (Adis Abeba)
AHMAR MTS
Ziway
Goba
Ginir

Léré
Laï
Sarh
Bahr Aouk
Kaña Kingi
AS SUDD
Mashra'er Raqq
Bahr al Ghazal
Bahr al Jabal
Shambe
Pibor
Shwan Gimira
Jima
Shola
SIDAMO

CENTRAL AFRICAN REPUBLIC
Fort Sibut
Fort Crampel
Yalinga
Ndélé
CHAÎNE DES MONGOS
BAHR AL GHAZĀL
Rumbek
Bor
Tambura
Mongallə
Jūba
Maji
Chamo
Wendo
Goba

Koundé
Bouar
Bossangoa
Rafaï
Zémio
Gwane
Dungu
Arua
Kapoeta
Lake Rudolf (Lake Stefanie) +1230
Mega
Moyale
El Wak

Carnot
Bangui
Mbaiki
Zango
Libenge
Mobaye
Bangassou
Bondo
Bambesa
Niangara
Watsa
Kitgum
Nimule

Yokaduma
Lomié
Dongou
Quessa
Mbandaka
Makanza
Bomongo
Basankusu
Isangi
Kisangani (Stanleyville)
Boyoma Falls
DEMOCRATIC REPUBLIC OF THE CONGO
Panga
Buta
Gombari
Mahagi Port
L. Albert
Kabalega Falls
Masindi
Ft Portal
Margherita Peak 16 763
Kampala
Entebbe
Jinja
Lake Victoria
UGANDA
Soroti
Mbale
Mt. Elgon 14 178
Eldoret
KENYA
Meru
SOMALIA
Doolow

CONGO

Equator

Scale:
0 50 100 200 300 400 500 Miles
0 100 200 400 600 800 Kilometers

Scale 1:16 000 000; one inch to 250 miles. Sinusoidal Projection
Elevations and depressions are given in feet

b

Continued on main map of Africa

EUROPE

ASIA

AFRICA

Location of area shown on the map

Scale 1:16 000 000; one inch to 250 miles.

c

Relief

Meters		Feet
3050		10 000
1525		5000
610		2000
305		1000
152.5		500
0	Sea Level	0
152.5		500
1525		5000
3050		10 000

Scale 1:4 000 000

0 10 20 30 40 Miles

0 10 20 30 40 50 60 Kilometers

Asia

Covering nearly one-third of the Earth's land surface, Asia is by far the largest of the seven continents. It is a land of extremes and dramatic physical contrasts, containing nearly every type of landform, and many of them on a vast scale. It boasts the world's lowest point (the Dead Sea), its highest point (Mt. Everest), its highest and largest plateau (the Plateau of Tibet), and its largest inland body of water (the Caspian Sea).

Wide belts of mountain systems cover much of Asia. The Himalayas, which form a great 1,500-mile (2,400-km) arc south of Tibet, are the highest mountains in the world: more than 90 Himalayan peaks rise above 24,000 feet (7,320 m).

The beginnings of civilization can be traced to three distinct areas of Asia: Mesopotamia, around 4000 BC; the Indus River valley, around 3000 BC; and China, around 2000 BC. Eight of the world's major religions—Buddhism, Christianity, Confucianism, Hinduism, Islam, Judaism, Shinto, and Taoism—originated in Asia.

Asia at a glance

Land area:
17,300,000 square miles
(44,900,000 sq km)

Estimated population
(January 1, 1995): 3,422,700,000

Population density:
198/square mile (76/sq km)

Mean elevation: 3,000 feet
(910 m)

Highest point: Mt. Everest,
China (Tibet)-Nepal, 29,028
feet (8,848 m)

Lowest point: Dead Sea,
Israel-Jordan, 1,339 feet
(408 m) below sea level

Longest river: Yangtze
(Chang), 3,900 mi (6,300 km)

Number of countries
(incl. dependencies): 50

Largest independent country:
Russia (Europe/Asia),
6,592,849 square miles
(17,075,400 sq km)

Smallest independent country:
Maldives, 115 square miles
(298 sq km)

**Most populous independent
country:** China, 1,196,980,000

**Least populous independent
country:** Maldives, 251,000

Largest city: Seoul, South
Korea, pop. 10,627,790 (1990)

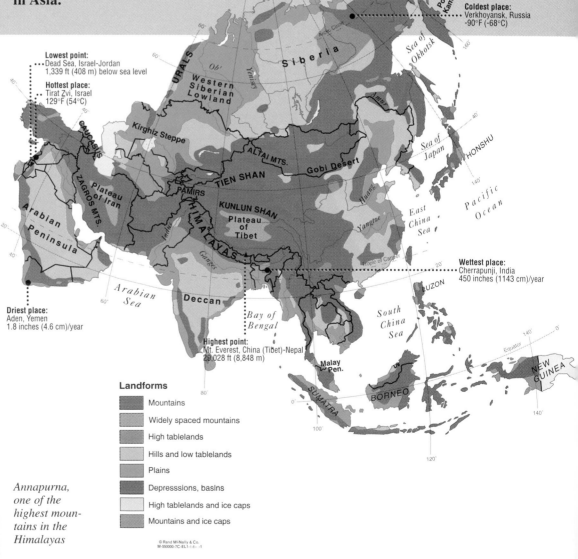

Coldest place:
Verkhoyansk, Russia
-90°F (-68°C)

Lowest point:
Dead Sea, Israel-Jordan
1,339 ft (408 m) below sea level

Hottest place:
Tirat Zvi, Israel
129°F (54°C)

Wettest place:
Cherrapunji, India
450 inches (1143 cm)/year

Driest place:
Aden, Yemen
1.8 inches (4.6 cm)/year

Highest point:
Mt. Everest, China (Tibet)-Nepal
29,028 ft (8,848 m)

Landforms

- Mountains
- Widely spaced mountains
- High tablelands
- Hills and low tablelands
- Plains
- Depresssions, basins
- High tablelands and ice caps
- Mountains and ice caps

© Rand McNally & Co.
M-550000-7C-EL1-1-1- -1

Annapurna, one of the highest mountains in the Himalayas

Climate

Climates vary greatly across Asia. In much of Siberia, temperatures average below -5°F (-20°C) in January, while the Persian Gulf region endures summer temperatures as high as 122°F (50°C). Monsoons interrupt hot dry spells with much-needed rain along the southeast and Indian Ocean coasts during the summer months. Between these extremes, almost every other type of climate on Earth can be found in Asia.

This climatic diversity can be explained by the continent's great expanse, from the Arctic to the tropics, and its great range in elevations.

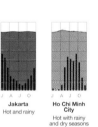

Tinted areas show temperature in degrees Fahrenheit. Vertical bars show precipitation in inches.

Jakarta	Ho Chi Minh City	Tehran	Riyadh	Beirut	Shanghai	Shenyang	Novosibirsk	Tomsk	Chokurdakh	Extensive uplands
Hot and rainy	Hot with rainy and dry seasons	Semiarid	Very dry	Hot, dry summer / mild, rainy winter	Warm, humid summer / cold, mild winter	Warm, humid summer / cold, snowy winter	Cool, humid summer / cold, snowy winter	Short, cool, humid summer / very cold, snowy winter	Cold and dry	Climate varies with elevation and latitude

Population

With 3.4 billion people, Asia is nearly five times as populous as any other continent and is home to six out of every ten people in the world. If its current 2% annual growth rate continues, Asia's population will double by the year 2030. The continent contains the two most populous countries in the world, China and India, as well as the most populous metropolitan area, Tōkyō-Yokohama, Japan.

Great concentrations of people are found in India, eastern China, Japan, Vietnam, and on the Indonesian island of Java. In contrast, vast stretches of northern Siberia, Mongolia, western China, and the Arabian Peninsula are only sparsely populated. Numerous desert regions, including Arabia's Rub' al Khālī and China's Takla Makān, are uninhabited.

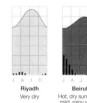

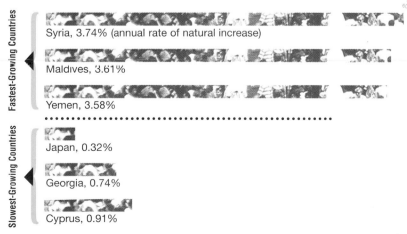

Fastest-Growing Countries
Syria, 3.74% (annual rate of natural increase)
Maldives, 3.61%
Yemen, 3.58%

Slowest-Growing Countries
Japan, 0.32%
Georgia, 0.74%
Cyprus, 0.91%

Inhabitants per sq. km. (mi.)
- Uninhabited
- <1 (2)
- 1-10 (2-25)
- 10-25 (25-60)
- 25-50 (60-125)
- 50-100 (125-250)
- >100 (250)

Environments and Land Use

Despite rapid industrialization in Japan, Korea, and Singapore, feeding the enormous and fast-growing population remains Asia's primary economic focus. In China, India, and Indonesia, two-thirds of the work force is engaged in farming. Where arable land exists, it is generally cultivated intensively. Rice is the most commonly grown crop: the continent produces more than 90% of the world's total. Other important crops include wheat, sorghum, millet, maize, and barley.

Asia's major agricultural regions are found in the fertile alluvial valleys, floodplains, and deltas of some of its greatest rivers, such as the Ganges and Brahmaputra in northern India, the Indus in Pakistan, the Huang (Yellow) and Yangtze in eastern China, the Irawaddy in Myanmar (Burma), the Mekong in Cambodia and Vietnam, and the Tigris and Euphrates in Iraq.

Tundra vegetation prevails across the arctic and subarctic regions of Siberia. Farther south, much of the land is densely forested. Deforestation, however, is rampant across the continent. In the colder central and northern areas, whole forests have been cut down to provide wood for heat and cooking. The tropical rain forests of the Indochina Peninsula, Malaysia, Indonesia, and the Philippines are rapidly being destroyed for their valuable hardwood, especially teak.

A wide sweep of semiarid grasslands across Central Asia covers one-quarter of the continent. These immense grazing lands are used by the people of many countries—notably Kazakstan and Mongolia—for livestock that include almost one-third of the world's cattle, nearly three-fifths of its goats, and half of its pigs. In recent decades, the tremendous petroleum reserves located in the arid west, around the Persian Gulf, have been both a source of wealth and a cause of turmoil. The continent also has less exploited, but sizable reserves of natural gas in Siberia and coal in China.

Urban
Cropland
Cropland and woodland
Cropland and grazing land
Grassland, grazing land
Forest, woodland
Swamp, marsh
Tundra
Shrub, sparse grass, wasteland
Barren land

© Rand McNally & Co.
M-560000-8L-EL1- - - -1

Harvesting rice from terraced paddies in China's Yunnan province

Asia's Economic Crisis

During the 1980s, economic growth was explosive for the countries of eastern Asia, sometimes referred to as the "Asian Tigers." In fact, many experts predicted that the 21st century would be "the Asian Century"—a time when the Asian Tigers would come of age internationally and would assert their economic, political, and cultural influence around the world. These optimistic projections changed radically in 1997 when what at first seemed to be a minor economic problem in Thailand sparked a global economic crisis.

At the time of the crisis Asian countries were benefiting from a huge influx of investment capital from the West as well as from Japan, Asia's wealthiest country. Fueled by foreign investment, their economies were characterized by rapid economic growth and prosperity. On the surface they seemed to be flourishing, but in reality most of the Asian Tigers were burdened with heavily indebted corporations, inflated stock and property prices, overvalued currencies, and bad loans.

When Thailand experienced a currency crisis in July 1997, few people took notice. But within a few months economic decline had spread to South Korea, Taiwan, Hong Kong, Indonesia, the Philippines, and Malaysia. In some countries, such as South Korea, the crisis necessitated a restructuring of all financial and economic institutions. In Indonesia, the crisis erupted into social unrest that resulted in the loss of more than a thousand lives.

By mid-1998 the Japanese economy was crippled by the worst recession in that country since World War II, and the rest of the world held its breath to see if the economies of Western Europe and the United States would also falter. The Western economies held steady, and in early 1999 the economies of Japan, South Korea, and Hong Kong were beginning to show signs of recovery. Other countries with developing economies, such as Brazil and Russia, continue to suffer from the global repercussions of the Asian economic crisis.

Busy shopping district in Seoul, South Korea, prior to that country's economic collapse.

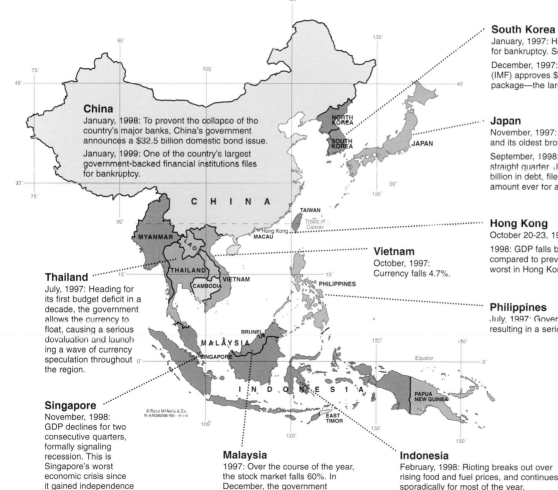

South Korea
January, 1997: Hanbo, a huge conglomerate, files for bankruptcy. Several others follow.
December, 1997: International Monetary Fund (IMF) approves $57 billion economic rescue package—the largest ever.

Japan
November, 1997: The country's 10th largest bank and its oldest brokerage house collapse.
September, 1998: Economy contracts for the third straight quarter. Japan Leasing Corp. with $16 billion in debt, files for bankruptcy—the largest amount ever for a corporate bankruptcy in Japan.

Hong Kong
October 20-23, 1997: Stock market falls 20%.
1998: GDP falls by 7% during third quarter compared to previous year. Recession is the worst in Hong Kong's history.

Philippines
July, 1997: Government allows currency to float, resulting in a serious devaluation.

China
January, 1998: To prevent the collapse of the country's major banks, China's government announces a $32.5 billion domestic bond issue.
January, 1999: One of the country's largest government-backed financial institutions files for bankruptcy.

Vietnam
October, 1997: Currency falls 4.7%.

Thailand
July, 1997: Heading for its first budget deficit in a decade, the government allows the currency to float, causing a serious devaluation and launching a wave of currency speculation throughout the region.

Singapore
November, 1998: GDP declines for two consecutive quarters, formally signaling recession. This is Singapore's worst economic crisis since it gained independence in 1965.

Malaysia
1997: Over the course of the year, the stock market falls 60%. In December, the government launches austerity measures.

Indonesia
February, 1998: Rioting breaks out over rising food and fuel prices, and continues sporadically for most of the year.

Scale 1:40 000 000; one inch to 630 miles. Lambert's Azimuthal, Equal Area Projection
Elevations and depressions are given in feet

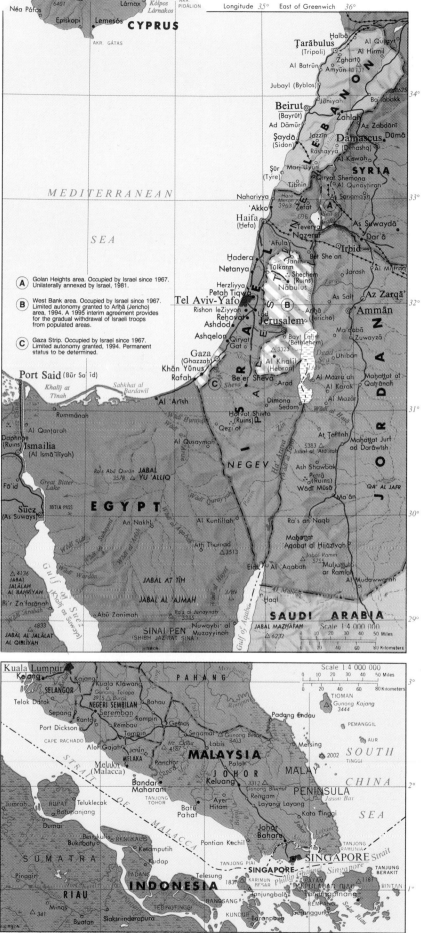

Relief

Meters		Feet
3050		10 000
1525		5000
610		2000
305		1000
0	Sea Level	0
152.5		500 Below
1525		5000 Sea Level
3050		10 000
6100		20 000

A-519695-76 1-20-21-44EL
COPYRIGHT BY
RAND McNALLY & COMPANY
MADE IN U.S.A.

Scale 1:40 000 000; one inch to 630 miles. Lambert's Azimuthal, Equal Area Projection
Elevations and depressions are given in feet

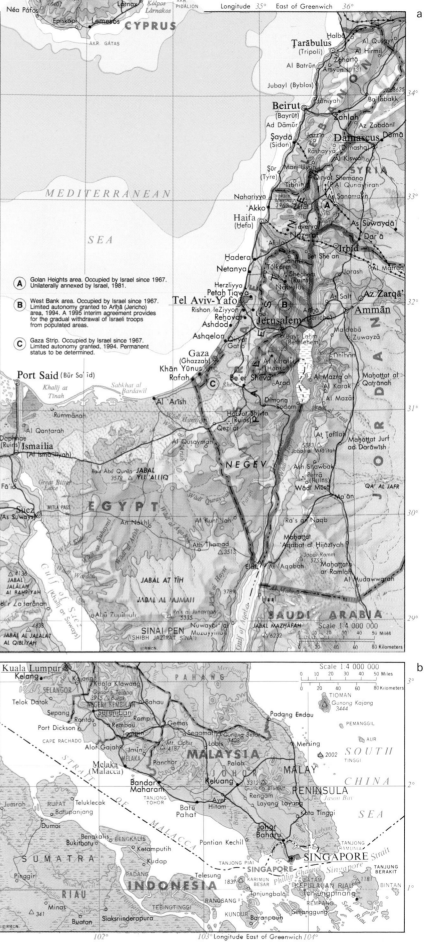

Ⓐ Golan Heights area. Occupied by Israel since 1967.
Unilaterally annexed by Israel, 1981.

Ⓑ West Bank area. Occupied by Israel since 1967.
Limited autonomy granted to Arīḥā (Jericho)
area, 1994. A 1995 interim agreement provides
for the gradual withdrawal of Israeli troops
from populated areas.

Ⓒ Gaza Strip. Occupied by Israel since 1967.
Limited autonomy granted, 1994. Permanent
status to be determined.

Scale 1:4 000 000

Scale 1:4 000 000

Cities and Towns

	0 to 50,000	o	500,000 to 1,000,000	⊚
	50,000 to 500,000	⊙	1,000,000 and over	∎

Scale 1:16 000 000; one inch to 250 miles Conic Projection
Elevations and depressions are given in feet.

SEVERNAYA ZEMLYA
(NORTHERN LAND)

MALYY TAIMYR

M.CHELYUSKIN

NOVOSIBIRSKIYE O-VA
(NEW SIBERIAN ISLANDS)

DE LONGA

NOVAYA SIBIR

FADDEYA

BEL'KOVSKIY

LYAKHOVSKIYE

MALYY
LYAKHOVSKIYE

VRANGELYA
WRANGEL

CHUKOTSKIY
P-OV

ANADYRSKIY
ZALIV

BYRRANGA
TAYMYR

KOTEL'NYY

STOLBOVOY

M SVYATOY
NOS

M SHELAGSKIY

AYON

Chaun
Guba

Arctic Circle

CHUKOTSKOYE NAGORYE

KORYAKSKIY KHREBET

KHATANGSKIY ZALIV
BOLSHOY
BEGICHEV

Nordvik

Ust'-Olenek

G. Sellya Khskaya

M BUOR
KHAYA

Tiksi

Kazach'ye

Ambarchik

Chaun

Medvezhi

Nizhne-Kolymsk

Arctic Circle

Amguema

Anadyr'

Thilichiki

KHATANGA

Anabar

Bulun

Sredne-
Kolymsk

Zaschiversk

Zyryanka

Omolon

Ust'-Penzhino

M. OLYUTORSKIY

Olenek

Olenek

Zhigansk

Verkhoyansk

Abyy

Luostakh

Oymyakon

Kolyma

Magadan

Penzhina

Gizhiga

KARAGIN

KHREBET KULAR

VERKHOYANSKIY KHREBET

KHREBET CHERSKOGO

Gora Chen
10,171

KHREBET GYDAN
(KOLYMSKIY)

ZALIV
SHELEKHOVA

POLUOSTROV

Marcha

Vilyuysk

YAKUTIA

Yakutsk

Aldan

Okhotsk

M. ALEVINA

KAMCHATKA

Verkhne-
Kamchatsk

Petropavlovsk-
Kamchatskiy

SAKHA

Suntar

Vilyuy

Olekminsk

Amga

Ust'-Maya

SEA OF
OKHOTSK

Kirensk

Mukhtuya

Tommot

DZHUGDZHUR KHREBET

Nel'kan

Ayan

Chumikan

SHANTAR

Ust'-Bol sheretsk

KURIL ISLANDS
(Russia)

PATOM
5577

G. Golets Purpula

PATOM
PLATEAU

Bodaybo

ALDAN
PLATEAU

Golets Skolistyy
9784

STANOVOY KHREBET

Nikolayevsk-
na-Amure

SAKHALIN
(Russia)

TATAR STRAIT

Okha

M TERPENIYA

Feleduy

Vitim

Nizhne-Angarsk

BURYATIA

Baley

Skovorodino

Beketova

Zeya

Aleksandrovsk

Uglegorsk

BAYKALSKIY KHREBET

Ozero
Baykal
Lake Baikal
Surface elev.1535 Ft.
above Sea Level

Barguzin

Chita

Nerchinsk

Nerchinskiy
Zavod

Zeya

Svobodnyy

Belogorsk

Komsomol'sk-
na-Amure

Sovetskaya
Gavan'

Poronaysk

Dolinsk

Yuzhno-Sakhalinsk

Ulan-Ude

Petrovsk-
Zabaykal'skiy

Sretensk

Ust'-Tyrma

Bureya

Khabarovsk

Kholmsk

Korsakov

YABLONOVYY KHREBET

Aginskoye

NERCHINSKIY KHREBET

MANCHURIAN RANGE

Zavitinsk

Raychikhinsk

Birobidzhan

SIKHOTE ALIN

Kyakhta

Aksha

Borzya

Blagoveshchensk

KHREBET BUREINSKIY

Dalnerechensk

HOKKAIDO

Sōya Kaikyō

SEA OF
JAPAN

Manzhouli

Hailar

GREATER KHINGAN RANGE

NEI MONGGOL

Goukou

Longzhen

LESSER KHINGAN RANGE

Ussuriysk KHREBET

Sōya Kaikyō

Choybalsan

Qiqihar

HEILUNGKIANG

Yitan

Spassk-Dal'niy

Olga

Arsen'yev

Suchan

Ulan Bator

Öndörhaan

Hulan

HARBIN

Sifenhou

Ning'an

Spassk-Dal'niy

Ussuriysk

Artëm

Nakhodka

Vladivostok

A-579300-76---11-9-21EL
COPYRIGHT BY
RAND McNALLY & COMPANY
MADE IN U.S.A.

Relief		
Meters		Feet
3050		10000
1525		5000
610		2000
305		1000
152.5		500
Sea Level		0
152.5		500
1525		5000
3050		10000

50 100   200   300   400   500 Miles

100   200   400   600   800 Kilometers

INDIA · POLITICAL

Scale 1:40.000.000

1-TRIPURA
2-MANIPUR
3-LAKSHADWEEP
4-DELHI
5-DĀDRA AND NAGAR HAVELI
6-PONDICHERRY
7-GOA, DAMĀN, AND DIU

Scale 1:4.000.000
0 10 20 30 40 Miles
0 20   40   60 Kilometers

A Area occupied by Pakistan and claimed by India.

B Area claimed and occupied by India; status disputed by Pakistan.

C Area occupied by China and claimed by India.

D Area occupied by India and claimed by China.

Same scale as main map

0 50 100 200 300 400 500 Miles
0 100 200 400 600 800 Kilometers

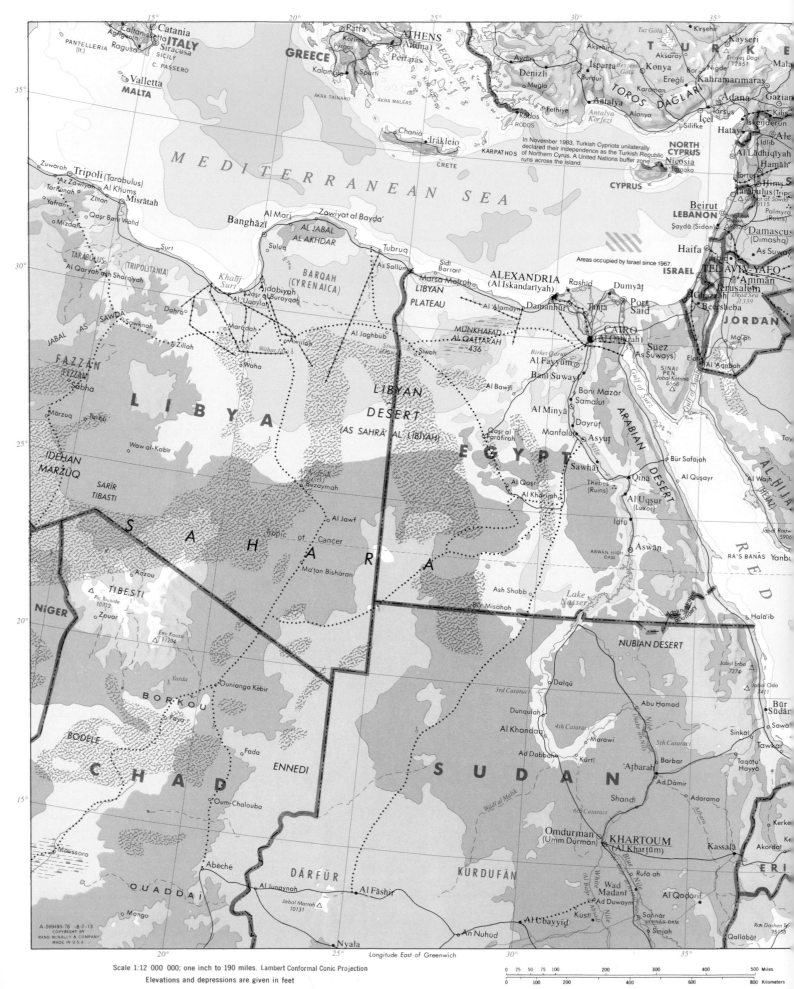

Scale 1:12 000 000; one inch to 190 miles. Lambert Conformal Conic Projection

Elevations and depressions are given in feet

0 25 50 75 100   200   300   400   500 Miles

0   100   200   400   600   800 Kilometers

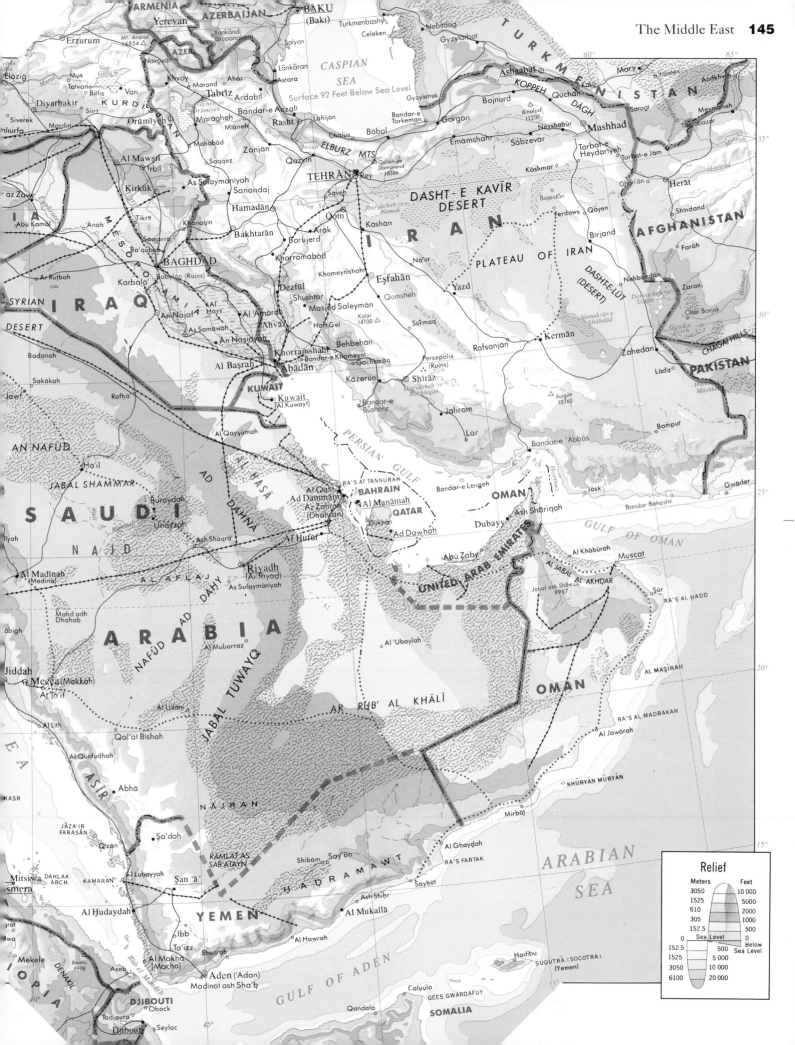

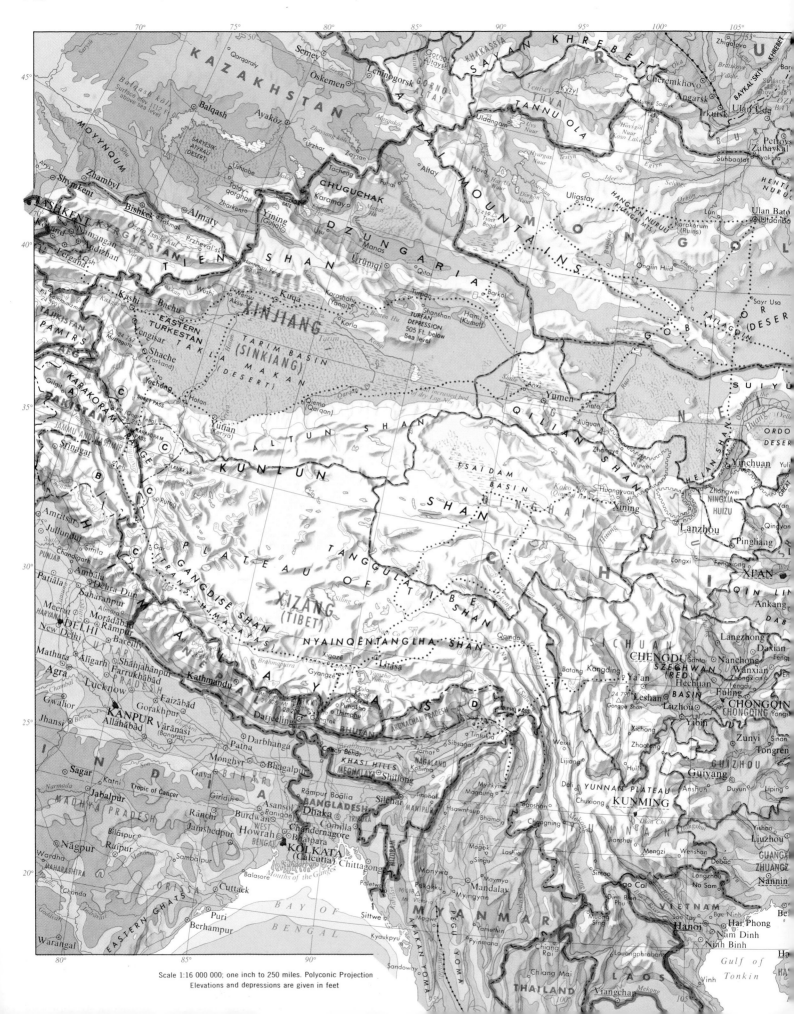

Scale 1:16 000 000; one inch to 250 miles. Polyconic Projection
Elevations and depressions are given in feet

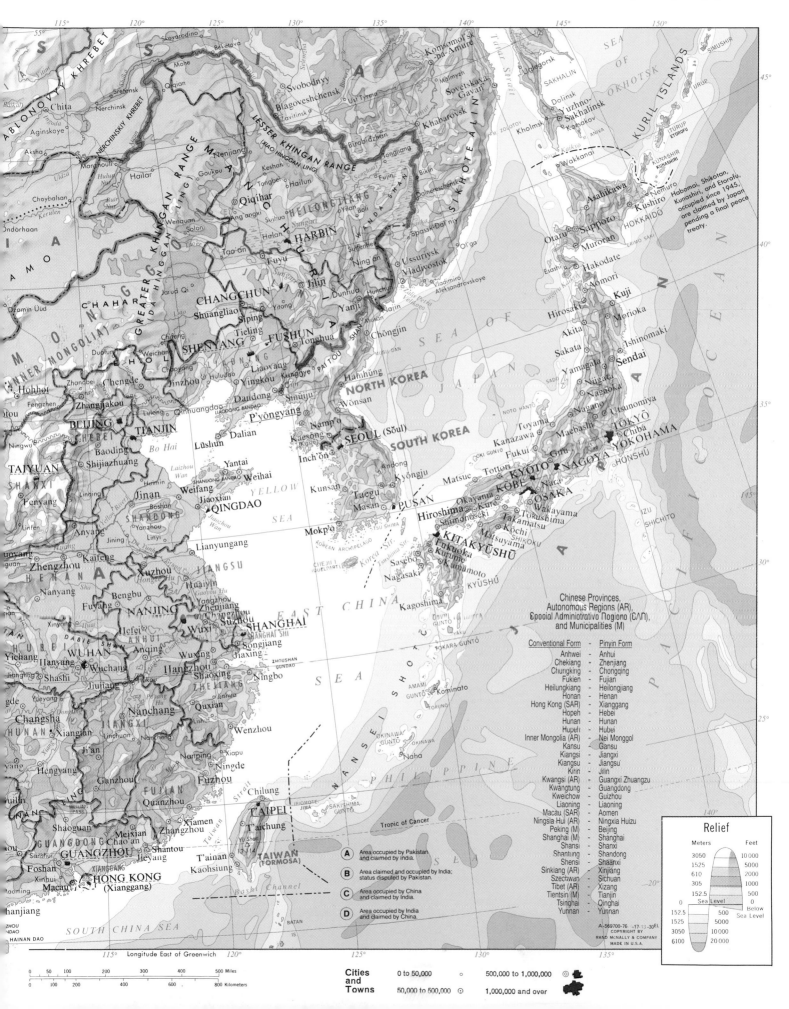

Chinese Provinces,
Autonomous Regions (AR),
Special Administrative Regions (SAR),
and Municipalities (M)

Conventional Form	Pinyin Form
Anhwei	Anhui
Chekiang	Zhenjiang
Chungking	Chongqing
Fukien	Fujian
Heilungkiang	Heilongjiang
Honan	Henan
Hong Kong (SAR)	Xianggang
Hopeh	Hebei
Hunan	Hunan
Hupeh	Hubei
Inner Mongolia (AR)	Nei Monggol
Kansu	Gansu
Kiangsi	Jiangxi
Kiangsu	Jiangsu
Kirin	Jilin
Kwangsi	Guangxi Zhuangzu
Kwangtung	Guangdong
Kweichow	Guizhou
Liaoning	Liaoning
Macau (SAR)	Aomen
Ningsia Hui (AR)	Ningxia Huizu
Peking (M)	Beijing
Shanghai (M)	Shanghai
Shansi	Shanxi
Shantung	Shandong
Shensi	Shaanxi
Sinkiang (AR)	Xinjiang
Szechwan	Sichuan
Tibet (AR)	Xizang
Tientsin (M)	Tianjin
Tsinghai	Qinghai
Yunnan	Yunnan

A Area occupied by Pakistan and claimed by India.

B Area claimed and occupied by India; status disputed by Pakistan.

C Area occupied by China and claimed by India.

D Area occupied by India and claimed by China.

Habomai, Shikotan, Kunashiri, and Etorofu, occupied since 1945, are claimed by Japan pending a final peace treaty.

Relief

Meters	Feet
3050	10 000
1525	5000
610	2000
305	1000
152.5	500
0 Sea Level	Below Sea Level
152.5	500
1525	5000
3050	10 000
6100	20 000

Cities and Towns

0 to 50,000	○
50,000 to 500,000	⊙
500,000 to 1,000,000	◉
1,000,000 and over	■

Longitude East of Greenwich

0 50 100 200 300 400 500 Miles
0 100 200 400 600 800 Kilometers

A-569700-76 -17-13-30EL
COPYRIGHT BY
RAND McNALLY & COMPANY
MADE IN U.S.A.

Relief

Meters	Feet
3050	10 000
1525	5000
610	2000
305	1000
152.5	500
Sea Level	
152.5	500
1525	5000
3050	10 000
6100	20 000

A-569800-76 -11-11-32
COPYRIGHT BY
RAND McNALLY & COMPANY
MADE IN U.S.A.

Scale 1:16 000 000; one inch to 250 miles. Polyconic Projection
Elevations and depressions are given in feet

Oceania (including Australia and New Zealand)

Oceania is comprised of Australia, New Zealand, eastern New Guinea, and approximately 25,000 other islands in the South Pacific, most of which are uninhabited. Many of the islands are coral atolls, formed by microscopic creatures over scores of centuries, while others are the result of volcanic action.

Bay of Islands, North Island, New Zealand

Oceania's largest landmass is Australia, which at three million square miles (7.7 million sq km) is the world's smallest continent. In fact, it is smaller than five countries—Russia, Canada, China, Brazil, and the United States. Australia is generally flat and dry. The interior is sparsely populated, with most people living in coastal cities such as Sydney.

The next-largest part of Oceania is Papua New Guinea, the country occupying the eastern half of the island of New Guinea, which has some of the most forbidding and remote terrain in the world. New Zealand, Oceania's third-largest country, is known for its natural beauty and its huge herds of sheep.

Oceania at a glance

Land area: 3,300,000 square miles (8,500,000 sq km)

Estimated population (January 1, 1995): 28,400,000

Population density: 8.6/square mile (3.3/sq km)

Mean elevation: 1,000 feet (305 m)

Highest point: Mt. Wilhelm, Papua New Guinea, 14,793 feet (4,509 m)

Lowest point: Lake Eyre, South Australia, 52 feet (16 m) below sea level

Longest river: Murray-Darling, 2,330 mi (3,750 km)

Number of countries (incl. dependencies): 33

Largest independent country: Australia, 2,966,155 square miles (7,682,300 sq km)

Smallest independent country: Nauru, 8.1 square miles (21 sq km)

Most populous independent country: Australia, 18,205,000

Least populous independent country: Tuvalu, 10,000

Largest city: Brisbane, pop. 1,334,017 (1991)

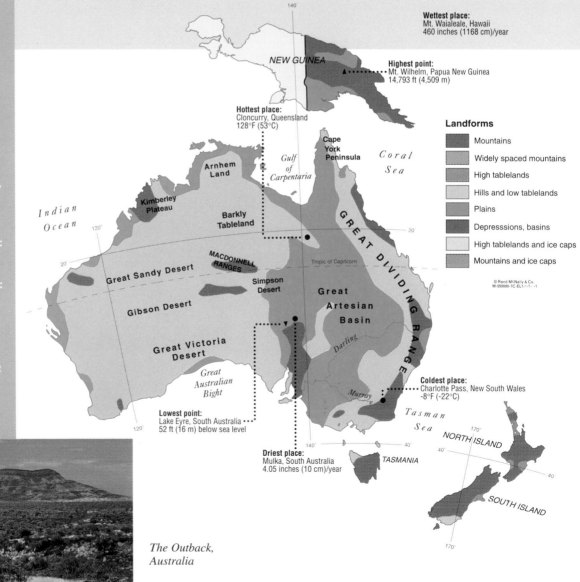

Wettest place:
Mt. Waialeale, Hawaii
460 inches (1168 cm)/year

Highest point:
Mt. Wilhelm, Papua New Guinea
14,793 ft (4,509 m)

Hottest place:
Cloncurry, Queensland
128°F (53°C)

Landforms
- Mountains
- Widely spaced mountains
- High tablelands
- Hills and low tablelands
- Plains
- Depresssions, basins
- High tablelands and ice caps
- Mountains and ice caps

© Rand McNally & Co.
M-550000-7C-EL1-1-1- -1

NEW GUINEA

Cape York Peninsula

Coral Sea

Gulf of Carpentaria

Arnhem Land

Kimberley Plateau

Indian Ocean

Barkly Tableland

GREAT DIVIDING RANGE

MACDONNELL RANGES

Great Sandy Desert

Tropic of Capricorn

Simpson Desert

Great Artesian Basin

Gibson Desert

Darling

Great Victoria Desert

Coldest place:
Charlotte Pass, New South Wales
-8°F (-22°C)

Great Australian Bight

Murray

Tasman Sea

Lowest point:
Lake Eyre, South Australia
52 ft (16 m) below sea level

NORTH ISLAND

Driest place:
Mulka, South Australia
4.05 inches (10 cm)/year

TASMANIA

SOUTH ISLAND

The Outback, Australia

Climate

A hot, dry desert climate prevails in central and western Australia, where summer temperatures regularly rise above 100°F (40°C). Toward the continent's northern, southern, and eastern coasts, the climate becomes more temperate and less arid. Southeastern Australia and New Zealand enjoy a milder, rainier climate similar to that of the Pacific Northwest of the United States. New Guinea, which has a tropical rain forest climate, experiences heavy rainfall and high temperatures throughout the year. Equatorial warmth and moderating tradewinds combine to make tropical paradises of many of Oceania's islands.

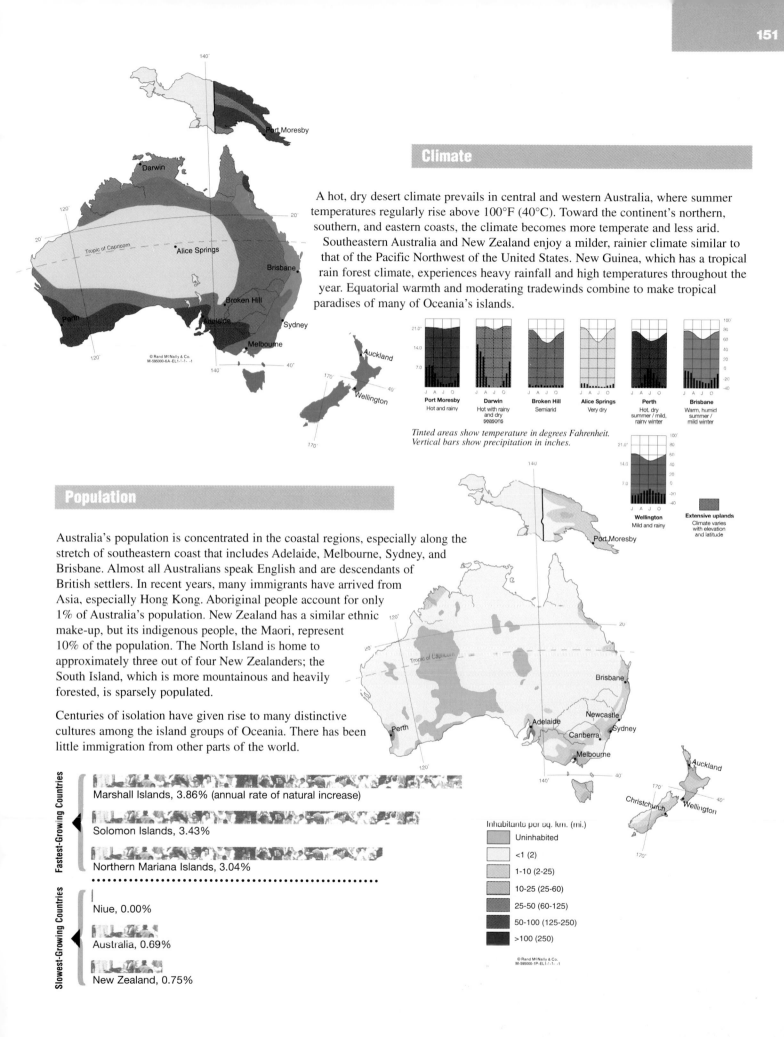

Port Moresby — Hot and rainy

Darwin — Hot with rainy and dry seasons

Broken Hill — Semiarid

Alice Springs — Very dry

Perth — Hot, dry summer / mild, rainy winter

Brisbane — Warm, humid summer / mild winter

Wellington — Mild and rainy

Tinted areas show temperature in degrees Fahrenheit. Vertical bars show precipitation in inches.

Extensive uplands — Climate varies with elevation and latitude

Population

Australia's population is concentrated in the coastal regions, especially along the stretch of southeastern coast that includes Adelaide, Melbourne, Sydney, and Brisbane. Almost all Australians speak English and are descendants of British settlers. In recent years, many immigrants have arrived from Asia, especially Hong Kong. Aboriginal people account for only 1% of Australia's population. New Zealand has a similar ethnic make-up, but its indigenous people, the Maori, represent 10% of the population. The North Island is home to approximately three out of four New Zealanders; the South Island, which is more mountainous and heavily forested, is sparsely populated.

Centuries of isolation have given rise to many distinctive cultures among the island groups of Oceania. There has been little immigration from other parts of the world.

Fastest-Growing Countries

Marshall Islands, 3.86% (annual rate of natural increase)

Solomon Islands, 3.43%

Northern Mariana Islands, 3.04%

Slowest-Growing Countries

Niue, 0.00%

Australia, 0.69%

New Zealand, 0.75%

Inhabitants per sq. km. (mi.)

- Uninhabited
- <1 (2)
- 1-10 (2-25)
- 10-25 (25-60)
- 25-50 (60-125)
- 50-100 (125-250)
- >100 (250)

© Rand McNally & Co.
M-595000-1P-EL1-1-1- -1

Environments and Land Use

Much of central and western Australia is a dry, inhospitable land of sand, rocks, and scrub vegetation. Surrounding this desert region is a broad band of semiarid grassland that covers more than half of the continent and supports a huge livestock industry. Australia has more sheep—132 million—than any other country in the world, as well as sizable herds of cattle. The dry climate and sparse plant life, however, mean that each animal requires a dozen or more acres to survive. Six percent of the continent is suitable for crops; most of the arable land is found on fertile plains in the southeast. Major crops include wheat, sugar cane, oats, barley, sorghum, and rice.

Farmland on North Island, New Zealand

Tourism plays an important role in Australia's economy. Among the continent's major attractions are its unusual wildlife, such as kangaroos, koalas, wombats, and platypuses; the Great Barrier Reef, which stretches for 1,250 miles (2,100 km) along the northeastern coast; and the ruggedly beautiful Outback, with its dramatic rock formations such as Ayers Rock (Uluru) and the Olga Rocks.

Thanks to its fertile land and temperate climate, New Zealand has a thriving livestock industry and is a leading world exporter of dairy products and lamb. Thinly populated and with little industry, it is one of the world's least polluted countries. Its pristine beauty encompasses a variety of scenery, including mountains, fjords, glaciers, rain forests, beaches and geysers. Only the country's relative isolation restrains its growing tourism industry.

Dense tropical rain forests blanket much of Papua New Guinea. These forests have thus far escaped the large-scale deforestation that is taking place in other tropical forests around the world.

Tourism is central to the economies of many of the islands throughout Oceania. Abundant sunshine, pleasant temperatures, and beautiful beaches draw millions of visitors each year to islands such as Tahiti and Fiji. For islands with little or no tourism, the economic scene is less promising: many islanders rely on subsistence fishing and foreign aid from former colonial powers.

Map labels:

NEW GUINEA
Darwin
Gulf of Carpentaria
Coral Sea
Indian Ocean
Great Sandy Desert
Gibson Desert
Great Victoria Desert
Great Artesian Basin
GREAT DIVIDING RANGE
Tropic of Capricorn
Brisbane
Perth
Great Australian Bight
Adelaide
Sydney
Tasman Sea
Melbourne
TASMANIA
NORTH ISLAND
Auckland
SOUTH ISLAND

Legend:

- Urban
- Cropland
- Cropland and woodland
- Cropland and grazing land
- Grassland, grazing land
- Forest, woodland
- Swamp, marsh
- Tundra
- Shrub, sparse grass, wasteland
- Barren land

0 100 200 300 400 500 Miles
0 200 400 600 800 Kilometers

© Rand McNally & Co.
M-590200-8L-EL1-1-1- -1

Herding sheep near Goulburn, New South Wales

The Original Australians and New Zealanders

Many anthropologists believe that Australia's Aborigines are the oldest race of people on Earth. During the 40,000 years since they migrated to the island continent from Asia, they have developed a rich culture with an intricate spiritual and social life.

The original New Zealanders, the Maoris, arrived from other Polynesian islands in the 10th century. At the beginning of large-scale immigration from Britain in the 1800s, the British government signed a treaty with the Maoris which granted them full rights as citizens. With the exception of some disputes over land, this agreement has paved the way for the historically harmonious relations between the races in New Zealand.

Aboriginal boy with elders, Western Australia

Relations between the Aborigines and whites in Australia have been less harmonious. The arrival of the first European colonists in 1788 set in motion a chain of events that decimated the Aborigines and threatened their unique culture. Disease and skirmishes killed Aborigines along the coast, and thousands of others were forced from their lands by settlers. Some sought refuge with Aborigines already living in Australia's interior, the Outback. Alcoholism and other social problems became common among the Aborigines as they found themselves confronted by a society they did not understand.

Australia was slow to recognize the rights of its first inhabitants. In the early 1960s, official attitudes began to change as public embarrassment grew over the decades of discrimination. A significant step occurred in 1962 when full rights of citizenship were extended to the Aborigines.

Questions of land ownership, however, remain problematic for both

Lands of Australia's Aborigines

Aboriginal reserves

© Rand McNally & Co.
M-595000-3R-EL1-1-1-   -1

sides. The government has set aside large reserves for the Aborigines, but much of the land is in the continent's hostile interior (see map above). Only in the past two decades has an agreement been reached allowing Aborigines to share in the vast mineral wealth of their northern lands. Recent court decisions have awarded individual Aborigines rights to ancestral lands which were seized by settlers, but many local governments continue to fight these decisions.

In the face of indifference and hostility, there has recently been an upsurge of interest in cultural traditions among the 240,000 Australians of aboriginal descent. Still, many of the traditions of the 500 different tribes that were present 200 years ago have been lost.

INDONESIA

Pasuruan
17 932
G: Mahameru
12 060

Singaraja Rinjani
Selat
Besar Rabbo
LOMBOK
SUMBAWA
Waingapu
SUMBA
SAWU
ROTI
Kupang
FLORES
LOMBLEN PANTAR
Alor
Dili
TIMOR
EAST TIMOR
(UN Admin.)

S U N D A I S L A N D S

SAVU
SEA

SELARU
TANJUNG VALS

A R A F U R A   S E A

S U N D A

SUNDA TRENCH

T I M O R   S E A

C. VAN DIEMEN
Van Diemen
Gulf
BATHURST
MELVILLE
CROKER
COBOURG PEN.
Darwin
Clarence Str.
Dundas
WESSEL IS.
CAPE ARNHEM
Blue Mud Bay
GROOTE
EYLANDT
GULF OF
CARPENTAR

I N D I A N

O C E A N

CAPE
LONDONDERRY
Joseph
Bonaparte Gulf
Anson Bay
Queen's
Chan.
ARNHEM LAND
Pine Creek
Katherine
Daly
Roper
Limmen
Bight
SIR EDWARD PELLEW
GROUP
WELLESLE

Wyndham
Mt. Hann
2800
KING LEOPOLD RANGES
Victoria River
Downs
Birdum
Daly Waters
Borroloola
BARKLY TABLELAND
Burketown

BUCCANEER   ARCH.
CAPE LEVEQUE
Sunday
ARCH.
King
DAMPIER
LAND
Broome
Derby
GEIKE
RANGE
Fitzroy
Crossing
Halls Creek
Newcastle Waters
Dobby
Camooweal

Roebuck Bay
LaGrange
Fitzroy
Stur
N O R T H E R N
Tanami
Tennant Creek
Mount Isa
Dajarin

EIGHTY MILE BEACH
LARREY POINT
DeGrey
RIPON
T E R R I T O R Y
Barrow Creek
Q U E

GREAT SANDY DESERT
Maekay
Q U

DAMPIER
ARCH.
Port Hedland
Roebourne
Marble Bar
Nullagine
Mt. Ziel
4955
RANGES
Arltunga
Hay

MONTE BELLO IS.
BARROW
Fortescue
Ashburton
Millstream
Onslow
HAMERSLEY RANGE
MT. Bruce
4052
Jiggalong
Macdonald
Amadeus
MACDONNELL
JAMES RANGE
Alice Springs
SIMPSON

NORTH WEST CAPE
Disappointment
GIBSON DESERT
Uluru
(Ayers Rock)
Finke
Charlotte
Waters
DESERT
Birdsville

POINT CLOATES
W E S T E R N
MUSGRAVE RANGES
Mt. Woodroffe
4724

Tropic of Capricorn
CAPE FARQUHAR
Geographe Chan.
Carnarvon
Gascoyne
Peak Hill
Carnegie
Wells
Gillen
EVERARD RANGES
The Alberga
Oodnadatta

BERNIER
DORRE
Shark Bay
Nabberu
S O U T H   A U S T R A L I A
Eyre

DIRK HARTOG
STEEP POINT
Meekatharra
Nannine
Cue
Wiluna
Yeo
STUART RANGE
William Creek
Marree

Ajana
Mount
Magnet
Sandstone
Laverton
A U S T R A L I A
Oodea Station
Torrens
Farina
Woomera
Parachil

HOUTMAN ROCKS
Northampton
Austin
Mingenew
Moore
Barlee
Menzies
Carey
GREAT VICTORIA DESERT
Hughes
Penong
Ceduna
Pimba
Whyalla
Port Pirie
FLINDERS RANGES
FLIN

Geraldton
Dongara
Pithara
Miling
Mogra
Lake Brown
Southern Cross
Kalgoorlie-Boulder
Coolgardie
Rawlinna
NULLARBOR   PLAIN
Eucla
POINT FOWLER
Whyalla
Port Augusta
Gladstone

DARLING   RANGE
SWANLAND
Norseman
Dundas
Cowan
Eyre
GREAT AUSTRALIAN BIGHT
Port Lincoln
EYRE
PENINSULA
Moonta
Port Wake
Gawle
Ade

Perth
Fremantle
Northam
York
Narrogin
Ravensthorpe
Salmon Gums
Esperance
KANGAROO

Collie
Bunbury
Busselton
Katanning
Hopetoun
ARCHIPELAGO
OF THE RECHERCHE
Nar
Kingst
CAPE JAFFA

CAPE NATURALISTE
Geographe Bay
Narrogin
CAPE LEEUWIN
Northalup
Albany
PT. D'ENTRECASTEAUX
WEST CAPE HOWE
King George Sd.
Mt. G

I N D I A N   O C E A N

40,000 SQ MI
AREA

0   100   200
Miles

A-590200-26
COPYRIGHT BY
RAND MCNALLY & COMPANY
MADE IN U.S.A.

Longitude 115°   East of Greenwich

Scale 1:16 000 000; one inch to 250 miles. Lambert's Azimuthal, Equal Area Projectio
Elevations and depressions are given in feet

Same scale as main map

| Cities and Towns | 0 to 50,000 | ○ | 500,000 to 1,000,000 | ◎ |
| | 50,000 to 500,000 | ⊙ | 1,000,000 and over | |

0 50 100 200 300 400 500 Miles

0 100 200 400 600 800 Kilometers

Relief

Meters		Feet
3050		10 000
1525		5000
610		2000
305		1000
152.5		500
0	Sea Level	0
152.5		500	Below
1525		5000	Sea Level
3050		10 000
6100		20 000

A-590200-76 6-5-17EL
COPYRIGHT BY
RAND McNALLY & COMPANY
MADE IN U.S.A.

Longitude 115°   East of Greenwich

Scale 1:16 000 000; one inch to 250 miles. Lambert's Azimuthal, Equal Area Projection
Elevations and depressions are given in feet

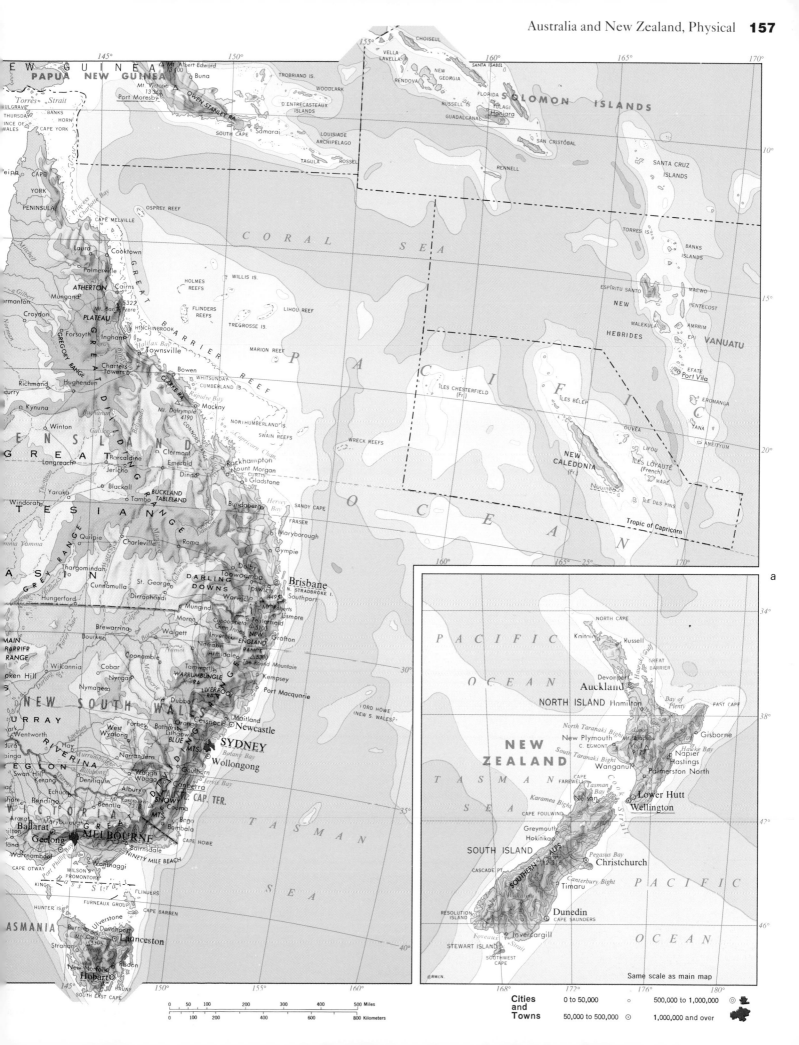

Relief

Meters		Feet
3050		10 000
1525		5000
610		2000
305		1000
152.5		500
0	Sea Level	0
152.5		500
1525		5000
3050		10 000
6100		20 000

A-598500-76 -11-27
COPYRIGHT BY
RAND McNALLY & COMPANY
MADE IN U.S.A.

Warm ocean currents
Cold ocean currents

Scale 1:50 000 000; one inch to 800 miles. Goode's Homolosine Equal Area Projection
Elevations and depressions are given in feet

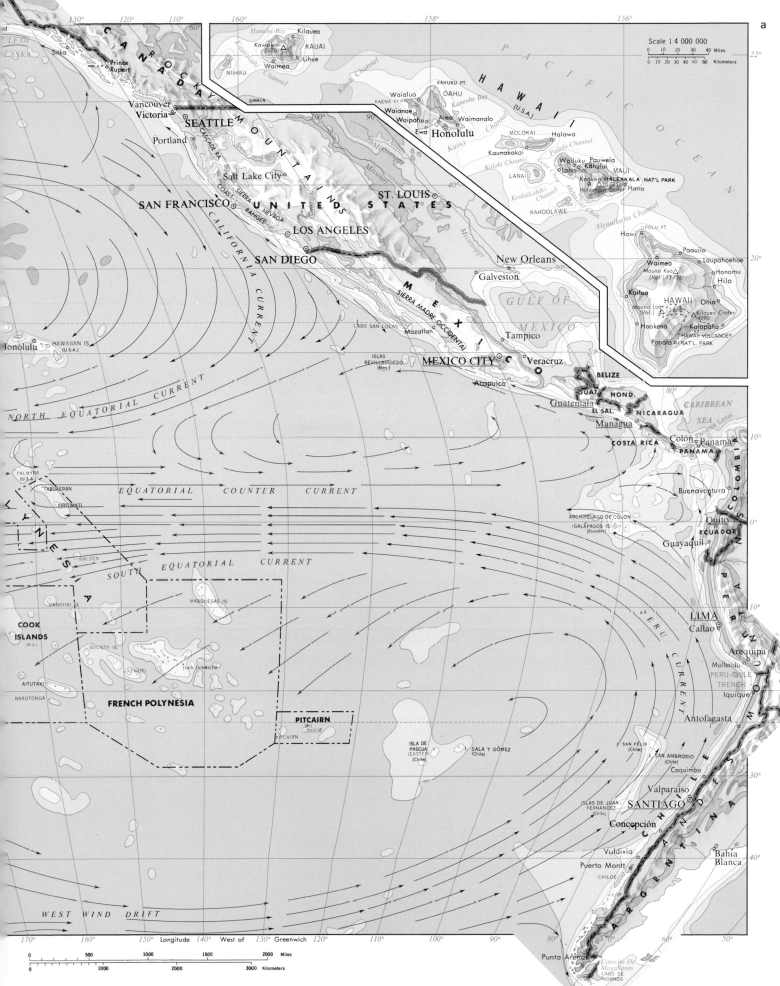

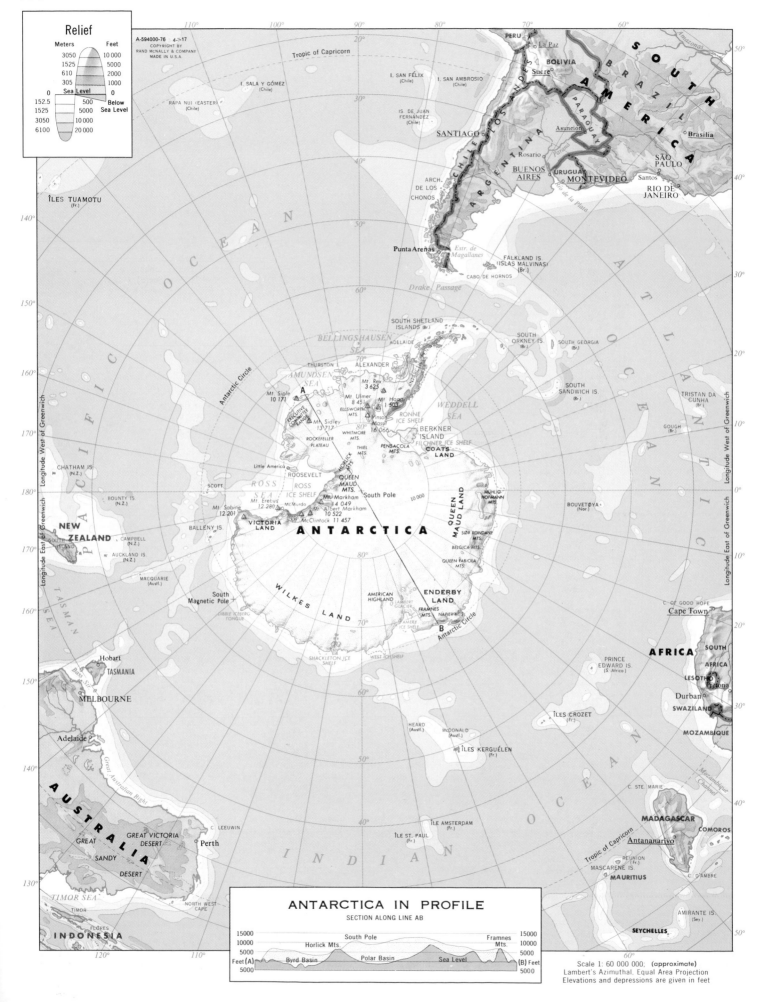

Relief

Meters		Feet
3050		10 000
1525		5000
610		2000
305		1000
0	Sea Level	0
152.5		500
		Below
1525		5000 Sea Level
3050		10 000
6100		20 000

A-594000-76 4-7-17
COPYRIGHT BY
RAND McNALLY & COMPANY
MADE IN U.S.A.

ANTARCTICA IN PROFILE
SECTION ALONG LINE AB

Scale 1: 60 000 000; (approximate)
Lambert's Azimuthal, Equal Area Projection
Elevations and depressions are given in feet

Glossary
Foreign Geographical Terms

Afk. ...... Afrikaans
Ara. ...... Arabic
Ber. ...... Berber
Blg. ...... Bulgarian
Bur. ...... Burmese
Cbd. ...... Cambodian
Ch. ...... Chinese
Czech ...... Czech
Dan. ...... Danish
Du. ...... Dutch
Est. ...... Estonian
Finn. ...... Finnish
Fr. ...... French
Gae. ...... Gaelic
Ger. ...... German
Gr. ...... Greek
Heb. ...... Hebrew
Ice. ...... Icelandic
Indon. ...... Indonesian
It. ...... Italian
Jpn. ...... Japanese
Kor. ...... Korean
Lao. ...... Laotian
Lapp. ...... Lappish
Mal. ...... Malay
Mong. ...... Mongolian
Nor. ...... Norwegian
Pas. ...... Pashto
Per. ...... Persian
Pol. ...... Polish
Port. ...... Portuguese
Rom. ...... Romanian
Rus. ...... Russian
S./C. ...... Serbo-Croatian
Slo. ...... Slovak
Sp. ...... Spanish
Swe. ...... Swedish
Thai ...... Thai
Tib. ...... Tibetan
Tur. ...... Turkish
Ukr. ...... Ukranian
Viet. ...... Vietnamese

-å, Dan., Nor., Swe. ...... river
āb, Per. ...... river
ada(lar), Tur. ...... island(s)
adrar, Ber. ...... mountains
ákra, akrotírion, Gr. ...... cape
altos, Sp. ...... mountains, hills
-älv,-älven, Swe. ...... river
-ån, Swe. ...... river
archipel, Fr. ...... archipelago
archipiélago, Sp. ...... archipelago
arquipélago, Port. ...... archipelago
arroyo, Sp. ...... brook
-ås,-åsen, Swe. ...... hills
baai, Du. ...... bay
bab, Ara. ...... strait
Bach, Ger. ...... brook, creek
-backen, Swe. ...... hill
bælt, Dan. ...... strait
bahía, Sp. ...... bay
bahr, baḥr, Ara. ...... river, sea
baía, Port. ...... bay
baie, Fr. ...... bay
-bana, Jpn. ...... cape
banco, Sp. ...... bank
bandao, Ch. ...... peninsula
bassin, Fr. ...... basin
batang, Indon. ...... river
bātlāq, Per. ...... marsh
ben, Gae. ...... mountain
Berg, Ger. ...... mountain, hill
-berg, Afk. ...... mountains
Berge, Ger. ...... mountains
bi'r, Ara. ...... well
birkat, Ara. ...... lake
bocca, It. ...... river mouth, pass
boğazı, Tur. ...... strait
bogd, Mong. ...... range
bolsón, Sp. ...... enclosed basin
-breen, Nor. ...... glacier
Brücke, Ger. ...... bridge
Bucht, Ger. ...... bay
bugt, Dan. ...... bay

bukit, Indon., Mal. ...... mountain, hill
-bukten, Swe. ...... bay
bulu, Indon. ...... mountain
Burg, Ger. ...... castle
burn, Gae. ...... brook
burnu, burun, Tur. ...... cape
cabezas, Sp. ...... peaks
cabo, Port., Sp. ...... cape
campo, It. ...... plain
cap, Fr., Cat. ...... cape
capo, It. ...... cape
catena, Sp. ...... range
cayo(s), Sp. ...... cay(s), islet(s)
cerro(s), Sp. ...... mountain(s), hill(s)
chaîne, Fr. ...... range
château, Fr. ...... castle
chiang, Ch. ...... harbor, harbour
chott, Ara. ...... intermittent lake, salt marsh
cima, It., Sp. ...... peak
città, It. ...... city
ciudad, Sp. ...... city
co, Tib. ...... lake
co., cerro, Sp. ...... mountain, hill
col, Fr. ...... pass
colina(s), Sp. ...... hill(s)
colline, It. ...... hills
collines, Fr. ...... hills
con, Viet. ...... islands
cord., cordillera, Sp. ...... range
costa, Sp. ...... coast
côte, Fr. ...... coast, hills
cuchilla, Sp. ...... hills, ridge
dağ, dağı, Tur. ...... mountain
dāgh, Per. ...... mountains
-dake, Jpn. ...... mountain
-dal, -dalen, Nor., Swe. ...... valley
danau, Indon. ...... lake
dao, Ch., Viet. ...... island
daryācheh, Per. ...... lake
dasht, Per. ...... desert
deniz, denizi, Tur. ...... sea
desierto, Sp. ...... desert
détroit, Fr. ...... strait
dijk, Du. ...... dike
distrito, Sp. ...... district
djebel, Ara. ...... mountain(s)
-do, Kor. ...... island
-elv,-elva, Nor. ...... river
embalse, Sp. ...... reservoir
erg, Ara. ...... sand desert
estrecho, Sp. ...... strait
étang, Fr. ...... pond
-ey, Ice. ...... island
fjäll(en), Swe. ...... mountain(s)
fjället, Swe. ...... mountain
fjärden, Swe. ...... fjord
-fjell, -fjellet, Nor. ...... mountain
-fjord, Nor. ...... fjord
-fjorden, Nor., Swe. ...... fjord, lake
-fjörur, Ice. ...... fjord, bay
-flói, Ice. ...... bay
foce, It. ...... river mouth, pass
forêt, Fr. ...... forest
-forsen, Swe. ...... waterfall
Forst, Ger. ...... forest
-foss, Ice. ...... waterfall
-fossen, Nor. ...... waterfall
g., gora, Rus. ...... mountain, hill
g., gunong, Mal. ...... mountain
gang, Ch. ...... bay
-gang, Kor. ...... river
gave, Fr. ...... mountain torrent
gebergte, Du. ...... range
Gebirge, Ger. ...... range
Gipfel, Ger. ...... peak
göl, Tur. ...... lake
golfe, Fr. ...... gulf
golfete, Sp. ...... bay
golfo, It., Sp. ...... gulf
gölu, Tur. ...... lake
gora, Rus. ...... mountain, hill
gora, S./C. ...... mountains
góra, Pol. ...... mountain
gory, Rus. ...... mountains, hills
góry, Pol. ...... mountains

gr'ada, Rus. ...... ridge
guba, Rus. ...... bay
gunong, Mal. ...... mountain
gunung, Indon. ...... mountain
-guntō, Jpn. ...... islands
Haff, Ger. ...... lagoon
hai, Ch. ...... sea, lake
-hama, Jpn. ...... beach
hamada, Ara. ...... desert
hāmūn, Per. ...... lake, marsh
-hantō, Jpn. ...... peninsula
hare, Heb. ...... mountains, hills
-hav, Swe. ...... sea
havre, Fr. ...... harbor, harbour
he, Ch. ...... river
ho, Ch. ...... river
-ho, Kor. ...... reservoir
-holm, Dan. ...... island
hora, Czech, Slo. ...... mountain
Horn, Ger. ...... point, peak
hu, Ch. ...... lake, reservoir
Hügel, Ger. ...... hill
-huk, Swe. ...... cape
ig., igarapé, Port. ...... river
île(s), Fr. ...... island(s)
îlet(s), Fr. ...... islet(s)
ilha(s), Port. ...... island(s)
ilhéu(s), Port. ...... islet(s)
Insel(n), Ger. ...... island(s)
isla(s), Sp. ...... island(s)
isola, It. ...... island
isole, It. ...... islands
istmo, Sp. ...... isthmus
jabal, Ara. ...... mountain(s)
järv, Est. ...... lake
-järvi, Finn. ...... lake
jazā'ir, Ara. ...... islands
jazirah, Indon. ...... peninsula
jiang, Ch. ...... river
-jima, Jpn. ...... island
-joki, Finn. ...... river
-jökull, Ice. ...... glacier
-kai, Jpn. ...... sea
-kaikyō, Jpn. ...... strait
-kaise, Lapp. ...... mountain
kali, Indon. ...... brook
kandao, Pas. ...... pass
-kang, Kor. ...... river
-kapp, Nor. ...... cape
kepulauan, Indon. ...... islands
khalīj, Ara. ...... gulf
khrebet, Russ., Ukr. ...... range
-ko, Jpn. ...... lake, lagoon
-kō, Jpn. ...... harbor, harbour
kólpos, Gr. ...... bay
Kopf, Ger. ...... peak
körfezi, Tur. ...... gulf, bay
kosa, Rus., Ukr. ...... spit
kou, Ch. ...... bay, pass
kuala, Mal. ...... bay
kūh(ha), Per. ...... mountain(s)
la, Tib. ...... pass
lac(s), Fr. ...... lake(s)
lag., laguna, Sp. ...... lagoon, lake
lago, It., Port., Sp. ...... lake
lagoa, Port. ...... lake, lagoon
laguna, Sp. ...... lagoon, lake
lagune, Fr. ...... lagoon
laht, Est. ...... bay
-lahti, Finn. ...... gulf
län, Swe. ...... county
laut, Indon. ...... sea
liedao, Ch. ...... islands
liman, Rus. ...... estuary
ling, Ch. ...... mountain(s), peak
llano(s), Sp. ...... plain(s)
loch, Gae. ...... lake, inlet
lomas, Sp. ...... hills
lough, Gae. ...... lake
lyman, Ukr. ...... estuary
-maa, Est. ...... island
-man, Kor. ...... bay
mar, Sp., It. ...... sea
marais, Fr. ...... marsh
mare, It. ...... sea
massif, Eng., Fr. ...... massif

Meer, Ger. ...... sea, lake
mer, Fr. ...... sea
mesa, Sp. ...... mesa
meseta, Sp. ...... plateau
-misaki, Jpn. ...... cape
mont, Fr. ...... mount
montagna, It. ...... mountain
montagne(s), Fr. ...... mountain(s)
montaña(s), Sp. ...... mountain(s)
monte, It., Port., Sp. ...... mount
montes, Port., Sp. ...... mountains
monti, It. ...... mountains
monts, Fr. ...... mountains
more, Rus., Ukr. ...... sea
morne, Fr. ...... mountain
morro, Port., Sp. ...... hill, mountain
mui, Viet. ...... point
munkhafad, Ara. ...... depression
munţii, Rom. ...... mountains
-nada, Jpn. ...... sea, gulf
nafūd, Ara. ...... desert
nagor'ye, Rus. ...... plateau, mountains
-näs, Swe. ...... peninsula
ness, Gae. ...... promontory
nos, Blg. ...... cape
nuruu, Mong. ...... mountains
nuur, Mong. ...... lake
-ø, Dan., Nor. ...... island
-ö, Swe. ...... island
o., ostrov, Rus. ...... island
óros, Gr. ...... mountain(s)
ostriv, Ukr. ...... island
ostrov(a), Rus. ...... island(s)
otok, S./C. ...... island
ouadi, Ara. ...... wadi
oued, Ara. ...... wadi
-øy, -øya, Nor. ...... island
oz., ozero, Rus., Ukr. ...... lake
pampa, Sp. ...... plain
pas, Fr. ...... strait
paso, Sp. ...... pass
Pass, Ger. ...... pass
passe, Fr. ...... passage
passo, It. ...... pass
peg., pegunungan, Indon. ...... mountains
pélagos, Gr. ...... sea
peña, Sp. ...... peak, rock
península, Sp. ...... peninsula
pertuis, Fr. ...... strait
peski, Rus. ...... sand desert
phnum, Cbd. ...... mountain
phou, Lao. ...... mountain
pic, Fr. ...... peak
pico(s), Port., Sp. ...... peak(s)
-piggen, Nor. ...... mountain
pik, Rus. ...... peak
pique, Fr. ...... peak
piton(s), Fr. ...... peak(s)
pivostriv, Ukr. ...... peninsula
planalto, Port. ...... plateau
planina, S./C. ...... mountain, range
plato, Afk., Blg., Rus. ...... plateau
playa, Sp. ...... beach
pointe, Fr. ...... point
polje, S./C. ...... plain, basin
poluostrov, Rus. ...... peninsula
pont, Fr. ...... bridge
ponta, pontal, Port. ...... point
porto, It. ...... port
presa, Sp. ...... reservoir, dam
presqu'île, Fr. ...... peninsula
proliv, Rus. ...... strait
puerto, Sp. ...... port
pulau, Indon., Mal. ...... island
puncak, Indon. ...... peak
punta, It., Sp. ...... point, peak
qundao, Ch. ...... islands
rão., ribeirão, Port. ...... river
ras, ra's, Ara. ...... cape
-retto, Jpn. ...... islands
ría, Sp. ...... ria (inlet)

rib., ribeira, Port. ...... brook
ribeirão, Port. ...... river
rio, Port. ...... river
río, Sp. ...... river
riviera, It. ...... coast
rivière, Fr. ...... river
roca, Sp. ...... rock
rocca, It. ...... rock, mountain
rt, S./C. ...... cape
sa., serra, Port. ...... range
sahrā', Ara. ...... desert
-saki, Jpn. ...... cape
salar, Sp. ...... salt flat
salina(s), Sp. ...... salt marsh, salt flat
salto(s), Port., Sp. ...... waterfall
-sammyaku, Jpn. ...... range
-san, Jpn., Kor. ...... mountain
-sanmaek, Kor. ...... mountains
Schloss, Ger. ...... castle
sebkha, Ara. ...... salt flat
See(n), Ger. ...... lake(s)
selat, Indon. ...... strait
seno, Sp. ...... sound
serra, Port. ...... range, mountain
serranía(s), Sp. ...... ridge(s)
shan, Ch. ...... mountain(s), island
shanmo, Ch. ...... mountains
-shima, Jpn. ...... island
-shotō, Jpn. ...... islands
sierra, Sp. ...... range, ridge
sjø, Nor. ...... lake
-sjön, Swe. ...... lake, bay
-sø, Dan. ...... lake
Spitze, Ger. ...... peak
sta., santa, Port., Sp. ...... saint
ste., sainte, Fr. ...... saint
step', Rus. ...... steppe
štít, Slo. ...... peak
sto., santo, Port., Sp. ...... saint
stretto, It. ...... strait
Strom, Ger. ...... stream
-ström, -strömmen, Swe. ...... stream
-su, Kor. ...... river
-suidō, Jpn. ...... channel
Sund, Ger. ...... sound
-sund, Swe. ...... sound
-take, Jpn. ...... mountain
Tal, Ger. ...... valley
tanjong, Mal. ...... cape
tanjung, Indon. ...... cape
tao, Ch. ...... island
teluk, Indon. ...... bay
thale, Thai ...... lagoon
-tō, Jpn. ...... island
tônlé, Cbd. ...... lake
-tunturi, Finn. ...... hill, mountain
ujung, Indon. ...... cape
-umi, Jpn. ...... lagoon
-ura, Jpn. ...... lagoon
valle, It., Sp. ...... valley
vallée, Fr. ...... valley
vârful, Rom. ...... mountain
-vatn, Ice., Nor. ...... lake
vdkhr., vodokhranilishche, Rus. ...... reservoir
-vesi, Finn. ...... lake
-viken, Swe. ...... gulf
vodokhranilishche, Rus. ...... reservoir
vodoskhovyshche, Ukr. ...... reservoir
vol., volcán, Sp. ...... volcano
wādī, Ara. ...... wadi
wāhat, wāḥāt, Ara. ...... oasis
wan, Ch., Jpn. ...... bay
-yama, Jpn. ...... mountain
yarımadası, Tur. ...... peninsula
yoma, Bur. ...... mountains
yumco, Tib. ...... lake
yunhe, Ch. ...... canal
-zaki, Jpn. ...... point
zaliv, Rus. ...... gulf, bay
zatoka, Ukr. ...... gulf, bay
zee, Du. ...... sea, lake

Abbreviations of Geographical Names and Terms

Ab., Can. ..... Alberta, Can.
Afg. .... Afghanistan
Afr. .... Africa
Ak., U.S. ..... Alaska, U.S.
Al., U.S. .... Alabama, U.S.
Alb. .... Albania
Alg. .... Algeria
Ang. .... Angola
Ant. .... Antarctica
Ar., U.S. .... Arkansas, U.S.
Arg. .... Argentina
Arm. .... Armenia
Aus. .... Austria
Austl. .... Australia
Az., U.S. .... Arizona, U.S.
Azer. .... Azerbaijan
B. .... Bay
Bah. .... Bahamas
Bahr. .... Bahrain
Barb. .... Barbados
B.C., Can. .... British
   Columbia, Can.
Bdi. .... Burundi
Bel. .... Belgium
Bela. .... Belarus
Bhu. .... Bhutan
Bngl. .... Bangladesh
Bol. .... Bolivia
Bos. .... Bosnia
   and Hercegovina
Bots. .... Botswana
Braz. .... Brazil
Bul. .... Bulgaria
Burkina ...... Burkina Faso
C. .... Cape
Ca., U.S. ... California, U.S.
Camb. .... Cambodia
Can. .... Canada
C.A.R. .... Central
   African Republic
Cay. Is. ..... Cayman Islands
C. Iv. .... Cote d'Ivoire
Co., U.S. .... Colorado, U.S.
Col. .... Colombia
C.R. .... Costa Rica
Cro. .... Croatia
Ct., U.S. ....
   Connecticut, U.S.

Ctry. .... Country
C.V. .... Cape Verde
Cyp. .... Cyprus
Czech Rep. .... Czech
   Republic
D.C., U.S. .... District of
   Columbia, U.S.
De., U.S. .. Delaware, U.S.
Den. .... Denmark
Dep. .... Dependency
Des. .... Desert
Dji. .... Djibouti
D.R.C. .... Democratic
   Republic of the Congo
Ec. .... Ecuador
El Sal. .... El Salvador
Eng., U.K. .England, U.K.
Eq. Gui. .... Equatorial
   Guinea
Erit. .... Eritrea
Est. .... Estonia
Eth. .... Ethiopia
E. Timor ...... East Timor
Eur. .... Europe
Falk. Is. ... Falkland Islands
Fin. .... Finland
Fl., U.S. ...... Florida, U.S.
Fr. .... France
Fr. Gu. ..... French Guiana
G. .... Gulf
Ga., U.S. .... Georgia, U.S.
Gam. .... The Gambia
Gaza Str. .... Gaza Strip
Geor. .... Georgia
Ger. .... Germany
Grc. .... Greece
Guad. .... Guadeloupe
Guat. .... Guatemala
Gui. .... Guinea
Gui.-B. ...... Guinea-Bissau
Guy. .... Guyana
Hi., U.S. ...... Hawaii, U.S.
Hond. .... Honduras
Hung. .... Hungary
I. .... Island
Ia., U.S. .... Iowa, U.S.
Ice. .... Iceland

Id., U.S. .... Idaho, U.S.
Il., U.S. ...... Illinois, U.S.
In., U.S. ..... Indiana, U.S.
Indon. .... Indonesia
Ire. .... Ireland
Is. .... Islands
Isr. .... Israel
Jam. .... Jamaica
Jord. .... Jordan
Kaz. .... Kazakhstan
Ks., U.S. .... Kansas, U.S.
Kuw. .... Kuwait
Ky., U.S. .. Kentucky, U.S.
Kyrg. .... Kyrgzstan
L. .... Lake
La., U.S. .. Louisiana, U.S.
Lat. .... Latvia
Leb. .... Lebanon
Leso. .... Lesotho
Lib. .... Liberia
Lith. .... Lithuania
Lux. .... Luxembourg
Ma., U.S. .. Massachusetts,
   U.S.
Mac. .... Macedonia
Madag. .... Madagascar
Malay. .... Malaysia
Mart. .... Martinique
Maur. .... Mauritania
Mb., Can. ....
   Manitoba, Can.
Md., U.S. .. Maryland, U.S.
Me., U.S. ...... Maine, U.S.
Mex. .... Mexico
Mi., U.S. .. Michigan, U.S.
Mn., U.S. .Minnesota, U.S.
Mo., U.S. .. Missouri, U.S.
Mol. .... Moldova
Mong. .... Mongolia
Monts. .... Montserrat
Mor. .... Morocco
Moz. .... Mozambique
Ms., U.S. ....
   Mississippi, U.S.
Mt. .... Mountain
Mt., U.S. .. Montana, U.S.
Mts. .... Mountains

Mwi. .... Malawi
Myan. .... Myanmar
N.A. .... North America
N.B., Can. .... New
   Brunswick, Can.
N.C., U.S. .... North
   Carolina, U.S.
N. Cal. ..... New Caledonia
N.D., U.S. .... North
   Dakota, U.S.
Ne., U.S. .. Nebraska, U.S.
Neth. .. Netherlands
Neth. Ant. ...Netherlands
   Antilles
Nf., Can... Newfoundland,
   Can.
N.H., U.S. .... New
   Hampshire, U.S.
Nic. .... Nicaragua
Nig. .... Nigeria
N. Ire., U.K. .... Northern
   Ireland, U.K.
N.J., U.S. ....
   New Jersey, U.S.
N. Kor. ...... Korea, North
N.M., U.S. .... New
   Mexico, U.S.
Nmb. .... Namibia
Nor. .... Norway
N.S., Can. .... Nova
   Scotia, Can.
N.T., Can. ......Northwest
   Territories, Can.
Nu., Can... Nunavut, Can.
Nv., U.S. .... Nevada, U.S.
N.Y., U.S. ....
   New York, U.S.
N.Z. .... New Zealand
Oc. .... Oceania
Oh., U.S. .... Ohio, U.S.
Ok., U.S. .Oklahoma, U.S.
On., Can.... Ontario, Can.
Or., U.S. ...... Oregon, U.S.
Pa., U.S. ....
   Pennsylvania, U.S.
Pak. .... Pakistan
Pan. .... Panama

Pap. N. Gui. .... Papua
   New Guinea
Para. .... Paraguay
P.E., Can. .Prince Edward
   Island, Can.
Pen. .... Peninsula
Phil. .... Philippines
Pk. .... Peak
Plat. .... Plateau
Pol. .... Poland
Polit. Reg. ...Political Region
Port. .... Portugal
P.Q., Can. ..Quebec, Can.
P.R. .... Puerto Rico
Prov. .... Province
R. .... River
Ra. .... Range
Region .... Reg.
Res. .... Reservoir
R.I., U.S. .... Rhode
   Island, U.S.
Rom. .... Romania
Rw. .... Rwanda
S.A. .... South America
S. Afr. .... South Africa
Sau. Ar. ....Saudi Arabia
S.C., U.S. .... South
   Carolina, U.S.
Scot., U.K. ....
   Scotland, U.K.
S.D., U.S. .... South
   Dakota, U.S.
Sen. .... Senegal
Sk., Can. .. Saskatchewan,
   Can.
S. Kor. ...... Korea, South
S.L. .... Sierra Leone
Slvk. .... Slovakia
Slvn. .... Slovenia
Som. .... Somalia
Sp. N. Afr. .... Spanish
   North Africa
Sri L. .... Sri Lanka
Str. .... Strait
St. Vin. .... St. Vincent
   and the Grenadines
Sur. .... Suriname

Swaz. .... Swaziland
Swe. .... Sweden
Switz. .... Switzerland
Tai. .... Taiwan
Taj. .... Tajikistan
Tan. .... Tanzania
Ter. .... Territory
Thai. .... Thailand
Tn., U.S. . Tennessee, U.S.
Trin. .... Trinidad
   and Tobago
Tun. .... Tunisia
Tur. .... Turkey
Turk. .... Turkmenistan
Tx., U.S. ...... Texas, U.S.
U.A.E. .... United
   Arab Emirates
Ug. .... Uganda
U.K. ...... United Kingdom
Ukr. ....Ukraine
Ur. .... Uruguay
U.S. .... United States
Ut., U.S. ...... Utah, U.S.
Uzb. .... Uzbekistan
Va., U.S. .... Virginia, U.S.
Ven. .... Venezuela
Viet. .... Vietnam
V.I.U.S. .... Virgin
   Islands (U.S.)
Vol. .... Volcano
Vt., U.S. ....Vermont, U.S.
Wa., U.S. ....
   Washington, U.S.
Wales, U.K. . Wales, U.K.
Wal./F.. Wallis and Futuna
W.B. .... West Bank
Wi., U.S. .. Wisconsin, U.S.
W. Sah. ... Western Sahara
W.V., U.S. .... West
   Virginia, U.S.
Wy., U.S...Wyoming, U.S.
Yk., Can. ....Yukon
   Territory, Can.
Yugo. .... Yugoslavia
Zam. .... Zambia
Zimb. ....Zimbabwe

Index

This universal index includes in a single alphabetical list approximately 4,100 names of features that appear on the reference maps. Each name is followed by geographical coordinates and a page reference.

Abbreviation and Capitalization

Abbreviations of names on the maps have been standardized as much as possible. Names that are abbreviated on the maps are generally spelled out in full in the index. Periods are used after all abbreviations regardless of local practice. The abbreviation "St." is used only for "Saint". "Sankt" and other forms of this term are spelled out.

Most initial letters of names are capitalized, except for a few Dutch names, such as "'s-Gravenhage." Capitalization of non-initial words in a name generally follows local practice.

Alphabetization

Names are alphabetized in the order of the letters of the English alphabet. Spanish ll and ch, for example, are not treated as distinct letters. Furthermore, diacritical marks are disregarded in alphabetization. German or Scandinavian ä or ö are treated as a or o.

The names of physical features may appear inverted, since they are always alphabetized under the proper, not the generic, part of the name, thus: "Gibraltar, Strait of." Otherwise every entry, whether consisting of one word or more, is alphabetized as a single continuous entity. "Lakeland," for example, appears after "Lake Forest" and before "La Línea." Names beginning with articles (Le Havre, Al Manāmah, Ad Dawhah) are not inverted. Names beginning "St.," "Ste." and "Sainte" are alphabetized as though spelled "Saint."

In the case of identical names, towns are listed first, then political divisions, then physical features.

Generic Terms

Except for cities, the names of all features are followed by terms that represent broad classes of features, for example, Mississippi, R. or Alabama, State.

Country names and names of features that extend beyond the boundaries of one country are followed by the name of the continent in which each is located. Country designations follow the names of all other places in the index. The locations of places in the United States and the United Kingdom are further defined by abbreviations that indicate the state or political division in which each is located.

Page References and Geographical Coordinates

The geographical coordinates and page references are found in the last columns of each entry.

Latitude and longitude coordinates for point features, such as cities and mountain peaks, indicate the locations of the symbols. For extensive areal features, such as countries or mountain ranges, or linear features, such as canals and rivers, locations are given for the position of the type as it appears on the map.

Index

A

Aachen, Ger. 51N 6E **117**
Aalborg, Den. 57N 10E **116**
Ābādān, Iran 30N 48E **142**
Abakan, Russia 54N 91E **140**
Abdulino, Russia 54N 54E **140**
Abeokuta, Nig. 7N 3E **128**
Aberdeen, Scot., U.K. 57N 2W **116**
Aberdeen, S.D., U.S. 45N 98W **88**
Aberdeen, Wa., U.S. 47N 124W **82**
Abidjan, C. Iv. 5N 4W **128**
Abilene, Tx., U.S. 32N 100W **94**
Abuja, Nig. 9N 7E **128**
Abū Kamāl, Syria 34N 41E **142**
Abū Zaby, U.A.E. 24N 54E **142**
Acapulco, Mex. 17N 100W **96**
Accra, Ghana 6N 0 **128**
Aconcagua, C., Mt., Arg. 33S 70W **106**
Acre, Isr. 33N 35E **121**
Adana, Tur. 37N 35E **121**
Adapazarı, Tur. 41N 30E **121**
Ad Dawhah, Qatar 25N 51E **142**
Ad Dilam, Sau. Ar. 24N 47E **142**
Addis Ababa, Eth. 9N 39E **129**
Adelaide, Austl. 35S 139E **156**
Aden, Yemen 13N 45E **142**
Aden, Gulf of, Asia-Afr. 12N 46E **142**
Adirondack Mts., N.Y., U.S. 44N 74W **91**
Adriatic Sea, Eur. 44N 14E **120**
Aegean Sea, Grc.-Tur. 39N 25E **121**
Afghanistan, Ctry., Asia 34N 65E **142**
Aflou, Alg. 34N 2E **120**
Afyon, Tur. 39N 30E **121**
Agadir, Mor. 30N 10W **128**
Aginskoye, Russia 51N 114E **141**
Āgra, India 27N 78E **143**
Agrínio, Grc. 39N 21E **121**
Aguascalientes, Mex. 22N 102W **96**
Agulhas, C., S. Afr. 35S 20E **130**
Ahaggar, Mts., Alg. 23N 6E **128**
Ahmadābād, India 23N 73E **143**
Ahmadnagar, India 19N 75E **143**
Ahvāz, Iran 31N 49E **142**
Aïn-Temouchent, Alg. 35N 1W **120**
Aitape, Pap. N. Gui. 3S 142E **149**
Aix en Provence, Fr. 44N 5E **117**
Ajaccio, Fr. 42N 9E **117**
Ajman, U.A.E. 25N 55E **142**
Ajmer, India 26N 75E **143**
Akhisar, Tur. 39N 28E **121**
Akhmīm, Egypt 27N 32E **129**
Akita, Japan 40N 140E **147**
Akjoujt, Maur. 20N 15W **128**
Aklavik, N.T., Can. 68N 135W **72**
Akola, India 21N 77E **143**
Akron, Oh., U.S. 41N 81W **90**
Aksu, China 41N 80E **146**
Alabama, State, U.S. 33N 87W **77**
Alameda, Ca., U.S. 38N 122W **84**
Alamogordo, N.M., U.S. 33N 106W **85**
Alanya, Tur. 37N 32E **121**
Alapayevsk, Russia 58N 62E **140**
Alaska, State, U.S. 65N 155W **76**
Alatyr', Russia 55N 46E **140**
Albacete, Spain 39N 2W **120**
Albania, Ctry., Eur. 41N 20E **121**
Albany, Ga., U.S. 32N 84W **92**
Albany, N.Y., U.S. 43N 74W **91**
Albany, Or., U.S. 45N 123W **82**
Albany, R., On., Can. 52N 84W **73**
Al Başrah, Iraq 30N 48E **142**
Albert, L., Ug.-Zaire 2N 30E **129**
Alberta, Prov., Can. 55N 117W **72**
Albi, Fr. 44N 2E **117**
Albuquerque, N.M., U.S. 35N 107W **85**
Al Buraymī, Oman 24N 56E **142**
Alcázar de San Juan, Spain 39N 3W **120**
Alcoy, Spain 39N 1W **120**
Aldan, Russia 59N 125E **141**
Aldanskaya, Russia 62N 135E **141**
Aleksandrovsk, Russia 51N 142E **141**
Aleppo, Syria 36N 37E **142**
Alès, Fr. 44N 4E **117**
Alessandria, Italy 45N 9E **117**
Aleutian Is., Ak., U.S. 52N 175W **76**
Alexandria (Al Iskandarīyah), Egypt 31N 30E **129**
Alexandria, La., U.S. 31N 92W **95**
Alexandria, Va., U.S. 39N 77W **91**
Alexandroúpoli, Grc. 41N 26E **121**
Al Fāshir, Sudan 14N 25E **129**
Al Fayyūm, Egypt 29N 31E **129**
Algeria, Ctry., Afr. 29N 1E **128**
Alghero, Italy 41N 8E **117**
Algiers (El Djazaïr), Alg. 37N 3E **128**
Al Ḩawṭah, Yemen 16N 48E **142**
Al Hudaydah, Yemen 15N 43E **142**
Al Hufūf, Sau. Ar. 25N 50E **142**
Alicante, Spain 38N 0 **120**
Alice Springs, Austl. 24S 134E **156**
Alīgarh, India 28N 78E **143**
Aliquippa, Pa., U.S. 41N 80W **91**
Al Ismā'īlīyah, Egypt 31N 32E **121**
Al Jawf, Sau. Ar. 30N 39E **142**
Al Jīzah, Egypt 30N 31E **121**
Al Khābūrah, Oman 24N 57E **142**
Al Kharṭūm Bahrī, Sudan 16N 33E **129**
Al Khums, Libya 33N 14E **129**
Al Khurmah, Sau. Ar. 22N 42E **142**
Al Lādhiqīyah (Latakia), Syria 36N 36E **142**
Allāhābād, India 26N 82E **143**
Allaykha, Russia 71N 149E **141**
Allegheny, R., U.S. 42N 79W **91**
Allentown, Pa., U.S. 41N 75W **91**
Alleppey, India 10N 76E **143**
Alliance, Ne., U.S. 42N 103W **88**
Alliance, Oh., U.S. 41N 81W **90**
Al Luḩayyah, Yemen 16N 43E **142**
Alma-Ata see Almaty, Kaz. 43N 77E **140**
Al Madīnah, Sau. Ar. 24N 40E **142**
Al Maḩallah al Kubrā, Egypt 31N 31E **129**
Al Manāmah, Bahr. 26N 51E **142**
Al Manṣūrah, Egypt 31N 31E **129**
Almaty, Kaz. 43N 77E **140**
Al Mawşil, Iraq 36N 41E **142**
Almería, Spain 37N 2W **120**
Al Minyā, Egypt 28N 31E **129**
Al Mubarraz, Sau. Ar. 23N 46E **142**
Al Mukallā, Yemen 14N 49E **142**
Al Mukhā (Mocha), Yemen 14N 43E **142**
Alor Setar, Malay. 6N 100E **148**
Alpena, Mi., U.S. 45N 83W **90**
Alps, Mts., Eur. 46N 9E **117**
Al Qaḑārif, Sudan 14N 35E **129**
Al Qaṭīf, Sau. Ar. 27N 50E **142**
Al Qayşūmah, Sau. Ar. 28N 46E **142**
Al Qunfudhah, Sau. Ar. 19N 41E **142**
Altai Mts., Asia 49N 87E **146**
Altamura, Italy 41N 17E **117**
Altay, China 48N 88E **146**
Altiplano, Plat., Bol. 19S 68W **104**
Alton, Il., U.S. 39N 90W **87**
Altoona, Pa., U.S. 40N 78W **91**
Al Ubayyid, Sudan 13N 30E **129**
Al Uqşur (Luxor), Egypt 26N 33E **129**
Al Wajh, Sau. Ar. 26N 37E **142**
Alwar, India 28N 77E **143**
Amarillo, Tx., U.S. 35N 102W **86**
Amazon (Amazonas), R., S.A. 2S 53W **105**
Ambāla, India 31N 77E **143**
Ambarchik, Russia 70N 162E **141**
Ambato, Ec. 1S 79W **104**
American Samoa, Dep., Oc. 15S 170W **158**
Americus, Ga., U.S. 32N 84W **92**
Amery, Mb., Can. 57N 94W **72**
Amga, Russia 61N 132E **141**
Amiens, Fr. 50N 2E **117**
Ammān, Jord. 32N 36E **142**
Amrāvati, India 21N 78E **143**
Amritsar, India 32N 75E **143**
Amsterdam, Neth. 52N 5E **117**
Amsterdam, N.Y., U.S. 43N 74W **91**
Amu Darya, R., Asia 40N 62E **142**
Amur, R., China-Russia 52N 126E **141**
Anaconda, Mt., U.S. 46N 113W **83**
Anadyr', Russia 65N 177E **141**
Anan'yiv, Ukr. 48N 30E **121**
Anchieta, Braz. 23S 43W **106**
Anchorage, Ak., U.S. 61N 150W **76**
Ancona, Italy 44N 14E **117**
Andaman Is., India 12N 92E **148**
Andaman Sea, Asia 13N 95E **148**
Anderson, In., U.S. 40N 86W **90**
Anderson, S.C., U.S. 34N 83W **93**
Andes Mts., S.A. 11S 75W **104**
Andizhan, Uzb. 41N 73E **140**
Andong, S. Kor. 37N 129E **147**
Andorra, Ctry., Eur. 42N 1E **120**
Andria, Italy 41N 16E **117**
Angarsk, Russia 53N 104E **141**
Angel, Salto, Falls, Ven. 6N 62W **104**
Angers, Fr. 47N 1W **117**
Angola, Ctry., Afr. 12S 18E **130**
Angoulême, Fr. 46N 0 **117**
Anguilla, Ctry., N.A. 18N 63W **97**
Ankang, China 33N 109E **146**
Ankara (Angora), Tur. 40N 33E **121**
Annaba, Alg. 37N 8E **128**
An Nafūd, Des., Sau. Ar. 28N 40E **142**
An Najaf, Iraq 31N 45E **142**
Annamese Cordillera, Mts., Laos-Viet. 18N 106E **148**
Annapolis, Md., U.S. 39N 76W **91**
Ann Arbor, Mi., U.S. 42N 84W **90**
Anniston, Al., U.S. 34N 86W **92**
Anqing, China 31N 117E **147**
Anshun, China 26N 106E **146**
Antalya (Adalia), Tur. 37N 31E **121**
Antananarivo, Madag. 19S 48E **131**
Antarctica, Cont. 90S 60W **160**
Antequera, Spain 37N 5W **120**
Antigua and Barbuda, Ctry., N.A. 17N 62W **97**
Antofagasta, Chile 24S 70W **106**
Antofalla, Salar de, Dry L., Arg. 26S 67W **106**
Antsiranana, Madag. 12S 49E **131**
Antwerp, Bel. 51N 4E **117**
Anxi, China 41N 96E **146**
Anzhero-Sudzhensk, Russia 56N 86E **140**
Aomori, Japan 41N 141E **147**
Aoraki, Mt., N.Z. 43S 170E **157**
Apeldoorn, Neth. 52N 6E **117**
Appalachian Mts., Can.-U.S. 38N 80W **77**
Appennino, Mts., Italy 44N 12E **117**
Appleton, Wi., U.S. 44N 88W **89**
Aqaba, Gulf of, Afr.-Asia 28N 35E **121**
Aqtöbe, Kaz. 50N 57E **115**
Arabian Sea, Asia 18N 63E **138**
Aracaju, Braz. 11S 37W **105**
Araçatuba, Braz. 21S 50W **105**
Arafura Sea, Austl.-Indon. 9S 133E **149**
Araguari, Braz. 19S 48W **105**
Arak, Iran 34N 50E **142**
Aral, Kaz. 47N 62E **140**
Aral Sea, L., Kaz.-Uzb. 45N 60E **115**
Araraquara, Braz. 22S 48W **105**
Ararat, Mt., Mt., Tur. 40N 44E **115**
Arcachon, Fr. 45N 1W **117**
Arctic Ocean 80N 150W **52**
Ardabīl, Iran 38N 48E **142**
Ardennes, Mts., Bel. 50N 5E **117**
Ardmore, Ok., U.S. 34N 97W **87**
Arecibo, P.R. 18N 67W **97**
Arequipa, Peru 16S 71W **104**
Arezzo, Italy 43N 12E **117**
Argentina, Ctry., S.A. 39S 67W **106**
Arhus, Den. 56N 10E **116**
Arizona, State, U.S. 34N 112W **76**
Arkansas, State, U.S. 35N 94W **77**
Arkansas, R., U.S. 35N 95W **86**
Arkhangelsk (Archangel), Russia 64N 40E **115**
Arlington, Tx., U.S. 33N 97W **95**
Arlington, Va., U.S. 39N 77W **91**
Armavir, Russia 45N 41E **115**
Armenia, Col. 5N 76W **104**
Armenia, Ctry., Asia 40N 45E **115**
Arnhem, Neth. 52N 6E **117**
Arras, Fr. 50N 3E **117**
Arsen'yev, Russia 44N 134E **141**
Árta, Grc. 39N 21E **121**
Artëm, Russia 43N 132E **141**
Aruba, Ctry., N.A. 12N 70W **97**
Arys, Kaz. 42N 68E **140**
Asansol, India 24N 87E **143**
Asbest, Russia 57N 61E **115**
Asheville, N.C., U.S. 36N 83W **93**
Ashkhabad, Turk. 38N 58E **142**
Ashland, Ky., U.S. 38N 83W **90**
Ash Shaqrā, Sau. Ar. 25N 45E **142**
Ash Shiḩr, Yemen 15N 50E **142**
Ashtabula, Oh., U.S. 42N 81W **90**
Asia Minor, Reg., Tur. 38N 33E **115**
Asmera, Erit. 15N 39E **129**
As Sallūm, Egypt 32N 25E **129**
Assiniboia, Sk., Can. 50N 106W **72**
As Sulaymānīyah, Iraq 36N 45E **142**
As Suwaydā', Syria 33N 37E **121**
Astana (Aqmola), Kaz. 51N 72E **140**
Asti, Italy 45N 8E **117**
Astoria, Or., U.S. 46N 124W **82**
Astrakhan', Russia 46N 48E **115**
Asunción, Para. 25S 57W **106**
Aswān, Egypt 24N 33E **129**
Asyūţ, Egypt 27N 31E **129**
Atbarah, Sudan 18N 30E **129**
Atbasar, Kaz. 52N 68E **140**
Atchison, Ks., U.S. 40N 95W **87**
Athabasca, Ab., Can. 55N 113W **72**
Athabasca, L., Can. 59N 109W **72**
Athabasca, R., Ab., Can. 57N 112W **72**
Athens, Ga., U.S. 34N 83W **92**
Athens (Athína), Grc. 38N 24E **121**
Atlanta, Ga., U.S. 34N 84W **92**
Atlantic City, N.J., U.S. 39N 74W **91**
Atlantic Ocean 20N 40W **52**
Atlas Mts., Afr. 33N 2W **88**
Atlin, L., Can. 60N 133W **72**
Aţ Ţā'if, Sau. Ar. 21N 41E **142**
Attleboro, Ma., U.S. 42N 71W **91**
Aţ Ţurayf, Sau. Ar. 32N 38E **142**
Atyraū, Kaz. 47N 52E **115**
Auburn, Me., U.S. 44N 70W **91**
Auckland, N.Z. 37S 175E **157**
Augsburg, Ger. 48N 11E **117**
Augusta, Ga., U.S. 33N 82W **93**
Augusta, Me., U.S. 44N 70W **77**
Aurangābād, India 20N 76E **143**
Aurillac, Fr. 45N 2E **117**
Aurora, Il., U.S. 42N 88W **90**
Austin, Tx., U.S. 30N 98W **95**
Australia, Ctry., Oc. 25S 135E **156**
Austria, Ctry., Eur. 47N 13E **117**
Avignon, Fr. 44N 5E **117**

Ayaköz, Kaz.	48N	80 E	140
Ayan, Russia	56N	138 E	141
Aydin, Tur.	38N	28 E	121
Ayers Rock, see Uluru, Mt., Austl.	25S	131 E	156
Aysha, Eth.	11N	43 E	129
Azerbaijan, Ctry., Asia	40N	47 E	115
Azores (Açores), Is., Port.	38N	29W	128
Azov, Sea of, Russia-Ukr.	46N	36 E	121
Az Ẓahrān (Dhahran), Sau. Ar.	26N	50 E	142
Az Zaqāzīq, Egypt	31N	32 E	129

B

Babanūsah, Sudan	12N	28 E	129
Bābol, Iran	36N	53 E	142
Babruysk, Bela.	53N	29 E	114
Babylon, Ruins, Iraq	32N	45 E	142
Bacău, Rom.	47N	27 E	121
Bachu, China	40N	78 E	146
Bac Lieu, Viet.	10N	106 E	148
Bacolod, Phil.	11N	123 E	148
Baden-Baden, Ger.	49N	8 E	117
Baffin Bay, B., N.A.	72N	65W	52
Baffin I., Nu., Can.	67N	69W	73
Bāfq, Iran	32N	55 E	142
Bagé, Braz.	31S	54W	106
Baghdād, Iraq	33N	44 E	142
Bago, Myan.	17N	96 E	148
Baguio, Phil.	16N	121 E	149
Bahamas, Ctry., N.A.	27N	77W	97
Bahāwalpur, Pak.	29N	72 E	143
Bahía Blanca, Arg.	39S	62W	106
Bahrain, Ctry., Asia	26N	51 E	142
Baia-Mare, Rom.	48N	24 E	121
Baker, Or., U.S.	45N	118W	82
Baker, L., Nu., Can.	64N	96W	72
Bakersfield, Ca., U.S.	35N	119W	84
Bakhtarān, Iran	34N	47 E	142
Baku (Bakı), Azer.	40N	50 E	115
Balashov, Russia	51N	43 E	115
Baleares, Islas, Is., Spain	39N	3 E	120
Baleine, Grande R. de la, R., P.Q., Can.	55N	76W	73
Bali, I., Indon.	8S	115 E	148
Balıkesir, Tur.	40N	28 E	121
Balkhash, Lake, see Balqash köli, L., Kaz.	47N	75 E	140
Ballarat, Austl.	38S	144 E	157
Balqash, Kaz.	47N	75 E	140
Balqash köli, L., Kaz.	47N	75 E	140
Balsas, R., Mex.	18N	101W	96
Balta, Ukr.	48N	30W	121
Bălţi, Mol.	48N	28 E	121
Baltic Sea, Eur.	55N	17 E	116
Baltimore, Md., U.S.	39N	77W	91
Bamako, Mali	13N	8W	128
Bamberg, Ger.	50N	11 E	117
Bampūr, Iran	27N	60 E	142
Bānda, India	26N	80 E	143
Banda, Laut (Banda Sea), Indon.	6S	127 E	149
Bandar-e Abbās, Iran	27N	56 E	142
Bandar-e Anzalī, Iran	37N	49 E	142
Bandar-e Būshehr, Iran	29N	51 E	142
Bandar-e Khomeynī, Iran	30N	49 E	142
Bandar-e Torkeman, Iran	37N	54 E	142
Bandar Lampung, Indon.	5S	105 E	148
Bandirma, Tur.	40N	28 E	121
Bandung, Indon.	7S	107 E	148
Bangalore, India	13N	75 E	143
Banghāzī (Bengasi), Libya	32N	20 E	129
Bangkok (Krung Thep), Thai.	14N	100 E	148
Bangladesh, Ctry., Asia	24N	90 E	143
Bangui, C.A.R.	4N	19 E	129
Bangweulu, L., Zam.	12S	30 E	130
Banī Suwayf, Egypt	29N	31 E	129
Banja Luka, Bos.	45N	17 E	121
Banjarmasin, Indon.	3S	115 E	148
Banjul, Gam.	13N	17W	128
Baotou, China	40N	110 E	147
Baraawe, Som.	1N	44 E	127
Baranavichy, Bela.	53N	26 E	114
Barbacena, Braz.	21S	44W	105
Barbados, Ctry., N.A.	14N	60W	97
Barberton, Oh., U.S.	41N	82W	90
Barcelona, Spain	41N	2 E	120
Bareilly, India	28N	79 E	143
Bari, Italy	41N	17 E	117
Barkol, China	44N	93 E	146
Bârlad, Rom.	46N	28 E	121
Barletta, Italy	41N	16 E	117
Barnaul, Russia	53N	83 E	140
Barquisimeto, Ven.	10N	69W	104
Barrancabermeja, Col.	7N	74W	104
Barranquilla, Col.	11N	75W	104
Barreiro, Port.	39N	9W	120
Barrhead, Ab., Can.	54N	114W	72
Barrow-in-Furness, Eng., U.K.	54N	3W	116
Basel, Switz.	48N	8 E	117
Basse Terre, Guad.	16N	62W	97
Bass Str., Austl.	40S	145 E	157
Bastia, Fr.	43N	9 E	117
Bata, Eq. Gui.	2N	10 E	128
Batang, China	30N	99 E	146
Batangas, Phil.	14N	121 E	149
Bătdâmbâng, Camb.	13N	103 E	148
Bath, Eng., U.K.	51N	2W	117
Batna, Alg.	36N	6 E	128
Baton Rouge, La., U.S.	30N	91W	95
Battle Creek, Mi., U.S.	42N	85W	90
Batumi, Geor.	42N	41 E	115
Bauang, Phil.	17N	120 E	149
Bauru, Braz.	22S	49W	105
Bay, Laguna de, L., Phil.	14N	121 E	149
Bay City, Mi., U.S.	44N	84W	90
Baykal, Ozero (L. Baikal), Russia	53N	109 E	141
Baykit, Russia	62N	97 E	141
Bayonne, Fr.	43N	1W	117
Bayonne, N.J., U.S.	41N	74W	91
Bayqongyr, Kaz.	48N	66 E	140
Beatrice, Ne., U.S.	40N	97W	87
Beaumont, Tx., U.S.	30N	94W	95
Bedford, Eng., U.K.	52N	0	117
Beihai, China	21N	109 E	146
Beijing (Peking), China	40N	116 E	147
Beirut, Leb.	34N	35 E	142
Beja, Tun.	37N	9 E	120
Bejaïa, Alg.	37N	5 E	128
Belarus, Ctry., Eur.	53N	28 E	114
Belcher Is., Nu., Can.	56N	79W	73
Belém (Pará), Braz.	1S	48W	105
Belfast, N. Ire., U.K.	55N	6W	116
Belfort, Fr.	48N	7 E	117
Belgium, Ctry., Eur.	51N	3 E	117
Belgrade (Beograd), Yugo.	45N	21 E	121
Belize, Ctry., N.A.	17N	89W	96
Belize City, Belize	17N	88W	96
Bellary, India	15N	77 E	143
Belle Isle, Str. of, Can.	51N	56W	73
Bellingham, Wa., U.S.	49N	122W	82
Belmopan, Belize	16N	89W	96
Belogorsk, Russia	51N	129 E	141
Belo Horizonte, Braz.	20S	44W	105
Beloit, Wi., U.S.	43N	89W	89
Beloretsk, Russia	54N	58 E	115
Bend, Or., U.S.	44N	121W	82
Benevento, Italy	41N	15 E	117
Bengal, Bay of, Asia	18N	88 E	138
Bengbu, China	33N	117 E	147
Benin, Ctry., Afr.	8N	2 E	128
Benin, Bight of, B., Afr.	5N	2 E	128
Benin City, Nig.	6N	6 E	128
Beni Saf, Alg.	35N	1W	128
Benoni, S. Afr.	26S	28 E	130
Benue, R., Cam.-Nig.	8N	8 E	128
Berbera, Som.	10N	45 E	127
Berdychiv, Ukr.	50N	29 E	114
Berëzovo, Russia	64N	65 E	140
Bergamo, Italy	46N	10 E	117
Bergen, Nor.	60N	5 E	116
Berhampur, India	19N	85 E	143
Bering Sea, Asia-N.A.	58N	179W	139
Berkeley, Ca., U.S.	38N	122W	84
Berlin, Ger.	52N	13 E	117
Bermuda, Dep., N.A.	32N	65W	97
Bern, Switz.	47N	7 E	117
Bernal, Arg.	34S	58W	106
Berwyn, Il., U.S.	42N	88W	90
Besançon, Fr.	47N	6 E	117
Beskra, Alg.	35N	6 E	128
Bessemer, Al., U.S.	33N	87W	92
Bethel, Ak., U.S.	61N	162W	76
Bethelehem, Pa., U.S.	41N	75W	91
Bethlehem, W.B.	32N	35 E	121
Beverly, Ma., U.S.	43N	71W	91
Beyşehir Gölü, L., Tur.	38N	32 E	121
Bezhitsa, Russia	53N	34 E	115
Béziers, Fr.	43N	3 E	117
Bhāgalpur, India	25N	87 E	143
Bhātpāra, India	23N	89 E	143
Bhaunagar, India	22N	73 E	143
Bhopāl, India	23N	77 E	143
Bhuj, India	24N	70 E	143
Bhutan, Ctry., Asia	27N	90 E	143
Biafra, Bight of, B., Afr.	3N	9 E	128
Białystok, Pol.	53N	23 E	116
Bielefeld, Ger.	52N	9 E	117
Bienville, Lac, L., P.Q., Can.	56N	73W	73
Bilāspur, India	22N	82 E	143
Bilbao, Spain	43N	3W	120
Billings, Mt., U.S.	46N	108W	83
Biloxi, Ms., U.S.	30N	89W	92
Binghamton, N.Y., U.S.	42N	76W	91
Bioko, I., Eq. Gui.	3N	8 E	128
Birmingham, Eng., U.K.	52N	2W	117
Birmingham, Al., U.S.	34N	87W	92
Birobidzhan, Russia	49N	133 E	141
Birsk, Russia	55N	55 E	140
Bisbee, Az., U.S.	31N	110W	85
Biscay, B. of, Fr.-Spain	45N	3W	120
Bishkek, Kyrg.	43N	75 E	140
Bisho, S. Afr.	33N	27W	130
Bismarck, N.D., U.S.	47N	101W	88
Bissau, Gui-B.	12N	16W	128
Bitola, Mac.	41N	21 E	121
Bitterroot Range, U.S.	47N	115W	82
Biysk, Russia	53N	85 E	140
Bizerte, Tun.	37N	10 E	128
Black Hills, U.S.	44N	104W	88
Black Sea, Eur.	43N	33 E	121
Blagoveshchensk, Russia	50N	128 E	141
Blanca, B., Arg.	39S	61W	106
Blantyre, Mwi.	16S	35 E	130
Bloemfontein, S. Afr.	29S	26 E	130
Blois, Fr.	48N	1 E	117
Bloomington, In., U.S.	39N	87W	90
Blue Mts., U.S.	46N	118W	82
Blue Nile, R., Eth.-Sudan	12N	34 E	129
Blue Ridge, U.S.	37N	81W	77
Bobo-Dioulasso, Burkina	11N	4W	128
Bodaybo, Russia	57N	115 E	141
Boden See, L., Ger.-Switz.	48N	9 E	117
Bogor, Indon.	7S	107 E	148
Bogotá, see Santa Fe de Bogotá, Col.	5N	74W	104
Bogotol, Russia	56N	89 E	140
Bo Hai, B., China	39N	119 E	147
Bohemian Forest, Mts., Ger.-Czech Rep.	50N	12 E	117
Boise, Id., U.S.	44N	116W	82
Boissevain, Mb., Can.	49N	100W	72
Bolivia, Ctry., S.A.	17S	64W	104
Bologna, Italy	44N	11 E	117
Bolzano, Italy	46N	11 E	117
Bombay, India	19N	73 E	143
Bomi Hills, Lib.	7N	11W	128
Bomongo, D.R.C.	2N	18 E	129
Bonn, Ger.	51N	7 E	117
Boothia Pen., N.T., Can.	71N	94W	72
Boras, Swe.	58N	13 E	116
Borāzjān, Iran	29N	51 E	142
Bordeaux, Fr.	45N	1W	117
Bordj-Bou-Arreridj, Alg.	36N	5 E	120
Borisoglebsk, Russia	51N	42 E	115
Borneo, I., Asia	1N	113 E	148
Borovichi, Russia	58N	34 E	140
Borūjerd, Iran	34N	49 E	142
Borzya, Russia	51N	117 E	141
Boshan, China	37N	118 E	147
Bosnia and Herzegovina, Ctry., Eur.	44N	18 E	121
Boston, Ma., U.S.	42N	71W	91
Bothnia, Gulf of, Fin.-Swe.	62N	19 E	116
Botosani, Rom.	48N	27 E	121
Botswana, Ctry., Afr.	22S	23 E	130
Bouaké, C. Iv.	8N	5W	128
Boulder, Co., U.S.	40N	105W	86
Boulder City, Nv., U.S.	36N	115W	84
Bourges, Fr.	47N	2 E	117
Bowling Green, Oh., U.S.	41N	84W	90
Bozeman, Mt., U.S.	46N	111W	83
Bradford, Eng., U.K.	54N	2W	116
Braga, Port.	42N	8W	120
Brahmaputra, R., Asia	27N	92 E	143
Brăila, Rom.	45N	28 E	121
Brandenburg, Ger.	52N	13 E	117
Brandon, Mb., Can.	50N	100W	72
Brasília, Braz.	16S	48W	105
Brasov, Rom.	46N	26 E	121
Bratislava, Slvk.	48N	17 E	117
Bratsk, Russia	56N	101 E	141
Braunschweig, Ger.	52N	11 E	117
Brawley, Ca., U.S.	33N	116W	84
Brazil, Ctry., S.A.	8S	60W	105
Brazzaville, Congo	4S	15 E	130
Bremen, Ger.	53N	9 E	117
Bremerhaven, Ger.	54N	9 E	117
Bremerton, Wa., U.S.	48N	123W	82
Brenner P., Aus.-Italy	47N	11 E	117
Brescia, Italy	46N	10 E	117
Brest, Fr.	48N	4W	117
Brest, Bela.	52N	24 E	114
Bridgeport, Ct., U.S.	41N	73W	91
Bridgetown, Barb.	13N	60W	97
Brig, Switz.	46N	8 E	117
Brighton, Eng., U.K.	51N	0	117
Brisbane, Austl.	27S	153 E	157
Bristol, Eng., U.K.	51N	3W	117
Bristol, Tn., U.S.	37N	82W	93
Bristol Chan., U.K.	51N	4W	117
British Columbia, Prov., Can.	56N	126W	72
British Isles, Eur.	55N	4W	116
Brno, Czech Rep.	49N	17 E	117
Brockton, Ma., U.S.	42N	71W	91
Brownsville, Tx., U.S.	26N	97W	95
Brownwood, Tx., U.S.	32N	99W	94
Brugge, Bel.	51N	3 E	117
Brunei, Ctry., Asia	5N	114 E	148
Brunswick, Ga., U.S.	31N	81W	93
Brussels, Bel.	51N	4 E	117
Bryansk, Russia	53N	34 E	115
Bucaramanga, Col.	7N	73W	104
Bucharest, Rom.	44N	26 E	121
Budapest, Hung.	47N	19 E	117
Buenaventura, Col.	4N	77W	104
Buenos Aires, Arg.	34S	58W	106
Buenos Aires, L., Arg.-Chile	46S	72W	106
Buffalo, N.Y., U.S.	43N	79W	91
Bug, R., Eur.	52N	21 E	116
Bugul'ma, Russia	55N	53 E	140
Bujumbura, Bdi.	3S	29 E	130
Bukavu, D.R.C.	3S	29 E	130
Bukhara, Uzb.	40N	64 E	142
Bula, Indon.	3S	130 E	149
Bulawayo, Zimb.	20S	29 E	130
Bulgaria, Ctry., Eur.	43N	25 E	121

Bulun, Russia	71N	127 E	**141**
Buna, Pap. N. Gui.	9S	148 E	**149**
Buraydah, Sau. Ar.	26N	44 E	**142**
Burdwān, India	23N	88 E	**143**
Bureya, Russia	50N	130 E	**141**
Burgas, Bul.	42N	27 E	**121**
Burgos, Spain	42N	4W	**120**
Burhānpur, India	21N	76 E	**143**
Burkina Faso, Ctry., Afr.	13N	3W	**128**
Burlington, Ia., U.S.	41N	91W	**89**
Burlington, Vt.	44N	73W	**91**
Burma, see Myanmar, Ctry., Asia	22N	95 E	**146**
Bursa, Tur.	40N	28 E	**121**
Būr Sūdān, Sudan	19N	37 E	**129**
Burundi, Ctry., Afr.	3S	30 E	**130**
Butler, Pa., U.S.	41N	80W	**91**
Butte, Mt., U.S.	46N	113W	**83**
Buy, Russia	58N	42 E	**140**
Buzău, Rom.	45N	27 E	**121**
Buzuluk, Russia	53N	52 E	**140**
Bydgoszcz, Pol.	53N	18 E	**116**
Bytom, Pol.	50N	19 E	**117**

C

Cabimas, Ven.	10N	71W	**104**
Cabinda, Ang.	6S	12 E	**130**
Cáceres, Spain	39N	6W	**120**
Cachoeiro do Itapemirim, Braz.	21S	41W	**105**
Cádiz, Spain	37N	6W	**120**
Caen, Fr.	49N	0	**117**
Cagliari, Italy	39N	9 E	**117**
Caguas, P.R.	18N	66W	**97**
Cairo (Al Qāhirah), Egypt	30N	31 E	**129**
Cairo, Il., U.S.	37N	89W	**90**
Calabar, Nig.	5N	8 E	**128**
Calais, Fr.	51N	2 E	**117**
Călărasi, Rom.	44N	27 E	**121**
Calcutta, see Kolkata, India	23N	88 E	**143**
Calexico, Ca., U.S.	33N	115W	**84**
Calgary, Ab., Can.	51N	114W	**72**
Cali, Col.	3N	76W	**104**
California, State, U.S.	38N	121W	**76**
California, G. de, Mex.	26N	110W	**96**
Callao, Peru	13S	77W	**104**
Caltanissetta, Italy	37N	14 E	**117**
Camagüey, Cuba	21N	78W	**97**
Cambodia, Ctry., Asia	12N	104 E	**148**
Cambrai, Fr.	50N	3 E	**117**
Cambridge, Eng., U.K.	52N	0	**117**
Cambridge, Ma., U.S.	42N	71W	**91**
Camden, N.J., U.S.	40N	75W	**91**
Cameroon, Ctry., Afr.	5N	12 E	**128**
Campeche, Mex.	19N	90W	**96**
Campinas, Braz.	23S	47W	**106**
Campo Grande, Braz.	20S	55W	**105**
Campos, Braz.	22S	41W	**105**
Canada, Ctry., N.A.	55N	100W	**72**
Canadian, R., U.S.	35N	97W	**86**
Çanakkale Boğazı (Dardanelles), Str., Tur.	40N	26 E	**121**
Canarias, Islas (Canary Is.), Spain	29N	18W	**128**
Canaveral, C., Fl., U.S.	28N	81W	**93**
Canberra, Austl.	35S	149 E	**157**
Caniapiscau, R., P.Q., Can.	57N	69W	**73**
Cannes, Fr.	44N	7 E	**117**
Canton, Oh., U.S.	41N	81W	**90**
Cape Girardeau, Mo., U.S.	37N	90W	**87**
Cape Town, S. Afr.	34S	18 E	**130**
Cape Verde, Ctry., Afr.	16N	25W	**128**
Cap-Haïtien, Haiti	20N	72W	**97**
Caprivi Strip, Reg., Nmb.	18S	23 E	**130**
Caracas, Ven.	10N	67W	**104**
Caravelas, Braz.	18S	39W	**105**
Carcassonne, Fr.	43N	2 E	**117**
Cardiff, Wales, U.K.	51N	3W	**117**
Caribbean Sea, N.A.-S.A.	15N	67W	**97**
Cariboo Mts., B.C., Can.	54N	122W	**72**
Carlisle, Eng., U.K.	55N	3W	**116**
Carpathians, Mts., Eur.	49N	22 E	**121**
Carpentaria, Gulf of, Austl.	15S	138 E	**156**
Carrara, Italy	44N	10 E	**117**
Carson City, Nv., U.S.	39N	120W	**84**
Cartagena, Col.	10N	76W	**104**
Cartagena, Spain	38N	1W	**120**
Carthage, Tun.	37N	10 E	**120**
Caruaru, Braz.	8S	36W	**105**
Casablanca, Mor.	34N	8W	**128**
Cascade Ra., N.A.	44N	122W	**82**
Casper, Wy., U.S.	43N	106W	**83**
Caspian Sea, Asia-Eur.	42N	49 E	**115**
Castellón de la Plana, Spain	40N	0	**120**
Catamarca, Arg.	28S	66W	**106**
Catania, Italy	37N	15 E	**117**
Caucasus Mts., Asia-Eur.	43N	42 E	**115**
Caxias do Sul, Braz.	29S	51W	**106**
Cayenne, Fr. Gu.	5N	52W	**105**
Cebu, Phil.	10N	124 E	**149**
Cedar, L., Mb., Can.	53N	101W	**72**
Cedar Rapids, Ia., U.S.	42N	92W	**89**
Cegléd, Hung.	47N	20 E	**117**
Celebes (Sulawesi), I., Indon.	2S	120 E	**148**
Celebes Sea, Asia	4N	122 E	**148**
Celle, Ger.	53N	10 E	**117**
Central, Cordillera, Ra., Bol.	21S	65W	**104**
Central African Republic, Ctry., Afr.	7N	20 E	**129**
České Budějovice, Czech Rep.	49N	14 E	**117**
Ceuta, Sp. N. Afr.	36N	5W	**120**
Chad, Ctry., Afr.	15N	17 E	**129**
Chad, L., Afr.	14N	14 E	**129**
Chalkida, Grc.	39N	24 E	**121**
Chalon-sur-Saône, Fr.	47N	5 E	**117**
Chaman, Pak.	31N	66 E	**143**
Champaign, Il., U.S.	40N	88W	**90**
Champlain, L., Can.-U.S.	45N	73W	**91**
Changchun, China	44N	125 E	**147**
Changde, China	29N	112 E	**147**
Changsha, China	28N	113 E	**147**
Changzhou, China	32N	120 E	**147**
Chania, Grc.	35N	24 E	**121**
Channel Is., Eur.	49N	3W	**117**
Chanthaburi, Thai.	13N	102 E	**148**
Chanute, Ks., U.S.	38N	95W	**87**
Chao'an, China	24N	117 E	**147**
Chao Phraya, R., Thai.	14N	100 E	**148**
Chapala, Lago de, L., Mex.	20N	103W	**96**
Chapel Hill, N.C., U.S.	36N	79W	**93**
Chardzhou, Turk.	39N	64 E	**142**
Charleroi, Bel.	50N	5 E	**117**
Charleston, S.C., U.S.	33N	80W	**93**
Charleston, W.V., U.S.	38N	82W	**90**
Charlotte, N.C., U.S.	35N	81W	**93**
Charlotte Amalie (St. Thomas), V.I.U.S.	18N	65W	**97**
Charlottesville, Va., U.S.	38N	78W	**91**
Charlottetown, P.E., Can.	46N	63W	**73**
Châteauroux, Fr.	47N	2 E	**117**
Châtellerault, Fr.	47N	1 E	**117**
Chattanooga, Tn., U.S.	35N	85W	**92**
Chau-phu, Camb.	11N	105 E	**148**
Cheboksary, Russia	56N	47 E	**115**
Chełm, Pol.	51N	23 E	**117**
Chelsea, Ma., U.S.	42N	71W	**91**
Chelyabinsk, Russia	55N	61 E	**140**
Chemnitz, Ger.	51N	13 E	**117**
Chengde, China	41N	118 E	**147**
Chengdu, China	30N	104 E	**146**
Cherbourg, Fr.	50N	2W	**117**
Cherdyn', Russia	60N	56 E	**140**
Cherepanovo, Russia	54N	83 E	**140**
Cherepovets, Russia	59N	38 E	**115**
Chernihiv, Ukr.	51N	31 E	**115**
Chernivtsi, Ukr.	48N	26 E	**114**
Chernyakhovsk, Russia	55N	22 E	**116**
Chesapeake Bay, U.S.	38N	76W	**91**
Chesnokovka, Russia	53N	84 E	**140**
Chester, Pa., U.S.	40N	75W	**91**
Cheyenne, Wy., U.S.	41N	105W	**86**
Chiang Rai, Thai.	20N	100 E	**148**
Chibougamau, P.Q., Can.	50N	74W	**73**
Chicago, Il., U.S.	42N	88W	**90**
Chicago Heights, Il., U.S.	41N	88W	**90**
Chickasha, Ok., U.S.	35N	98W	**86**
Chiclayo, Peru	7S	80W	**104**
Chicopee, Ma., U.S.	42N	73W	**91**
Chicoutimi, P.Q., Can.	48N	71W	**73**
Chieti, Italy	42N	14 E	**117**
Chifeng, China	42N	119 E	**147**
Chihuahua, Mex.	29N	106W	**96**
Chikishlyar, Turk.	38N	54 E	**142**
Chile, Ctry., S.A.	38S	72W	**106**
Chillán, Chile	37S	72W	**106**
Chillicothe, Oh., U.S.	39N	83W	**90**
Chilung, Tai.	25N	122 E	**147**
Chimbote, Peru	9S	78W	**104**
Chimkent, see Shymkent, Kaz.	42N	70 E	**140**
China, Ctry., Asia	34N	101 E	**146**
Chingola, Zam.	13S	28 E	**130**
Chisinău, Mol.	47N	29 E	**114**
Chistopol', Russia	55N	50 E	**140**
Chita, Russia	52N	114 E	**141**
Chitrāl, Pak.	36N	72 E	**143**
Chittagong, Bngl.	22N	91 E	**143**
Chŏngjin, N. Kor.	42N	130 E	**147**
Chongqing, China	30N	107 E	**146**
Choybalsan, Mong.	48N	114 E	**147**
Christchurch, N.Z.	43S	173 E	**157**
Christmas I., Dep., Oc.	10S	105 E	**148**
Chumikan, Russia	55N	135 E	**141**
Chuquicamata, Chile	22S	69W	**106**
Churchill, Mb., Can.	59N	94W	**72**
Churchill, R., Can.	58N	95W	**72**
Chusovoy, Russia	58N	58 E	**115**
Chust, Uzb.	41N	71 E	**140**
Cicero, Il., U.S.	42N	88W	**90**
Cide, Tur.	42N	33 E	**121**
Ciénaga, Col.	11N	74W	**104**
Cienfuegos, Cuba	22N	80W	**97**
Cincinnati, Oh., U.S.	39N	84W	**90**
Cirebon, Indon.	7S	109 E	**148**
Ciudad Bolívar, Ven.	8N	64W	**104**
Ciudad Chetumal (Payo Obispo), Mex.	18N	88W	**96**
Ciudad Guayana, Ven.	9N	63W	**104**
Ciudad Juárez, Mex.	32N	106W	**96**
Ciudad Obregón, Mex.	28N	110W	**96**
Ciudad Real, Spain	39N	4W	**120**
Ciudad Victoria, Mex.	24N	99W	**96**
Clarksburg, W.V., U.S.	39N	80W	**91**
Clearwater, Fl., U.S.	28N	83W	**93**
Cleburne, Tx., U.S.	32N	97W	**95**
Clermont-Ferrand, Fr.	46N	3 E	**117**
Cleveland, Oh., U.S.	41N	82W	**90**
Cleveland Heights, Oh., U.S.	41N	82W	**90**
Clifton, N.J., U.S.	41N	74W	**91**
Clovis, N.M., U.S.	34N	103W	**86**
Cluj-Napoca, Rom.	47N	24 E	**121**
Coast Mts., Can.-U.S.	57N	131W	**72**
Coast Ranges, U.S.	40N	123W	**76**
Cod, Cape, Ma., U.S.	42N	70W	**91**
Coeur d'Alene, Id., U.S.	48N	117W	**82**
Coffeyville, Ks., U.S.	37N	96W	**87**
Coimbra, Port.	40N	8W	**120**
Colima, Mex.	19N	104W	**96**
Colmar, Fr.	49N	7 E	**117**
Cologne (Köln), Ger.	51N	7 E	**117**
Colombia, Ctry., S.A.	3N	74W	**104**
Colombo, Sri L.	7N	80 E	**143**
Colón, Pan.	9N	80W	**97**
Colon, Archipiélago de (Galápagos Is.), Ec.	0	90W	**104**
Colorado, State, U.S.	39N	105W	**76**
Colorado, R., Arg.	39S	65W	**106**
Colorado, R., Mex.-U.S.	36N	113W	**76**
Colorado, R., Tx., U.S.	30N	98W	**95**
Colorado Springs, Co., U.S.	39N	105W	**86**
Columbia, Mo., U.S.	39N	92W	**87**
Columbia, S.C., U.S.	34N	81W	**93**
Columbia, R., Can.-U.S.	46N	120W	**72**
Columbus, Ga., U.S.	32N	85W	**92**
Columbus, Oh., U.S.	40N	83W	**90**
Comilla, Bngl.	24N	91 E	**143**
Como, Italy	46N	9 E	**117**
Comodoro Rivadavia, Arg.	46S	68W	**106**
Comoros, Ctry., Afr.	12S	44 E	**131**
Conakry, Gui.	9N	14W	**128**
Concepción, Chile	37S	73W	**106**
Concepción del Uruguay, Arg.	33S	58W	**106**
Concord, N.H., U.S.	43N	71W	**91**
Concordia, Arg.	31S	58W	**106**
Congo, Ctry., Afr.	3S	14 E	**130**
Congo, R., Afr.	4S	16 E	**130**
Congo, Democratic Republic of the, Ctry., Afr.	1S	23 E	**130**
Connecticut, R., U.S.	44N	72W	**91**
Connecticut, State, U.S.	42N	73W	**77**
Constanta, Rom.	44N	29 E	**121**
Constantine, Alg.	36N	7 E	**128**
Cooch Behār, India	26N	90 E	**143**
Cook Islands, Dep., Oc.	20S	158W	**158**
Cook, Mt., see Aoraki, N.Z.	43S	170 E	**157**
Copenhagen (København), Den.	56N	12 E	**116**
Coral Gables, Fl., U.S.	26N	80W	**93**
Coral Sea, Oc.	14S	155 E	**157**
Córdoba, Arg.	32S	64W	**106**
Córdoba, Mex.	19N	97W	**96**
Córdoba, Spain	38N	5W	**120**
Cork, Ire.	52N	8W	**117**
Coro, Ven.	11N	70W	**104**
Corpus Christi, Tx., U.S.	28N	97W	**95**
Corrientes, Arg.	27S	59W	**106**
Corsica, I., Fr.	42N	9 E	**117**
Corsicana, Tx., U.S.	32N	96W	**95**
Çorum, Tur.	41N	35 E	**121**
Corvallis, Or., U.S.	45N	123W	**82**
Costa Rica, Ctry., N.A.	10N	85W	**97**
Cote d'Ivoire, Ctry., Afr.	7N	6W	**120**
Cotonou, Benin	7N	3 E	**128**
Cottbus, Ger.	52N	14 E	**117**
Council Bluffs, Ia., U.S.	41N	96W	**88**
Covington, Ky., U.S.	39N	85W	**90**
Craiova, Rom.	44N	24 E	**121**
Cranston, R.I., U.S.	42N	71W	**91**
Crater L., Or., U.S.	43N	122W	**82**
Cremona, Italy	45N	10 E	**117**
Crete, I., Grc.	35N	25 E	**121**
Crimean Peninsula, see Kryms'kyy pivostriv, Ukr.	45N	34 E	**115**
Croatia, Ctry., Eur.	15N	15 E	**120**
Croydon, Eng., U.K.	51N	0	**117**
Cuba, Ctry., N.A.	22N	79W	**97**
Cúcuta, Col.	8N	72W	**104**
Cuddalore, India	12N	80 E	**143**
Cuddapah, India	14N	79 E	**143**
Cuenca, Ec.	3S	79W	**104**
Cuernavaca, Mex.	19N	99W	**96**
Cuiabá, Braz.	16S	56W	**105**
Culiacán, Mex.	25N	107W	**96**
Cullera, Spain	39N	0	**120**
Cumaná, Ven.	10N	64W	**104**
Curico, Chile	35S	71W	**106**
Curitiba, Braz.	26S	49W	**106**
Cusco, Peru	14S	72W	**104**
Cuttack, India	21N	86 E	**143**
Cuyahoga Falls, Oh., U.S.	41N	81W	**90**
Cyprus, Ctry., Asia	35N	33 E	**121**

Cyprus, North, Ctry., Asia 36N 33 E 121
Czech Republic, Ctry., Eur. 49N 15 E 117
Czestochowa, Pol. 51N 19 E 117

D

Dakar, Sen. 15N 17W 128
Dakhla, W. Sah. 24N 16W 128
Dali, China 35N 110 E 146
Dalian (Lüda), China 39N 121 E 147
Dallas, Tx., U.S. 33N 97W 95
Dalnerechensk, Russia 46N 134 E 141
Damān, India 21N 73 E 143
Damanhūr, Egypt 31N 31 E 129
Damascus (Dimashq), Syria 34N 36 E 142
Dāmghān, Iran 36N 54 E 142
Da Nang (Tourane), Viet. 16N 108 E 148
Dandong, China 40N 124 E 147
Danube, R., Eur. 43N 24 E 121
Danville, Il., U.S. 40N 88W 90
Danville, Va., U.S. 37N 80W 93
Danzig, Gulf of, Pol.-Russia 54N 19 E 116
Darbhanga, India 26N 86 E 143
Dar es Salaam, Tan. 7S 39 E 131
Darjeeling, India 27N 88 E 143
Darling, R., Austl. 33S 143 E 157
Darling Ra., Austl. 31S 116 E 156
Darmstadt, Ger. 50N 9 E 117
Darnah, Libya 33N 23 E 129
Darwin, Austl. 12S 131 E 156
Daugavpils, Lat. 56N 26 E 114
Dauphin, Mb., Can. 51N 100W 72
Davao, Phil. 7N 125 E 149
Davenport, Ia., U.S. 42N 91W 89
David, Pan. 8N 82W 97
Dawei, Myan. 14N 98 E 148
Dawson, Yk., Can. 64N 139W 72
Dawson Creek, B.C., Can. 56N 120W 72
Daxian, China 31N 107 E 146
Dayr az Zawr, Syria 35N 40 E 142
Dayton, Oh., U.S. 40N 84W 90
Daytona Beach, Fl., U.S. 29N 81W 93
Da Yunhe (Grand Canal), China 35N 117 E 147
Dead Sea, Asia 32N 35 E 121
Deadwood, S.D., U.S. 44N 104W 88
Dearborn, Mi., U.S. 42N 83W 90
Death Valley, Ca., U.S. 36N 117W 84
Debrecen, Hung. 48N 22 E 117
Decatur, Al., U.S. 34N 87W 92
Decatur, Il., U.S. 40N 89W 90
Deccan Plat., India 19N 77 E 143
Dehra Dūn, India 30N 78 E 143
Delaware, State, U.S. 39N 75W 77
Delaware, R., U.S. 42N 75W 91
Delaware Bay, U.S. 39N 75W 91
Delhi, India 29N 77 E 143
Del Rio, Tx., U.S. 29N 101W 94
Deming, N.M., U.S. 32N 108W 85
Denison, Tx., U.S. 34N 97W 87
Denizli, Tur. 38N 29 E 121
Denmark, Ctry., Eur. 56N 10 E 116
Denver, Co., U.S. 40N 105W 86
Dera Ghāzi Khān, Pak. 30N 71 E 143
Dera Ismāīl Khān, Pak. 32N 71 E 143
Derby, Eng., U.K. 53N 1W 117
Dese, Eth. 11N 40 E 129
Des Moines, Ia., U.S. 42N 94W 89
Des Moines, R., U.S. 41N 93W 89
Des Plaines, Il., U.S. 42N 88W 90
Dessau, Ger. 52N 12 E 117
Detroit, Mi., U.S. 42N 83W 90
Devils L., N.D., U.S. 48N 99W 88
Dezfūl, Iran 32N 49 E 142
Dhaka (Dacca), Bngl. 24N 90 E 143
Dhawalāgiri, Mt., Nepal 28N 84 E 143
Dhule, India 21N 75 E 143
Dickinson, N.D., U.S. 47N 103W 88
Dijon, Fr. 47N 5 E 117
Dikson, Russia 73N 80 E 140
Dili, E. Timor 9S 126 E 149
Dire Dawa, Eth. 10N 42 E 129
District of Columbia, U.S. 39N 77W 91
Diu, India 21N 71 E 143
Diyarbakir, Tur. 38N 40 E 142
Djerid, Chott, L., Tun. 33N 8 E 120
Djibouti, Dji. 12N 43 E 129
Djibouti, Ctry., Afr. 12N 43 E 129
Dniprodzerzhyns'k, Ukr. 48N 34 E 115
Dnipropetrovs'k, Ukr. 48N 35 E 115
Dnister, R., Mol.-Ukr. 46N 30 E 121
Dobo, Indon. 6S 134 E 149
Dobrich, Bul. 44N 28 E 121
Dodge City, Ks., U.S. 38N 100W 86
Dodoma, C., Tan. 6S 36 E 131
Dominica, Ctry., N.A. 15N 61W 97
Dominican Republic, Ctry., N.A. 19N 71W 97
Don, R., Russia 47N 39 E 115
Donets'k, Ukr. 48N 38 E 115
Dong Hoi, Viet. 17N 107 E 148
Dortmund, Ger. 52N 7 E 117
Dothan, Al., U.S. 31N 85W 92
Douala, Cam. 4N 10 E 128
Douglas, Az., U.S. 31N 109W 85
Douro (Duero), R., Port.-Spain 41N 8W 120
Dover, Eng., U.K. 51N 1 E 117
Dover, De., U.S. 39N 75W 91
Dover, Str. of, Eng.-Fr. 50N 1 E 117
Drakensberg, Mts., Afr. 29S 29 E 130
Dráma, Grc. 41N 24 E 121
Dresden, Ger. 51N 14 E 117
Drohobych, Ukr. 49N 24 E 114
Drumheller, Ab., Can. 51N 113W 72
Dryden, On., Can. 50N 93W 73
Dubayy, U.A.E. 25N 55 E 142
Dublin (Baile Átha Cliath), Ire. 53N 6W 116
Dubrovnik, Cro. 43N 18 E 121
Dubuque, Ia., U.S. 42N 91W 89
Dudinka, Russia 69N 86 E 140
Dudley, Eng., U.K. 53N 2W 117
Duisburg, Ger. 51N 7 E 117
Duluth, Mn., U.S. 47N 92W 89
Dumyāṭ (Damietta), Egypt 31N 32 E 129
Dundalk, Ire. 54N 6W 116
Dundalk, Md., U.S. 39N 77W 91
Dundee, Scot., U.K. 56N 3W 116
Dunedin, N.Z. 46S 171 E 157
Dun Laoghaire, Ire. 53N 6W 116
Durango, Mex. 24N 105W 96
Durazno, Ur. 33S 57W 106
Durban, S. Afr. 30S 31 E 130
Durham, N.C., U.S. 36N 79W 93
Durrës, Alb. 41N 19 E 121
Dushanbe, Taj. 39N 69 E 140
Düsseldorf, Ger. 51N 7 E 117
Dzerzhinsk, Russia 56N 44 E 115
Dzhambul, see Zhambyl, Kaz. 43N 71 E 140

E

Eagle Pass, Tx., U.S. 29N 100W 94
East Chicago, In., U.S. 42N 87W 90
East China Sea, Asia 29N 124 E 147
East Cleveland, Oh., U.S. 41N 82W 90
Eastern Ghāts, Mts., India 16N 79 E 143
East Hartford, Ct., U.S. 42N 73W 91
East Liverpool, Oh., U.S. 41N 81W 90
East London, S. Afr. 33S 28 E 130
Easton, Pa., U.S. 41N 75W 91
East Orange, N.J., U.S. 41N 74W 91
East Providence, R.I., U.S. 42N 71W 91
East St. Louis, Il., U.S. 39N 90W 87
East Timor, Dep., Asia 9S 126 E 149
Ebro, R., Spain 41N 0 120
Ech Cheliff, Alg. 36N 2 E 128
Écija, Spain 37N 5W 120
Ecuador, Ctry., S.A. 1S 79W 104
Édessa, Grc. 41N 22 E 121
Edinburgh, Scot., U.K. 56N 3W 116
Edirne, Tur. 42N 27 E 121
Edmonton, Ab., Can. 54N 114W 72
Edson, Ab., Can. 54N 117W 72
Edward, L., Ug.-Zaire 0 29 E 130
Egypt, Ctry., Afr. 27N 30 E 129
Eisenach, Ger. 51N 10 E 117
El Aaiún, W. Sah. 27N 13W 128
Elazığ, Tur. 38N 39 E 121
Elblag, Pol. 54N 19 E 116
El Boulaïda, Alg. 37N 3 E 128
El'brus, Gora, Mt., Russia 43N 42 E 115
Elburz Mts., Iran 37N 51 E 142
El Djelfa, Alg. 35N 3 E 128
El Dorado, Ar., U.S. 33N 93W 87
El Ferrol, Spain 43N 8W 120
Elgin, Il., U.S. 42N 88W 90
Elizabeth, N.J., U.S. 41N 74W 91
El Jadida, Mor. 33N 9W 128
El Kairouan, Tun. 36N 10 E 128
Elkhart, In., U.S. 42N 86W 90
Elko, Nv., U.S. 41N 116W 82
Ellensburg, Wa., U.S. 47N 120W 82
Elmhurst, Il., U.S. 42N 88W 90
Elmira, N.Y., U.S. 42N 77W 91
El Pao, Ven. 8N 63W 104
El Paso, Tx., U.S. 32N 106W 94
El Qala, Alg. 37N 8 E 120
El Salvador, Ctry., N.A. 14N 89W 96
Elūru, India 17N 80 E 143
El Wad, Alg. 33N 7 E 128
Ely, Nv., U.S. 39N 115W 84
Elyria, Oh., U.S. 41N 82W 90
Emāmshahr, Iran 36N 55 E 142
Emporia, Ks., U.S. 38N 96W 87
Engel's, Russia 51N 46 E 115
England, Polit. Reg., U.K. 52N 2W 117
English Channel, Eur. 50N 2W 117
Enid, Ok., U.S. 36N 98W 86
Enschede, Neth. 52N 7 E 117
Ensenada, Mex. 32N 116W 96
Entebbe, Ug. 0 32 E 129
Enugu, Nig. 6N 7 E 128
Épinal, Fr. 48N 6 E 117
Equatorial Guinea, Ctry., Afr. 3N 9 E 128
Ereğli, Tur. 38N 34 E 121
Erfurt, Ger. 51N 11 E 117
Erie, Pa., U.S. 42N 80W 91
Erie, L., Can.-U.S. 42N 81W 90
Eritrea, Ctry., Afr. 16N 38 E 129
Ernākulam, India 10N 76 E 143
Erne, L., N. Ire., U.K. 55N 8W 116
Erzgebirge (Ore Mts.), Ger.-Czech Rep. 50N 13 E 117
Erzurum, Tur. 40N 41 E 142
Esbjerg, Den. 55N 8 E 116
Eşfahān, Iran 33N 51 E 142
Eskifjördur, Ice. 65N 14W 116
Eskilstuna, Swe. 59N 17 E 116
Eskişehir, Tur. 40N 30 E 121
Esquel, Arg. 43S 71W 106
Essen, Ger. 52N 7 E 117
Estonia, Ctry., Eur. 59N 26 E 114
Ethiopia, Ctry., Afr. 9N 38 E 129
Etna, Mt., Vol., Italy 38N 15 E 117
Etoshapan, L., Nmb. 19S 16 E 130
Euclid, Oh., U.S. 42N 82W 90
Eugene, Or., U.S. 44N 123W 82
Euphrates, R., Asia 36N 40 E 142
Eureka, Ca., U.S. 41N 124W 82
Evanston, Il., U.S. 42N 88W 90
Evansville, In., U.S. 38N 87W 90
Everest, Mt., China-Nepal 28N 87 E 143
Everett, Wa., U.S. 48N 122W 82
Évora, Port. 39N 8W 120
Exeter, Eng., U.K. 51N 4W 117
Eyre, L., Austl. 28S 136 E 156

F

Faeroe Is., Ctry., Eur. 62N 6W 116
Fairmont, W.V., U.S. 39N 80W 91
Faisalabad, Pak. 31N 73 E 143
Faizābād, India 27N 83 E 143
Fakfak, Indon. 3S 132 E 149
Falkland Islands, Dep., S.A. 51S 59W 106
Fall River, Ma., U.S. 42N 71W 91
Famagusta, Cyp. 35N 34 E 121
Farāh, Afg. 32N 62 E 142
Fargo, N.D., U.S. 47N 97W 88
Faro, Port. 37N 8W 120
Farrukhābād, India 27N 80 E 143
Fayetteville, N.C., U.S. 35N 79W 93
Felanitx, Spain 39N 3 E 120
Fenyang, China 37N 112 E 147
Feodosiya, Ukr. 45N 35 E 121
Ferdows, Iran 34N 58 E 142
Fergana, Uzb. 40N 72 E 140
Fergus Falls, Mn., U.S. 46N 96W 88
Ferrara, Italy 45N 12 E 117
Fès, Mor. 34N 5W 128
Feyzābād, Afg. 37N 71 E 143
Fiji, Ctry., Oc. 19S 175 E 159
Findlay, Oh., U.S. 41N 84W 90
Finland, Ctry., Eur. 65N 27 E 116
Finland, Gulf of, Eur. 60N 24 E 114
Fitchburg, Ma., U.S. 43N 72W 91
Flagstaff, Az., U.S. 35N 112W 85
Flint, Mi., U.S. 43N 84W 90
Florence, Al., U.S. 35N 88W 92
Florence (Firenze), Italy 44N 11 E 117
Flores, I., Indon. 8S 121 E 148
Flores, Laut (Flores Sea), Indon. 7S 120 E 148
Florianópolis, Braz. 27S 48W 106
Florida, State, U.S. 30N 84W 77
Florida, Strs. of, N.A. 25N 80W 97
Florida Keys, Is., Fl., U.S. 25N 81W 93
Flórina, Grc. 41N 21 E 121
Foggia, Italy 41N 16 E 117
Fond du Lac, Wi., U.S. 44N 88W 89
Fonseca, Golfo de, G., N.A. 13N 88W 96
Forli, Italy 44N 12 E 117
Formosa, Arg. 27S 58W 106
Formosa, Braz. 15S 47W 105
Fortaleza (Ceará), Braz. 4S 39W 105
Fort Collins, Co., U.S. 41N 105W 86
Fort-de-France, Mart. 15N 61W 97
Fort Dodge, Ia., U.S. 43N 94W 89
Fort Good Hope, N.T., Can. 66N 129W 72
Forth, Firth of, Str., Scot., U.K. 56N 3W 116
Fort Lauderdale, Fl., U.S. 26N 80W 93
Fort Macleod, Ab., Can. 50N 113W 72
Fort McPherson, N.T., Can. 68N 135W 72
Fort Myers, Fl., U.S. 27N 82W 93
Fort Nelson, R., B.C., Can. 58N 122W 72
Fort Sandeman, Pak. 31N 69 E 143

Fort Saskatchewan, Ab., Can. 54N 113W 72
Fort Scott, Ks., U.S. 38N 95W 87
Fort Severn, On., Can. 57N 88W 73
Fort Simpson, N.T., Can. 62N 122W 72
Fort Smith, N.T., Can. 60N 112W 72
Fort Smith, Ar., U.S. 35N 94W 87
Fort Wayne, In., U.S. 41N 85W 90
Fort Worth, Tx., U.S. 33N 97W 95
Foxe Chan., Nu., Can. 69N 80W 73
Franca, Braz. 21S 47W 105
France, Ctry., Eur. 47N 2 E 117
Frankfort, Ky., U.S. 38N 85W 90
Frankfurt am Main, Ger. 50N 9 E 117
Frankfurt an der Oder, Ger. 52N 15 E 117
Fraser, R., B.C., Can. 52N 122W 72
Fredericton, N.B., Can. 46N 67W 73
Freeport, Il., U.S. 42N 89W 90
Freeport, N.Y., U.S. 41N 74W 91
Freetown, S.L. 8N 13W 128
Freiberg, Ger. 51N 13 E 117
French Guiana, Ctry., S.A. 5N 53W 105
French Polynesia, Dep., Oc. 20S 140W 158
Fresnillo, Mex. 23N 103W 96
Fresno, Ca., U.S. 37N 120W 84
Fribourg, Switz. 47N 7 E 117
Frisian Is., Eur. 54N 5 E 117
Fujin, China 47N 132 E 147
Fuji San, Mt., Japan 36N 139 E 147
Fukui, Japan 36N 136 E 147
Fukuoka, Japan 34N 130 E 147
Fulda, Ger. 51N 10 E 117
Fuling, China 30N 107 E 146
Funchal, Port. 33N 16W 128
Fundy, B. of, Can. 44N 67W 73
Fürth, Ger. 49N 11 E 117
Fushun, China 42N 125 E 147
Fuyang, China 33N 116 E 147
Fuyu, China 45N 125 E 147
Fuzhou, China 26N 119 E 147

G

Gabon, Ctry., Afr. 2S 12 E 130
Gaborone, Bots. 25S 25 E 130
Gadsden, Al., U.S. 34N 86W 92
Gainesville, Fl., U.S. 30N 82W 93
Galapagos Is., see Colón, Archipiélago de, Ec. 1S 90W 104
Galati, Rom. 45N 28 E 121
Galle, Sri L. 6N 80 E 143
Gällivare, Swe. 68N 20 E 116
Gallup, N.M., U.S. 35N 109W 85
Galveston, Tx., U.S. 29N 95W 95
Gambia, The, Ctry., Afr. 13N 17W 128
Gäncä, Azer. 41N 46 E 115
Ganges, R., Bngl.-India 24N 98 E 143
Ganges, Mouths of the, Bngl.-India 22N 88 E 143
Gangtok, India 27N 89 E 143
Ganzhou, China 26N 115 E 147
Gar, China 31N 81 E 146
Garin, Arg. 34S 59W 106
Garm, Taj. 39N 70 E 140
Garonne, R., Fr.-Spain 45N 0 117
Gary, In., U.S. 42N 87W 90
Gatun, Pan. 9N 80W 96
Gävle, Swe. 61N 17 E 116
Gaya, India 25N 85 E 143
Gaziantep, Tur. 37N 37 E 121
Gdańsk (Danzig), Pol. 54N 19 E 116
Gdynia, Pol. 54N 18 E 116
Geelong, Austl. 38S 144 E 157
Gelibolu, Tur. 40N 27 E 121
Gemena, D.R.C. 3N 19 E 129
General San Martín, Arg. 34S 59W 106
Geneva, Switz. 46N 6 E 117
Geneva, L., Fr.-Switz. 46N 6 E 117
Genoa (Genova), Italy 44N 9 E 117
Gent, Bel. 51N 4 E 117
Geographe Chan., Austl. 24S 113 E 156
Georgetown, Guy. 8N 58W 105
George Town (Pinang), Malay. 5N 100 E 148
Georgia, Ctry., Asia 42N 44 E 115
Georgia, State, U.S. 33N 83W 77
Georgian B., On., Can. 46N 82W 73
Gera, Ger. 51N 12 E 117
Germantown, Oh., U.S. 40N 84W 90
Germany, Ctry., Eur. 51N 10 E 117
Germiston, S. Afr. 26S 28 E 130
Gerona, Spain 42N 3 E 120
Ghana, Ctry., Afr. 8N 2W 128
Ghanzi, Bots. 22S 22 E 130
Ghardaïa, Alg. 32N 4 E 128
Ghazaouet, Alg. 35N 2W 128
Ghaznī, Afg. 34N 68 E 143
Ghazzah (Gaza), Gaza Str. 32N 34 E 129
Ghilizane, Alg. 36N 1 E 128
Gibraltar, Ctry., Eur. 36N 5W 120
Gibraltar, Str. of, Afr.-Eur. 36N 6W 120
Gien, Fr. 48N 3 E 117
Gifu, Japan 35N 137 E 147
Gijón, Spain 43N 6W 120
Gila, R., U.S. 33N 114W 85
Girardot, Col. 4N 76W 104
Gizhiga, Russia 62N 161 E 141
Glama, R., Nor. 61N 11 E 116
Glasgow, Scot., U.K. 56N 4W 116
Glazov, Russia 58N 53 E 140
Glendale, Ca., U.S. 34N 118W 84
Gliwice, Pol. 50N 19 E 117
Globe, Az., U.S. 33N 111W 85
Gloucester, Eng., U.K. 52N 2W 117
Gloucester, Ma., U.S. 43N 71W 91
Gloversville, N.Y., U.S. 43N 74W 91
Gniezno, Pol. 53N 18 E 117
Gobi (Shamo), Des., China-Mong. 43N 102 E 146
Godāvari, R., India 19N 78 E 143
Goiânia, Braz. 17S 49W 105
Gómez Palacio, Mex. 26N 103W 96
Gonaïves, Haiti 19N 73W 97
Gonder, Eth. 13N 37 E 129
Good Hope, Cape of, S. Afr. 34S 19 E 130
Goodwood, S. Afr. 34S 19 E 130
Gorakhpur, India 27N 84 E 143
Gorgān, Iran 37N 54 E 142
Gorkiy, see Nizhniy Novgorod, Russia 56N 44 E 115
Görlitz, Ger. 51N 15 E 117
Gorno-Altaysk, Russia 52N 86 E 140
Gorodok, Russia 51N 104 E 141
Göteborg, Swe. 58N 12 E 116
Gotha, Ger. 51N 11 E 117
Gotland, I., Swe. 58N 19 E 116
Goukou, China 49N 122 E 147
Gradačac, Bos. 45N 18 E 121
Grampian Mts., Scot., U.K. 57N 5W 116
Granada, Spain 37N 4W 120
Granby, P.Q., Can. 45N 73W 73
Gran Chaco, Reg., S.A. 24S 62W 106
Grande-Prairie, Ab., Can. 55N 119W 72
Grand Erg Occidental, Dunes, Alg. 30N 1W 120
Grand Erg Oriental, Dunes, Alg. 30N 6 E 120
Grand Forks, N.D., U.S. 48N 97W 88
Grand Island, Ne., U.S. 41N 98W 86
Grand Junction, Co., U.S. 39N 109W 85
Grand Rapids, Mi., U.S. 43N 86W 90
Granite City, Il., U.S. 39N 90W 87
Granville, L., Mb., Can. 57N 100W 72
Gravelbourg, Sk., Can. 50N 107W 72
Graz, Aus. 47N 15 E 117
Great Artesian Basin, Austl. 23S 143 E 157
Great Australian Bight, Austl. 34S 127 E 156
Great Barrier Reef, Austl. 19S 148 E 157
Great Bear L., N.T., Can. 67N 120W 72
Great Dividing Ra., Austl. 25S 148 E 157
Greater Antilles, Is., N.A. 18N 75W 97
Greater Khingan Range, China 46N 120 E 147
Greater Sunda Is., Asia 4S 110 E 148
Great Falls, Mt., U.S. 47N 111W 83
Great Indian (Thar) Des., India-Pak. 27N 71 E 143
Great Karroo, Plat., S. Afr. 34S 21 E 130
Great Sandy Des., Austl. 22S 125 E 156
Great Slave L., N.T., Can. 62N 115W 72
Great Salt L., Ut., U.S. 41N 113W 83
Great Victoria Des., Austl. 30S 127 E 156
Great Wall, China 38N 108 E 146
Great Yarmouth, Eng., U.K. 53N 2 E 117
Greece, Ctry., Eur. 40N 22 E 121
Greeley, Co., U.S. 40N 105W 86
Green, R., U.S. 39N 110W 76
Green Bay, Wi., U.S. 44N 88W 89
Greenland, Ctry., N.A. 75N 39W 52
Green Mts., Vt. 44N 73W 91
Greenock, Scot., U.K. 56N 5W 116
Green River, Wy., U.S. 42N 110W 83
Greensboro, N.C., U.S. 36N 80W 93
Greenville, Ms., U.S. 33N 91W 92
Greenville, S.C., U.S. 35N 82W 93
Grenada, Ctry., N.A. 12N 62W 97
Grenoble, Fr. 45N 6 E 117
Grimsby, Eng., U.K. 54N 0 117
Groningen, Neth. 53N 6 E 117
Groot Vloer, Dry L., S. Afr. 30S 20 E 130
Grossglockner, Mt., Aus. 47N 13 E 117
Groton, Ct., U.S. 41N 72W 91
Guadalajara, Mex. 21N 103W 96
Guadeloupe, Ctry., N.A. 16N 62W 97
Guadiana, R., Port.-Spain 38N 8W 120
Gualeguay, Arg. 33S 59W 106
Gualeguaychú, Arg. 33S 58W 106
Guam, Dep., Oc. 14N 144 E 159
Guangzhou (Canton), China 23N 113 E 147
Guantánamo, Cuba 20N 75W 97
Guaporé, R., Bol.-Braz. 12S 64W 104
Guatemala, Guat. 15N 91W 96
Guatemala, Ctry., N.A. 15N 90W 96
Guayaquil, Ec. 2S 80W 104
Guayaquil, Golfo de, G., Ec. 3S 83W 104
Guernsey, Ctry., Eur. 50N 3W 117
Guilin, China 25N 110 E 147
Guinea, Ctry., Afr. 11N 12W 128
Guinea, Gulf of, Afr. 3N 3 E 128
Guinea-Bissau, Ctry., Afr. 12N 15W 128
Guiyang, China 27N 107 E 146
Gujrānwāla, Pak. 32N 74 E 143
Gulbarga, India 17N 77 E 143
Gulfport, Ms., U.S. 30N 89W 92
Guntūr, India 16N 80 E 143
Gur'yevsk, Russia 54N 86 E 140
Gusau, Nig. 12N 7 E 128
Gusev, Russia 55N 22 E 116
Guyana, Ctry., S.A. 5N 59W 105
Gwādar, Pak. 25N 62 E 142
Gwalior, India 26N 78 E 143
Gwardafuy, Gees, C., Som. 12N 51 E 127
Gyangzê, China 29N 89 E 146
Gydan, Khrebet (Kolymskiy Mts.), Russia 62N 155 E 141
Gyöngyös, Hung. 48N 20 E 117
Gyor, Hung. 48N 18 E 117
Gyumri, Arm. 41N 44 E 115

H

Hackensack, N.J., U.S. 41N 74W 91
Hadibū, Yemen 13N 54 E 142
Hagerstown, Md., U.S. 40N 78W 91
Haifa, Isr. 33N 35 E 142
Haikou, China 20N 110 E 148
Hā'il, Sau. Ar. 27N 42 E 142
Hailar, China 49N 119 E 147
Hainan Dao, I., China 19N 110 E 147
Hai Phong, Viet. 21N 107 E 148
Haiti, Ctry., N.A. 19N 73W 97
Hakodate, Japan 42N 141 E 147
Halethorpe, Md., U.S. 39N 77W 91
Halifax, N.S., Can. 45N 64W 73
Halle, Ger. 51N 12 E 117
Halmahera, I., Indon. 1N 128 E 149
Halmstad, Swe. 57N 13 E 116
Hamadān, Iran 35N 48 E 142
Hamburg, Ger. 54N 10 E 116
Hamden, Ct., U.S. 41N 73W 91
Hamhŭng, N. Kor. 40N 128 E 147
Hami (Kumul), China 43N 93 E 146
Hamilton, On., Can. 43N 80W 73
Hamilton, Oh., U.S. 39N 85W 90
Hammond, In., U.S. 42N 88W 90
Hampton, Va., U.S. 37N 76W 91
Hamtramck, Mi., U.S. 42N 83W 90
Hangzhou, China 30N 120 E 147
Hannibal, Mo., U.S. 40N 91W 87
Hannover, Ger. 52N 10 E 117
Hanoi, Viet. 21N 106 E 148
Hanyang, China 30N 114 E 147
Haparanda, Swe. 66N 24 E 116
Harare, Zimb. 18S 31 E 130
Harbin, China 46N 126 E 147
Hardwār, India 30N 78 E 143
Harer, Eth. 10N 42 E 129
Hargeysa, Som. 9N 44 E 127
Harlingen, Tx., U.S. 26N 98W 95
Harrisburg, Pa., U.S. 40N 77W 91
Hartford, Ct., U.S. 42N 73W 91
Hartlepool, Eng., U.K. 55N 1W 116
Harvey, Il., U.S. 42N 88W 90
Hastings, Eng., U.K. 51N 0 117
Hastings, Ne., U.S. 41N 99W 86
Hatay, Tur. 36N 36 E 121
Hatteras, C., N.C., U.S. 35N 76W 93
Hattiesburg, Ms., U.S. 31N 89W 92
Havana, Cuba 23N 82W 97
Havre, Mt., U.S. 49N 110W 83
Hawaii, State, U.S. 20N 157W 76
Hawaiian Islands, Is., U.S. 22N 158W 158
Hay River, N.T., Can. 61N 116W 72
Hazleton, Pa., U.S. 41N 76W 91
Hebrides, Is., Scot., U.K. 58N 6W 116
Hebron, Jord. 32N 35 E 121
Hecate Str., B.C., Can. 54N 131W 72
Hechuan, China 30N 106 E 146
Hefei, China 32N 117 E 147
Heidelberg, Ger. 49N 9 E 117
Heilbronn, Ger. 49N 9 E 117
Hekla, Vol., Ice. 64N 19W 116
Helena, Ar., U.S. 35N 91W 87
Helena, Mt., U.S. 47N 112W 83
Hellín, Spain 38N 2W 120
Helsingborg, Swe. 56N 13 E 116
Helsingør, Den. 56N 13 E 116
Helsinki, Fin. 60N 25 E 116

Hengyang, China 27N 112 E 147
Herāt, Afg. 34N 62 E 142
Hermosillo, Mex. 29N 111W 96
Hibbing, Mn., U.S. 47N 93W 89
Hidalgo del Parral, Mex. 27N 106W 96
Highland Park, Il., U.S. 42N 88W 90
High Prairie, Ab., Can. 55N 117W 72
Himalayas, Mts., Asia 29N 85 E 146
Ḩims, Syria 35N 36 E 142
Hindu Kush, Mts., Afg.-Pak. 35N 69 E 143
Hirosaki, Japan 41N 141 E 147
Hiroshima, Japan 34N 132 E 147
Hispaniola, I., N.A. 19N 72W 97
Hobart, Austl. 43S 147 E 157
Ho Chi Minh City (Saigon), Viet. 11N 107 E 148
Hódmezovásárhely, Hung. 46N 20 E 117
Hohhot, China 41N 112 E 147
Hokkaidō, I., Japan 43N 144 E 147
Holguín, Cuba 21N 76W 97
Hollywood, Fl., U.S. 26N 80W 93
Holyoke, Ma., U.S. 42N 72W 91
Homyel', Bela. 52N 31 E 115
Honduras, Ctry., N.A. 15N 87W 96
Honduras, Gulf of, N.A. 16N 87W 96
Hong Kong, China 22N 114 E 147
Hongshui, R., China 25N 108 E 146
Honolulu, Hi., U.S. 21N 158W 76
Honshū, I., Japan 34N 140 E 147
Hood, Mt., Or., U.S. 45N 122W 82
Hood River, Or., U.S. 46N 121W 82
Horlivka, Ukr. 48N 38 E 115
Hormuz, Strait of, Asia 26N 56 E 142
Hornos, Cabo de (C. Horn), Chile 56S 67W 106
Hotan, China 37N 80 E 146
Hot Springs, Ar., U.S. 34N 93W 87
Houston, Tx., U.S. 30N 95W 95
Hovd, Mong. 48N 92 E 146
Howrah, India 23N 88 E 143
Hrodna, Bela. 54N 24 E 114
Huaiyin, China 34N 119 E 147
Huambo, Ang. 13S 16 E 130
Huancayo, Peru 12S 75W 104
Huang (Yellow), R., China 36N 116 E 147
Huangyuan, China 37N 101 E 146
Huaral, Peru 11S 77W 104
Huascarán, Nevs., Pk., Peru 9S 77W 104
Hubli, India 15N 75 E 143
Hudson, R., U.S. 42N 74W 91
Hudson B., Can. 60N 85W 73
Hudson Str., Can. 63N 72W 73
Hue, Viet. 16N 108 E 148
Huelva, Spain 37N 7W 120
Hulan, China 46N 127 E 147
Hull, P.Q., Can. 45N 76W 73
Huludao, China 41N 121 E 147
Humboldt, Sk., Can. 52N 105W 72
Humboldt, R., Nv., U.S. 40N 118W 84
Hungary, Ctry., Eur. 47N 19 E 117
Huntington, W.V., U.S. 38N 82W 90
Huntsville, Al., U.S. 35N 87W 92
Huron, S.D., U.S. 44N 98W 88
Huron, L., Can.-U.S. 45N 83W 90
Hutchinson, Ks., U.S. 38N 98W 86
Hyderābād, India 17N 79 E 143
Hyderābād, Pak. 25N 68 E 143
Hyères, Fr. 43N 6 E 117

I

Ibadan, Nig. 7N 4 E 128
Ibagué, Col. 4N 75W 104
Icel, Tur. 37N 35 E 121
Iceland, Ctry., Eur. 65N 19W 116
Idaho, State, U.S. 44N 115W 76
Idaho Falls, Id., U.S. 43N 112W 83
Ife, Nig. 8N 5 E 128
Ifôghas, Adrar des, Reg., Alg.-Mali 20N 2 E 128
Igarka, Russia 67N 86 E 140
Iglesias, Italy 39N 9 E 117
Igluligaarjuk, Nu., Can. 63N 91W 72
Iguassu Falls, Arg.-Braz. 25S 54W 106
Ijebu Ode, Nig. 7N 4 E 128
Ilesha, Nig. 8N 5 E 128
Ilimsk, Russia 57N 104 E 141
Illinois, State, U.S. 40N 90W 77
Iloilo, Phil. 11N 123 E 148
Imperia, Italy 44N 8 E 117
Inch'ŏn, S. Kor. 37N 127 E 147
India, Ctry., Asia 24N 78 E 143
Indiana, State, U.S. 40N 86W 77
Indianapolis, In., U.S. 40N 86W 90
Indian Head, Sk., Can. 51N 104W 72
Indian Ocean 10S 75 E 53
Indonesia, Ctry., Asia 5S 115 E 148
Indore, India 23N 75 E 143
Indus, R., Asia 27N 68 E 143
Inn, R., Eur. 48N 13 E 117
Innsbruck, Aus. 47N 11 E 117
International Falls, Mn., U.S. 49N 93W 89
Inuvik, N.T., Can. 69N 134W 72
Inverness, Scot., U.K. 57N 4W 116
Ioánnina, Grc. 40N 21 E 121
Ionian Sea, Eur. 39N 18 E 121
Iowa, State, U.S. 42N 94W 77
Iowa City, Ia., U.S. 42N 92W 89
Ipoh, Malay. 5N 101 E 148
Ipswich, Eng., U.K. 52N 1 E 117
Iqaluit, Nu., Can. 63N 68W 73
Iquique, Chile 20S 70W 104
Iquitos, Peru 4S 73W 104
Irákleio, Grc. 35N 25 E 121
Iran, Ctry., Asia 33N 53 E 142
Iran, Plat. of, Iran 33N 56 E 142
Iraq, Ctry., Asia 32N 44 E 142
Irbit, Russia 58N 63 E 140
Ireland, Ctry., Eur. 53N 8W 116
Irkutsk, Russia 52N 104 E 141
Iron Mountain, Mi., U.S. 46N 88W 89
Irrawaddy, R., Myan. 20N 95 E 148
Irtysh, R., Asia 59N 70 E 140
Iseyin, Nig. 8N 3 E 128
Ishim, Russia 56N 69 E 140
Ishinomaki, Japan 38N 141 E 147
Isiro, D.R.C. 3N 28 E 129
Iskenderun, Tur. 37N 36 E 121
Islāmābād, Pak. 34N 73 E 143
Island, L., Mb., Can. 54N 96W 72
Isle of Man, Ctry., Eur. 54N 5W 116
Isparta, Tur. 38N 31 E 121
Israel, Ctry., Asia 32N 35 E 142
İstanbul, Tur. 41N 29 E 121
İstanbul Boğazı (Bosporus), Str., Tur. 41N 29 E 121
Itabuna, Braz. 15S 39W 105
Italy, Ctry., Eur. 43N 13 E 117
Ithaca, N.Y., U.S. 42N 76W 91
Ivano-Frankivs'k, Ukr. 49N 25 E 114
Ivory Coast, see Cote d'Ivoire, Ctry., Afr. 7N 6W 128
Iwo, Nig. 8N 4 E 128
Izhevsk, Russia 57N 53 E 115
Izmayil, Ukr. 45N 29 E 121
Izmir, Tur. 38N 27 E 121
İzmit, Tur. 41N 30 E 121

J

Jabalpur, India 23N 80 E 143
Jaboatão, Braz. 8S 35W 105
Jackson, Mi., U.S. 42N 84W 90
Jackson, Ms., U.S. 32N 90W 92
Jackson, Tn., U.S. 36N 89W 92
Jacksonville, Fl., U.S. 30N 82W 93
Jaén, Spain 38N 4W 120
Jaffna, Sri L. 10N 80 E 143
Jaipur, India 27N 76 E 143
Jakarta, Indon. 6S 107 E 148
Jakobstad, Fin. 64N 23 E 116
Jamaica, Ctry., N.A. 18N 77W 97
Jambi, Indon. 2S 103 E 148
James, R., U.S. 45N 98W 88
James, R., Va., U.S. 38N 78W 91
James B., Can. 54N 81W 73
Jamestown, N.Y., U.S. 42N 79W 91
Jamestown, N.D., U.S. 47N 99W 88
Jāmnagar, India 23N 70 E 143
Jamshedpur, India 23N 86 E 143
Janesville, Wi., U.S. 43N 89W 89
Japan, Ctry., Asia 34N 139 E 147
Japan, Sea of, Asia 41N 132 E 147
Jaroslaw, Pol. 50N 23 E 117
Jāsk, Iran 26N 58 E 142
Jasper, Ab., Can. 53N 118W 72
Java (Jawa), I., Indon. 9S 111 E 148
Jawa, Laut (Java Sea), Indon. 5S 110 E 148
Jayapura, Indon. 3S 141 E 149
Jefferson City, Mo., U.S. 39N 92W 87
Jelgava, Lat. 57N 24 E 116
Jena, Ger. 51N 12 E 117
Jerome, Az., U.S. 35N 112W 85
Jersey, Ctry., Eur. 49N 2W 117
Jersey City, N.J., U.S. 41N 74W 91
Jerusalem, Isr. 32N 35 E 142
Jhelum, Pak. 33N 74 E 143
Ji'an, China 27N 115 E 147
Jiaoxian, China 36N 120 E 147
Jiaxing, China 31N 121 E 147
Jiddah, Sau. Ar. 21N 39 E 142
Jihlava, Czech Rep. 49N 16 E 117
Jilin, China 44N 127 E 147
Jinan, China 37N 117 E 147
Jinhua, China 29N 120 E 147
Jining, China 35N 117 E 147
Jinja, Ug. 0 33 E 129
Jinta, China 40N 99 E 146
Jinzhou, China 41N 121 E 147
Jiujiang, China 30N 116 E 147
Jiuquan, China 40N 98 E 146
João Pessoa (Paraíba), Braz. 7S 35W 105
Jodhpur, India 26N 73 E 143
Johannesburg, S. Afr. 26S 28 E 130
Johnson City, Tn., U.S. 36N 82W 93
Johnstown, Pa., U.S. 40N 79W 91
Johor Baharu, Malay. 1N 104 E 148
Joliet, Il., U.S. 42N 88W 90
Jonesboro, Ar., U.S. 36N 91W 87
Jönköping, Swe. 58N 14 E 116
Jonquière, P.Q., Can. 48N 72W 73
Joplin, Mo., U.S. 37N 95W 87
Jordan, Ctry., Asia 30N 36 E 142
Juan de Fuca, Str. of, Can.-U.S. 48N 124W 82
Jubba, R., Afr. 0 42 E 131
Juiz de Fora, Braz. 22S 43W 105
Jujuy, Arg. 23S 66W 106
Jullundur, India 31N 76 E 143
Junagādh, India 22N 70 E 143
Juneau, Ak., U.S. 58N 134W 76
Junín, Arg. 35S 61W 106

K

K2 (Qogir Feng), Mt., China-Pak. 36N 76 E 143
Kabelega Falls, Ug. 3N 32 E 129
Kābul, Afg. 35N 69 E 143
Kachuga, Russia 54N 106 E 141
Kaduna, Nig. 10N 7 E 128
Kaesŏng (Kaijo), N. Kor. 38N 127 E 147
Kagoshima, Japan 32N 131 E 147
Kahramanmaras, Tur. 38N 37 E 121
Kaifeng, China 35N 114 E 147
Kaimana, Indon. 4S 134 E 149
Kaiserslautern, Ger. 49N 8 E 117
Kakhovs'ke vodoskhovyshche, Res., Ukr. 47N 34 E 121
Kākināda, India 17N 82 E 143
Kalahari Des., Afr. 23S 21 E 130
Kalamáta, Grc. 37N 22 E 121
Kalamazoo, Mi., U.S. 42N 86W 90
Kalāt, Pak. 29N 67 E 143
Kalemie, D.R.C. 6S 29 E 130
Kaliningrad (Königsberg), Russia 55N 21 E 114
Kalispell, Mt., U.S. 48N 114W 83
Kalisz, Pol. 52N 18 E 117
Kaluga, Russia 54N 36 E 115
Kama, R., Russia 56N 52 E 115
Kamchatka, Poluostrov, Pen., Russia 55N 159 E 141
Kamen-na-Obi, Russia 54N 81 E 140
Kamensk-Ural'skiy, Russia 56N 62 E 115
Kamloops, B.C., Can. 51N 120W 72
Kampala, Ug. 0 33 E 129
Kâmpóng Thum, Camb. 13N 105 E 148
Kamsack, Sk., Can. 52N 102W 72
Kam'yanets'-Podil's'kyy, Ukr. 49N 27 E 121
Kamyshin, Russia 50N 45 E 115
Kananga, D.R.C. 6S 22 E 130
Kanazawa, Japan 37N 137 E 147
Kānchipuram, India 13N 80 E 143
Kandahār, Afg. 32N 66 E 143
Kandalaksha, Russia 67N 32 E 114
Kanding, China 30N 102 E 146
Kandy, Sri L. 7N 81 E 143
Kangāvar, Iran 35N 47 E 142
Kankakee, Il., U.S. 41N 88W 90
Kano, Nig. 12N 9 E 128
Kānpur, India 27N 80 E 143
Kansas, State, U.S. 39N 98W 76
Kansas City, Ks., U.S. 39N 95W 87
Kansas City, Mo., U.S. 39N 95W 87
Kansk, Russia 56N 96 E 140
Kaohsiung, Tai. 23N 120 E 147
Kaolack, Sen. 14N 16W 128
Kapoeta, Sudan 5N 34 E 129
Kapuskasing, On., Can. 49N 82W 73
Kara, Russia 69N 65 E 140
Karāchi, Pak. 25N 66 E 143
Karaganda, see Qaraghandy, Kaz. 50N 73 E 140
Karakoram Ra., Asia 36N 76 E 143
Karaman, Tur. 37N 33 E 121
Karashahr (Yanqi), China 42N 86 E 146
Karbalā', Iraq 33N 44 E 142
Kargat, Russia 55N 80 E 140
Kargopol', Russia 61N 39 E 118
Karlovac, Cro. 45N 15 E 120
Karlovy Vary, Czech Rep. 50N 13 E 117
Karlsruhe, Ger. 49N 8 E 117
Karlstad, Swe. 59N 13 E 116
Kars, Tur. 41N 43 E 142
Karshi, Uzb. 38N 66 E 143
Karskoye More, Sea, Russia 72N 75 E 140
Kartaly, Russia 53N 61 E 140
Kasaï, R., Ang.-Zaire 4S 19 E 130
Kāshān, Iran 34N 51 E 142
Kashi, China 39N 76 E 146
Kassalā, Sudan 15N 36 E 129
Kassel, Ger. 51N 9 E 117
Kastoría, Grc. 40N 21 E 121
Katanga, Reg., D.R.C. 9S 25 E 130
Kathmandu, Nepal 28N 85 E 143
Katowice, Pol. 50N 19 E 117

Katsina Ala, Nig. ...7N 9 E **128**
Kattegat, Str., Den.-Swe. ...57N 11 E **116**
Kaunas (Kovno), Lith. ...55N 24 E **114**
Kavála, Grc. ...41N 24 E **121**
Kavieng, Pap. N. Gui. ...3S 151 E **149**
Kavir, Dasht-e, Des., Iran ...34N 53 E **142**
Kayes, Mali ...14N 12W **128**
Kayseri, Tur. ...39N 35 E **121**
Kazach'ye, Russia ...71N 136 E **141**
Kazakhstan, Ctry., Asia ...48N 68 E **140**
Kazan', Russia ...56N 49 E **115**
Kazbek, Gora, Mt., Russia ...43N 45 E **115**
Kāzerūn, Iran ...30N 52 E **142**
Kecskemét, Hung. ...47N 20 E **117**
Kem', Russia ...65N 35 E **140**
Kemerovo, Russia ...55N 86 E **140**
Kemi, Fin. ...66N 25 E **116**
Kenitra (Port Lyautey), Mor. ...34N 7W **120**
Kenora, On., Can. ...50N 94W **73**
Kenosha, Wi., U.S. ...43N 88W **89**
Kentucky, State, U.S. ...37N 85W **77**
Kentucky, R., U.S. ...38N 85W **90**
Kenya, Ctry., Afr. ...2N 38 E **131**
Kenya, Mt. (Kirinyaga), Kenya ...0 37 E **131**
Keokuk, Ia., U.S. ...40N 92W **87**
Kerch, Ukr. ...45N 36 E **115**
Kerguélen, Îles, Is., Afr. ...50S 69 E **53**
Kerki, Turk. ...38N 65 E **143**
Kérkyra, I., Grc. ...40N 20 E **121**
Kermān, Iran ...30N 57 E **142**
Kettering, Oh., U.S. ...40N 84W **90**
Key West, Fl., U.S. ...25N 82W **93**
Khabarovsk, Russia ...48N 135 E **141**
Khal'mer-Yu, Russia ...68N 64 E **140**
Khambhāt, Gulf of, India ...21N 72 E **143**
Kharagpur, India ...22N 87 E **143**
Kharkiv, Ukr. ...50N 36 E **115**
Khartoum, Sudan ...16N 33 E **129**
Khāsh, Iran ...28N 61 E **142**
Khasi Hills, India ...26N 93 E **143**
Khaskovo, Bul. ...42N 26 E **121**
Khatanga, Russia ...72N 102 E **141**
Kherson, Ukr. ...47N 33 E **115**
Khmel'nyts'kyy, Ukr. ...49N 27 E **121**
Kholmsk, Russia ...47N 142 E **141**
Khon Kaen, Thai. ...17N 103 E **148**
Khorog, Taj. ...37N 72 E **143**
Khorramshahr, Iran ...31N 48 E **142**
Khudzhand, Taj. ...40N 70 E **143**
Khulna, Bngl. ...23N 90 E **143**
Khvoy, Iran ...39N 45 E **142**
Khyber P., Afg.-Pak. ...34N 70 E **143**
Kiel, Ger. ...54N 10 E **116**
Kiev (Kyyiv), Ukr. ...50N 31 E **115**
Kigali, Rw. ...2S 30 E **130**
Kilimanjaro, Mt., Tan. ...3S 37 E **101**
Kimberley, S. Afr. ...29S 25 E **130**
Kindersley, Sk., Can. ...51N 109W **72**
King Leopold Ranges, Austl. ...17S 126 E **156**
Kingston, On., Can. ...44N 76W **73**
Kingston, Jam. ...18N 77W **97**
Kingston, N.Y., U.S. ...42N 74W **91**
Kingstown, St. Vin. ...13N 61W **97**
Kinshasa (Léopoldville), D.R.C. ...4S 15 E **130**
Kirensk, Russia ...58N 108 E **141**
Kiribati, Ctry., Oc. ...1N 175 E **158**
Kirklareli, Tur. ...42N 27 E **121**
Kirksville, Mo., U.S. ...40N 93W **87**
Kirkūk, Iraq ...35N 44 E **142**
Kirkwall, Scot., U.K. ...59N 3W **116**
Kirov, Russia ...59N 50 E **115**
Kirovohrad, Ukr. ...49N 32 E **115**
Kirovsk, Russia ...68N 34 E **114**
Kirthar Ra., Pak. ...27N 67 E **143**
Kiruna, Swe. ...68N 20 E **116**
Kisangani (Stanleyville), D.R.C. ...1N 25 E **129**
Kiselëvsk, Russia ...54N 86 E **140**
Kitayūshū, Japan ...34N 130 E **147**

Kitchener, On., Can. ...43N 81W **73**
Kivu, L., Rw.-Zaire ...2S 28 E **130**
Kizil Irmak, R., Tur. ...40N 34 E **121**
Klaipeda, Lith. ...56N 21 E **116**
Klamath Falls, Or., U.S. ...42N 122W **82**
Knoxville, Tn., U.S. ...36N 84W **92**
Kōbe, Japan ...34N 135 E **147**
Koblenz, Ger. ...50N 8 E **117**
Kōchi, Japan ...34N 134 E **147**
Koko Nor (Qinghai Hu), L., China ...37N 98 E **146**
Kokomo, In., U.S. ...41N 86W **90**
Kokopo, Pap. N. Gui. ...4S 152 E **149**
Koksoak, R., Can. ...58N 70W **73**
Kolār, India ...14N 79 E **143**
Kolhāpur, India ...17N 74 E **143**
Kolkata (Calcutta), India ...23N 88 E **143**
Kolomna, Russia ...55N 39 E **115**
Kolomyya, Ukr. ...49N 25 E **121**
Kolpashevo, Russia ...58N 83 E **140**
Kol'skiy Poluostrov (Kola Pen.), Russia ...67N 37 E **115**
Kolwezi, D.R.C. ...11S 26 E **130**
Kominato, Japan ...28N 129 E **147**
Komotiní, Grc. ...41N 25 E **121**
Komsomol'sk na-Amure, Russia ...51N 137 E **141**
Konya, Tur. ...37N 32 E **121**
Korçë, Alb. ...41N 21 E **121**
Korea, North, Ctry., Asia ...40N 127 E **147**
Korea, South, Ctry., Asia ...37N 127 E **147**
Korea Str., S. Kor.-Japan ...33N 128 E **147**
Korla, China ...42N 86 E **146**
Korsakov, Russia ...47N 143 E **141**
Kosciuszko, Mt., Austl. ...36S 118 E **157**
Košice, Slvk. ...49N 21 E **117**
Kostroma, Russia ...58N 41 E **115**
Koszalin, Pol. ...54N 16 E **116**
Kota Baharu, Malay. ...6N 102 E **148**
Kota Kinabalu, Malay. ...6N 116 E **148**
Kotka, Fin. ...60N 27 E **116**
Kotlas, Russia ...61N 47 E **115**
Koudougou, Burkina ...12N 2W **128**
Koussi, Emi, Mt., Chad ...20N 18 E **129**
Kovrov, Russia ...56N 41 E **115**
Kowloon, H.K. ...22N 114 E **147**
Kozáni, Grc. ...40N 22 E **121**
Kozhikode, India ...11N 76 E **143**
Kra, Isthmus of, Myan.-Thai. ...10N 99 E **148**
Kragujevac, Yugo. ...44N 21 E **121**
Kraków, Pol. ...50N 20 E **117**
Kraljevo, Yugo. ...44N 21 E **121**
Kranj, Slvn. ...46N 14 E **120**
Krasnodar, Russia ...45N 39 E **115**
Krasnokamsk, Russia ...58N 56 E **115**
Krasnotur'insk, Russia ...60N 60 E **140**
Krasnoural'sk, Russia ...58N 60 E **115**
Krasnovodsk, Turk. ...40N 53 E **142**
Krasnoyarsk, Russia ...56N 93 E **140**
Kremenchuk, Ukr. ...49N 33 E **115**
Kristiansand, Nor. ...58N 8 E **116**
Kronshtadt, Russia ...60N 30 E **114**
Kropotkin, Russia ...45N 41 E **121**
Krugersdorp, S. Afr. ...26S 28 E **130**
Kryms'kyy pivostriv (Crimean Pen.), Ukr. ...45N 34 E **115**
Kryvyy Rih, Ukr. ...48N 33 E **115**
Ksar el Kebir, Mor. ...35N 6W **120**
Kuala Lumpur, Malay. ...3N 102 E **148**
Kuching, Malay. ...1N 110 E **148**
Kudymkar, Russia ...59N 55 E **140**
Kuji, Japan ...40N 142 E **147**
Kumamoto, Japan ...33N 131 E **147**
Kumasi, Ghana ...7N 2W **128**
Kungur, Russia ...57N 57 E **140**
Kunlun Shan, Mts., China ...36N 87 E **146**
Kunming, China ...25N 103 E **146**
Kunsan, S. Kor. ...36N 127 E **147**
Kupang, Indon. ...10S 124 E **149**
Kupino, Russia ...54N 78 E **140**

Kuqa, China ...42N 83 E **146**
Kurgan, Russia ...55N 65 E **140**
Kurgan-Tyube, Taj. ...38N 69 E **143**
Kuril Is., Russia ...46N 147 E **147**
Kursk, Russia ...52N 36 E **115**
Kurume, Japan ...33N 130 E **147**
Kushiro, Japan ...43N 144 E **147**
Kushva, Russia ...58N 60 E **140**
Kustanay, see Qostanay, Kaz. ...53N 64 E **140**
Kütahya, Tur. ...39N 30 E **121**
Kutaisi, Geor. ...42N 43 E **115**
Kutch, Gulf of, India ...22N 68 E **143**
Kutch, Rann of, Swamp, India-Pak. ...24N 69 E **143**
Kutulik, Russia ...53N 103 E **141**
Kuwait (Al Kuwayt), Kuw. ...29N 48 E **142**
Kuwait, Ctry., Asia ...29N 48 E **142**
Kuybyshev, see Samara, Russia ...53N 50 E **115**
Kuybyshevskoye, Res., Russia ...54N 48 E **115**
Kyakhta, Russia ...51N 107 E **141**
Kyŏngju, S. Kor. ...36N 129 E **147**
Kyōto, Japan ...35N 136 E **147**
Kyrgyzstan, Ctry., Asia ...41N 75 E **143**
Kyūshū, I., Japan ...32N 132 E **147**
Kyustendil, Bul. ...42N 23 E **121**
Kyzyl, Russia ...52N 94 E **140**

L

Labrador, Reg., Nf., Can. ...53N 62W **73**
Lackawanna, N.Y., U.S. ...43N 79W **91**
Lac La Biche, Ab., Can. ...55N 112W **72**
La Coruña, Spain ...43N 8W **120**
La Crosse, Wi., U.S. ...44N 91W **89**
Lae, Pap. N. Gui. ...6S 147 E **149**
La Fayette, In., U.S. ...40N 87W **90**
Lafayette, La., U.S. ...30N 92W **95**
Laghouat, Alg. ...34N 3 E **128**
Lagos, Nig. ...7N 3 E **128**
La Grande, Or., U.S. ...45N 118W **82**
LaGrange, Ga., U.S. ...33N 85W **92**
Lahore, Pak. ...32N 74 E **143**
Lahti, Fin. ...61N 26 E **116**
Lake Charles, La., U.S. ...30N 93W **95**
Lake Forest, Il., U.S. ...42N 88W **90**
Lakeland, Fl., U.S. ...28N 82W **93**
Lakewood, Oh., U.S. ...41N 82W **90**
La Línea, Spain ...36N 5W **120**
Lalitpur, Nepal ...27N 85 E **143**
Lamía, Grc. ...39N 22 E **121**
Lanús, Arg. ...34S 58W **106**
Lancaster, Eng., U.K. ...54N 3W **116**
Lancaster, Oh., U.S. ...40N 83W **90**
Lancaster, Pa., U.S. ...40N 76W **91**
Lang Son, Viet. ...22N 107 E **148**
Langzhong, China ...32N 106 E **146**
Lanigan, Sk., Can. ...52N 105W **72**
Länkäran, Azer. ...39N 49 E **142**
Lansing, Mi., U.S. ...43N 85W **90**
Lanzhou, China ...36N 104 E **146**
Laoag, Phil. ...18N 121 E **148**
Laos, Ctry., Asia ...20N 102 E **148**
La Paz, Bol. ...17S 68W **104**
La Paz, Mex. ...24N 110W **96**
Lapland, Reg., Eur. ...68N 25 E **116**
La Plata, Arg. ...35S 58W **106**
Laptev Sea, Russia ...75N 125 E **141**
L'Aquila, Italy ...42N 13 E **117**
Larache, Mor. ...35N 6W **128**
Laramie, Wy., U.S. ...41N 106W **76**
Laredo, Tx., U.S. ...28N 99W **94**
La Rioja, Arg. ...29S 67W **106**
Lárisa, Grc. ...40N 22 E **121**
Larnaka, Cyp. ...35N 34 E **121**

Las Cruces, N.M., U.S. ...32N 107W **85**
La Serena, Chile ...30S 71W **106**
La Seyne, Fr. ...43N 6 E **117**
La Spezia, Italy ...44N 10 E **117**
Las Vegas, Nv., U.S. ...36N 115W **84**
Las Vegas, N.M., U.S. ...36N 105W **86**
Latvia, Ctry., Eur. ...57N 25 E **114**
Launceston, Austl. ...42S 147 E **157**
Laurel, Ms., U.S. ...32N 89W **92**
Lausanne, Switz. ...47N 7 E **117**
Laval, Fr. ...48N 1W **117**
Lawrence, Ks., U.S. ...39N 95W **87**
Lawrence, Ma., U.S. ...43N 71W **91**
Lawton, Ok., U.S. ...35N 98W **86**
Lead, S.D., U.S. ...44N 104W **88**
Leavenworth, Ks., U.S. ...39N 95W **87**
Lebanon, Pa., U.S. ...40N 76W **91**
Lebanon, Ctry., Asia ...34N 36 E **121**
Lecce, Italy ...40N 18 E **117**
Leeds, Eng., U.K. ...54N 2W **116**
Leeuwarden, Neth. ...52N 6 E **117**
Legazpi, Phil. ...13N 124 E **149**
Legnica, Pol. ...51N 16 E **117**
Le Havre, Fr. ...50N 0 **117**
Leicester, Eng., U.K. ...53N 1W **116**
Leipzig, Ger. ...51N 12 E **117**
Le Mans, Fr. ...48N 0 **117**
Lemdiyya, Alg. ...36N 3 E **128**
Lena, R., Russia ...72N 127 E **141**
Leningrad, see St. Petersburg, Russia ...60N 30 E **114**
Leninogorsk, Kaz. ...50N 83 E **140**
Leominster, Ma., U.S. ...43N 72W **91**
León, Mex. ...21N 102W **96**
León, Spain ...43N 6W **120**
Le Puy, Fr. ...45N 4 E **117**
Lérida, Spain ...42N 1 E **120**
Lerwick, Scot., U.K. ...60N 1W **116**
Leshan, China ...30N 104 E **146**
Lesotho, Ctry., Afr. ...30S 28 E **130**
Lesser Antilles, Is., N.A.-S.A. ...15N 61W **97**
Lesser Khingan Range (Xiao Hinggan Ling), China ...48N 128 E **147**
Lesser Sunda Is., Asia ...9S 120 E **148**
Leszno, Pol. ...52N 17 E **117**
Lewiston, Id., U.S. ...46N 117W **82**
Lewiston, Me., U.S. ...44N 70W **91**
Lewistown, Mt., U.S. ...47N 109W **83**
Lexington, Ky., U.S. ...38N 84W **90**
Lhasa, China ...30N 91 E **146**
Liaoyang, China ...41N 123 E **147**
Liberec, Czech Rep. ...51N 15 E **117**
Liberia, Ctry., Afr. ...6N 9W **128**
Libreville, Gabon ...0 9 E **130**
Libya, Ctry., Afr. ...28N 18 E **129**
Libyan Des., Afr. ...28N 24 E **129**
Liechtenstein, Ctry., Eur. ...47N 9 E **117**
Liège, Bel. ...51N 3 E **117**
Liepāja, Lat. ...57N 21 E **116**
Ligurian Sea, Fr.-Italy ...43N 8 E **117**
Likasi, D.R.C. ...11S 27 E **130**
Lille, Fr. ...51N 3 E **117**
Lima, Oh., U.S. ...41N 84W **90**
Lima, Peru ...12S 77W **104**
Limassol, Cyp. ...35N 33 E **121**
Limbe, Mt., Cam. ...4N 9 E **148**
Limerick, Ire. ...52N 9W **117**
Limoges, Fr. ...46N 1 E **117**
Limpopo, R., Afr. ...23S 28 E **130**
Linares, Spain ...38N 4W **120**
Lincoln, Eng., U.K. ...53N 1W **117**
Lincoln, Ne., U.S. ...41N 97W **87**
Lingayen, Phil. ...16N 120 E **149**
Linköping, Swe. ...58N 16 E **116**
Linyi, China ...35N 118 E **147**
Linz, Aus. ...48N 14 E **117**
Lipetsk, Russia ...52N 40 E **115**
Lisbon, Port. ...39N 9W **120**
Lithuania, Ctry., Eur. ...56N 24W **114**
Little Karroo, Plat., S. Afr. ...34S 21 E **130**
Little Rock, Ar., U.S. ...35N 92W **87**
Liuzhou, China ...24N 109 E **146**
Liverpool, Eng., U.K. ...53N 3W **116**
Livingston, Mt., U.S. ...46N 111W **83**

Livingstone, Zam. 18S 26 E 130
Livno, Bos. 44N 17 E 121
Livorno, Italy 44N 11 E 117
Ljubljana, Slvn. 46N 14 E 120
Llanelli, Wales, U.K. 52N 4W 117
Llanos, Reg., Col.-Ven. 5N 70W 104
Lloydminster, Sk., Can. 53N 110W 72
Lobamba, Swaz. 34N 32 E 130
Lobatse, Bots. 25S 26 E 130
Lockport, N.Y., U.S. 43N 79W 91
Loc Ninh, Viet. 12N 107 E 148
Łódź, Pol. 52N 19 E 117
Logan, Ut., U.S. 42N 112W 83
Logan, Mt., Yk., Can. 61N 141W 72
Logroño, Spain 42N 2W 120
Loire, R., Fr. 48N 2 E 117
Lomas de Zamora, Arg. 34S 58W 106
Lomé, Togo 6N 1 E 128
London, On., Can. 43N 82W 73
London, Eng., U.K. 51N 0 117
Londonderry, N. Ire., U.K. 55N 7W 116
Londrina, Braz. 23S 51W 106
Long Beach, Ca., U.S. 34N 118W 84
Long I., N.Y., U.S. 41N 73W 91
Long Range Mts., Nf., Can. 48N 57W 73
Long Xuyen, Viet. 11N 105 E 148
Lorain, Oh., U.S. 41N 82W 90
Loralai, Pak. 31N 69 E 143
Lorca, Spain 38N 2W 120
Lorient, Fr. 48N 3W 117
Los Alamos, N.M., U.S. 36N 106W 85
Los Ángeles, Chile 37S 72W 106
Los Angeles, Ca., U.S. 34N 118W 84
Los Teques, Ven. 10N 67W 105
Lota, Chile 37S 73W 106
Louangphrabang, Laos 20N 102 E 148
Louisiana, State, U.S. 31N 92W 77
Louisville, Ky., U.S. 38N 86W 90
Lowell, Ma., U.S. 43N 71W 91
Lower Hutt, N.Z. 41S 175 E 157
Loznica, Yugo. 45N 19 E 121
Lualaba, R., D.R.C. 10S 25 E 130
Luanda, Ang. 9S 13 E 130
Lubbock, Tx., U.S. 34N 102W 86
Lübeck, Ger. 54N 11 E 116
Lubilash, R., D.R.C. 8S 24 E 130
Lublin, Pol. 51N 23 E 117
Lubumbashi (Elizabethville), D.R.C. 12S 28 E 130
Lucca, Italy 44N 10 E 117
Lucena, Spain 37N 4W 120
Lucknow, India 27N 81 E 143
Ludhiāna, India 31N 76 E 143
Lugo, Spain 43N 8W 120
Lugoj, Rom. 46N 22 E 121
Luleå, Swe. 66N 22 E 116
Lun, Mong. 48N 105 E 146
Lund, Swe. 56N 13 E 116
Luoyang, China 35N 113 E 147
Lurgan, N. Ire., U.K. 54N 6W 116
Lusaka, Zam. 15S 28 E 130
Lüshun, China 39N 121 E 147
Luxembourg, Lux. 50N 6 E 117
Luxembourg, Ctry., Eur. 50N 6 E 117
Luzern, Switz. 47N 8 E 117
Luzhou, China 29N 105 E 146
Luzon, I., Phil. 17N 120 E 148
L'viv (Lvov), Ukr. 50N 24 E 114
Lynchburg, Va., U.S. 37N 79W 91
Lynn, Ma., U.S. 42N 71W 91
Lynn Lake, Mb., Can. 57N 101W 72
Lyon, Fr. 46N 5 E 117
Lys'va, Russia 58N 58 E 115

M

Macapá, Braz. 0 51W 105
Macau, China 22N 114 E 147
Macdonnell Ranges, Austl. 24S 133 E 156
Macedonia, Ctry., Eur. 42N 22 E 121
Maceió, Braz. 10S 36W 105
Macímboa da Praia, Moz. 11S 40 E 131
Mackenzie, R., N.T., Can. 63N 124W 72
Mackenzie Mts., Can. 64N 130W 72
Mackinaw City, Mi., U.S. 46N 85W 90
Macon, Ga., U.S. 33N 84W 92
Madagascar, Ctry., Afr. 20S 46 E 131
Madeira, R., Bol.-Braz. 7S 63W 104
Madeira, Arquipélago da, Is., Port. 33N 16W 128
Madison, Wi., U.S. 43N 89W 89
Madras, India 13N 80 E 143
Madre del Sur, Sierra, Mts., Mex. 18N 101W 96
Madre Occidental, Sierra, Mts., Mex. 23N 105W 96
Madre Oriental, Sierra, Mts., Mex. 23N 100W 96
Madrid, Spain 40N 4W 120
Madurai, India 10N 78 E 143
Maebashi, Japan 36N 139 E 147
Mafeking, S. Afr. 26S 25 E 130
Magadan, Russia 60N 151 E 141
Magallanes, Estrecho de, Str., Arg.-Chile 53S 69W 106
Magdalena, R., Col. 8N 74W 104
Magdeburg, Ger. 52N 12 E 117
Magé, Braz. 23S 43W 106
Maghniyya, Alg. 35N 2W 120
Magnitogorsk, Russia 53N 59 E 115
Mahajanga, Madag. 15S 46 E 131
Mahilyou, Bela. 54N 30 E 114
Mahón, Spain 40N 4 E 120
Maiduguri, Nig. 12N 13 E 129
Main Barrier Ra., Austl. 31S 142 E 157
Mai-Ndombe, L., D.R.C. 2S 19 E 130
Maine, State, U.S. 45N 69W 77
Mainz, Ger. 50N 8 E 117
Maiquetía, Ven. 11N 67W 105
Makasar, Selat, Str., Indon. 3S 118 E 148
Makgadikgadi Pans, Dry L., Bots. 21S 26 E 130
Makiyivka, Ukr. 48N 38 E 115
Makushino, Russia 55N 68 E 140
Malabo, Eq. Gui. 4N 9 E 128
Málaga, Spain 37N 4W 120
Malatya, Tur. 38N 38 E 121
Malawi, Ctry., Afr. 11S 34 E 130
Malaya Vishera, Russia 59N 32 E 140
Malay Pen., Asia 8N 101 E 148
Malaysia, Ctry., Asia 4N 102 E 148
Malbork, Pol. 54N 19 E 116
Malden, Ma., U.S. 42N 71W 91
Maldives, Ctry., Asia 5N 70 E 53
Mali, Ctry., Afr. 16N 2W 128
Mallawī, Egypt 28N 31 E 121
Mallorca, I., Spain 40N 3 E 120
Malmö, Swe. 56N 13 E 116
Malta, Ctry., Eur. 36N 14 E 120
Maluku (Moluccas), Is., Indon. 3S 127 E 149
Maluku, Laut (Molucca Sea), Indon. 0 125 E 149
Manado, Indon. 1N 125 E 149
Managua, Nic. 12N 86W 96
Manakara, Madag. 22S 48 E 131
Manas, China 44N 86 E 146
Manaus (Manaos), Braz. 3S 60W 105
Manchester, Eng., U.K. 53N 2W 116
Manchester, Ct., U.S. 42N 72W 91
Manchester, N.H., U.S. 43N 71W 91
Manchuria, Reg., China 46N 126 E 147
Mandalay, Myan. 22N 96 E 146
Mandan, N.D., U.S. 47N 101W 88
Mandeb, Bab el, Str., Afr.-Asia 13N 43 E 142
Māndvi, India 23N 69 E 143
Mangalore, India 13N 75 E 143
Manhattan, Ks., U.S. 39N 97W 87
Manila, Phil. 15N 121 E 149
Manisa, Tur. 39N 27 E 121
Manitoba, L., Mb., Can. 51N 99W 72
Manitoba, Prov., Can. 55N 98W 72
Manitowoc, Wi., U.S. 44N 88W 89
Manizales, Col. 5N 76W 104
Mankato, Mn., U.S. 44N 94W 89
Mannar, G. of, India-Sri L. 9N 79 E 143
Mannheim, Ger. 49N 9 E 117
Mansfield, Oh., U.S. 41N 82W 90
Manzanillo, Cuba 20N 77W 97
Manzhouli, China 49N 117 E 147
Maputo, Moz. 26S 33 E 130
Maracaibo, Ven. 11N 72W 104
Maracaibo, Lago de, L., Ven. 10N 72W 104
Maracay, Ven. 10N 68W 104
Marajó, Ilha de, I., Braz. 1S 50W 105
Marañón, R., Peru 5S 75W 104
Mar del Plata, Arg. 38S 58W 106
Mardin, Tur. 37N 41 E 142
Marianao, Cuba 23N 82W 97
Maribor, Slvn. 47N 16 E 121
Marilia, Braz. 23S 50W 105
Marion, In., U.S. 41N 86W 90
Marion, Oh., U.S. 41N 83W 90
Mariupol', Ukr. 47N 38W 115
Mariveles, Phil. 14N 120 E 149
Markovo, Russia 65N 170 E 141
Marmara Denizi, Sea, Tur. 41N 28 E 121
Maroua, Cam. 11N 14 E 129
Marquette, Mi., U.S. 46N 88W 89
Marrakech, Mor. 32N 8W 128
Marsala, Italy 38N 12 E 117
Marseille, Fr. 43N 5 E 117
Marshall, Tx., U.S. 33N 94W 95
Marshall Is., Ctry., Oc. 10N 170 E 159
Martha's Vineyard, I., Ma., U.S. 41N 70W 91
Martinique, Ctry., N.A. 15N 61W 97
Martre, Lac la, L., N.T., Can. 64N 120W 72
Mary, Turk. 38N 62 E 142
Maryland, State, U.S. 39N 76W 77
Masan, S. Kor. 35N 129 E 147
Maseru, Leso. 29S 27 E 130
Mashhad, Iran 36N 59 E 142
Masjed Soleymān, Iran 32N 49 E 142
Mason City, Ia., U.S. 43N 93W 89
Massachusetts, State, U.S. 42N 72W 77
Masset, B.C., Can. 54N 132W 72
Massillon, Oh., U.S. 41N 82W 90
Matadi, D.R.C. 6S 14 E 130
Matamoros, Mex. 26N 97W 96
Matanzas, Cuba 23N 82W 97
Matara, Sri L. 6N 81 E 143
Mataram, Indon. 9S 116 E 148
Mathura, India 28N 78 E 143
Matochkin Shar, Russia 74N 56 E 140
Maţraḩ, Oman 24N 58 E 142
Matsue, Japan 35N 133 E 147
Matsuyama, Japan 34N 133 E 147
Maturin, Ven. 10N 63W 104
Maun, Bots. 20S 24 E 130
Mauritania, Ctry., Afr. 19N 12W 128
Mauritius, Ctry., Afr. 20S 58 E 53
Mawlamyine, Myan. 16N 98 E 148
Mayagüez, P.R. 18N 67W 97
Maykop, Russia 45N 40 E 115
Mayo, Yk., Can. 64N 136W 72
Mayran, Laguna de, L., Mex. 26N 103W 96
Mazār-e Sharīf, Afg. 37N 67 E 143
Mazatlán, Mex. 23N 106W 96
Mbabane, Swaz. 26S 31 E 130
Mbandaka, D.R.C. 0 18 E 130
M'banza Congo, Ang. 7S 14 E 130
McAlester, Ok., U.S. 35N 96W 87
McAllen, Tx., U.S. 26N 98W 94
McGrath, Ak., U.S. 63N 155W 76
McKeesport, Pa., U.S. 40N 80W 91
McKinley, Mt., Ak., U.S. 63N 150W 76
McLennan, Ab., Can. 56N 117W 72
Mecca (Makkah), Sau. Ar. 21N 40 E 142
Medan, Indon. 4N 99 E 148
Medellín, Col. 6N 76W 104
Medford, Or., U.S. 42N 123W 82
Mediterranean Sea, Afr.-Asia-Eur. 38N 10 E 120
Mednogorsk, Russia 51N 57 E 140
Meerut, India 29N 78 E 143
Meknès, Mor. 34N 6W 128
Mekong, R., Asia 18N 104 E 148
Melaka, Malay. 2N 102 E 148
Melbourne, Austl. 38S 145 E 157
Melfort, Sk., Can. 53N 105W 72
Melilla, Afr. 35N 3W 120
Melitopol', Ukr. 47N 35 E 115
Melville, Sk., Can. 51N 103W 72
Melville Pen., Nu., Can. 68N 85W 73
Memphis, Tn., U.S. 35N 90W 92
Mendoza, Arg. 33S 69W 106
Menorca, I., Spain 40N 4 E 120
Menzel Bourguiba, Tun. 37N 10 E 120
Merano, Italy 46N 11 E 117
Merauke, Pap. N. Gui. 9S 140 E 149
Mercedario, C., Mt., Arg.-Chile 32S 70W 106
Mercedes, Arg. 29S 58W 106
Mergui, Myan. 12N 99 E 148
Mérida, Mex. 21N 90W 96
Mérida, Ven. 8N 71W 104
Meriden, Ct., U.S. 41N 73W 91
Meridian, Ms., U.S. 32N 89W 92
Mesopotamia, Reg., Iraq 34N 44 E 142
Messina, Italy 38N 16 E 117
Metairie, La., U.S. 30N 90W 95
Metz, Fr. 49N 6 E 116
Mexicali, Mex. 32N 115W 96
Mexico, Ctry., N.A. 24N 102W 96
Mexico, G. of, N.A. 25N 90W 96
Mexico City, Mex. 19N 99W 96
Mezen', Russia 66N 44 E 115
Miami, Az., U.S. 33N 111W 85
Miami, Fl., U.S. 26N 80W 93
Miami Beach, Fl., U.S. 26N 80W 93
Michigan, State, U.S. 44N 85W 77
Michigan, L., U.S. 44N 87W 90
Michigan City, In., U.S. 42N 87W 90
Michikamau, L., Nf., Can. 54N 63W 73
Michurinsk, Russia 53N 41 E 115
Micronesia, Federated States of, Ctry., Oc. 5N 153 E 159
Middlesbrough, Eng., U.K. 55N 1W 116
Middletown, Ct., U.S. 42N 73W 91
Middletown, Oh., U.S. 39N 84W 90
Midland, Tx., U.S. 32N 102W 94
Midway Is., Dep., Oc. 30N 175W 158
Milan, Italy 45N 9 E 117
Miles City, Mt., U.S. 46N 106W 83
Milwaukee, Wi., U.S. 43N 88W 89
Minas, Ur. 34S 55W 106
Minatitlán, Mex. 18N 95W 96
Mindanao, I., Phil. 8N 125 E 149
Mindoro, I., Phil. 13N 120 E 149
Minneapolis, Mn., U.S. 45N 93W 89
Minnedosa, Mb., Can. 50N 100W 72
Minnesota, State, U.S. 46N 95W 77
Minnesota, R., Mn., U.S. 45N 96W 88
Minot, N.D., U.S. 48N 101W 88
Minsk, Bela. 54N 28 E 114
Minusinsk, Russia 54N 92 E 140
Mirbāṭ, Oman 17N 55 E 142

Mirim, L., Braz. 33S 54W **106**
Mirzāpur, India 25N 83E **143**
Mishawaka, In., U.S. 42N 86W **90**
Miskolc, Hung. 48N 21E **117**
Misrātah, Libya 32N 15E **129**
Mississippi, State, U.S. 33N 90W **77**
Mississippi, R., U.S. 32N 92W **77**
Missoula, Mt., U.S. 47N 114W **83**
Missouri, State, U.S. 38N 93W **77**
Missouri, R., U.S. 41N 96W **77**
Misti, Volcán, Vol., Peru 16S 71W **104**
Mitchell, S.D., U.S. 44N 98W **88**
Mitsiwa, Erit. 16N 39E **129**
Mmabatho, S. Afr. 26S 26E **130**
Moberly, Mo., U.S. 39N 92W **87**
Mobile, Al., U.S. 31N 88W **92**
Modena, Italy 45N 11E **117**
Mogadishu, Som. 2N 45E **127**
Mogi das Cruzes, Braz. 24S 46W **106**
Mohyliv-Podil's'kyy, Ukr. 48N 28E **121**
Moldova, Ctry., Eur. 47N 29E **121**
Molfetta, Italy 41N 17E **117**
Moline, Il., U.S. 42N 90W **89**
Mombasa, Kenya 4S 40E **131**
Monaco, Ctry., Eur. 44N 8E **117**
Monastir, Tun. 36N 11E **120**
Moncton, N.B., Can. 46N 65W **73**
Monghyr, India 25N 87E **143**
Mongolia, Ctry., Asia 46N 100E **146**
Monroe, La., U.S. 32N 92W **95**
Monroe, Mi., U.S. 42N 83W **90**
Monrovia, Lib. 6N 11W **128**
Mons, Bel. 50N 4E **117**
Montana, State, U.S. 47N 109W **76**
Montauban, Fr. 44N 1E **117**
Montego Bay, Jam. 18N 78W **97**
Monterey, Ca., U.S. 37N 122W **84**
Montería, Col. 9N 76W **104**
Monterrey, Mex. 26N 100W **96**
Monte Sant'Angelo, Italy 42N 16E **117**
Montevideo, Ur. 35S 56W **106**
Montgomery, Al., U.S. 32N 86W **92**
Montluçon, Fr. 46N 3E **117**
Montpelier, Vt. 44N 73W **91**
Montpellier, Fr. 44N 4E **117**
Montréal, P.Q., Can. 45N 74W **73**
Montserrat, Dep., N.A. 17N 63W **97**
Monywa, Myan. 22N 95E **146**
Moose Jaw, Sk., Can. 50N 106W **72**
Moosonee, On., Can. 51N 81W **73**
Morādābād, India 29N 79W **143**
Morden, Mb., Can. 49N 98W **72**
Morelia, Mex. 20N 101W **96**
Morena, Sa., Mts., Spain 38N 6W **120**
Morgan City, La., U.S. 30N 91W **95**
Morioka, Japan 40N 141E **147**
Morlaix, Fr. 49N 4W **117**
Morocco, Ctry., Afr. 32N 6W **128**
Morombe, Madag. 22S 44E **131**
Morón, Arg. 34S 59W **106**
Morris, Mb., Can. 49N 98W **72**
Morshansk, Russia 53N 42E **115**
Moscow, Id., U.S. 47N 117W **82**
Moscow (Moskva), Russia 56N 38E **115**
Mosquitos, Golfo de los, G., Pan. 9N 81W **97**
Mostar, Bos. 43N 18E **121**
Motherwell, Scot., U.K. 56N 4W **116**
Mouaskar, Alg. 35N 0 **128**
Moulins, Fr. 47N 3E **117**
Mount Carmel, Il., U.S. 38N 88W **90**
Mount Vernon, N.Y., U.S. 41N 74W **91**
Mozambique, Ctry., Afr. 18S 35E **130**
Mozambique Chan., Afr. 20S 40E **131**
Mukacheve, Ukr. 48N 23E **121**
Mukhtuya, Russia 61N 113E **141**
Mulhouse, Fr. 48N 7E **117**
Multān, Pak. 30N 71E **143**
Muncie, In., U.S. 40N 85W **90**
Munich (München), Ger. 48N 12E **117**
Münster, Ger. 52N 8E **117**
Murcia, Spain 38N 1W **120**
Murmansk, Russia 69N 33E **114**
Murom, Russia 55N 42E **140**
Muroran, Japan 42N 141E **147**
Murray Bridge, Austl. 35S 140E **156**
Muscat, Oman 23N 58E **142**
Muskegon, Mi., U.S. 43N 86W **90**
Muskogee, Ok., U.S. 36N 95E **87**
Myanmar, Ctry., Asia 22N 95E **146**
Myitkyina, Myan. 26N 97E **146**
Mykolayiv, Ukr. 47N 32E **115**
Mymensingh, Bngl. 25N 90E **143**
Mysore, India 13N 77E **143**
Mytilíni, Grc. 39N 27E **121**

N

Naberezhnyye Chelny, Russia 56N 52E **115**
Nabeul, Tun. 37N 11E **128**
Nabulus, Jord. 32N 35E **121**
Nacala, Moz. 15S 41E **131**
Naestved, Den. 55N 12E **116**
Naga, Phil. 14N 123E **149**
Nagano, Japan 37N 138E **147**
Nagaoka, Japan 37N 139E **147**
Nâgappattinam, India 11N 80E **143**
Nagasaki, Japan 33N 130E **147**
Nagoya, Japan 35N 137E **147**
Nâgpur, India 21N 79E **143**
Nagykanizsa, Hung. 46N 17E **117**
Naha, Japan 26N 128E **147**
Naiguatá, Ven. 11N 67W **104**
Nairobi, Kenya 1S 37E **131**
Najin, N. Kor. 42N 130E **147**
Nakhodka, Russia 43N 133E **141**
Nakhon Ratchasima, Thai. 15N 102E **148**
Nakskov, Den. 55N 11E **116**
Namangan, Uzb. 41N 72E **143**
Nam Co, L., China 31N 91E **146**
Nam Dinh, Viet. 20N 106E **148**
Namib Des., Nmb. 24S 15E **130**
Namibia, Ctry., Afr. 21S 16E **130**
Nampa, Id., U.S. 44N 117W **82**
Namp'o, N. Kor. 39N 125E **147**
Namur, Bel. 50N 5E **117**
Nanchang, China 29N 116E **147**
Nanchong, China 31N 106E **146**
Nancy, Fr. 49N 6E **117**
Nanda-Devi, Mt., India 30N 80E **143**
Nanjing, China 32N 119E **147**
Nanning, China 23N 108E **146**
Nanping, China 26N 118E **147**
Nansei Shotō, Is., Japan 28N 128E **147**
Nantes, Fr. 47N 2W **117**
Nanyang, China 33N 113E **147**
Napa, Ca., U.S. 38N 122W **84**
Naples, Italy 41N 14E **117**
Nara, Japan 35N 136E **147**
Narbonne, Fr. 43N 3E **117**
Narvik, Nor. 68N 17E **116**
Nar'yan-Mar, Russia 68N 53E **115**
Narym, Russia 59N 82E **140**
Naryn, Kyrg. 41N 76E **140**
Nashua, N.H., U.S. 43N 71W **91**
Nashville, Tn., U.S. 36N 87W **92**
Našice, Cro. 45N 18E **121**
Nāsik, India 20N 74E **143**
Nassau, Bah. 25N 77W **97**
Natal, Braz. 6S 35W **105**
Natchez, Ms., U.S. 32N 91W **92**
Nazareth, Isr. 33N 35E **121**
N'Djamena, Chad 12N 15E **129**
Ndola, Zam. 13S 29E **130**
Neagh, L., N. Ire., U.K. 55N 7W **116**
Nebit-Dag, Turk. 39N 54E **142**
Nebraska, State, U.S. 42N 101W **76**
Neepawa, Mb., Can. 50N 100W **72**
Negro, R., S.A. 0 64W **104**
Neiva, Col. 3N 75W **104**
Nelson, B.C., Can. 49N 117W **72**
Nelson, R., Can. 56N 94W **72**
Nepal, Ctry., Asia 28N 84E **143**
Nerchinsk, Russia 52N 116E **141**
Netherlands, Ctry., Eur. 53N 5E **117**
Neuchâtel, Switz. 47N 7E **117**
Neumünster, Ger. 54N 10E **116**
Neuquén, Arg. 39S 68W **106**
Neusiedler See, L., Aus.-Hung. 48N 16E **117**
Nevada, State, U.S. 39N 117W **76**
Nevada, Sa., Mts., Spain 37N 3W **120**
Nevers, Fr. 47N 3E **117**
Nev'yansk, Russia 57N 60E **140**
New Albany, In., U.S. 38N 86W **90**
Newark, N.J., U.S. 41N 73W **91**
Newark, Oh., U.S. 40N 82W **90**
New Bedford, Ma., U.S. 42N 71W **91**
New Bern, N.C., U.S. 35N 77W **93**
New Britain, Ct., U.S. 42N 73W **91**
New Brunswick, N.J., U.S. 40N 74W **91**
New Brunswick, Prov., Can. 47N 66W **73**
New Caledonia, Dep., Oc. 21S 164E **157**
Newcastle, Austl. 33S 152E **157**
New Castle, Pa., U.S. 41N 80W **91**
Newcastle upon Tyne, Eng., U.K. 55N 2W **116**
New Delhi, India 29N 77E **143**
Newfoundland, Prov., Can. 48N 56W **73**
New Guinea, I., Asia-Oc. 5S 140E **149**
New Hampshire, State, U.S. 44N 72W **77**
New Haven, Ct., U.S. 41N 73W **91**
New Jersey, State, U.S. 40N 74W **77**
New London, Ct., U.S. 41N 72W **91**
New Mexico, State, U.S. 35N 108W **76**
New Orleans, La., U.S. 30N 90W **95**
Newport, Eng., U.K. 51N 1W **117**
Newport, R.I., U.S. 41N 71W **91**
Newport News, Va., U.S. 37N 76W **91**
Newton, Ma., U.S. 42N 71W **91**
New York, N.Y., U.S. 41N 74W **91**
New York, State, U.S. 43N 76W **77**
New Zealand, Ctry., Oc. 39S 170E **157**
Neyshābūr, Iran 36N 59E **142**
Nha Trang, Viet. 12N 109E **148**
Niagara Falls, N.Y., U.S. 43N 79W **91**
Niamey, Niger 14N 2E **128**
Nicaragua, Ctry., N.A. 13N 86W **96**
Nicastro, Italy 39N 16E **117**
Nice, Fr. 44N 7E **117**
Nicobar Is., India 8N 94E **148**
Nicosia, Cyp. 35N 33E **121**
Niğde, Tur. 38N 35E **121**
Niger, Ctry., Afr. 16N 8E **128**
Niger, R., Afr. 8N 6E **128**
Nigeria, Ctry., Afr. 9N 8E **128**
Niigata, Japan 38N 139E **147**
Nikolayev, see Mykolayiv, Ukr. 47N 32E **115**
Nikol'sk, Russia 59N 46E **140**
Nikopol, Bul. 44N 25E **121**
Nikopol', Ukr. 48N 34E **115**
Nile, R., Egypt-Sudan 28N 30E **129**
Nilopólis, Braz. 23S 43W **106**
Nîmes, Fr. 44N 4E **117**
Nineveh, Ruins, Iraq 36N 43E **142**
Ningbo, China 30N 121E **147**
Ningde, China 26N 120E **147**
Nipigon, On., Can. 49N 88W **73**
Nipigon, L., On., Can. 50N 89W **73**
Niš, Yugo. 43N 22E **121**
Niterói, Braz. 23S 43W **106**
Nizhne-Angarsk, Russia 56N 109E **141**
Nizhne-Kolymsk, Russia 69N 161E **141**
Nizhniy Novgorod, Russia 56N 44E **115**
Nizhniy Tagil, Russia 58N 60E **115**
Nizhnyaya Tunguska, R., Russia 64N 92E **141**
Nizhyn, Ukr. 51N 32E **115**
Noākhāli, Bngl. 23N 91E **143**
Noākhāli, Bngl. 23N 91E **143**
Nogales, Az., U.S. 31N 111W **85**
Nogales, Mex. 31N 111W **96**
Noginsk, Russia 56N 38E **115**
Nome, Ak., U.S. 64N 165W **76**
Nordvik, Russia 74N 111E **141**
Norfolk, Ne., U.S. 42N 97W **88**
Norfolk, Va., U.S. 37N 76W **91**
Noril'sk, Russia 69N 87E **140**
Norristown, Pa., U.S. 40N 75W **91**
Norrköping, Swe. 59N 16E **116**
Northampton, Eng., U.K. 52N 1W **117**
Northampton, Ma., U.S. 42N 73W **91**
North Carolina, State, U.S. 36N 79W **77**
North Channel, B., Can. 46N 83W **90**
North Chicago, Il., U.S. 42N 88W **90**
North Dakota, State, U.S. 48N 100W **76**
Northern Ireland, Polit. Reg., U.K. 55N 7W **116**
Northern Mariana Is., Ctry., Oc. 16N 146E **159**
North Gamboa, Pan. 9N 80W **96**
North I., N.Z. 38S 171E **157**
North Judson, In., U.S. 41N 87W **90**
North Little Rock, Ar., U.S. 35N 92W **87**
North Platte, R., Ne., U.S. 41N 101W **86**
North Saskatchewan, R., Can. 54N 111W **72**
North Sea, Eur. 56N 2E **116**
North Tonawanda, N.Y., U.S. 43N 79W **91**
North Vancouver, B.C., Can. 49N 105W **72**
Northwest Territories, Can. 65N 120W **72**
Norwalk, Ct., U.S. 41N 73W **91**
Norway, Ctry., Eur. 65N 13E **116**
Norwegian Sea, Eur. 66N 1E **116**
Norwich, Eng., U.K. 53N 1E **117**
Norwich, Ct., U.S. 41N 72W **91**
Norwood, Oh., U.S. 39N 84W **90**
Nottingham, Eng., U.K. 53N 1W **117**
Nouakchott, Maur. 18N 16W **128**
Noumea, N. Cal. 22S 167E **157**
Nova Iguaçu, Braz. 23S 43W **106**
Nova Mambone, Moz. 21S 35E **130**
Novara, Italy 45N 9E **117**
Nova Scotia, Prov., Can. 45N 64W **73**
Novaya Zemlya, Is., Russia 72N 54E **140**
Nové Zámky, Slvk. 48N 18E **117**
Novgorod, Russia 59N 31E **114**
Novi-Pazar, Yugo. 43N 20E **121**
Novi Sad, Yugo. 45N 20E **121**
Novocherkassk, Russia 47N 40E **115**
Novokuznetsk, Russia 54N 87E **140**
Novomoskovsk, Russia 54N 38E **115**
Novorossiysk, Russia 45N 38E **115**
Novosibirsk, Russia 55N 83E **140**
Novosibirskiye Ostrava (New Siberian Is.), Russia 75N 141E **141**
Novyy Port, Russia 67N 72E **140**
Nowy Sacz, Pol. 50N 21E **117**

Ntwetwe Pan, Basin, Bots. ...20S 25 E **130**
Nubian Des., Sudan ...21N 33 E **129**
Nuevo Laredo, Mex. ...27N 99W **96**
Nuevo San Juan, Pan. ...9N 80W **96**
Nullarbor Plain, Austl. ...32S 128 E **156**
Nunavut, Ter., Can. ...70N 95W **73**
Nurata, Uzb. ...41N 65 E **140**
Nürnberg, Ger. ...49N 11 E **117**
Nushki, Pak. ...29N 66 E **143**
Nyala, Sudan ...12N 25 E **129**
Nyasa, L., Afr. ...12S 35 E **130**
Nyíregyháza, Hung. ...48N 22 E **117**

O

Oakland, Ca., U.S. ...38N 122W **84**
Oak Park, Il., U.S. ...42N 88W **90**
Oak Ridge, Tn., U.S. ...36N 84W **92**
Oaxaca, Mex. ...17N 97W **96**
Ob', R., Russia ...63N 67 E **140**
Occidental, Cordillera, Ra., Peru ...10S 77W **104**
Odemiş, Tur. ...38N 28 E **121**
Odense, Den. ...55N 10 E **116**
Odesa (Odessa), Ukr. ...46N 31 E **115**
Ogbomosho, Nig. ...8N 4 E **128**
Ogden, Ut., U.S. ...41N 112W **83**
Ogilvie Mts., Yk., Can. ...65N 139W **72**
Ohio, State, U.S. ...40N 83W **77**
Ohio, R., U.S. ...37N 88W **90**
Okayama, Japan ...35N 134 E **147**
Okha, Russia ...54N 143 E **141**
Okhotsk, Sea of, Japan-Russia ...57N 147 E **141**
Oklahoma, State, U.S. ...36N 98W **76**
Oklahoma City, Ok., U.S. ...35N 98W **87**
Okovango Swamp, Bots. ...19S 23 E **130**
Olavarría, Arg. ...37S 60W **106**
Old Crow, Yk., Can. ...68N 140W **72**
Oldenburg, Ger. ...53N 8 E **117**
Olds, Ab., Can. ...52N 114W **72**
Olean, N.Y., U.S. ...42N 78W **91**
Olekminsk, Russia ...61N 121 E **141**
Ol'ga, Russia ...44N 136 E **141**
Olhão, Port. ...37N 8W **120**
Olinda, Braz. ...8S 35W **105**
Olivos, Arg. ...34S 58W **106**
Olomouc, Czech Rep. ...50N 17 E **117**
Olot, Spain ...42N 3 E **120**
Olsztyn, Pol. ...54N 20 E **116**
Olympia, Wa., U.S. ...47N 123W **82**
Omaha, Ne., U.S. ...41N 96W **87**
Oman, Ctry., Asia ...19N 57 E **142**
Oman, G. of, Asia ...25N 57 E **142**
Omdurman, Sudan ...16N 32 E **129**
Omsk, Russia ...55N 73 E **140**
Öndörhaan, Mong. ...47N 111 E **147**
Onega, Russia ...64N 38 E **115**
Onezhskoye Ozero (L. Onega), Russia ...62N 37 E **115**
Onitsha, Nig. ...6N 6 E **128**
Ontario, Prov., Can. ...50N 89W **73**
Ontario, L., Can.-U.S. ...44N 78W **91**
Oostende, Bel. ...51N 3 E **117**
Opole, Pol. ...51N 18 E **117**
Oradea, Rom. ...47N 22 E **121**
Oral, Kaz. ...51N 51 E **115**
Oran, Alg. ...36N 1W **128**
Orange, R., Afr. ...29S 18 E **130**
Oranjemund, Nmb. ...29S 16 E **130**
Ordu, Tur. ...41N 38 E **121**
Örebro, Swe. ...59N 15 E **116**
Oregon, State, U.S. ...44N 120W **76**
Orekhovo-Zuyevo, Russia ...56N 39 E **140**
Orël, Russia ...53N 36 E **115**
Orenburg, Russia ...52N 55 E **115**
Oriental, Cordillera, Ra., S.A. ...14S 68W **104**
Orinoco, R., Col.-Ven. ...8N 65W **104**
Oristano, Italy ...40N 9 E **117**

Orizaba, Mex. ...19N 97W **96**
Orkney Is., Scot., U.K. ...59N 2W **116**
Orlando, Fl., U.S. ...29N 81W **93**
Orléans, Fr. ...48N 2 E **117**
Orsk, Russia ...51N 59 E **115**
Oruro, Bol. ...18S 67W **104**
Ōsaka, Japan ...35N 135 E **147**
Osh, Kyrg. ...40N 73 E **140**
Oshawa, On., Can. ...44N 79W **73**
Oshkosh, Wi., U.S. ...44N 89W **89**
Oshogbo, Nig. ...8N 4 E **128**
Osijek, Cro. ...46N 19 E **121**
Oslo, Nor. ...60N 11W **116**
Osorno, Chile ...41S 73W **106**
Ostrava, Czech Rep. ...50N 18 E **117**
Ostrowiec Swietokrzyski, Pol. ...51N 21 E **117**
Ostrów Wielkopolski, Pol. ...52N 18 E **117**
Otaru, Japan ...43N 141 E **147**
Ottawa, On., Can. ...45N 76W **73**
Ottawa, R., Can. ...46N 77W **73**
Ottumwa, Ia., U.S. ...41N 92W **89**
Ouagadougou, Burkina ...12N 2W **128**
Oujda, Mor. ...35N 2W **128**
Oulu, Fin. ...65N 26 E **116**
Outardes, R. aux, R., P.Q., Can. ...52N 70W **73**
Oviedo, Spain ...43N 6W **120**
Owensboro, Ky., U.S. ...38N 87W **90**
Oxford, Eng., U.K. ...52N 1W **117**
Oxford, Oh., U.S. ...39N 85W **90**
Oyo, Nig. ...8N 4 E **128**
Ozieri, Italy ...41N 9 E **117**

P

Pachuca, Mex. ...20N 99W **96**
Pacific Ocean ...10S 150W **52**
Padang, Indon. ...1S 100 E **148**
Padova, Italy ...45N 12 E **117**
Padre I., Tx., U.S. ...27N 97W **95**
Paisley, Scot., U.K. ...56N 4W **116**
Pakistan, Ctry., Asia ...30N 71 E **143**
Pakokku, Myan. ...21N 95 E **146**
Palana, Russia ...59N 160 E **141**
Palau, Ctry., Oc. ...8N 135 E **159**
Palembang, Indon. ...3S 105 E **148**
Palencia, Spain ...42N 5W **120**
Palermo, Italy ...38N 13 E **117**
Palestine, Reg., Asia ...32N 35 E **139**
Palma, Spain ...40N 3 E **120**
Palmira, Col. ...4N 76W **104**
Palúa, Ven. ...9N 63W **104**
Pamirs, Mts., Asia ...38N 73 E **142**
Pampa, Tx., U.S. ...36N 101W **86**
Pampa, Reg., Arg. ...35S 64W **106**
Panaji (Panjim), India ...16N 74 E **143**
Panamá, Pan. ...9N 80W **97**
Panama, Ctry., N.A. ...8N 80W **97**
Panama, G. of, Pan. ...8N 80W **97**
Panama City, Fl., U.S. ...30N 86W **92**
Pančevo, Yugo. ...45N 21 E **121**
Pápa, Hung. ...47N 17 E **117**
Papua New Guinea, Ctry., Oc. ...7S 142 E **149**
Paraguay, Ctry., S.A. ...24S 57W **106**
Paraguay, R., S.A. ...25S 58W **106**
Paramaribo, Sur. ...5N 55W **105**
Paraná, Arg. ...32S 60W **106**
Paraná, R., S.A. ...25S 54W **106**
Paris, Fr. ...49N 2 E **117**
Paris, Tx., U.S. ...34N 96W **87**
Parkersburg, W.V., U.S. ...39N 82W **90**
Parma, Italy ...45N 10 E **117**
Parma, Oh., U.S. ...41N 82W **90**
Parnaíba, Braz. ...3S 42W **105**
Pärnu, Est. ...58N 24 E **116**
Parsons, Ks., U.S. ...37N 95W **87**
Pasadena, Ca., U.S. ...34N 118W **84**
Passaic, N.J., U.S. ...41N 74W **91**
Pasto, Col. ...1N 77W **104**

Patagonia, Reg., Arg. ...44S 46W **106**
Pathein, Myan. ...17N 95 E **148**
Patiāla, India ...30N 76 E **143**
Patna, India ...26N 85 E **143**
Patos, Lago dos, L., Braz. ...31S 53W **106**
Pátra, Grc. ...38N 22 E **121**
Patterson, N.J., U.S. ...41N 74W **91**
Pau, Fr. ...43N 0 **117**
Pavia, Italy ...45N 9 E **117**
Pavlodar, Kaz. ...52N 77 E **140**
Pavlovsk, Russia ...49N 36 E **121**
Pawtucket, R.I., U.S. ...42N 71W **91**
Paysandú, Ur. ...32S 58W **106**
Peabody, Ma., U.S. ...43N 71W **91**
Peace, R., Can. ...57N 117W **72**
Pebane, Moz. ...17S 38 E **131**
Peć, Yugo. ...43N 20 E **117**
Pechenga, Russia ...70N 31 E **114**
Pecos, R., U.S. ...31N 103W **76**
Pécs, Hung. ...46N 18 E **121**
Peiraiás, Grc. ...38N 24 E **121**
Peleduy, Russia ...60N 113 E **141**
Pelly Mts., Yk., Can. ...62N 134W **72**
Pelotas, Braz. ...32S 52W **106**
Pembroke, On., Can. ...46N 77W **73**
Pendleton, Or., U.S. ...46N 119W **82**
Pennsylvania, State, U.S. ...41N 78W **77**
Pensacola, Fl., U.S. ...30N 87W **92**
Penticton, B.C., Can. ...49N 119W **72**
Penza, Russia ...53N 45 E **115**
Penzhino, Russia ...64N 168 E **141**
Peoria, Il., U.S. ...41N 90W **90**
Pereira, Col. ...5N 76W **104**
Pergamino, Arg. ...34S 61W **106**
Perigueux, Fr. ...45N 1 E **117**
Perm', Russia ...58N 56 E **115**
Pernik, Bul. ...43N 23 E **121**
Perpignan, Fr. ...43N 3 E **117**
Persian G., Asia ...28N 50 E **142**
Perth, Austl. ...32S 116 E **156**
Perth, Scot., U.K. ...56N 3W **116**
Perth Amboy, N.J., U.S. ...41N 74W **91**
Peru, Ctry., S.A. ...10S 75W **104**
Perugia, Italy ...43N 12 E **117**
Pervomays'k, Ukr. ...48N 31 E **121**
Pesaro, Italy ...44N 13 E **117**
Peshāwar, Pak. ...34N 72 E **143**
Peterborough, On., Can. ...44N 78W **73**
Petersburg, Va., U.S. ...37N 78W **93**
Petrich, Bul. ...41N 23 E **121**
Petropavlovsk, Kaz. ...55N 69 E **140**
Petropavlovsk-Kamchatskiy, Russia ...53N 159 E **141**
Petrópolis, Braz. ...23S 43W **106**
Petrozavodsk, Russia ...62N 34 E **115**
Phenix City, Al., U.S. ...32N 85W **92**
Philadelphia, Pa., U.S. ...40N 75W **91**
Philippines, Ctry., Asia ...14N 125 E **149**
Philippine Sea, Asia ...25N 129 E **147**
Phitsanulok, Thai. ...17N 100 E **148**
Phnom Penh, Camb. ...12N 105 E **148**
Phoenix, Az., U.S. ...33N 112W **85**
Phra Nakhon Si Ayutthaya, Thai. ...14N 101 E **148**
Piacenza, Italy ...45N 10 E **117**
Piatra-Neamt, Rom. ...47N 26 E **121**
Piedras Negras, Mex. ...29N 101W **96**
Pierre, S.D., U.S. ...44N 100W **88**
Pietermaritzburg, S. Afr. ...30S 30 E **130**
Pieve, Italy ...46N 12 E **120**
Pilcomayo, R., S.A. ...24S 60W **106**
Pinar del Río, Cuba ...22N 84W **97**
Pine Bluff, Ar., U.S. ...34N 92W **87**
Pinega, Russia ...65N 43 E **140**
Pinsk, Bela. ...52N 26 E **114**
Piombino, Italy ...43N 11 E **117**
Piotrkow Trybunalski, Pol. ...51N 20 E **117**
Piracicaba, Braz. ...23S 48W **105**
Pirot, Yugo. ...43N 23 E **121**
Pisa, Italy ...44N 10 E **117**
Pistoia, Italy ...44N 12 E **117**
Pitesti, Rom. ...45N 25 E **121**
Pittsburg, Ks., U.S. ...37N 95W **87**

Pittsburgh, Pa., U.S. ...40N 80W **91**
Pittsfield, Ma., U.S. ...42N 73W **91**
Piura, Peru ...5S 81W **104**
Plainfield, N.J., U.S. ...41N 74W **91**
Plata, R. de la, Arg.-Ur. ...35S 58W **106**
Platte, R., Ne., U.S. ...41N 100W **88**
Plauen, Ger. ...50N 12 E **117**
Pleven, Bul. ...43N 24 E **121**
Pljevlja, Yugo. ...43N 19 E **121**
Ploiesti, Rom. ...45N 26 E **121**
Plovdiv, Bul. ...42N 25 E **121**
Plymouth, Eng., U.K. ...50N 4W **117**
Plzeň, Czech Rep. ...50N 13 E **117**
Po, R., Italy ...45N 11 E **117**
Pocatello, Id., U.S. ...43N 112W **83**
Podgorica, Yugo. ...42N 19 E **121**
Pointe-à-Pitre, Guad. ...16N 62W **97**
Pointe Noire, Congo ...5S 12 E **130**
Poitiers, Fr. ...47N 0 **117**
Poland, Ctry., Eur. ...52N 18 E **117**
Poltava, Ukr. ...50N 35 E **115**
Pomona, Ca., U.S. ...34N 118W **84**
Ponce, P.R. ...18N 67W **97**
Pondicherry, India ...12N 80 E **143**
Ponta Delgada, Port. ...38N 26W **128**
Ponta Grossa, Braz. ...25S 50W **106**
Ponta Pora, Braz. ...22S 56W **105**
Pontiac, Mi., U.S. ...43N 83W **90**
Pontianak, Indon. ...0 109 E **148**
Poopo, Lago de, L., Bol. ...18S 68W **104**
Popayán, Col. ...2N 77W **104**
Porbandar, India ...22N 70 E **143**
Pori, Fin. ...61N 22 E **116**
Poronaysk, Russia ...49N 143 E **141**
Port Alice, B.C., Can. ...50N 127W **72**
Port Angeles, Wa., U.S. ...48N 123W **82**
Port Antonio, Jam. ...18N 76W **97**
Port Arthur, Tx., U.S. ...30N 94W **95**
Port-au-Prince, Haiti ...19N 72W **97**
Port Elizabeth, S. Afr. ...34S 26 E **130**
Port Harcourt, Nig. ...5N 7 E **128**
Port Huron, Mi., U.S. ...43N 82W **90**
Portland, Me., U.S. ...44N 70W **91**
Portland, Or., U.S. ...46N 123W **82**
Port Moresby, Pap. N. Gui. ...10S 147 E **149**
Porto, Port. ...41N 9W **120**
Porto Alegre, Braz. ...30S 51W **106**
Port of Spain, Trin. ...11N 61W **97**
Porto-Novo, Benin ...7N 3 E **128**
Porto Velho, Braz. ...9S 64W **104**
Port Said, Egypt ...31N 32 E **129**
Portsmouth, Eng., U.K. ...51N 1W **117**
Portsmouth, N.H., U.S. ...43N 71W **91**
Portsmouth, Oh., U.S. ...39N 83W **90**
Portsmouth, Va., U.S. ...37N 76W **91**
Portugal, Ctry., Eur. ...40N 8W **120**
Posadas, Arg. ...28S 56W **106**
Potenza, Italy ...41N 16 E **117**
Poti, Geor. ...42N 42 E **115**
Potomac, R., U.S. ...38N 77W **91**
Potosí, Bol. ...20S 66W **104**
Potsdam, Ger. ...52N 13 E **117**
Pottstown, Pa., U.S. ...40N 76W **91**
Pottsville, Pa., U.S. ...41N 76W **91**
Poughkeepsie, N.Y., U.S. ...42N 74W **91**
Poyang Hu, L., China ...29N 117 E **147**
Poznan, Pol. ...52N 17 E **117**
Prague (Praha), Czech Rep. ...50N 14 E **117**
Praia, C.V. ...15N 23W **128**
Přerov, Czech Rep. ...49N 17 E **117**
Prescott, Az., U.S. ...34N 112W **85**
Prešov, Slvk. ...49N 21 E **117**
Pretoria, S. Afr. ...26S 28 E **130**
Prilep, Mac. ...41N 22 E **121**
Prince Albert, Sk., Can. ...53N 106W **72**
Prince Edward Island, Prov., Can. ...47N 63W **73**
Prince George, B.C., Can. ...54N 123W **72**

Prince Rupert, B.C., Can.	54N	130W	**72**
Priština, Yugo.	43N	21E	**121**
Prizren, Yugo.	42N	21E	**121**
Prome (Pye), Myan.	19N	95E	**148**
Providence, R.I., U.S.	42N	71W	**91**
Provo, Ut., U.S.	40N	112W	**85**
Przemysl, Pol.	50N	23E	**117**
Przheval'sk, Kyrg.	42N	78E	**146**
Pskov, Russia	58N	28E	**114**
Puebla, Mex.	19N	98W	**96**
Pueblo, Col.	38N	105W	**86**
Puerto Aisén, Chile	46S	73W	**106**
Puerto Cabello, Ven.	10N	68W	**104**
Puerto Deseado, Arg.	48S	66W	**106**
Puerto la Cruz, Ven.	10N	65W	**104**
Puertollano, Spain	39N	4W	**120**
Puerto Natales, Chile	52S	72W	**106**
Puerto Rico, Ctry., N.A.	18N	67W	**97**
Puerto Santa Cruz, Arg.	50S	69W	**106**
Puerto Suárez, Bol.	19S	58W	**105**
Puget Sound, Wa., U.S.	48N	122W	**82**
Pula, Cro.	45N	14E	**120**
Punakha, Bhu.	28N	90E	**143**
Pune, India	18N	72E	**143**
Punta Arenas, Chile	53S	71W	**106**
Punto Fijo, Ven.	12N	70W	**104**
Puri, India	20N	86E	**143**
Pusan, S. Kor.	35N	129E	**147**
Pyatigorsk, Russia	44N	43E	**115**
Pyinmana, Myan.	20N	96E	**148**
P'yŏngyang, N. Kor.	39N	126E	**147**
Pyrenees, Mts., Fr.-Spain	43N	0	**120**

Q

Qamdo, China	31N	97E	**146**
Qaraghandy, Kaz.	50N	73E	**140**
Qarqaraly, Kaz.	49N	75E	**140**
Qaşr al Burayqah, Libya	30N	19E	**129**
Qatar, Ctry., Asia	25N	51E	**142**
Qeshm, Iran	27N	56E	**142**
Qinā, Egypt	26N	33E	**129**
Qingdao, China	36N	120E	**147**
Qinhuangdao, China	40N	120E	**147**
Qiqihar, China	47N	124E	**147**
Qitai, China	44N	89E	**146**
Qom, Iran	34N	51E	**142**
Qomsheh, Iran	32N	52E	**142**
Qostanay, Kaz.	53N	64E	**140**
Quanzhou, China	25N	119E	**147**
Québec, P.Q., Can.	47N	71W	**73**
Quebec, Prov., Can.	52N	70W	**73**
Queen Charlotte Is., B.C., Can.	54N	133W	**72**
Querétaro, Mex.	21N	100W	**96**
Quetta, Pak.	30N	67E	**143**
Quezaltenango, Guat.	15N	91W	**96**
Quezon City, Phil.	15N	121E	**149**
Quibdó, Col.	6N	77W	**104**
Quilmes, Arg.	34S	58W	**106**
Quilon, India	9N	76E	**143**
Quimper, Fr.	48N	4W	**117**
Quincy, Ma., U.S.	42N	71W	**91**
Quito, Ec.	0	79W	**104**
Quxian, China	29N	119E	**147**
Qyzylorda, Kaz.	45N	66E	**140**

R

Rabat, Mor.	34N	7W	**128**
Racine, Wi., U.S.	43N	88W	**89**
Radom, Pol.	51N	21E	**117**
Rafaela, Arg.	31S	61W	**106**
Rafḥā, Sau. Ar.	30N	43E	**142**
Ragusa, Italy	37N	15E	**120**
Raigarh, India	22N	84E	**143**
Rainier, Mt., Wa., U.S.	47N	122W	**82**
Rainy River, On., Can.	49N	94W	**73**
Raipur, India	21N	82E	**143**
Rājahmundry, India	17N	82E	**143**
Rājkot, India	22N	71E	**143**
Rājshāhi, Pak.	24N	89E	**143**
Raleigh, N.C., U.S.	36N	79W	**93**
Rāmpur, India	29N	79E	**143**
Rancagua, Chile	34S	71W	**106**
Rānchī, India	23N	85E	**143**
Randers, Den.	56N	10E	**116**
Ranger, Tx., U.S.	32N	99W	**94**
Rangoon (Yangon), Myan.	17N	96E	**148**
Rangpur, Bngl.	26N	89E	**143**
Rapid City, S.D., U.S.	44N	103W	**88**
Ras Dashen Terara, Mt., Eth.	13N	38E	**129**
Rashīd, Egypt	31N	30E	**121**
Rasht, Iran	37N	50E	**142**
Raton, N.M., U.S.	37N	104W	**86**
Ravenna, Italy	44N	12E	**117**
Rāwalpindi, Pak.	34N	73E	**143**
Rawāndūz, Iraq	37N	44E	**142**
Rawlins, Wy., U.S.	42N	107W	**83**
Rawson, Arg.	43S	65W	**106**
Reading, Eng., U.K.	51N	1W	**117**
Reading, Pa., U.S.	40N	76W	**91**
Recife (Pernambuco), Braz.	8S	35W	**105**
Red, R., Can.-U.S.	48N	97W	**72**
Red, R., China-Viet.	21N	104E	**148**
Red, R., U.S.	32N	93W	**76**
Red Deer, Ab., Can.	52N	114W	**72**
Redding, Ca., U.S.	40N	122W	**82**
Red Sea, Afr.-Asia	24N	37E	**142**
Regensburg, Ger.	49N	12E	**117**
Reggio di Calabria, Italy	38N	16E	**117**
Reggio nell'Emilia, Italy	45N	11E	**117**
Regina, Sk., Can.	51N	104W	**72**
Reims, Fr.	49N	4E	**117**
Reindeer L., Can.	58N	102W	**72**
Rennes, Fr.	48N	1W	**117**
Reno, Nv., U.S.	40N	120W	**84**
Resistencia, Arg.	27S	59W	**106**
Reunion, Dep., Afr.	22S	56E	**53**
Reus, Spain	41N	1E	**120**
Rewa, India	25N	81E	**143**
Reykajavik, Ice.	64N	22W	**116**
Rhein, R., Eur.	51N	7E	**117**
Rhode Island, State, U.S.	42N	72W	**77**
Rhône, R., Fr.-Switz.	44N	5E	**120**
Ribeirão Prêto, Braz.	21S	48W	**105**
Richland, Wa., U.S.	46N	119W	**82**
Richmond, Va., U.S.	38N	77W	**91**
Rieti, Italy	42N	13E	**117**
Riga, Lat.	57N	24E	**114**
Rīgān, Iran	29N	59E	**142**
Rijeka, Cro.	45N	13E	**120**
Rimini, Italy	44N	13E	**117**
Ringkobing, Den.	56N	8E	**116**
Ríobamba, Ec.	2S	79W	**104**
Rio Branco, Braz.	10S	68W	**104**
Río Cuarto, Arg.	33S	64W	**106**
Rio de Janeiro, Braz.	23S	43W	**106**
Río Gallegos, Arg.	52S	68W	**106**
Rio Grande, Braz.	31S	52W	**106**
Rio Grande, R., Mex.-U.S.	26N	98W	**76**
Rio Muni, Polit. Reg., Eq. Gui.	2N	10E	**128**
Riverside, Ca., U.S.	34N	117W	**84**
Riyadh, Sau. Ar.	25N	47E	**142**
Rize, Tur.	41N	40E	**121**
Roanne, Fr.	46N	4E	**117**
Roanoke, Va., U.S.	37N	80W	**93**
Rocha, Ur.	34S	54W	**106**
Rochefort, Fr.	46N	1W	**117**
Rochester, Mn., U.S.	44N	92W	**89**
Rochester, N.Y., U.S.	43N	78W	**91**
Rockford, Il., U.S.	42N	89W	**90**
Rockhampton, Austl.	23S	150E	**157**
Rock Hill, S.C., U.S.	35N	81W	**93**
Rock Island, Il., U.S.	42N	96W	**89**
Rock Springs, Wy., U.S.	42N	109W	**83**
Rockville Centre, N.Y., U.S.	41N	74W	**91**
Rocky Mts., N.A.	45N	110W	**76**
Ródos, Grc.	36N	28E	**121**
Romania, Ctry., Eur.	46N	23E	**121**
Rome, Ga., U.S.	34N	85W	**92**
Rome, Italy	42N	13E	**117**
Rosario, Arg.	33S	61W	**106**
Roseburg, Or., U.S.	43N	123W	**82**
Rosenheim, Ger.	48N	12E	**117**
Rostock, Ger.	54N	12E	**116**
Rostov-na-Donu, Russia	47N	40E	**115**
Roswell, N.M., U.S.	33N	105W	**86**
Rotterdam, Neth.	52N	4E	**117**
Rouen, Fr.	49N	22E	**117**
Royal Oak, Mi., U.S.	42N	83W	**90**
Ruapehu, Mt., Vol., N.Z.	39S	176E	**157**
Rubtsovsk, Russia	52N	81E	**140**
Rudolf, L., Eth.-Kenya	4N	36E	**129**
Rufisque, Sen.	15N	17W	**128**
Ruse, Bul.	44N	26E	**121**
Russell, Mb., Can.	51N	101W	**72**
Russia, Ctry., Asia-Eur.	60N	80E	**140**
Rwanda, Ctry., Afr.	2S	30E	**130**
Ryazan', Russia	55N	40E	**115**
Rybinsk, Russia	58N	39E	**115**
Rzeszow, Pol.	50N	22E	**117**
Rzhev, Russia	56N	34E	**115**

S

Saarbrücken, Ger.	49N	7E	**117**
Šabac, Yugo.	45N	20E	**121**
Sabah, Polit. Reg., Malay.	5N	116E	**148**
Sabine, R., U.S.	30N	94W	**95**
Sacramento, Ca., U.S.	39N	121W	**84**
Sacramento, R., Ca., U.S.	38N	122W	**84**
Safad, Isr.	33N	35E	**121**
Safi (Asfi), Mor.	32N	9W	**128**
Sāgar, India	24N	79E	**143**
Saginaw, Mi., U.S.	43N	84W	**90**
Saguenay, R., P.Q., Can.	48N	71W	**73**
Sagunto, Spain	40N	0	**120**
Sahara, Des., Afr.	23N	10E	**128**
Sahāranpur, India	30N	78E	**143**
Saïda, Alg.	35N	0	**128**
St. Agustine, Fl., U.S.	30N	81W	**93**
St. Brieuc, Fr.	49N	3W	**117**
St. Catharines, On., Can.	43N	79W	**73**
St. Clair, L., Can.-U.S.	42N	83W	**91**
St. Cloud, Mn., U.S.	46N	94W	**89**
St. Denis, Fr.	40N	2E	**117**
St. Étienne, Fr.	45N	4E	**117**
St. George's, Nf., Can.	48N	58W	**73**
St. George's Chan., Eur.	52N	7W	**117**
St. Helens, Mt., Vol., Wa., U.S.	46N	122W	**82**
St. Hyacinthe, P.Q., Can.	46N	73W	**73**
St. John, N.B., Can.	45N	66W	**73**
St. John's, Nf., Can.	48N	53W	**73**
St. Joseph, Mo., U.S.	40N	95W	**87**
St. Kitts and Nevis, Ctry., N.A.	17N	63W	**97**
St. Lawrence, R., Can.-U.S.	48N	69W	**73**
St. Lawrence, G. of, Can.	48N	62W	**73**
St. Louis, Sen.	16N	16W	**128**
St. Louis, Mo., U.S.	39N	90W	**87**
St. Lucia, Ctry., N.A.	14N	61W	**97**
St. Malo, Fr.	49N	2W	**117**
St. Nazaire, Fr.	48N	2W	**117**
St. Paul, Ab., Can.	54N	111W	**72**
St. Paul, Mn., U.S.	45N	93W	**89**
St. Petersburg, Fl., U.S.	28N	83W	**93**
St. Petersburg (Leningrad), Russia	60N	30E	**114**
St. Pierre and Miquelon, Ctry., N.A.	47N	57W	**73**
St. Quentin, Fr.	50N	3E	**117**
St. Vincent and the Grenadines, Ctry., N.A.	13N	61W	**97**
Sakākah, Sau. Ar.	30N	40E	**142**
Salamanca, Spain	41N	6W	**120**
Salé, Mor.	34N	7W	**128**
Salekhard, Russia	67N	67E	**140**
Salem, India	12N	78E	**143**
Salem, Ma., U.S.	43N	71W	**91**
Salem, Or., U.S.	45N	123W	**82**
Salerno, Italy	40N	15E	**117**
Salina, Ks., U.S.	39N	98W	**87**
Salina Cruz, Mex.	16N	95W	**96**
Salinas, Ca., U.S.	37N	122W	**84**
Salisbury, Eng., U.K.	51N	2W	**117**
Salta, Arg.	25S	65W	**106**
Salt Lake City, Ut., U.S.	41N	112W	**85**
Salto, Ur.	31S	58W	**106**
Salton Sea, L., Ca., U.S.	33N	116W	**84**
Salvador (Bahia), Braz.	13S	38W	**105**
Salween, R., Asia	21N	98E	**148**
Salzburg, Aus.	48N	13E	**117**
Samara, Russia	53N	50E	**115**
Samarkand, Uzb.	40N	67E	**140**
Samoa, Ctry., Oc.	15S	177W	**158**
Samsun, Tur.	41N	36E	**121**
Sanā', Yemen	16N	44E	**142**
Sanandaj, Iran	36N	47E	**142**
San Angelo, Tx., U.S.	31N	100W	**94**
San Antonio, Tx., U.S.	29N	98W	**94**
San Antonio Oeste, Arg.	41S	65W	**106**
San Bernardino, Ca., U.S.	34N	117W	**84**
San Bernardo, Chile	34S	71W	**106**
Sánchez, Dom. Rep.	19N	70W	**97**
San Cristóbal, Ven.	8N	72W	**104**
Sancti Spíritus, Cuba	22N	79W	**97**
San Diego, Ca., U.S.	33N	117W	**84**
Sandpoint, Id., U.S.	48N	116W	**82**
Sandusky, Oh., U.S.	41N	83W	**90**
San Fernando, Arg.	34S	59W	**106**
San Fernando, Phil.	17N	120E	**149**
Sanford, Fl., U.S.	29N	81W	**93**
San Francisco, Arg.	31S	62W	**106**
San Francisco, Ca., U.S.	38N	122W	**84**
Sāngli, India	17N	75E	**143**
San Isidro, Arg.	34S	59W	**106**
San Joaquin, R., Ca., U.S.	37N	121W	**83**
San José, C.R.	10N	84W	**97**
San Jose, Ca., U.S.	37N	122W	**84**
San Juan, P.R.	18N	66W	**97**
San Justo, Arg.	34S	59W	**106**
Sankt Gallen, Switz.	47N	9E	**117**
Sanlıurfa, Tur.	37N	39E	**121**
Sanlúcar de Barrameda, Spain	37N	6W	**120**
San Luis, Arg.	33S	66W	**106**
San Luis Obispo, Ca., U.S.	35N	121W	**84**
San Luis Potosí, Mex.	22N	101W	**96**
San Marino, Ctry., Eur.	44N	13E	**117**
San Miguel, El Sal.	13N	88W	**96**
San Nicolas, Arg.	33S	60W	**106**
San Rafael, Arg.	34S	68W	**106**
San Salvador, El Sal.	14N	89W	**96**
San Sebastián, Spain	43N	2W	**120**
Santa Ana, El Sal.	14N	90W	**96**
Santa Ana, Ca., U.S.	34N	118W	**84**
Santa Barbara, Ca., U.S.	34N	120W	**84**
Santa Clara, Cuba	22N	80W	**97**
Santa Cruz, Bol.	18S	63W	**104**
Santa Cruz, Braz.	30S	52W	**106**

Santa Cruz, Ca., U.S.	37N	122W	84
Santa Cruz de Tenerife, Spain	28N	15W	128
Santa Fe, Arg.	32S	61W	106
Santa Fe, N.M., U.S.	35N	106W	85
Santa Fe de Bogotá, Col.	5N	74W	104
Santa Lucia, Ur.	34S	56W	106
Santa Maria, Braz.	30S	54W	106
Santa Marta, Col.	11N	74W	104
Santa Monica, Ca., U.S.	34N	118W	84
Santander, Spain	43N	4W	120
Santa Rosa, Arg.	37S	64W	106
Santa Rosa, Ca., U.S.	38N	123W	84
Santiago, Chile	33S	71W	106
Santiago de Campostela, Spain	43N	9W	120
Santiago de Cuba, Cuba	20N	76W	97
Santiago del Estero, Arg.	28S	64W	106
Santo Domingo, Dom. Rep.	18N	70W	97
Santos, Braz.	24S	46W	106
São Carlos, Braz.	22S	48W	105
São Francisco, R., Braz.	9S	40W	105
São Gonçalo, Braz.	23S	43W	106
São João del Rei, Braz.	21S	44W	106
São João de Meriti, Braz.	23S	43W	106
São Luis (Maranhão), Braz.	3S	43W	105
Saone, R., Fr.	46N	5E	117
São Paulo, Braz.	24S	47W	106
São Vicente, Braz.	24S	46W	106
Sapele, Nig.	6N	5E	128
Sapporo, Japan	43N	141E	147
Sarajevo, Bos.	43N	18E	121
Sarandi, Arg.	34S	58W	106
Saransk, Russia	54N	45E	115
Sarapul, Russia	56N	54E	115
Sarasota, Fl., U.S.	27N	83W	93
Saratov, Russia	52N	45E	115
Sarawak, Polit. Reg., Malay.	3N	113E	148
Sardinia, I., Italy	40N	9E	117
Sarnia, On., Can.	43N	82W	73
Sasarām, India	25N	84E	143
Sasebo, Japan	33N	130E	147
Saskatchewan, Prov., Can.	55N	108W	72
Saskatchewan, R., Can.	54N	103W	72
Saskatoon, Sk., Can.	52N	107W	72
Sassari, Italy	41N	9E	117
Satu Mare, Rom.	48N	23E	121
Saudarkrokur, Ice.	66N	20W	116
Saudi Arabia, Ctry., Asia	27N	42E	142
Savannah, Ga., U.S.	32N	81W	93
Savannah, R., U.S.	33N	82W	93
Savona, Italy	44N	8E	117
Sawhāj, Egypt	27N	32E	129
Sayḩūt, Yemen	15N	51E	142
Sayr Usa, Mong.	45N	107E	146
Say'un, Yemen	16N	49E	142
Schaffhausen, Switz.	48N	9E	117
Schenectady, N.Y., U.S.	43N	74W	91
Schleswig, Ger.	55N	10E	116
Scotland, Polit. Reg., U.K.	57N	3W	116
Scottsbluff, Ne., U.S.	42N	104W	88
Scranton, Pa., U.S.	42N	76W	91
Seattle, Wa., U.S.	48N	122W	82
Sedalia, Mo., U.S.	39N	93W	87
Segovia, Spain	41N	4W	120
Seine, R., Fr.	49N	1E	117
Sekondi-Takoradi, Ghana	5N	2W	128
Selkirk Mts., B.C., Can.	51N	117W	72
Selma, Al., U.S.	32N	87W	92
Selvas, Reg., Braz.	5S	64W	104
Semarang, Indon.	7S	110E	148
Semey, Kaz.	50N	80E	140
Semipalatinsk, see Semey, Kaz.	50N	80E	140
Sendai, Japan	38N	141E	147
Senegal, Ctry., Afr.	15N	15W	128
Seoul (Sŏul), S. Kor.	38N	127E	147
Sept-Îles, P.Q., Can.	50N	66W	73
Serov, Russia	60N	60E	115
Serpukhov, Russia	55N	37E	115
Sérres, Grc.	41N	24E	121
Settat, Mor.	33N	7W	128
Setúbal, Port.	39N	9W	120
Sevastopol', Ukr.	45N	34E	115
Severnaya Zemlya, Is., Russia	79N	100E	141
Sevilla, Spain	37N	6W	120
Seychelles, Ctry., Afr.	4S	55E	53
Sezela, S. Afr.	30S	30E	131
Sfax, Tun.	35N	11E	128
Shache (Yarkand), China	38N	77E	146
Shāhjahānpur, India	28N	80E	143
Shakhrisyabz, Uzb.	39N	68E	140
Shakhty, Russia	48N	40E	115
Shalqar, Kaz.	48N	60E	140
Shanghai, China	31N	121E	147
Shanshan, China	43N	90E	146
Shantou, China	23N	117E	147
Shaoguan, China	25N	114E	147
Shaoxing, China	30N	121E	147
Shaoyang, China	27N	112E	147
Sharon, Pa., U.S.	41N	80W	90
Shaunavon, Sk., Can.	50N	108W	72
Shawnee, Ok., U.S.	35N	97W	87
Sheboygan, Wi., U.S.	44N	88W	89
Sheffield, Eng., U.K.	53N	1W	117
Shenkursk, Russia	62N	43E	140
Shenyang, China	42N	123E	147
Sherbrooke, P.Q., Can.	45N	72W	73
Sheridan, Wy., U.S.	45N	107W	83
Sherman, Tx., U.S.	34N	97W	87
Shetland Is., Scot., U.K.	60N	2W	116
Shibām, Yemen	16N	49E	142
Shibīn al Kawm, Egypt	31N	31E	121
Shijiazhuang, China	38N	115E	147
Shikārpur, Pak.	28N	69E	143
Shikoku, I., Japan	33N	135E	147
Shillong, India	26N	92E	143
Shimonoseki, Japan	34N	131E	147
Shīrāz, Iran	30N	52E	142
Shivpuri, India	26N	78E	143
Shkoder, Alb.	42N	19E	121
Sholāpur, India	18N	76E	143
Shreveport, La., U.S.	32N	94W	95
Shuangliao, China	44N	123E	147
Shumen, Bul.	43N	27E	121
Shuqrah, Yemen	14N	46E	142
Shūshtar, Iran	32N	49E	142
Shuya, Russia	57N	41E	140
Shymkent, Kaz.	42N	70E	140
Siālkot, Pak.	33N	74E	143
Šiauliai, Lith.	56N	23E	116
Šibenik, Cro.	44N	16E	121
Sibiu, Rom.	46N	24E	121
Sibolga, Indon.	2N	99E	148
Sicily, I., Italy	37N	14E	117
Sidi bel Abbès, Alg.	35N	1W	128
Sidi Ifni, Mor.	29N	10W	128
Siena, Italy	43N	11E	117
Sierra Leone, Ctry., Afr.	9N	13W	128
Sierra Nevada, Mts., Ca., U.S.	38N	120W	84
Silifke, Tur.	36N	34E	121
Silistra, Bul.	44N	27E	121
Silver Spring, Md., U.S.	39N	77W	91
Simferopol', Ukr.	45N	34E	115
Simla, India	31N	77E	143
Singapore, Ctry., Asia	1N	104E	148
Sinop, Tur.	42N	35E	121
Sinŭiju, N. Kor.	40N	125E	147
Sioux City, Ia., U.S.	42N	96W	88
Sioux Falls, S.D., U.S.	44N	97W	88
Sioux Lookout, On., Can.	50N	92W	73
Sipiwesk, Mb., Can.	56N	97W	72
Siracusa, Italy	37N	15E	121
Sirājganj, Bngl.	25N	90E	143
Sisak, Cro.	45N	16E	121
Sittwe, Myan.	20N	93E	146
Sivas, Tur.	40N	37E	121
Skagerrak, Str., Den.-Nor.	57N	8E	116
Skelleftea, Swe.	65N	21E	116
Skikda, Alg.	37N	7E	128
Skopje, Mac.	42N	21E	121
Skovorodino, Russia	54N	124E	141
Slavgorod, Russia	53N	79E	140
Slavonski Brod, Cro.	45N	18E	121
Sligo, Ire.	54N	8W	116
Sliven, Bul.	43N	26E	121
Slobodskoy, Russia	59N	50E	140
Slovakia, Ctry., Eur.	48N	20E	117
Slovenia, Ctry., Eur.	46N	15E	120
Slupsk, Pol.	54N	17E	116
Smila, Ukr.	49N	32E	121
Smith, Ab., Can.	55N	114W	72
Smolensk, Russia	55N	32E	115
Snake, R., U.S.	45N	117W	82
Sochi, Russia	44N	40E	115
Sofia (Sofiya), Bul.	43N	23E	121
Söke, Tur.	38N	27E	121
Sokoto, Nig.	13N	5E	128
Solikamsk, Russia	60N	57E	115
Sol'-Iletsk, Russia	51N	55E	140
Solomon Islands, Ctry., Oc.	7S	160E	157
Somalia, Ctry., Afr.	3N	43E	131
Sombor, Yugo.	46N	19E	121
Somerville, Ma., U.S.	42N	71W	91
Songjiang, China	31N	121E	147
Songkhla, Thai.	7N	101E	148
Sopron, Hung.	48N	17E	117
Sortavala, Russia	62N	31E	140
Sosnogorsk, Russia	63N	54E	140
Souq-Ahras, Alg.	36N	8E	120
Souris, Mb., Can.	50N	100W	72
Sousse, Tun.	36N	11E	128
South Africa, Ctry., Afr.	28S	28E	130
South Bend, In., U.S.	42N	86W	90
South Carolina, State, U.S.	34N	81W	77
South China Sea, Asia	20N	114E	147
South Dakota, State, U.S.	44N	102W	76
Southern Alps, Mts., N.Z.	44S	169E	157
South Georgia, Dep., S.A.	54S	37W	52
Southhampton, Eng., U.K.	51N	1W	117
Southhampton, I., Nu., Can.	65N	85W	73
South I., N.Z.	43S	167E	157
South Orkney Islands, Is., S.A.	60S	45W	52
South Saskatchewan, R., Can.	50N	110W	72
South Shields, Eng., U.K.	55N	1W	116
Sovetsk (Tilsit), Russia	55N	22E	116
Sovetskaya Gavan', Russia	49N	140E	141
Spain, Ctry., Eur.	40N	4W	120
Spartanburg, S.C., U.S.	35N	82W	93
Spassk-Dal'niy, Russia	44N	133E	141
Split, Cro.	43N	16E	121
Spokane, Wa., U.S.	48N	117W	82
Spola, Ukr.	49N	32E	121
Springfield, Il., U.S.	40N	90W	90
Springfield, Ma., U.S.	42N	73W	91
Springfield, Mo., U.S.	37N	93W	87
Springfield, Oh., U.S.	40N	84W	90
Sredne-Kolymsk, Russia	68N	155E	141
Sri Lanka (Ceylon), Ctry., Asia	7N	79E	143
Srīnagar, India	34N	75E	143
Stamford, Ct., U.S.	41N	74W	91
Stanley, Falk. Is.	52S	58W	106
Stara Zagora, Bul.	42N	26E	121
Stargard Szczeciński, Pol.	53N	15E	116
Stavanger, Nor.	59N	6E	116
Sterling, Col.	41N	103W	86
Sterlitamak, Russia	54N	56E	115
Stettler, Ab., Can.	52N	113W	72
Steubenville, Oh., U.S.	40N	81W	90
Stewart, I., N.Z.	47S	168E	157
Stif, Alg.	36N	5E	128
Stockholm, Swe.	59N	18E	116
Stockton, Ca., U.S.	38N	121W	84
Stoke-on-Trent, Eng., U.K.	53N	2W	117
Stralsund, Ger.	54N	13E	116
Strasbourg, Fr.	49N	8E	117
Stratford, On., Can.	43N	81W	90
Stratford, Ct., U.S.	41N	73W	91
Strumica, Mac.	41N	23E	121
Stryy, Ukr.	49N	24E	121
Stuttgart, Ger.	49N	9E	117
Subic, Phil.	15N	120E	149
Subotica, Yugo.	46N	20E	121
Sucre, Bol.	19S	65W	104
Sudan, Ctry., Afr.	15N	29E	129
Sudbury, On., Can.	46N	81W	73
Sudetes, Mts., Czech Rep.-Pol.	51N	16E	117
Suez (As Suways), Egypt	30N	33E	129
Suez, G. of, Egypt	29N	33E	129
Suez Canal, Egypt	30N	32E	129
Suifenhe, China	45N	131E	147
Sukabumi, Indon.	7S	107E	148
Sukhumi, Geor.	43N	41E	115
Sukkur, Pak.	28N	69E	143
Sulina, Rom.	45N	30E	121
Sulu Sea, Malay.-Phil.	9N	119E	148
Sumatra (Sumatera), I., Indon.	2N	100E	148
Sumba, I., Indon.	10S	119E	148
Sunderland, Eng., U.K.	55N	1W	116
Sundsvall, Swe.	62N	19E	116
Sumy, Ukr.	51N	35E	115
Suntar, Russia	62N	118E	141
Superior, Wi., U.S.	47N	92W	89
Superior, L., Can.-U.S.	48N	88W	89
Şūr (Tyre), Leb.	33N	35E	121
Şūr, Oman	22N	59E	142
Surabaya, Indon.	7S	113E	148
Surakarta, Indon.	8S	111E	148
Surat, India	21N	73E	143
Surgut, Russia	61N	74E	140
Suriname, Ctry., S.A.	4N	56W	105
Surt, Libya	31N	17E	129
Susquehanna, R., U.S.	40N	76W	91
Suzhou, China	31N	121E	147
Svalbard, Is., Nor.	74N	20E	53
Sverdlovsk, see Yekaterinburg, Russia	57N	61E	115
Svobodnyy, Russia	51N	128E	141
Swansea, Wales, U.K.	52N	4W	117
Swaziland, Ctry., Afr.	27S	31E	130
Sweden, Ctry., Eur.	60N	14E	116
Sweetwater, Tx., U.S.	32N	100W	94
Switzerland, Ctry., Eur.	47N	8E	117
Sydney, Austl.	34S	151E	157
Syktyvkar, Russia	61N	50E	140
Synel'nykove, Ukr.	48N	36E	121
Syracuse, N.Y., U.S.	43N	76W	91
Syr Darya, R., Asia	46N	61E	140
Syria, Ctry., Asia	34N	38E	142
Syzran', Russia	53N	48E	115
Szczecin (Stettin), Pol.	53N	15E	116
Szczecinek, Pol.	54N	17E	116
Szeged, Hung.	46N	20E	117
Székesfehérvár, Hung.	47N	18E	117
Szolnok, Hung.	47N	20E	117
Szombathely, Hung.	47N	17E	117

T

Tabrīz, Iran	38N	46E	142
Tacheng, China	47N	83E	146
Tacloban, Phil.	11N	125E	149
Tacoma, Wa., U.S.	47N	122W	82
Tacuarembó, Ur.	32S	56W	106
Tadjoura, Dji.	12N	43E	142

Taegu, S. Kor. 36N 129E 147
Taganrog, Russia 47N 39E 115
Tagus, R., Port.-Spain 39N 8W 120
Tahiti, I., Oc. 17S 149W 158
Tahoe, L., U.S. 39N 120W 84
T'aichung, Tai. 24N 121E 147
T'ainan, Tai. 23N 120E 147
T'aipei, Tai. 25N 121E 147
Taiwan (Formosa), Ctry., Asia 23N 122E 147
Taiwan Strait, China-Tai. 25N 120E 147
Taiyuan, China 38N 113E 147
Tajikistan, Ctry., Asia 39N 71E 143
Tak, Thai. 16N 99E 148
Takamatsu, Japan 34N 134E 147
Takla Makan, Des., China 39N 82E 146
Talasea, Pap. N. Gui. 5S 150E 149
Talca, Chile 35S 72W 106
Talcahuano, Chile 37S 73W 106
Tallahassee, Fl., U.S. 30N 84W 92
Tallinn, Est. 59N 25E 114
Tambov, Russia 53N 41E 115
Tampa, Fl., U.S. 28N 82W 93
Tampere, Fin. 62N 24W 116
Tampico, Mex. 22N 98W 96
Tandil, Arg. 37S 59W 106
Tanganyika, L., Afr. 6S 30E 130
Tanger, Mor. 36N 6W 128
Tannūrah, Ra's at, C., Sau. Ar. 27N 50E 142
Ţanţā, Egypt 31N 31E 129
Tanzania, Ctry., Afr. 7S 33E 130
Tao'an, China 45N 123E 147
Tapajós, R., Braz. 3S 56W 105
Tara, Russia 57N 74E 140
Ţarābulus (Tripoli), Leb. 34N 36E 142
Taranto, Italy 40N 17E 117
Tarbes, Fr. 43N 0 117
Târgoviste, Rom. 45N 25E 121
Târgu-Mures, Rom. 47N 25E 121
Tarifa, Spain 36N 6W 120
Tarīm, Yemen 16N 49E 142
Tarkwa, Ghana 5N 2W 128
Tarnow, Pol. 50N 21E 117
Tarragona, Spain 41N 1E 120
Tarsus, Tur. 37N 35E 121
Tartu, Est. 58N 27E 114
Ţarţūs, Syria 35N 36E 121
Tashkent, Uzb. 41N 69E 140
Tasmania, I., Austl. 42S 147E 157
Tasman Sea, Oc. 37S 155E 157
Tatarsk, Russia 55N 75E 140
Tatar Str., Russia 50N 141E 147
Taubate, Braz. 23S 46W 105
Taunton, Ma., U.S. 42N 71W 91
Tavda, Russia 58N 65E 140
Taymā', Sau. Ar. 28N 39E 142
Tazovskoye, Russia 67N 78E 140
Tbessa, Alg. 35N 8E 128
Tbilisi, Geor. 42N 45E 115
Tczew, Pol. 54N 19E 116
Tecuci, Rom. 46N 27E 121
Tegucigalpa, Hond. 14N 87W 96
Tehrān, Iran 36N 51E 142
Tehuantepec, Golfo de, G., Mex. 16N 95W 96
Tekirdağ, Tur. 41N 27E 121
Tel Aviv-Yafo, Isr. 32N 35E 142
Temir, Kaz. 49N 57E 140
Temirtaū, Kaz. 50N 73E 140
Tempe, Az., U.S. 33N 112W 85
Temple, Tx., U.S. 31N 97W 95
Temryuk, Russia 45N 37E 121
Temuco, Chile 39S 73W 106
Tennessee, State, U.S. 36N 88W 77
Tepic, Mex. 22N 105W 96
Teresina, Braz. 5S 43W 105
Teresópolis, Braz. 22S 43W 106
Termez, Uzb. 37N 67E 143
Terni, Italy 43N 13E 117
Ternopil', Ukr. 50N 26E 121
Terrace, B.C., Can. 55N 129W 72
Terracina, Italy 41N 13E 117
Terre Haute, In., U.S. 39N 87W 90
Tetouan, Mor. 36N 6W 128
Tetovo, Mac. 42N 21E 121
Texarkana, Ar., U.S. 33N 94W 87
Texas, State, U.S. 31N 101W 76
Texas City, Tx., U.S. 29N 95W 95
Thailand, Ctry., Asia 16N 101E 148
Thailand, G. of, Asia 12N 101E 148
Thames, R., Eng., U.K. 51N 1E 117
Thanh Hoa, Viet. 20N 106E 148
Thanjāvūr, India 11N 79E 143
The Dalles, Or., U.S. 46N 121W 82
The Everglades, Swamp, Fl., U.S. 26N 81W 93
The Hague ('s Gravenhage), Neth. 52N 4E 117
Thessaloníki, Grc. 41N 23E 121
Thiès, Sen. 15N 17W 128
Thimphu, Bhu. 28N 90E 146
Thionville, Fr. 49N 6E 117
Thíva (Thebes), Grc. 38N 23E 121
Thohoyandou, S. Afr. 23S 31E 130
Thompson, Mb., Can. 56N 98W 72
Thunder Bay, On., Can. 48N 89W 73
Tianjin, China 39N 117E 147
Tiberias, Isr. 33N 36E 121
Tibet, Plateau of, China 32N 83E 146
Tieling, China 42N 124E 147
Tien Shan, Mts., Asia 43N 80E 146
Tierra del Fuego, I., Arg.-Chile 54S 68W 106
Tigre, Arg. 34S 58W 106
Tigris, R., Asia 35N 44E 142
Tihert, Alg. 35N 1E 128
Tijuana, Mex. 33N 117W 96
Tikhoretsk, Russia 46N 40E 121
Tikhvin, Russia 60N 34E 140
Tikrīt, Iraq 35N 44E 142
Tiksi, Russia 72N 129E 141
Tilburg, Neth. 52N 5E 117
Tilimsen, Alg. 35N 1W 128
Timashevskaya, Russia 46N 38E 121
Timisoara, Rom. 46N 21E 121
Timmins, On., Can. 48N 81W 73
Timor, I., Asia 10S 125E 149
Timor Sea, Asia-Austl. 10S 128E 149
Tindouf, Alg. 28N 8W 128
Tiranë, Alb. 41N 20E 121
Tiraspol, Mol. 47N 30E 121
Tiruchchirāppalli, India 11N 79E 143
Tirunelveli, India 8N 78E 143
Tisdale, Sk., Can. 53N 104W 72
Tisza, R., Eur. 46N 20E 117
Titicaca, Lago, L., Bol.-Peru 16S 69W 104
Tivoli, Italy 42N 13E 117
Tlaxcala, Mex. 19N 98W 96
Toamasina, Madag. 18S 49E 131
Tobol'sk, Russia 59N 68E 138
Tocantins, R., Braz. 3S 50W 105
Tocopilla, Chile 22S 70W 106
Togo, Ctry., Afr. 8N 1E 128
Tokat, Tur. 40N 36E 121
Tokmak, Kyrg. 43N 76E 140
Tokushima, Japan 34N 135E 147
Tōkyō, Japan 36N 140E 147
Toledo, Oh., U.S. 42N 84W 90
Toledo, Spain 40N 4W 120
Toluca, Mex. 19N 100W 96
Tommot, Russia 59N 126E 141
Tomsk, Russia 56N 85E 140
Tonga, Ctry., Oc. 20S 173W 158
Tonghua, China 42N 126E 147
Tongren, China 27N 110E 146
Tonk, India 26N 76E 143
Tonkin, G. of, China-Viet. 20N 107E 148
Tonopah, Nv., U.S. 38N 117W 84
Topeka, Ks., U.S. 39N 96W 87
Torghay, Kaz. 50N 64E 140
Toronto, On., Can. 44N 79W 73
Torreón, Mex. 26N 103W 96
Torrington, Ct., U.S. 42N 73W 91
Torun, Pol. 53N 19E 116
Touggourt, Alg. 33N 6E 128
Toul, Fr. 49N 6E 117
Toulon, Fr. 43N 6E 117
Toulouse, Fr. 44N 1E 117
Toungoo, Myan. 19N 96E 148
Tours, Fr. 47N 1E 117
Toyama, Japan 37N 137E 147
Trabzon, Tur. 41N 40E 121
Trapani, Italy 38N 12E 117
Traverse City, Mi., U.S. 45N 86W 90
Trento, Italy 46N 11E 117
Trenton, N.J., U.S. 40N 75W 91
Tres Arroyos, Arg. 38S 60W 106
Treviso, Italy 46N 12E 117
Trier, Ger. 50N 7E 117
Trieste, Italy 46N 14E 117
Trikala, Grc. 40N 22E 121
Trincomalee, Sri L. 9N 81E 143
Trinidad, Col. 37N 105W 86
Trinidad and Tobago, Ctry., N.A. 11N 61W 97
Trinity, R., Tx., U.S. 31N 95W 95
Tripoli, Libya 33N 13E 129
Trivandrum, India 8N 77E 143
Trois-Rivières, P.Q., Can. 46N 73W 73
Troitsk, Russia 54N 62E 115
Troitsko-Pechorsk, Russia 62N 56E 140
Trondheim (Nidaros), Nor. 63N 12E 116
Troy, N.Y., U.S. 43N 74W 91
Troyes, Fr. 48N 4E 117
Trstenik, Yugo. 44N 20E 121
Trujillo, Peru 8S 79W 104
Trujillo, Ven. 9N 70W 104
Tsiafajovona, Mt., Madag. 19S 47E 131
Tuapse, Russia 44N 39E 121
Tubruq (Tobruk), Libya 32N 24E 129
Tucacas, Ven. 11N 68W 104
Tucson, Az., U.S. 32N 111W 85
Tucumán, Arg. 27S 65W 106
Tula, Russia 54N 38E 115
Tulcea, Rom. 45N 29E 121
Tulsa, Ok., U.S. 36N 96W 87
Tulun, Russia 54N 101E 141
Tunis, Tun. 37N 10E 128
Tunisia, Ctry., Afr. 35N 10E 128
Tunja, Col. 5N 73W 104
Tupungato, Cerro, Mt., Arg.-Chile 33S 70W 106
Tura, Russia 64N 100E 141
Turin, Italy 45N 8E 117
Turkestan, Reg., Asia 43N 65E 142
Turkey, Ctry., Asia-Eur. 38N 33E 115
Turkmenistan, Ctry., Asia 40N 60E 142
Turku, Fin. 60N 22E 116
Turpan, China 43N 89E 146
Turukhansk, Russia 66N 89E 140
Tuscaloosa, Al., U.S. 33N 88W 92
Tuxtla Gutiérrez, Mex. 17N 93W 96
Tuzla, Bos. 45N 19E 121
Tver', Russia 57N 36E 115
Twin Falls, Id., U.S. 43N 114W 83
Tyler, Tx., U.S. 32N 95W 95
Tyndinskiy, Russia 55N 125E 141
Tynemouth, Eng., U.K. 55N 2W 116
Tyrrhenian Sea, Fr.-Italy 40N 11E 117
Tyukalinsk, Russia 56N 72E 140
Tyumen', Russia 57N 65E 140

U

Ubangi, R., Afr. 3N 18E 129
Uberaba, Braz. 20S 48W 105
Uberlândia, Braz. 19S 48W 105
Udaipur, India 25N 74E 143
Udine, Italy 46N 13E 117
Ufa, Russia 55N 56E 115
Uganda, Ctry., Afr. 2N 32E 129
Uiju, N. Kor. 40N 125E 147
Ujjain, India 23N 76E 143
Ujungpandang (Makasar), Indon. 5S 119E 148
Ukraine, Ctry., Eur. 49N 32E 115
Ulaangom, Mong. 50N 92E 146
Ulan Bator, Mong. 47N 107E 146
Ulan-Ude, Russia 52N 108E 141
Ulcinj, Yugo. 42N 19E 121
Uliastay, Mong. 48N 97E 146
Ulm, Ger. 48N 10E 117
Uluru, Mt., Austl. 25S 131E 156
Ul'yanovsk, Russia 54N 48E 115
Umtata, S. Afr. 32S 28E 130
Unayzah, Sau. Ar. 26N 44E 142
United Arab Emirates, Ctry., Asia 23N 53E 142
United Kingdom, Ctry., Eur. 55N 3W 116
United States, Ctry., N.A. 38N 100W 76
Uppsala, Swe. 60N 18E 116
Ural, R., Kaz.-Russia 50N 52E 115
Urals, Mts., Russia 62N 60E 115
Uranium City, Sk., Can. 60N 109W 72
Urbana, Il., U.S. 40N 88W 90
Uruguaiana, Braz. 30S 57W 106
Uruguay, Ctry., S.A. 33S 56W 106
Uruguay, R., S.A. 28S 55W 106
Ürümqi, China 44N 88E 146
Usak, Tur. 39N 29E 121
Ushuaia, Arg. 55S 68W 106
Ussuriysk, Russia 44N 132E 141
Ust'-Kulom, Russia 62N 54E 140
Ust'-Maya, Russia 61N 135E 141
Ust'-Olenek, Russia 73N 120E 141
Ust' Port, Russia 69N 84E 140
Ust'-Tsil'ma, Russia 65N 52E 140
Ust' Tyrma, Russia 50N 131E 141
Usu, China 44N 84E 146
Utah, State, U.S. 39N 113W 76
Utica, N.Y., U.S. 43N 75W 91
Utrecht, Neth. 52N 5E 117
Utrera, Spain 37N 6W 120
Utsunomiya, Japan 37N 140E 147
Uttaradit, Thai. 18N 100E 148
Uzbekistan, Ctry., Asia 41N 64E 142

V

Vaasa, Fin. 63N 22E 116
Vác, Hung. 48N 19E 117
Vadodara, India 22N 73E 143
Vadsö, Nor. 70N 30E 116
Valdepeñas, Spain 39N 3W 120
Valdivia, Chile 40S 73W 106
Valdosta, Ga., U.S. 31N 83W 92
Valence, Fr. 45N 5E 117
Valencia, Spain 39N 0 120
Valencia, Ven. 10N 68W 104
Valentine, Ne., U.S. 43N 101W 88
Valladolid, Spain 42N 5W 120
Vallejo, Ca., U.S. 38N 122W 84
Valletta, Malta 36N 15E 120
Valley City, N.D., U.S. 47N 98W 88
Valparaíso, Chile 33S 72W 106
Vancouver, B.C., Can. 49N 123W 72
Vancouver, Wa., U.S. 46N 123W 82
Vancouver I., B.C., Can. 50N 127W 72
Vannes, Fr. 48N 3W 117
Vanuatu, Ctry., Oc. 17S 169E 157
Vārānāsi (Benaras), India 25N 83E 143
Varaždin, Cro. 46N 16E 121
Varna (Stalin), Bul. 43N 28E 121
Vasterås, Swe. 60N 17E 116
Vatican City, Ctry., Eur. 42N 12E 117
Vegreville, Ab., Can. 53N 112W 72
Velikiy Ustyug, Russia 61N 47E 140
Veliko Turnovo, Bul. 43N 26E 121
Vellore, India 13N 79E 143

Vel'sk, Russia..............61N 42 E **140**
Venezuela, Ctry., S.A........8N 65W **104**
Venice, Italy..............45N 12 E **117**
Ventspils, Lat.............57N 21 E **116**
Veracruz, Mex..............19N 96W **96**
Veräval, India.............21N 70 E **143**
Verdun, Fr.................49N 5 E **117**
Vermilion, Ab., Can........53N 111W **72**
Vermont, State, U.S.......44N 73W **77**
Verona, Italy..............45N 11 E **117**
Versailles, Fr.............49N 2 E **117**
Vesuvio, Vol., Italy......41N 15 E **117**
Viangchan, Laos............18N 103 E **148**
Vicente López, Arg.........34S 58W **106**
Vicenza, Italy.............46N 12 E **117**
Vichy, Fr..................46N 3 E **117**
Vicksburg, Ms., U.S........32N 91W **92**
Victoria, B.C., Can........48N 123W **72**
Victoria, L., Afr..........1S 33 E **130**
*Victoria Falls, Zam.-
    Zimb.*..................18S 25 E **130**
Victoria I., Nu., Can.....70N 110W **72**
Vidin, Bul.................44N 23 E **121**
Viedma, Arg................41S 63W **106**
Vienna (Wien), Aus.........48N 16 E **117**
Vietnam, Ctry., Asia......18N 108 E **148**
Vigo, Spain................42N 9W **120**
Vijayawâda, India..........17N 81 E **143**
Vila, Vanuatu..............18S 168 E **157**
Villa Bella, Bol...........10S 65W **104**
Villach, Aus...............47N 14 E **117**
Villahermosa, Mex..........18N 93W **96**
Villa María, Arg...........32S 63W **106**
Villa Mercedes, Arg........34S 65W **106**
Villeurbanne, Fr...........46N 5 E **117**
Vilnius, Lith..............55N 25 E **114**
Vilyuysk, Russia...........64N 122 E **141**
Viña del Mar, Chile........33S 72W **106**
Vindeln, Swe...............64N 20 E **116**
Vineland, N.J., U.S........39N 75W **91**
Vinnytsya, Ukr.............49N 29 E **114**
Virden, Mb., Can...........50N 101W **72**
Virginia, Mn., U.S.........48N 93W **89**
Virginia, State, U.S......37N 81W **77**
Virginia Beach, Va.,
    U.S....................37N 76W **91**
Virgin Is., N.A...........18N 63W **97**
Viterbo, Italy.............42N 12 E **117**
Vitim, Russia..............59N 113 E **141**
Vitória, Braz..............20S 40W **105**
Vitoria, Spain.............43N 3W **120**
Vitsyebsk, Bela............55N 30 E **114**
Vladikavkaz, Russia........43N 45 E **142**
Vladimir, Russia...........56N 40 E **115**
Vladivostok, Russia........43N 132 E **141**
Vlorë (Valona), Alb........40N 20 E **121**
Volga, R., Russia.........46N 48 E **115**
Volgograd (Stalingrad),
    Russia.................49N 44 E **115**
Vologda, Russia............59N 40 E **115**
Volos, Grc.................39N 23 E **121**
Vol'sk, Russia.............52N 47 E **115**
Vorkuta, Russia............67N 64 E **140**
Voronezh, Russia...........52N 39 E **115**
Votkinsk, Russia...........57N 54 E **115**
Voznesens'k, Ukr...........48N 31 E **121**
Vratsa, Bul................43N 24 E **121**
Vršac, Yugo................45N 21 E **121**
Vyborg, Russia.............61N 29 E **114**
Vylkove, Ukr...............45N 30 E **121**
Vytegra, Russia............61N 36 E **140**

W
Wabash, R., U.S...........38N 88W **90**
Waco, Tx., U.S.............32N 97W **95**
Waingapu, Indon............10S 120 E **148**
Wainwright, Ab., Can.......53N 111W **72**
Wakayama, Japan............34N 135 E **147**
Wake, I., Oc.............19N 167 E **159**
Wakkanai, Japan............45N 142 E **147**
Waku Kundo, Ang............11S 15 E **130**

Wales, Polit. Reg., U.K.....52N 4W **117**
Walla Walla, Wa., U.S......46N 118W **82**
Walvis Bay, Nmb............23S 14 E **130**
Walworth, Wi., U.S.........43N 89W **89**
Wanxian, China.............31N 108 E **146**
Warangal, India............18N 80 E **143**
Wargla, Alg................32N 5 E **128**
Warren, Mi., U.S...........43N 83W **90**
Warren, Oh., U.S...........41N 81W **90**
Warren, Pa., U.S...........42N 79W **91**
Warsaw (Warszawa),
    Pol....................52N 21 E **117**
Warwick, R.I., U.S.........42N 71W **91**
Washington, D.C.,
    U.S....................39N 77W **91**
Washington, Pa., U.S.......40N 80W **91**
Washington, State, U.S....47N 121W **76**
Waterbury, Ct., U.S........41N 73W **91**
Waterloo, Ia., U.S.........42N 92W **89**
Watertown, N.Y., U.S.......44N 76W **91**
Watertown, S.D., U.S.......45N 97W **88**
Watrous, Sk., Can..........52N 106W **72**
Watson Lake, Yk.,
    Can....................60N 129W **72**
Waukegan, Il., U.S.........42N 88W **90**
Waukesha, Wi., U.S..........4N 88W **89**
Wausau, Wi., U.S...........45N 90W **89**
Wauwatosa, Wi., U.S........43N 88W **89**
Waycross, Ga., U.S.........31N 82W **93**
Weddell Sea, Sea, Ant.....73S 45W **52**
Weifang, China.............37N 119 E **147**
Weimar, Ger................51N 11 E **117**
Weirton, W.V., U.S.........40N 81W **90**
Wellington, N.Z............41S 175 E **157**
Wels, Aus..................48N 14 E **117**
Wensu, China...............42N 80 E **146**
Wenzhou, China.............28N 121 E **147**
West Allis, Wi., U.S.......43N 88W **89**
*Western Ghâts, Mts.,
    India*.................16N 74 E **143**
*Western Sahara, Dep.,
    Afr.*..................25N 14W **128**
*Western Samoa, see
    Samoa, Ctry., Oc.*.....15S 177W **158**
West Hartford, Ct.,
    U.S....................42N 73W **91**
West Indies, Is., N.A.....18N 73W **97**
West Lafayette, In.,
    U.S....................40N 87W **90**
West Palm Beach, Fl.,
    U.S....................27N 80W **93**
*West Virginia, State,
    U.S.*..................39N 81W **77**
Wewak, Pap. N. Gui........4S 143 E **149**
Wexford, Ire...............52N 6W **117**
Weymouth, Ma., U.S.........43N 71W **91**
Wheaton, Md., U.S..........39N 77W **91**
Wheeling, W.V., U.S........40N 81W **90**
Whitecourt, Ab., Can......54N 116W **72**
Whitehorse, Yk., Can......61N 135W **72**
White Nile, R., Sudan....13N 33 E **129**
White Plains, N.Y.,
    U.S....................41N 74W **91**
White Sea, Russia..........66N 39 E **115**
Whiting, In., U.S..........42N 87W **90**
Whitney, Mt., Ca., U.S....36N 118W **84**
Wichita, Ks., U.S..........38N 97W **87**
Wichita Falls, Tx.,
    U.S....................34N 98W **86**
Wiener-Neustadt, Aus.......48N 16 E **117**
Wiesbaden, Ger.............50N 8 E **117**
Wilhelmshaven, Ger.........53N 8 E **117**
Wilkes-Barre, Pa., U.S.....41N 76W **91**
Willemstad, Neth.
    Ant....................12N 69W **97**
Williamsport, Pa., U.S.....41N 77W **91**
Williston, N.D., U.S.......48N 104W **88**
Wilmette, Il., U.S.........42N 88W **90**
Wilmington, De., U.S.......40N 76W **91**
Wilmington, N.C.,
    U.S....................34N 78W **93**
Windhoek, Nmb..............22S 17 E **130**
Windsor, Nf., Can..........49N 56W **73**
Windsor, On., Can..........42N 83W **73**
Winnemucca, Nv.,
    U.S....................41N 118W **82**
Winnetka, Il., U.S.........42N 88W **90**
Winnipeg, Mb., Can........50N 97W **72**

Winnipeg, L., Mb.,
    Can....................53N 98W **72**
Winona, Mn., U.S...........44N 92W **89**
Winston-Salem, N.C.,
    U.S....................36N 80W **93**
Wisconsin, R., Wi., U.S....43N 90W **89**
Wisconsin, State, U.S.....44N 91W **77**
Wisconsin Dells, Wi.,
    U.S....................44N 90W **89**
Wisla (Vistula), R., Pol....53N 19 E **116**
Wismar, Ger................54N 11 E **116**
Włocławek, Pol.............52N 19 E **117**
Wollongong, Austl..........34S 151 E **157**
Wolverhampton, Eng.,
    U.K....................53N 2W **117**
Wŏnsan, N. Kor............39N 127 E **147**
*Woods, Lake of the,
    Can.-U.S.*.............49N 95W **89**
Woonsocket, R.I., U.S......42N 71W **91**
Worcester, Eng., U.K.......52N 2W **117**
Worcester, Ma., U.S........42N 72W **91**
Worms, Ger.................50N 8 E **117**
Wrocław (Breslau),
    Pol....................51N 17 E **117**
Wuchang, China.............31N 114 E **147**
Wuhan, China...............30N 114 E **147**
Wuppertal, Ger.............51N 7 E **117**
Wushi, China...............41N 79 E **146**
Wuxi, China................32N 120 E **147**
Wuxing, China..............31N 120 E **147**
Wuzhou, China..............24N 111 E **147**
Wyandotte, Mi., U.S........42N 83W **90**
Wyoming, State, U.S.......43N 108W **76**

X
Xalapa, Mex................20N 97W **96**
Xanthi, Grc................41N 25 E **121**
Xiamen, China..............24N 118 E **147**
Xi'an, China...............34N 109 E **146**
Xiang, R., China..........26N 113 E **147**
Xiangtan, China............28N 113 E **147**
Xingu, R., Braz...........7S 53W **105**
Xinhui, China..............23N 113 E **147**
Xining, China..............37N 102 E **146**
Xinyang, China.............32N 114 E **147**
Xuzhou, China..............34N 117 E **147**

Y
Yakima, Wa., U.S...........47N 120W **82**
Yakutsk, Russia............62N 130 E **140**
Yalta, Ukr.................44N 34 E **115**
*Yalu, R., China-N.
    Kor.*..................41N 126 E **147**
Yamagata, Japan............38N 140 E **147**
Yambol, Bul................42N 27 E **121**
Yamoussoukro, C. Iv........7N 4W **128**
Yamsk, Russia..............60N 154 E **141**
Yanbu, Sau. Ar.............24N 38 E **142**
*Yangtze (Chang), R.,
    China*.................30N 117 E **147**
Yankton, S.D., U.S.........43N 97W **88**
Yantai, China..............38N 121 E **147**
Yaoundé, Cam...............4N 12 E **128**
Yaransk, Russia............57N 48 E **140**
Yaroslavl', Russia.........58N 40 E **115**
Yatung, China..............27N 89 E **143**
Yazd, Iran.................32N 54 E **142**
Ye, Myan...................15N 98 E **148**
Yecheng, China.............37N 79 E **146**
Yekaterinburg
    (Sverdlovsk), Russia...57N 61 E **115**
Yelets, Russia.............53N 38 E **115**
Yellowknife, N.T.,
    Can....................62N 115W **72**
Yellow Sea, Asia.........37N 123 E **147**

Yellowstone, R., U.S......46N 106W **83**
Yemen, Ctry., Asia........15N 47 E **142**
Yenisey, R., Russia.......72N 83 E **140**
Yeniseysk, Russia..........58N 92 E **140**
Yerevan, Arm...............40N 44 E **115**
Yevpatoriya, Ukr...........45N 33 E **121**
Yeysk, Russia..............47N 38 E **121**
Yibin, China...............29N 105 E **146**
Yichang, China.............31N 111 E **147**
Yinchuan, China............38N 106 E **146**
Yingkou, China.............41N 123 E **147**
Yining (Gulja), China......44N 81 E **146**
Yogyakarta, Indon..........8S 110 E **148**
Yokohama, Japan............36N 140 E **147**
Yonkers, N.Y., U.S.........41N 74W **91**
York, Eng., U.K............54N 1W **116**
York, Pa., U.S.............40N 77W **91**
Yorkton, Sk., Can..........51N 103W **72**
Yoshkar-Ola, Russia........57N 48 E **115**
Youngstown, Oh., U.S.......41N 81W **90**
Yrghyz, Kaz................48N 61 E **140**
Yugoslavia, Ctry., Eur....45N 17 E **121**
Yukon, Ter., Can.........63N 135W **72**
Yukon, R., Can.-U.S......63N 160W **76**
Yuma, Az., U.S.............33N 115W **85**
Yumen, China...............40N 97 E **146**
Yutian (Keriya), China.....37N 82 E **146**

Z
Zabrze, Pol................50N 19 E **117**
Zacatecas, Mex.............23N 103W **96**
Zadar, Cro.................44N 15 E **120**
Zagreb, Cro................46N 16 E **121**
Zagros Mts., Iran.........34N 48 E **142**
Zähedän, Iran..............30N 61 E **142**
Zahlah, Leb................34N 36 E **121**
*Zaire, see Congo,
    Democratic Republic
    of the, Ctry., Afr.*....1S 23 E **130**
Zambezi, R., Afr.........16S 30 E **130**
Zambia, Ctry., Afr.......15S 28 E **130**
Zamboanga, Phil............7N 122 E **148**
Zamora, Spain..............42N 6W **120**
Zamość, Pol................51N 23 E **117**
Zanesville, Oh., U.S.......40N 82W **90**
Zanjân, Iran...............36N 48 E **142**
Zanzibar, I., Tan.........6S 39 E **131**
*Zapadnaya Dvina, R.,
    Eur.*..................57N 24 E **114**
Zaporizhzhya
    (Zaporozh'ye), Ukr.....48N 35 E **115**
Zaragoza, Spain............42N 1W **120**
Zarate, Arg................34S 59W **106**
Zashiversk, Russia.........67N 143 E **141**
Zavitinsk, Russia..........50N 130 E **147**
*Zemla Franca-Iosifa,
    Is., Russia*...........80N 50 E **53**
Zemun, Yugo................45N 20 E **121**
Zeya, Russia...............54N 127 E **141**
Zhambyl, Kaz...............43N 71 E **140**
Zhangaqazaly, Kaz..........46N 62 E **140**
Zhangjiakou, China.........41N 115 E **147**
Zhangzhou, China...........25N 118 E **147**
Zhanjiang, China...........21N 110 E **147**
Zhengzhou, China...........35N 114 E **147**
Zhenjiang, China...........32N 119 E **147**
Zhigansk, Russia...........67N 123 E **141**
Zhytomyr, Ukr..............50N 29 E **114**
Žilina, Slvk...............49N 19 E **117**
Zimbabwe, Ctry., Afr.....19S 30 E **130**
Zomba, Mwi.................15S 35 E **130**
Zonguldak, Tur.............41N 32 E **121**
Zunyi, China...............28N 107 E **146**
Zürich, Switz..............47N 9 E **117**
Zvenyhorodka, Ukr..........49N 31 E **121**
Zwickau, Ger...............51N 12 E **117**
Zwolle, Neth...............13N 6 E **117**
Zyryanovsk, Kaz............50N 84 E **140**